WATFIV
For Humans

Rex Page

Rich Didday

WEST PUBLISHING CO.
St. Paul • New York • Boston
Los Angeles • San Francisco

Page & Didday–WATFIV For Humans

Library of Congress Cataloging in Publication Data

Page, Rex L
    WATFIV for humans.
    Includes index.
    1. FORTRAN (Computer program language) I. Didday,
Richard L., joint author. II. Title.
QA76.73.F25P33   001.6'424   76-3433
ISBN 0-8299-0100-0

PREFACE

There are two basically different kinds of texts about WATFIV programming. One kind is the text wholly oriented toward the Waterloo version of Fortran, and the other is the text about standard Fortran programming which contains a few references to format-free I/O in the early chapters and includes the WATFIV error messages in an appendix. Our text falls into the first category. We feel that the format-free I/O and character string facilities of WATFIV make it possible to teach a more effective introductory programming course in WATFIV than in standard Fortran. In addition, the excellent WATFIV error messages make it possible for the student to do more on his own than he can with most other Fortran compilers. The text used in such a course, in order to take full advantage of these WATFIV facilities, must approach the introductory material in a different manner from standard Fortran texts, making it difficult to integrate the two approaches in one text. For these reasons we have written this new version of our existing text, *Fortran for Humans.*

The use of character string constants and arithmetic expressions, in addition to the usual variable names in format-free I/O lists, makes it possible to delay the introduction of FORMATs until very late in a WATFIV course. In fact, unless literacy in standard Fortran is a goal of the course, FORMATs could be omitted entirely without unduly restricting the I/O facilities available to the students. This eliminates a major stumbling block for novice Fortran programmers, most of whom could well do without the extra burden of learning the intricate interplay between FORMAT and I/O list. Therefore, we have placed the material on FORMATs in a chapter which is independent of the rest of the text. This material can be introduced at any point in the course after the student has learned about assignment statements and expressions. All the examples in the text, other than those in the chapter on FORMATs (Chapter 10), are written using format-free I/O. This doesn't make the examples less complicated from an algorithmic point of view, nor does it make them less illustrative of the topic of discussion. In fact, it makes them more pertinent by avoiding the confusion that FORMATs often create.

The early introduction of character string variables (Chapter 2) makes it easier for the student to write programs which don't have numerical computation as their central theme, thus broadening the spectrum of interesting elementary problems.

We have arranged the material in the order which we feel is the most pedagogically sound. In many cases this means introducing restricted versions of certain statements a chapter or two ahead of the more general versions. This can have an unfortunate side effect: it makes the text more difficult to use as a reference. We have included four features in this text which we hope will alleviate this problem. (1) We have prepared an extensive alphabetical index. (2) We have written a WATFIV manual summarizing the language definitions in one place for easy reference, with non-ANSI Fortran features marked in gray. (3) We have prepared a quick reference index which lists examples of each type of statement keyed to relevant pages in the text. (4) We have included optional sections on advanced topics in relevant chapters, thus keeping similar material together for easy reference.

> *Boxes throughout the text summarize important points and provide additional information.*

DO loops are introduced in Chapter 8. We feel it is best to delay their introduction until the student is well versed in the construction of all kinds of loops; otherwise, there is a tendency to terminate loops with counters when other termination conditions would be more appropriate. However, Chapter 8 doesn't depend on any material beyond assignments, expressions, and arrays, and can therefore be covered quite early in the course. In fact, the first section of the chapter introduces the notion of a DO loop without mentioning arrays, so that DO loops could be introduced in the course simultaneously with Chapter 3 without having to deviate from the text in any important way.

This text is intended for an introductory course in programming. Accordingly, it emphasizes algorithm design, program organization, and clarity of expression more than statement syntax and semantic detail. The syntax and semantics are all there, but we spend more time discussing ideas which are more difficult to learn. We have tried, by example more than by essay, to emphasize internal program documentation (proper commenting, indentation, and the like). Such things are, to some extent, a matter of taste and style, but we think it is important for the student to develop a feeling for the importance of good program design and documentation.

The material in the first ten chapters can be covered adequately in about 25 fifty-minute lectures, with time for the students to ask plenty of questions. In longer courses, much of the material in the remaining chapters can also be covered. The choice of topics is, of course, left to the instructor.

The compiler for WATFIV, the Waterloo version of Fortran IV, was developed by the Applied Analysis and Computer Science Department of the University of Waterloo. We would like to thank Professor J. Wesley Graham, one of the compiler designers, for his permission to reproduce the WATFIV error messages in this text. We would also like to thank John O'Loughlin and the other helpful people at the Digital Computing Center, Wichita State University for their assistance in debugging the programs appearing in the text.

R. L. Page
R. L. Didday

Larimer County, Colorado

CONTENTS

*

WATFIV
For Humans

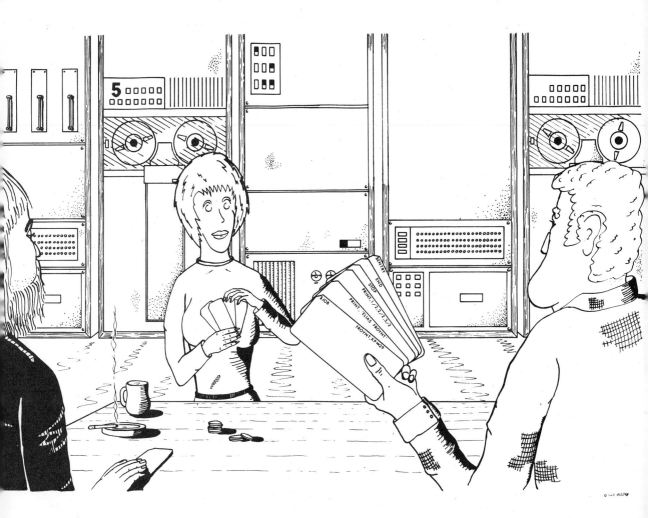

1 BASIC IDEAS

Section 1 1

Advice to You Who Are About to Learn WATFIV

You will probably find learning to program a new kind of experience. Insofar as programming is like planning a task, it is a familiar process. What makes it difficult is that the planning must be much more complete than most people are used to.

For example, suppose a carpenter decides to write a set of directions for hanging a door. The difficulty of his task would depend to a large extent on his audience. It would be much easier for him to write a set of directions addressed to another carpenter than it would be to write directions addressed to the general public. For the public the directions would have to be much more complete because most people would know little about carpentry. In fact, a layman who happened to know how to hang a door would probably write better instructions for the general public than would the expert carpenter. While the carpenter might be tempted to say "rout strike box in jamb", the layman would realize that he would have to explain what a door jamb is, what the strike of a lock is, and what routing is before he could make any such statement.

It is usually the case that the programmer, like the carpenter, knows much more than his audience, the computer, about the process he is trying to describe. The computer does know some things in the sense that it can perform a set of operations, but it is up to the programmer to describe the process in terms the computer understands. If a computer system accepts WATFIV, then it already knows how to perform all the operations specified in WATFIV. It is up to the programmer to describe the process in terms of those operations.

To learn to do this is not easy for most people. However, it seems easier once you get the hang of it. It is also fun. Since it is easy and fun for those who know, you will no doubt have lots of friends who want to help you learn to program. Most of them will help you by writing a program which solves the problem you are working on. It should be fairly obvious that this does *not* help you learn to program. You can't learn to swim by having your friend do it for you. But it may not be so obvious that this form of help is often detrimental rather than merely unhelpful. It is detrimental primarily because your helper is likely to use statements you have never seen before. (It might be interesting for you to keep track of the number of times someone says to you "Oh, that's no good. Why

1

don't you do it this way?") These things you've never seen before will fall into one of four categories:

1 (OK) They are described in the text and you will learn them soon.
2 (POOR) They are advanced constructions and shouldn't be used until you know more about the basics.
3 (BAD) They are outmoded ways of doing things which are holdovers from more primitive languages.
4 (FREQUENT) They don't exist at all.

We offer this advice: Listen politely to friends who want to help, but always try to write the program yourself using techniques you know about from the part of the text you have read.

In writing this text we have tried to make no assumptions about educational backgrounds beyond expecting you to have had the usual high school courses, including a course in basic algebra. However, some of the problems at the ends of the chapters provide the opportunity for people to use specialized knowledge in mathematics, business, science, and engineering. Each chapter has several problems, so you can choose a problem that you understand.

The exercises at the end of each section should help you confirm that you understand the material in the section. Answers for virtually all the exercises appear at the end of the book. If you do all the exercises and check them with the answers, you will learn the material much more thoroughly.

Although the first few chapters contain many new concepts, you will probably be able to grasp them quickly. Later chapters contain more and more complex combinations of these basic concepts and will probably require more thought. You can't learn to program in a day. It will take lots of thought and practice, but we think you will find it an enjoyable experience.

---

blanks: Although people rarely draw attention to them, blank characters are very important in written communications. A blank serves as an unobtrusive separator.

////Imagine/reading/a/sentence/like/this.////
Oronewithnoseparatorsatalllikethis.

You may not be used to thinking of a blank character as the same sort of thing as an "a" or "b" or a "!". But on a line printer (as on a typewriter) it takes a definite action to produce a blank just as it requires a definite action to produce an "a".

One of the reasons we have numbered sections the way we have in this book is to draw attention to the blank as a legitimate character.

A typical usage is "Figure 13 4 1", read "figure thirteen four one", identifying the first figure in the fourth section of Chapter 13.

Section 1 2

Background

This book is intended to help you learn to program computers using the programming language WATFIV. In practice, the only way to learn to program is to do it, so this book is really only an aid to reduce the number of errors in your trial-and-error learning process.

WATFIV is a **computer language**, a language with which to communicate commands to a computer. A **computer** is a machine which manipulates symbols by following the instructions in a computer program (written in a computer language, of course). Humans may interpret these symbols as they please. For example, a person might want to interpret a certain set of

> **computer:** *a machine which can perform arithmetic operations, make logical decisions, and perform many other symbol manipulation tasks automatically following the instructions in a computer program*

symbols as the results of a number of questionnaires, and he might write a program (a sequence of commands) in WATFIV which would cause some of the symbols to be matched up in pairs. He might then call this process "computer dating" and make a lot of money.

Motivation for development of computers comes from efforts to mechanize symbol manipulation tasks. An adding machine is a familiar device which manipulates symbols and, in so doing, winds up with symbols that we call the sum of the symbols we put in.

> **program:** *a sequence of instructions*

Early computers were little more than assemblages of devices which added, multiplied, divided, etc., and could do these operations in sequence. Thus, a person who wanted to add a large list of numbers, then divide the sum by another number, then subtract this from yet another number, could write down a series of commands which would be *stored in the machine* and carried out in order automatically. The key word here is "stored". The instructions which the computer is to follow are stored in the machine, and they can be changed by the user of the computer, the programmer.

> **machine language:** *a set of commands which a computer is built to perform. Different computers have different machine languages. A machine language program runs with no need for translation. Most machine languages bear little similarity to human languages.*

In the early days, one of the programmer's biggest problems was keeping up with changes in computers. There was, and still is, a continuing introduction of newer, faster, different computers. In the early fifties a group of programmers began an attempt to get around this problem. It had become apparent that if something weren't done, programmers would be spending large portions of their lives just learning the language for one new computer after another. Since the process of learning new languages was both gruesome and time-consuming, they designed a computer language closer to English than typical machine languages. They called their new language **Fortran.** It was a higher-level language. Since there had never been any widely used higher-level languages before that time, and since the problems involved in translating complex higher-level statements into efficient machine language programs had only begun to be studied, their first successful effort didn't look very much like English. They wanted Fortran to provide a way of giving commands to computers that was easy for programmers to learn, general enough to handle a great variety of problems, and designed so that the commands would be meaningful in terms of any computer's internal workings. Hopefully, manufacturers of new computers would provide machine language programs for translating Fortran programs into commands for their new machines. Programmers, then, wouldn't have to learn too much about the new machine to be able to program it and could continue to write their programs in Fortran, relying on the company's translation program to convert Fortran statements to machine commands.

> *higher-level language: a computer language which appears more like a human language than does machine language and is designed to be used on many different brands of computers*

Even though the new language wasn't really much like English, it was a big improvement over machine languages. It was concerned largely with arithmetic computing, and it promised to bring the use of the computer within the reach of a large number of technically oriented people who would not have been willing to write programs before. Although the first version of Fortran was never widely available, Fortran II (introduced in 1958), became the first popular, commercially available higher-level language.

Through the years, as people have become more and more familiar with what is involved in programming, they have found certain types of statements more useful than others. *Higher-level languages have evolved.* WATFIV, the language you will be learning, is a version of Fortran developed by the Applied Analysis and Computer Science Department of the University of Waterloo, Ontario, and is widely available at computing installations using IBM 360 or 370 equipment. It has several features which make it easier for the novice programmer to use than standard Fortran systems. Yet it is so much like standard Fortran systems that students who have learned WATFIV can write programs for other Fortran systems simply by learning to restrict themselves to standard Fortran statements. Virtually every computing installation has some Fortran system available, and nearly all of these systems accept a certain set of standard features described in a publication by the American National Standards Institute. (See *Fortran,* ANSI X3.9–1966, American National Standards Institute, Inc., 1430 Broadway, New York, New York 10018.)

Many higher-level languages in addition to Fortran have been designed and used, and it is probable that sooner or later Fortran will no longer be so popular— a more modern language will take its place. At this time, however, Fortran is very widely used, and computer companies have spent a lot of time and effort making programs which translate Fortran into their machine languages. These programs are called **compilers**, perhaps because they work by compiling a long list of machine commands which will do just what your Fortran statements ask. Of all the compilers available at your computer center, it is likely that the 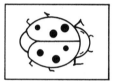 Fortran compiler is the most reliable and the most convenient to use. As you learn more about computer programming, you will see why there are likely to be mistakes (or **bugs** as they are called) in any large computer program including a compiler. It is hard enough to write programs without having to worry about bugs in the compiler, so it is important to use a language whose compiler is as accurate as possible. Since this language will, on

> *compiler: a program which translates a higher-level language into machine language*

most computer systems, be Fortran, it is a valuable language to know.

It is important to understand what it is that you are to learn about programming. We are not going to try to teach you to "think in WATFIV"—in fact, this is undesirable. What you are encouraged to learn is first how to analyze a problem from the real world, to divide it into subproblems each of which you know how to solve, and second, how to state the results of your analysis to a computer in terms of a WATFIV program. Figure 1 2 1 illustrates the process.

Phases 2 and 3 are the most important to learn—and if you do learn them, you will be in a much better position to understand what can be done with computers. Unfortunately, they are virtually impossible to learn out of context. You will have to learn about reasonable analogies between real world processes and computer processes by learning about computers through programming.

Let's apply the scheme shown in Figure 1 2 1 to a specific problem. Figure 1 2 2 suggests a concrete example of a case in which it is very easy to make appropriate analogies. We don't expect you to understand all the details of the program, just the general idea.

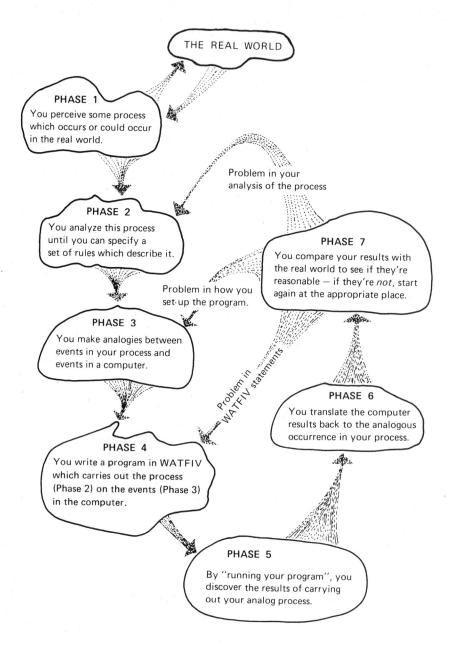

Figure 1·2·1   The Big Picture

Phase 1   You decide you want to know the average price per pound of laundry detergent.

Phase 2   The process you wish to carry out is to sum the individual brand prices and divide by the total number of brands.

$$\text{Average price} = \frac{\text{Sum of prices}}{\text{total number of brands}}$$

Phase 3　You decide to let data locations in the computer represent the price per pound for each brand and the number of brands, and to use the addition and division operations to carry out your process.

Phase 4

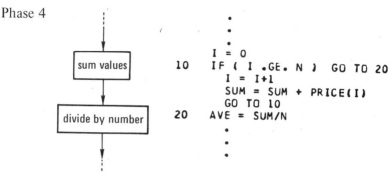

```
                              .
                              .
                              .
                        I = 0
              10   IF ( I .GE. N )  GO TO 20
                        I = I+1
                        SUM = SUM + PRICE(I)
                        GO TO 10
              20   AVE = SUM/N
                              .
                              .
                              .
```

Phase 5　You run your program and get the computed value.

Phase 6　That value should be the average price per pound.

Phase 7　If that number seems reasonable, accept it. If it doesn't, try to see where the problem lies, and start in again at the appropriate place.

Figure 1 2 2　Selecting a Laundry Detergent

Writing programs and using the results of computations is (or should be) a very logical process. The stories about credit card foul-ups, statements like "we have student numbers because that's easier for the computer", and the assumptions that computers are like people only dumber and faster, show that unfortunately, many people don't understand the BIG PICTURE. As you go through this book, recalling the ideas in Figure 1 2 1 may help you to keep your perspective.

While the process of using the computer is basically logical, Phase 4, in which your ideas are translated into WATFIV commands may not seem to be. Don't worry if certain requirements in WATFIV don't seem rational to you—they're probably not. Don't forget that Fortran was designed before anyone had used high-level languages. Since then, committees and special interest groups have added parts, usually trying to keep the new version enough like the old so that old programs will run on the new compilers. Such an evolution is bound to produce some clumsy appendages, and WATFIV has inherited all of the strange quirks which have developed in Fortran. In this book we are trying to protect you from as many idiosyncrasies as possible; in fact, we will occasionally lie to you. That is, initially we will leave certain details out of the language we describe. But these will be only little white lies, and we think that they're for your own good (the details often add little but confusion at first). We fill in details when it becomes necessary so that, by the end of Chapter 11, you have the whole picture.

By the way, you might consider that English, which was developed by a *huge* committee, isn't exactly logical either.

EXERCISES 1 2

1   Write down some of your current opinions about computers, how they work, what they do, what they will be able to do, how they affect the life of the average person. Attach what you've written to the last page of this book so that when you've finished the book, you can see in what ways your ideas about computers have changed.

2   Read more about the history of Fortran in the chapter on Fortran in *Programming Languages: History and Fundamentals* by Jean E. Sammet, New York, Prentice-Hall, 1969, pp. 143–172.

Section 1 3

Algorithms

Algorithm is a special word used by computer scientists to mean a rule, procedure, or sequence of instructions. An algorithm is a description of how to do some task, and each step of the description, while incompletely specified, is understood by the person or machine which is to perform the task. Each step will always be incompletely specified simply because it's impossible to describe anything *completely*. You just hope to be understood most of the time. Our first example of an algorithm is so incompletely specified that one important instruction is totally left out. Look at Figure 1 3 1 and see if you can discover what is missing.

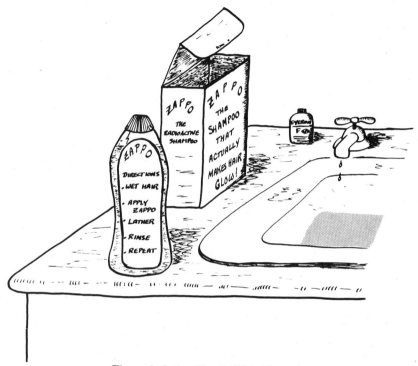

Figure 1 3 1   The ZAPPO Algorithm

Since the **ZAPPO** instructions fail to tell you when to stop, you would wash your hair forever if you followed them unswervingly. There is little doubt that sometime, someone you know, maybe even (perish the thought) *you,* will write a program for the computer which acts like the **ZAPPO** directions in Figure 1 3 1. Saying "but that isn't what I *meant*" will get you sympathy but not results. Fear not, however; your program will not run forever. The infinite loop is a universal problem, and for that reason all programs are given some time limit. They run just so long, then they are thrown out whether they seem to be finished or not.

> *infinite loop: a list of instructions which cannot be performed in a finite amount of time*

The most important things to notice in the **ZAPPO** algorithm are:

1   when performed in order, the instructions lead you through the process of "washing your hair with **ZAPPO**"—presumably this is a difficult task which must be explained;

2 each instruction is incompletely specified—if you don't know how to "lather", this algorithm is of no use to you; and

3 every step within the algorithm seems reasonable, but the overall effect is not reasonable (namely, it never stops).

A popular and useful way of depicting algorithms is **flowcharting**. Writing a flowchart helps people visualize how the individual parts of an algorithm fit together.

> *flowchart: a pictorial presentation of an algorithm*

Figure 1 3 2 shows a flowchart of the ZAPPO algorithm.

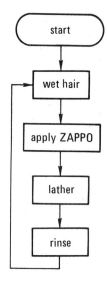

Figure 1 3 2

You will note that instruction 5 ("repeat") is not written out in the flowchart, and if you think about it a bit, you will realize that it is a different kind of instruction from the other four. Instructions 1 through 4 tell you to perform a specific act, whereas number 5 tells you where to get your next instruction. In a flowchart, arrows are used to indicate where to go next. We also added a box with "START" in it. If we read directions on a bottle, we assume we start at the top. In flowcharts this isn't always true.

So that you will be more comfortable thinking in terms of algorithms, we'll show you a few more examples. In each case we'll present a verbal description and a flowchart of the algorithm involved. Try to see how one relates to the other and see which is easier for you to use. Probably you'll want to use a combination of the two techniques.

VERBAL DESCRIPTION

Starting at lower edge, cast on 116 sts. 1st row: *K2, P2. Repeat from * across. Repeat first row until total length is 60 inches.

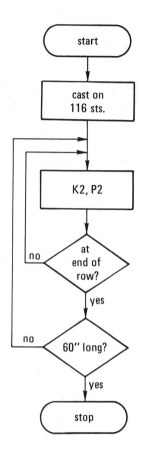

Figure 1 3 3   Knitting a Scarf

The verbal description in the knitting algorithm may look strange to you, especially if you don't know that "sts." means "stitches" and that "K2, P2" means "knit 2, purl 2", but this is a characteristic of programming languages—they contain symbols which mean a precise thing to the person or computer being instructed.

You will notice that "*" is used to identify a place to repeat from and that the "repeat from * across" instruction has become an arrow in the flowchart. Also you will notice that, unlike the ZAPPO algorithm, the commands to "repeat" are conditional. You don't repeat forever; you repeat to the end of the row ("across"), or until the total length is 60 inches.

The flowchart for the knitting algorithm is relatively complicated, yet it is easy to understand. You probably won't write a program as complicated as this flowchart until you have read Chapter 3.

Get a Job (sha nana na sha nanananana)

Suppose you were out of work and wanted to get a job. One scheme would be:

VERBAL DESCRIPTION

START: Get the "help wanted" section of the newspaper, and look at the first listing.

DECIDE: If you couldn't stand the job, go to instruction LOOP. If you could stand the job, then call the people who placed the ad. If they seem reluctant to talk to you, try to convince them how great you would be at that job, and check their response again. If they agree to talk to you, set up an appointment. If they turn you down, then proceed to the next step.

LOOP: See if there are any more listings. If there are, look at the next one and go to instruction DECIDE. If there aren't, be bitter, complain about the economy, and file for unemployment.

It may seem silly to you to write down an elaborate set of instructions for getting a job—after all, "everybody knows how to do that". That may be, but the point is most computer languages have been designed to do one fairly simple thing at a time, based on very little information, so when you are writing a computer program it is *you* who must figure out how to fit a number of basic instructions together to do a useful overall task. You will have to learn to describe the things you want done in simple terms. If you start thinking about all the little things you have to know to accomplish everyday tasks, it will give you some idea of the level of detail needed in computer programs.

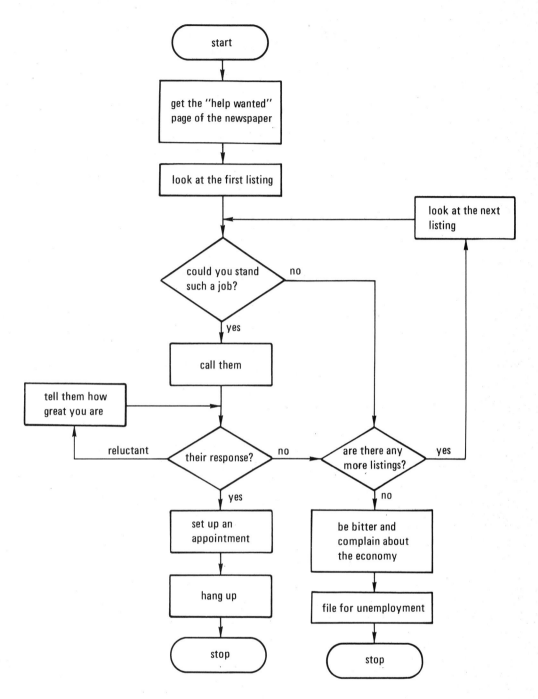

Figure 1 3 4 Getting a Job

Computing Compound Interest

Suppose you want to put some money in a savings account, and you want to decide whether it would be better to get 5% interest compounded quarterly or 4.85% interest compounded weekly. One way to find out which is better is to compute your interest for one year at each rate and then compare the results. There are several reasonable ways to do such a thing; we'll take a naive approach.

VERBAL DESCRIPTION

SETUP: Compute how many times a year you will receive interest (four times with quarterly interest, 52 for weekly compounding). Call the number of times N.

UPDATE: Update the current principal by multiplying it by

$$1 + \frac{\text{interest rate}}{100 \times N}$$

Repeat this updating step until you have done it N times.

PROFIT: Subtract the initial deposit from the final principal to get the interest received.

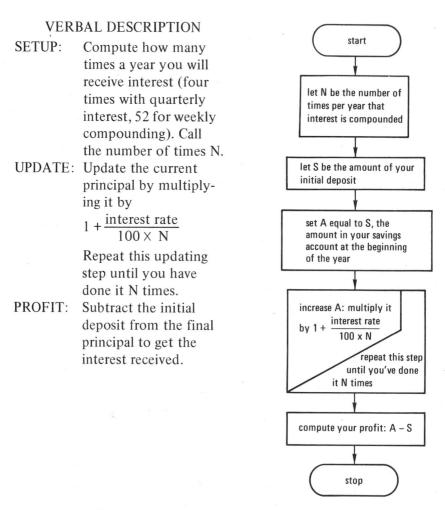

Figure 1 3 5   Computing Compound Interest

This algorithm has a characteristic which is common to many algorithms; it repeats one of its statements several times. Computers are often used to perform difficult tasks by repeating many simple tasks as in this example. Possibly this is where the characterization of computers as "high speed idiots" comes from. This seems a little unfair since the computer *is* able to perform its program, and this is all we expect of it. Perhaps the program could be characterized as intelligent or idiotic, but the terms don't apply to the computer itself.

EXERCISES 1 3

1 Write a verbal description of and a flow chart for one or two of the
following:

    making a dessert (following a recipe)
    fixing a flat rear tire on a bicycle
    computing your income tax
    writing a haiku verse
    buying a pair of shoes
    figuring your grade-point average
    getting a driver's license

Section 1 4

Machine Ideas

You will recall from Section 2 that Fortran was designed for use on many
different computers. Fortran, and therefore WATFIV also, assumes that every
computer has certain characteristics. These assumed characteristics can be described in simple terms and are helpful to know. The WATFIV statements you
will soon be learning will make sense if you visualize them as affecting the various
parts of the **conceptual computer** shown in Figure 1 4 1.

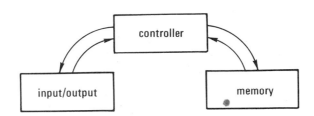

Figure 1 4 1   The Conceptual Computer

The conceptual computer has three parts, a controller which carries out the
commands which make up your program, a memory which stores your program
and any values it may use or produce, and input-output devices through which
values are fed in and printed out. We'll describe each part in concrete terms.

The **memory** consists of some number of words or **cells**. A memory cell is a
collection of two-state elements. At any point in time each element is in one or the
other state. These two states are commonly named

*memory: part of a computer
which stores programs and data*

"0" and "1" by machine designers, and although
we'll rarely think of memory cells in these terms,
the size of a memory cell is invariably given in **bits** (binary digits), the number of
two-state elements making up the cell.

Each cell in memory has an **address** (denoting where it is) and a **value** (the particular pattern of 1's and 0's that it contains). In WATFIV programs we give a **name** to each memory cell we wish to store a value in; the name can be thought of as the address of the memory cell. We can issue commands which will copy the value from a particular memory cell into another part of the machine by using

> *We use the terms* word, cell, memory word, memory location, *and* memory cell *interchangeably.*

the name of that memory cell. As the term "copy" implies, doing this does not disturb the value in the memory cell. We will also be able to store values in memory cells, and since there is only a fixed storage capacity (a fixed number of bits) in a cell, the value that used to be there is destroyed when a new value is stored.

The **controller** is the central coordinator of the conceptual computer. Your program, being stored in the memory, is really just a bunch of values (patterns of 1's and 0's) in a bunch of memory cells. The values that make up your program are examined by the controller, and the 1's and 0's work like electrical switches turning on the various subunits required to carry out the command. We're not trying to say that a computer is just a lot of 1's and 0's. That would be a vast over-simplification. But we want to emphasize that

> *controller: part of a computer which carries out commands from a program*

the controller simply carries out the instructions or commands specified by bit patterns in memory cells. The controller can get values from memory cells, can manipulate them, can put new values back in memory, and can supervise the input and output devices.

Input and output devices **(I/O devices)** are the means of communication between human users and the machine. You will probably punch commands to the computer on cards, and these cards will be "read" by a **card reader,** an input device. The other I/O device you will use frequently is the **printer** which will print your program and its results. TV and movie scenes involving computers always seem to focus on card readers, line printers, magnetic tape devices, or card sorters. The

> *input/output: part of a computer which allows communication between users and the computer*

first three are I/O devices often used to help communicate with a computer. A card sorter, on the other hand, stands alone, not connected to a computer. It can do several information processing tasks, but it cannot be considered a general purpose computer. Probably these devices are shown because they move at a spectacular rate of speed. In the controller and the memory, on the other hand, nothing moves at all except electrons, and they're hard to see.

There are other types of I/O devices, but until you know much more about computers, you'll be able to get by with just a card reader and a line printer. If you think we're being elusive, look at the manual describing the computer you will be using. Then you'll think we're as clear as Frank Zappa is weird.

Anyway, lest you think a card reader can actually *read,* let us emphasize that a card reader converts the holes in the card into electrical signals. These signals are put into the memory by the controller. Hence they become the values associated with those memory cells.

The card reader is commanded to "read" a card by the controller (when the controller has been instructed by your program). Similarly the controller can send values to the printer and direct the printer to print them.

EXERCISES 1 4

1 Tour the computer you will be using and look at the various I/O devices, the controller (or **processor**), the various types of memory, etc.

2 Find out something about the machine you will be using—the number of bits per word, the number of words in the memory, the brand and model number, the price, etc.

3 List the parts of the "conceptual computer" and their functions.

4 What is the difference between the name of a memory cell and its value?

Section 1 5
A Program for the Conceptual Computer

To get an idea of how computers operate, it will be helpful for you to simulate a computer running a program. The idea is to play the roles of the various parts of the conceptual computer as it goes through the steps of a program. This is a realistic simulation. Every command is directly analogous to a WATFIV statement, and all of the parts of the conceptual computer are used. The program you'll be simulating takes in two values and raises the first to the power designated by the second, using repeated multiplication. If the two values are 2 and 4, for example, the program will eventually arrive at the result 16 (two times two times two times two).

Begin as follows:

1 Get a stack of cards and label nine of them with the names STATEMENT 1, STATEMENT 2, . . . , STATEMENT 9. Label three more with the names A, B, and EXP. These twelve cards represent the memory. Spread them out so you can see them all at once, or at least so you can get to them easily.

2 Get a piece of paper and a pencil to use to write the output sent to the "printer".

3 Take three more cards and write

      2   3   on the first

      5   0   on the second

and 2 −1 on the third.

Place these cards face up in a stack with the first card on top for use by the "card reader".

4 Write the instructions (program statements) below on the cards labeled STATEMENT 1 through STATEMENT 9.

COMMENT: this program computes one number raised to the power of a second number.

STATEMENT 1   Remove the top card on the card reader stack, copy the first number on it into memory cell A, copy the second number into memory cell B, and then throw the card away.

STATEMENT 2   Look at the value in memory cell A and send it to the printer followed by the phrase "TO THE POWER", then send the value of B to the printer, and finally send the word "IS".

STATEMENT 3   Store the value 1 in memory cell EXP.

STATEMENT 4   Look at the value in memory cell B. If it is zero, take your next instruction from STATEMENT 8, otherwise go on to STATEMENT 5.

STATEMENT 5   Look at the values in memory cells EXP and A, multiply them together, and store the result in EXP.

STATEMENT 6   Take the value from memory cell B, subtract one from it, and place the new value back in B, erasing the old value.

STATEMENT 7   Get your next instruction from STATEMENT 4.

STATEMENT 8   Look at the value in memory cell EXP and send it to the printer.

STATEMENT 9   Get your next instruction from STATEMENT 1.

The program you will carry out does a fairly simple task; it reads in two numbers, a and b, and then multiplies a by itself b times. Figure 1 5 1 is a flowchart for the process.

> **exponentiation:** *to compute a^b, just take*
> $$\underbrace{a \times a \times \ldots \times a}_{b \; factors}$$

In order to carry out the program, simply start with the instruction in memory cell STATEMENT 1, carry out exactly what it says, and then proceed to the next memory cell in sequence (*i.e.,* to STATEMENT 2, and so on). Some of the instructions say to break the sequence. In this case, you again proceed sequentially after starting from the new STATEMENT. Go!

There are a great many things to be learned from what you just did (assuming that you did the above simulation). The STATEMENTs that you (simulating the controller) carried out are very similar to the commands which can be written as statements in WATFIV, so you now have a feeling for the degree of explicitness required to write programs. In addition, the algorithm we used has an unfortunate but altogether too common property—it works fine for some input values, and lousy for others. Hope you didn't go on too long with the last pair of input values

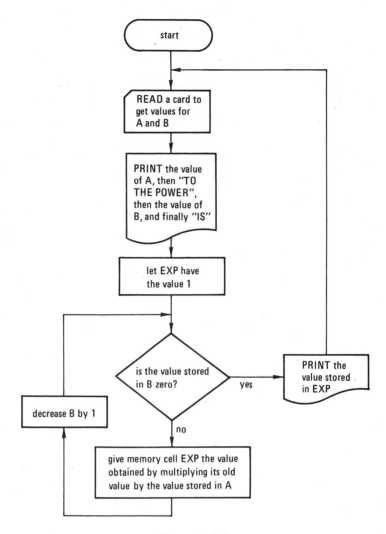

Figure 1 5 1

before you realized that something was desperately wrong. To be realistic, we should have given you a time limit, after which you (the controller) would stop executing the program whether you were finished or not.

The exercises below will give you a little more practice in choosing and expressing commands; Exercise 4 will help in making the transition from the simulated computer to the mechanics of running real programs.

EXERCISES 1 5

1 Add another command into the exponentiation program so that it will just stop if the value for memory cell B is negative.

2 Write a program for the conceptual computer which computes the average of a bunch of numbers.

3   Write a program which finds the longest name in a list of names. Write a bunch of your friends' names on cards, and simulate a computer executing the program to find the longest name.

4   Punch up a deck of cards, making an exact copy of the cards shown in the drawing at the front of this book with these two exceptions:

a   replace the name in apostrophes on the card which begins with the word PRINT by your name. For example, if your name is Chester Farnsworthy, change the card to read

PRINT, 'CHESTER FARNSWORTHY'

b   Replace the control cards

$JOB
and $ENTRY

by cards appropriate to your computer center.

(The control cards for running WATFIV programs will be written on the walls somewhere in the computer center. Look around the place; you'll be spending a lot of time there.)

2 SIMPLE PROGRAMS

Section 2 1
Memory Cells

Of the three parts of the conceptual computer, the memory is probably the most confusing. The I/O apparatus's purpose is straightforward, the controller carries out commands, some of which you can imagine from your class simulation, and the memory is used to store values. This seems simple enough, but confusion seems to arise from the fact that each memory cell has a name. Because of the way computer programs are written, many people tend to confuse the name of a memory cell with the value stored in it, a mistake similar to confusing a box with its contents. Try to keep in mind that a memory cell is a container for a value.

We've said a number of things about memory already (that it's made up of cells, each of which has an address or name and a value, and that both your program and data are stored there). In this chapter we'll make these ideas more concrete and begin to get some ideas of how we use the computer's memory.

In order to use the memory in the WATFIV language, you need a name for each memory cell you intend to use. The language is very considerate in that it allows you to name the memory cells in any way you like, as long as you follow a few rules.

> *rules for naming memory cells*
> *start with a letter*
> *use* only *letters and numerals*
> *use no more than six characters*

As long as you follow these rules you have *complete freedom*! For example, you may name a memory cell DARN, if you like, or any other four letter word, or POT or CELL12 or COFFEE. But you may not name a memory cell MARI-JUANA or ASPIRINS because these names have too many characters, nor can

> *If you are using the* KP=29 *option (the light gray, modern-looking keypunches) you may use $ signs in memory cell names.*

you name one D--N because two of the characters in that name are neither letters nor numerals.

Once you have named a memory cell, the natural question arises: "What can you do with it?" The answer is that you can store any kind of information you want in it, as long as you can devise a way to represent the information.

By the time you get through this book, you will be able to create representations for whatever types of information you want to deal with. However, certain features of WATFIV make it easier to deal with a few specific types of information. So, for a while we'll use only those types. In fact, in this chapter you'll see only two of those **data types**, as they are called.

> *A **data type** is a well defined collection of items of information. A computer system or the programmer associates a special representation with each data type. Since a particular item of information, when stored in the computer's memory, is actually a string of 0's and 1's, this associated representation is essential for correct interpretation of the information item. Two different items of information may be stored in the computer's memory as the same string of 0's and 1's if the items have different data types. In this case the difference between them is determined solely by the difference in their associated representations.*

When you want to use a memory cell in a WATFIV program, you must decide what kind of information it will contain; that is, you must choose its **type**. Within a program you may use many memory cells containing many different types of information, but any *one* memory cell is allowed to contain only *one* kind of information. That is, you will associate *one* name and *one* data type with each memory cell you use.

> FORTRAN *is not a legal memory cell name. But* WATFIV *is.*

In this chapter, to keep things simple, the only data types we will deal with will be **integer numbers**, like 1, 2, 3, 7, 11, −4, −1, and 0, and **character strings**, like 'CAT', 'DOG', 'ZEBRA', and 'BOGGLE YOUR MIND'.

> *In* WATFIV *programs each* INTEGER *must be written as a series of digits which may be preceded by a + or a −sign:*
>
> 1492
> +83
> −194
> +0047
>
> *A* WATFIV INTEGER *may not contain any other kinds of symbols.*
>
> 1,492 *won't work.*
> +83.0 *won't work either.*

At the beginning of each WATFIV program we use declaration statements to name the memory cells we intend to use and we say what type of information we intend to store in them. For example, the declaration statement

```
INTEGER TWO, THREE, A, Q1
```
gives names to four memory cells whose contents will be INTEGERs. On the other hand, the declaration statement

```
CHARACTER*10 X, Y, Z
```

gives names to three memory cells, X, Y, and Z, and decrees that each will be used to store a string of ten characters. The declaration statement

```
CHARACTER*1 WOK, FOO
```

attaches names to two memory cells, each of which will contain one character. A memory cell may contain only one kind of information. It can't contain an INTEGER value at one point and a CHARACTER*1 value at another point.

In WATFIV programs, each **CHARACTER*n** *constant must be enclosed in quote marks (single quotes, like apostrophes, rather than double quotes).*
   'HOUSE'
   'FARM'
   'K7 SPOT REMOVER'
   '$43.27***TOTAL'
The quote marks aren't part of the CHARACTER string. They only serve to delimit the ends of the string which may contain any characters, including blanks.

---

declaration statement

form
   type list
   type is the name of a WATFIV data type (INTEGER or CHARACTER*n for example)
   list is a list of memory cell names, separated by commas
   Note: In the case of the CHARACTER*n data type, the *type* name CHARACTER is followed by a string length indicator of the form *n where *n* is an INTEGER between 1 and 255. If *n* is 1, the *1 may be omitted.

meaning
   instructs the compiler to attach the names in *list* to memory cells which will be used to store information of the *type* declared at the beginning of the statement

examples

```
INTEGER A, B, C, TWO, THREE, Q1
CHARACTER*10 W, ALPHA, Z27, STUDNT
CHARACTER*3 R, SP, TRACK
```

EXERCISES 2 1

1 Which of the following are legal names for memory locations? If not, why not?

23SKIDOO   JUICE
SKIDOO23   TONY THE TIGER
TORQUE   FORTRAN
BATMAN13

2 Which of the following are legal declaration statements?

```
INTEGER A
INTEGER A, B
INTEGER VERYLONG
INTERGER Q
CHARACTER*3 J, Z, BETA
CHARACTER HIGH, LOW
```

3 Write a declaration statement naming two memory cells called AJAX and FOAM to be used to store INTEGERs.

4 Give an example of a number that is *not* an INTEGER.

5 Write a declaration statement attaching three names to memory cells to be used for storing CHARACTER strings of length 47.

6 Which of the following are legitimate CHARACTER*n strings and what are the length and contents of each legitimate string?
'MERRY GO ROUND'
'C'
'1,472'
'392 + 932'
'75 CHICKENS'
'23 CENTS/CHICKEN'

Section 2 2

The Assignment Statement

The question of how to get information into the memory cells you have named still remains. There are two ways. One is to assign values to the cells directly in the program; the other is to get their values from some source of data such as punched cards. Each method has its advantages in different contexts, but the former is the more important in learning to program. We will discuss it first.

An **assignment statement** gives values to memory cells directly in the program. The general form of the assignment statement is a memory cell name followed by the assignment operator (the equal sign, =), followed by the value which you wish to place into the memory cell. The assignment operator transfers the value on its right into the memory cell named on its left.

The assignment statement confuses many people, perhaps because the assignment operator (=) is a familiar sign, but the operation it designates is *not* familiar. The action in an assignment statement proceeds from *right to left:* the value on the right is placed into the memory cell named on the left. This is an important thing to remember, so important that you should probably read this paragraph again.

> =   *Remember! In* WATFIV *the equal sign does not mean equals in the mathematical sense. A statement like* A = B *places the value in the memory cell* B *into the memory cell* A. *It is true that immediately after the statement is executed the values in* A *and* B *are the same, but at some later time the values in the two memory cells may be different. For example, the next statement in the program may assign a different value to* B. *This won't affect the value of* A, *so at that point* A's *value will be different from* B's.

Examples

```
TWO = 2
```
the value 2 is placed into the memory cell named TWO

```
THREE = -1
```
the value −1 is placed into the memory cell named THREE. (This is a lousy name for a cell containing the value −1, but WATFIV doesn't care.)

```
STUDNT = 'JOHN SMITH'
```
the ten-character string 'JOHN SMITH' is placed into the memory cell named STUDNT

```
TRACK = '.'
```
a period is placed into the memory cell named TRACK.

Of course, in order for the above assignment statements to work properly, the declaration statements

```
INTEGER TWO, THREE
CHARACTER*10 STUDNT
CHARACTER*1 TRACK
```

must appear at the beginning of the program.

---

assignment statement

form
    v = *e*
    v is a memory cell name
    e is an expression

meaning
    computes the value of *e* and places it in *v*

examples
```
A = 3
T = 'LONG'
C = 3*A + 47
```

It would soon get boring just writing programs that assigned values to a bunch of memory locations. Fortunately, the right hand side of an assignment statement can be more complex than just a single number or CHARACTER string. It may be an **expression** involving some arithmetic computations. In WATFIV, the familiar operations of addition, subtraction, multiplication, division, and exponentiation may be used in the usual way (see TABLE).

(Table)

operation	standard symbols	example	WATFIV symbol	examples
addition	+	a + b	+	A+B 1+1
subtraction	−	a − b	−	A−B 3−2
multiplication	×	a × b	*	A*B 4*4
division	÷ — /	a ÷ b $\frac{a}{b}$ a/b	/	A/B 10/2
exponentiation	superscript	a^b	**	A**B 2**10

The reason the multiplication and exponentiation symbols aren't the same as usual will become apparent if you look at a punched card. There would be no way of telling the multiply sign × from the letter X, so * is used instead. In addition, there's no way of punching superscript symbols, so we use ** instead.

Example

    A = 18427 - (14*639)

The value of the arithmetic expression above (namely 9481) is placed into the memory cell named A.

Expressions can be considerably more general than the ones you have seen so far, which have involved only constants. It is also permissible to use memory cell names in an expression. Thus, names of memory cells may appear on both sides of an assignment statement, but the names are used in very different ways. As you already know, the name on the *left* side tells where to *store* the value which results from the computation on the right side. Memory cell names on the *right* side mean "go to this place in memory, and use whatever value is stored there in the computation." It is important to realize that the values of memory cells on the right remain unchanged.

Example

```
Q1 = (TWO*THREE) + (A - THREE)
```

The value of the arithmetic expression on the right is placed into the memory cell named Q1. To compute the value of the expression, the controller must first determine the contents of each of the memory cells TWO, THREE, and A, then execute the indicated arithmetic operations. If we assume the values of the memory cells TWO, THREE, and A haven't changed since the last time we used them in this chapter, then TWO has the value 2, THREE has the value −1, and A has the value 9481, so Q1 will be assigned the value 9480.

Example

```
Q1 = Q1 + 1
```

The value of the expression on the right is placed into the memory cell named Q1. This example may appear odd at first because the memory cell to be given a value is involved in the expression on the right. This is one time when it is especially important to remember that the action goes from right to left. First the computer looks up the current value of Q1; our last assignment made that value 9480. Adding 1 to 9480, the value of the expression is 9481, and this value is put into the memory cell Q1. This assignment destroys the old value of Q1, of course.

In most cases writing arithmetic expressions to make computations is quite natural and the results fit in pretty well with your past experience. However, there is one big difference to keep in mind. Remember that each memory cell is made up of a fixed number of elements or symbols, 0's and 1's. That means that some numbers will be too long to fit. For example, INTEGER memory cells in IBM 360 or 370 computers can only handle INTEGERs in the range −2149531648 to +2149531647. This may not seem particularly restrictive, and usually it isn't, but it is important to realize that this doesn't include *all* integers. There is an infinite number of (mathematical) integers. If you are not careful, this restricted INTEGER range may cause you to get results you don't expect. For example, if you multiply two big numbers together, the result may be too big to fit in one memory cell. If this happens, the part that doesn't fit is lost!

> INTEGERs *vs. integers: You have probably noticed that when we refer to* WATFIV *values of type* INTEGER, *we write* "INTEGER". *When we want to refer to "counting numbers", i.e., mathematical numbers, we'll write "integers".*

Another problem arises in evaluating expressions like 29/7. The result certainly cannot be computed to infinite precision, but what value should be computed? WATFIV settles this question by convention: the value of an arithmetic operation involving only INTEGERs must be an INTEGER. Therefore, if the value 4 1/7 comes up as the quotient of two INTEGERs, the fractional part is dropped. Hence 29/7 equals 4 (in WATFIV).

Arithmetic expressions will be dealt with in more detail later. For now, rely on your past experience with mathematics to guide you in using parentheses to denote groups of operations which are to be done before others. For example, 1 + (7 * 3) is 22, but (1 + 7) * 3 is 24. You may also rely on the usual algebraic rules of precedence: exponentiations are performed first, then multiplications and divisions, then additions and subtractions. For example, 10 + 7**2/12 equals 10 + [(7**2)]/12), which is 14. When you are uncertain about how an expression will be evaluated, use parentheses to make it perfectly clear.

EXERCISES 2 2

1 At the end of the following program fragment, what are the values of A and B?

```
INTEGER A, B
B = 10
A = B
B = 2
```

2 What values would be stored in INTEGER memory cell B by these assignment statements?

```
B = 2*3*4
B = (2/1) + 1
B = -19*2
```

3 Which of these are legal assignment statements? If not, why not? (Assume all variable names have been declared to be INTEGERs.

```
A = A*A + A
BO = 2
-AT = 2
AT = -AT
CAT + DOG = FIGHT
CAT + DOG - 3
FIGHT = CAT + DOG
```

4 What value will be stored in INTEGER memory cell SOUP by these assignment statements?

```
SOUP = 1 + (7*4)/2
SOUP = 123/2
SOUP = (19/20) + 1
SOUP = (21/20) + 1
SOUP = (8/16)*1024
```

5 Write statements which will
   a declare an INTEGER memory cell named FIRST and assign FIRST the value 2,
   b assign FIRST its old value times 4, and
   c assign FIRST its old value plus 1.

28

6 At the end of the following program fragment, what will be the contents of the memory cells?

```
CHARACTER*4 A, B
CHARACTER*1 P
A = 'WAIT'
B = 'WALK'
P = ','
```

7 One of the statements in the following program fragment is not proper. Which one?

```
CHARACTER*6 A, B
A = 'TUMBLE'
B = 'RUMPLESTILTSKIN'
```

8 At the end of the following program, what will be the contents of the memory cells?

```
CHARACTER*6 A, B, C, D
A = 'TO OWE'
B = 'TOO WE'
C = ' BATS '
D = 'BATS  '
```

Section 2 3

The PRINT Statement

So far you have learned how to attach names to memory cells and to place values into them. You can also make the computer perform computations involving INTEGER numbers. Unfortunately, however, you have no way at this point of finding out the results of the computations. The PRINT statement will solve this problem as the following example demonstrates.

Suppose you are buying a car, and you want to compute the total price, including an optional FM radio and supersport airfoil spoiler. The computation might proceed like this:

1 note the base price
2 note the price of the FM radio option
3 note the price of the airfoil spoiler option
4 add the above three figures to get a subtotal
5 compute 2 percent sales tax (2% = 1/50)
6 add tax to subtotal to get total cost

The program below makes these computations. Actually, due to the truncation involved in INTEGER division, the tax computation may be as much as 49 cents short, but we won't worry about that at this point. You should be able to understand everything in the program except, possibly, the PRINT, STOP, and END statements. We'll explain those after you've looked the program over carefully.

```
INTEGER BASEPR, RADIO, SPOILR
INTEGER SUBTOT, TAX, TOTAL
BASEPR = 4127
RADIO = 232
SPOILR = 248
SUBTOT = BASEPR + RADIO + SPOILR
TAX = SUBTOT/50
TOTAL = SUBTOT + TAX
PRINT, 'BASE PRICE     $', BASEPR
PRINT, '     RADIO     $', RADIO
PRINT, '   SPOILER     $', SPOILR
PRINT, ' '
PRINT, 'TOTAL PRICE    $', SUBTOT
PRINT, '          TAX  $', TAX
PRINT, ' '
PRINT, 'PLEASE PAY CASHIER    $', TOTAL
STOP
END
```

Each of the PRINT statements in the program instructs the controller to send one line to the printer. The first line printed will contain the CHARACTER*15 constant listed after the word PRINT and the value of memory cell BASEPR.

```
BASE PRICE     $         4127
```

The second and third PRINT statements have a similar form with different CHARACTER*n constants and memory cells, and together they cause the controller to print two more lines. The fourth PRINT statement may seem a little strange. It says to print a blank and nothing else. This causes a blank line to be printed so that different sections of the output will be separated on the page. This isn't strictly necessary, of course, but it makes the output from the program easier to read. You will probably want to use similar formatting tricks in your programs. The complete output from our program appears below.

```
BASE PRICE     $         4127
     RADIO     $          232
   SPOILER     $          248

TOTAL PRICE    $         4607
        TAX    $           92

PLEASE PAY CASHIER    $         4699
```

A PRINT statement causes a line to be printed. In general a PRINT statement begins with the word PRINT, followed by a comma, then by a list of values to be printed. If there is more than one of these values, then they are separated by commas. It is important to realize that each PRINT statement starts a new line, so that, in order to print more than one thing on a single line, a PRINT statement must have a list consisting of more than one value. These values may be simply constants, like 'TAX $', or they may be the names of memory cells whose values are to be printed, or, more generally, they may be expressions whose values are to be computed and printed.

The above program, for example, would have printed exactly the same results if the last PRINT statement had been

```
PRINT, 'PLEASE PAY CASHIER    $', SUBTOT + TAX
```

In fact, this PRINT would have simplified the program in a sense because it avoids the need for the assignment statementTOTAL = SUBTOT + TAX. Actually, you can rewrite the above program without using any memory cells at all simply by including all the computations as expressions in the PRINT lists. If you rewrite the program in this way, you will notice that the computer will need to perform some computations more than once, and this is one of the reasons we used memory cells in our version. Another reason is that the program is easier to understand when the computations are separated into small pieces and their results assigned to memory cells whose names indicate the purpose of the computations.

PRINT statement

form

PRINT, *list*

list, an **output list**, contains one or more values (*i.e.,* constants, memory cell names, or expressions) separated by commas. One restriction: the expressions in *list* must not begin with parentheses.

meaning

The controller directs the printer to print each of the values in the *list* on a line. If the values won't all fit on one line, as many lines are used as are needed to complete the printing of the entire *list.*

examples

```
PRINT, X
PRINT, C
PRINT, X, X+Y, 'STRING'
PRINT, +(X*Y-X)
```

Getting back to the program, you are probably still wondering about its last two lines—the STOP and END statements. The STOP statement instructs the controller to stop executing your program and proceed to someone else's. The END statement instructs the compiler that there are no more statements in your program. The END statement must be, physically, the last card in your program, but the STOP statement may appear anywhere. Of course, after the STOP is executed, no other statement in your program will be executed, so it's difficult to see why you would want to put it anywhere except immediately preceding the END statement, but in Chapter 3 we'll see examples where the difference between STOP and END is clearer. For now, just remember that the compiler, in translating your program to machine language, translates STOP into a command for the controller, but END is an instruction for the compiler itself and is not translated into a machine language command.

STOP statement

form
    STOP

meaning
    instructs controller to stop executing your program and begin
    to execute someone else's program

END statement

form
    END

meaning
    instructs compiler that there are no more statements in your
    program

Now that you have seen a complete program, you will no doubt want to write a program to do some computation and print the results. In order to prepare the program on punched cards, you'll need to know the format for a WATFIV statement card. In general each statement goes on a separate card and is placed in the statement field; that is, in columns seven through seventy-two. Other fields on the WATFIV statement card are used for purposes that we will discuss later.

Conventions concerning the physical appearance of WATFIV statements are based on the assumption that the statements are punched on 80 column cards. Certain columns are used for certain purposes. There are four fields on a WATFIV statement card:

1. the label field (columns 1-5)
2. the continuation field (column 6)
3. the statement field (columns 7-72)
4. the identification field (columns 73-80).

The identification field is completely ignored by the compiler but it is printed on your program listing and is often used for card numbering. In all fields, blanks are ignored; you should use blanks freely to make your program readable.

You write one statement on each card. However, if your statement is too long to fit in the statement field of one card, you may continue it into the statement field of the next card by placing any mark (other than zero) in the continuation field (column 6) of the second card.

There is one additional convention: a C in column 1 will cause the compiler to ignore the entire card. Since the card will be printed on the program listing, you may use this convention to intersperse your program with comments.

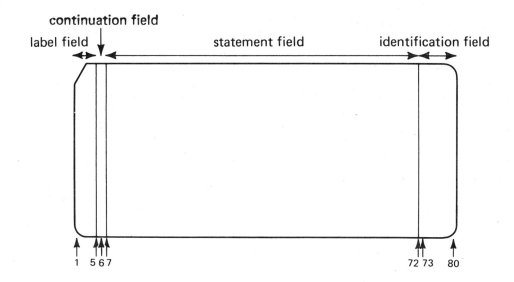

continuation field

label field   statement field   identification field

1   5 6 7   72 73   80

EXERCISES 2 3

1 Are all of the following statements legal?

```
PRINT, X + (2*Y), 3*7415+1
PRINT, 'WHY NOT', (X+Y)*2
PRINT, 'OK', +(X+Y)*2
```

2 Rewrite the program of this section without using any memory cells.

Section 2 4

The READ Statement

In most cases the most convenient and efficient way to place values into memory cells is to use the assignment statement which we have just discussed. There is, however, a second way to give values to memory cells which, in certain cases, makes a program easier to use. We are speaking of the READ statement. Its main advantage is that it allows you to change the data that the program uses in its computations without changing the program itself. The following example illustrates the point.

Suppose you are tired of balancing your checkbook each month, especially since your balance often disagrees with the bank's. You know the bank uses a computer to figure your balance, so maybe if you use a computer too, you will have a better chance of agreeing with the bank. Let's try to think of a way to write a program to compute your bank balance.

Basically, the program must assign the old balance and amounts of the month's transactions to memory cells, compute the new balance, and print the result. One approach to writing such a program is described below.

1. for each check you wrote, declare one memory cell to store the amount
2. for each deposit you made declare one memory cell to store the amount
3. declare a memory cell to store the old balance and one to store the new balance
4. assign values for the old balance and all the checks and deposits using assignment statements
5. write an expression which computes the new balance and assign its value to the memory cell to be used for that purpose
6. print the new balance

The big disadvantage to a program like this one is that it must be changed every month. Each month you will write a different number of checks for different amounts, make a different number of deposits, and have a different old balance. Therefore, you will have to declare a different number of memory cells in each month's program and assign them different values.

A second approach would be to keep a running balance rather than to do all the totaling at the end. Then, instead of needing a memory cell for each check and deposit, you need only one cell for the current transaction (check or deposit) and one cell for the current balance. This approach is described in Figure 2 4 1.

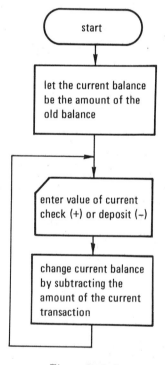

Figure 2 4 1

Although this approach is closer to what we want, there is still a problem; there is no way to stop and PRINT the final balance. The program just keeps going. You will learn a way to exit the loop to print results in Chapter 3, but for now we'll try another approach.

We are trying to avoid changing the program each month. Of course it is clear that something must be changed since the amounts of the transactions will be different each month, but it would be nice to have some way to give the program this information without having to change the program itself. To give data to the program from an outside source, in other words. This can be accomplished by using the READ statement. The READ statement directs the card reader to place values into memory cells. These values are taken from data cards which are not part of the program itself. A READ statement consists of the word READ followed by a comma, followed by a list of memory cell names. The memory cell names in the list must be separated by commas, just as they were in the declaration statements you saw in Section 2 1.

The READ statement places a value into each memory cell in the **input list,** getting these values from a data card following your program. The first value on the card goes into the first memory cell in the input list, the second value into the second memory cell, and so on. The values must be separated by spaces or commas, and each value must be a constant of the same data type as the corresponding memory cell in the READ list. If the first data card does not contain enough values to fill all the memory cells in the list, then the next card will be used, and so on until all the memory cells in the input list have values.

READ statement

form
    READ, *list*
    list, an **input list,** is a list of memory cell names separated by commas

meaning
    Places values into the memory cells in *list* taking the values from a data card or cards. If there is more than one memory cell in *list*, the values on the data card(s) must be separated by commas or spaces. The first value on the card(s) will be stored in the first cell in the list, the second value in the second cell, etc.

examples
```
READ, TCELL
READ, A, B, C
```

If there are leftover values on a card used by a READ statement, they will be totally ignored by the program. The next READ statement will start over on the next card.

No data card can be read twice. Each time a READ *statement is performed, it starts at the beginning of a new card.*

You may recall that in Chapter 1, when you were simulating a computer, the controller executed some statements similar to READ. It was a two step process: first the controller told the card reader to read a card, then told certain memory cells to remember the values on that card. The WATFIV READ statement is executed in the same way.

> **data cards**: *cards with values punched on them which follow your program. They are not statements in your program, but they contain values to be stored in memory cells used by your program.*

These data cards are placed after a special card put after the end of your program. This card, which for most systems contains only the phrase $ENTRY, tells the compiler that there are no more statements in your program and signals the controller to start executing your program. The exact form of this signal card varies from one installation to another so you should consult your reference manual or local experts.

> *Since data cards come after your program and are not part of it, their use is not bound by the rules for punching* WATFIV *statements. You may use any or all of the 80 columns available.*

Now let's see how we can use the READ statement to solve the bank balance problem. Recall that we wanted to write the program in such a way that we could use it every month without change. Thus the program itself can neither depend on the actual amounts of the checks and deposits nor on the number of transactions. This calls for careful planning, and we will take several stabs at the problem before coming up with a complete solution.

Our first approach is to READ the amounts of the transactions one by one and keep a running total representing the current balance. Our program will assume that there are no more than five transactions in any one month. If you are a heavy check writer, you could easily change the program so that it will handle 25 or 50 transactions, but this dependence on a maximum number of checks is an objectionable feature which we will remove later in an improved version of the program. Read the program carefully, and try to understand what it does. We'll describe it in detail after you've read through it.

```
COMMENT--THIS PROGRAM CALCULATES A NEW BANK BALANCE GIVEN
C        THE OLD BALANCE AND TRANSACTIONS.
C        TO USE THE PROGRAM, PUNCH SIX DATA CARDS.
C          CARD 1  --OLD BALANCE  (ALL AMOUNTS IN PENNIES)
C          CARDS 2-6--TRANSACTIONS (POSITIVE FOR CHECKS AND
C                                   NEGATIVE FOR DEPOSITS)
        INTEGER BALNCE, TRANS
        READ, BALNCE
        READ, TRANS
        BALNCE = BALNCE - TRANS
        READ, TRANS
        BALNCE = BALNCE - TRANS
        READ, TRANS
        BALNCE = BALNCE - TRANS
        READ, TRANS
        BALNCE = BALNCE - TRANS
        READ, TRANS
        BALNCE = BALNCE - TRANS
        PRINT, 'NEW BALANCE IS', BALNCE, 'CENTS'
        STOP
        END
```

data
```
    45603
    7836
   -2539
    4525
     4522
   -7542
```

output
```
NEW BALANCE IS          38801 CENTS
```

There are several things to notice about the above program. The most important is the high degree of redundancy. That is, the statements READ, TRANS and BALNCE = BALNCE – TRANS are repeated over and over again. There are always ways to avoid repeating the same statements over and over again, and you will learn one in the next chapter, but for now this will have to suffice.

The second important feature is the technique of computing the sum of the transactions using a single memory cell in which the running sum builds up. In this case, that memory cell is called BALNCE. First we put the amount of the old balance into BALNCE. This step is called **initialization**. Each time we got the amount of a new transaction from a data card, we changed BALNCE by that amount. This technique, called **accumulating a sum,** is very common in computer programming. You will see it again and again. In this case the sum accumulates one term at a time in the memory cell BALNCE.

EXERCISES 2 4

1 Prepare some data cards for the above WATFIV program assuming that you wrote four checks in the amounts \$4.27, \$27.92, \$132.00, and \$9.42, made one deposit in the amount of \$237.26, and had an old balance of \$1.25. What results would be printed if the program were executed with these data cards?

2 Which of the following are legal WATFIV I/O statements? If a statement is not legal, explain why.

```
READ, A, B, D
PRINT, A, B, D
READ, A, A+B, 2
PRINT, A, A+B, 2
PRINT A, B
PRINT, A, 2
PRINT, (A+B)
PRINT, +(A+B)
```

3 Write a program which READs four INTEGERs from a card and PRINTs out their sum.

PROBLEMS 2

1 Write a program to (a) print your name (b) assign the result of a computation to an INTEGER memory cell, *e.g.,* N = 1 + 2 − (3*4)/5, and (c) print the value of this INTEGER variable below your name.

2 Write a program which READs INTEGERs representing miles driven and gallons of gas used. Compute your car's mileage and print out miles driven, gallons used, and gas mileage.

3 Write a program which computes and PRINTs the sum of the squares of the first twenty integers: $1^2 + 2^2 + \ldots + 20^2$.

4 Write a program which READs the lengths of the sides of a rectangle from a data card and PRINTs those lengths along with the area of the rectangle.

5 Write a program which READs a person's name (twenty characters) from a data card along with five INTEGERs representing the amounts of the named person's credit card purchases for the month and PRINTs the sum of these amounts along with the person's name.

3 SIMPLE LOOPS

Section 3 1

Introduction

By now you know enough WATFIV statements to write programs which perform numerical computations and PRINT out the results. You also know that the numbers used in the computations can either be written within the program itself or gotten from data cards outside the program. Thus you are able to use a computer to do computations similar to those you might do on a desk calculator. In some cases it might actually be more convenient to use a computer to do these calculations, but most of the time it would be easier to use the desk calculator. In one case, the numbers and arithmetic operation symbols are punched on cards; in the other case, entered directly into the machine through its keyboard—about the same amount of work. The computer might have a slight advantage if the expression is written with lots of parentheses which make it hard to untangle; and the calculator might have a slight advantage in simply totaling up a list of numbers (as in our checking account problem) since the procedure is simple enough to be remembered without being written down in the form of a program. Thus, the computer may not seem particularly useful to you right now, but by the end of this chapter you will begin to see how useful it can be.

Totaling a list of numbers on a calculator is a very repetitious task: enter a number, punch the add key, enter a number, punch the add key, etc. The WATFIV program we wrote in Chapter 2 to total a list of numbers was also very repetitious:

```
        .
        .
        .
READ, TRANS
BALNCE = BALNCE - TRANS
        .
        .
        .
```

It turns out that a repetitious program can always be written in a much more compact way using a program structure known as a **loop**. Instead of writing the same statements over and over, we tell the computer to repeat the statements. In order to tell the computer to repeat, we need to know a new kind of WATFIV statement.

loop:

Section 3 2

Transfer of Control

If we come to a point in a program where we want to repeat a previous statement instead of proceeding in the usual sequence to the next statement, we must have some way of telling the controller where to begin that repetition. In WATFIV this is done by placing a **label** on the statement to be repeated and referring to that label to effect the repeat. To tell the controller to repeat from the statement whose label is *s*, we write

GO TO s

The label *s* is an unsigned INTEGER between 1 and 99999. The statement to be repeated will have the number *s* in its label field, columns one through five (see the box at the end of Section 2 3 describing the statement card format). Almost any statement may be labeled, but it is wise to put a label on a statement only if it is necessary to refer to the statement from some other point in the program.

> *The only statements we've seen so far which may not be labeled are the declaration statements*
>> INTEGER *list*
>> CHARACTER*n list
>> *and the* END *statement.*
>
> *These are commands to the* compiler, *not to the controller.*

Examine the following rewritten version of Chapter 2's bank balancing program.

```
column 7
    |
    INTEGER BALNCE, TRANS
    READ, BALNCE
20  READ, TRANS
      BALNCE = BALNCE - TRANS
      GO TO 20
    END
```

This version avoids having to rewrite statements in the program. Instead, the GO TO statement causes them to be repeated. Unfortunately, the program suffers from the same malady as the flowchart in Figure 2 4 1: it never stops to print the final balance.

We need some way to avoid repeating the important steps in the program indefinitely. We want to add a new transaction to the balance only if we haven't already finished adding all of this month's transactions. In other words, instead of always returning to statement 20, we want to return only under certain *conditions*. A conditional GO TO would solve the problem. You may recall that in Section 1 3 we had a similar problem with the ZAPPO algorithm, but there was no problem with the knitting algorithm because it had a conditional repeat.

Fortunately, WATFIV provides a way to construct a **conditional statement**: the IF statement. For our current purposes, the **IF statement** has the form

$$\text{IF } (e_1 \; rel \; e_2) \text{ GO TO } s$$

where s is a statement label, e_1 and e_2 are arithmetic expressions like the right hand side of an assignment statement, and rel expresses a relation between e_1 and e_2. The six possibilities for rel are shown in the accompanying box.

relation	usual symbol	WATFIV symbol
less than	$<$	.LT.
less than or equal to	$\leqslant$	.LE.
equal to	$=$	.EQ.
not equal to	$\neq$	.NE.
greater than or equal to	$\geqslant$	.GE.
greater than	$>$	.GT.

(Actually the IF statement can be more general than this, but we'll get to that later.) If $e_2 \; rel \; e_2$ is true, then the controller proceeds to statement s; otherwise, the controller continues from the statement following the IF statement in the usual sequence. For instance, the IF statement below

$$\text{IF (TRANS .NE. 0) GO TO 20}$$

means "IF the value of memory cell TRANS is not equal to 0, then GO TO statement 20; otherwise, just go on to the next statement."

IF statement (restricted version)

form
> IF $(e_1 \; rel \; e_2)$ GO TO s
> e_1 and e_2 are arithmetic expressions
> rel is a relational operator
> s is a statement label

meaning
> instructs the controller to decide whether or not the expressed relationship between the arithmetic expressions is true; if so, the controller proceeds from statement s; otherwise it continues from the next statement as usual

examples
```
IF ( A+B .GT. 0 )  GO TO 130
IF ( 3*(A/B) .GT. C*B )  GO TO 500
```

Now let's see how we can use the IF statement to fix our program. We want to say,

"If the last transaction has not yet been added
to the balance, repeat from statement 20."

There is no way to say this directly using the IF statement, so we will have to find a way to say it in the language we have available. To do this we need some way to tell when we have reached the last transaction. Of course, we have no way of knowing in advance exactly what the amount of the last transaction will be, but with a little thought we realize that we know something the last transaction won't be: it will *not* be zero. How can we use this fact?

Suppose that, after punching all of the month's transactions on cards, we punch one more card containing the transaction *zero*. When we come to a card containing the transaction zero, we will know that it must be the last transaction. Our program can use that fact to determine whether or not to continue the loop.

```
        INTEGER BALNCE, TRANS
        READ, BALNCE
 20     READ, TRANS
          BALNCE = BALNCE - TRANS
          IF ( TRANS .NE. 0 ) GO TO 20
        PRINT, BALNCE
        STOP
        END
```

> Note that we've indent-
> ed the statements that
> make up the loop.

data
```
    45603
    7836
   -2539
    4525
     4522
   -7542
          0
```

output
```
        38801
```

The program places the beginning balance in BALNCE, then adds each transaction into the balance until it reaches the last transaction (zero). At that point, instead of returning to statement 20 to add in another transaction, it prints the final balance and stops.

Perhaps we should note that the program actually adds the phony zero transaction into the balance. Since zero doesn't change a sum, it doesn't affect the result, but that is really a fortunate coincidence. It would be better not to add the phony transaction into the balance at all. Can you think of a way to change the program so that is doesn't add the phony transaction (see Exercise 3 2 2)?

Simple as it seems, the IF statement you have just learned about adds a great deal of power to the language. In fact, there is a mathematical theorem which says that any computation which can be done at all, no matter how complicated, can be programmed using statements you already know: the assignment statement, the PRINT statement, the GO TO statement, and the IF statement. The rest of the WATFIV statements you will learn won't make the language any more powerful, but they will help you write programs in a more concise, efficient, and readable way than you could using only what you know now. Nevertheless, using only the statements you know now, you can program the computer to do a large variety of useful tasks, and these programs can be both efficient and clearly expressed. We hope this will give you some confidence when you attack the problems at the end of this chapter.

EXERCISES 3 2

1 Are any of the following IF statements illegal?

```
IF ( X .GT. Y )  GO TO 35
IF ( X*2 + 17 .LE. Y**2 )  GO TO 100
IF ( 14 .EG. 2 )  GO TO 10
IF ( X .SGT. A )  GO TO 15
IF Y .EQ. 0, GO TO 20
```

2 Rewrite the bank balancing program so that it doesn't add in the phony transaction.

Hint: You will need to move the IF statement, change its GO TO statement, add another GO TO statement in the place where the IF now stands, and put a label on the PRINT statement.

Section 3 3

Loops

To become more familiar with the IF statement, let's try to write a WATFIV program to do the computations of the laundry detergent problem of Figure 1 2 2. In that problem we wanted to average the price per pound of a number of laundry detergents. Imagine that you had a bunch of cards and each card contained the price and the weight of a different brand of detergent. The flowchart in Figure 3 3 1 shows what we want to do. Briefly, we want to accumulate a sum of prices, counting the number of terms in the sum as we go along, and divide the total by the number of terms to get the average price. You are already aware of a technique for accumulating a sum, so the part of the program which computes the sum of the prices should be easy to follow.

> *Counting the number of times some event happens (number of cards read, for instance) is just a special case of accumulating a sum, namely the case in which each term in the sum is 1.*

Follow the flowchart in Figure 3 3 1 and try to see what it does. If you don't quite get it, make up some data cards and follow the instructions, performing the computations as you go. Once you understand the flowchart, try to see how you'd convert each part of it to WATFIV statements. Hopefully the only place you'll have any trouble at all is in translating the statement "does the card contain a price and weight?"

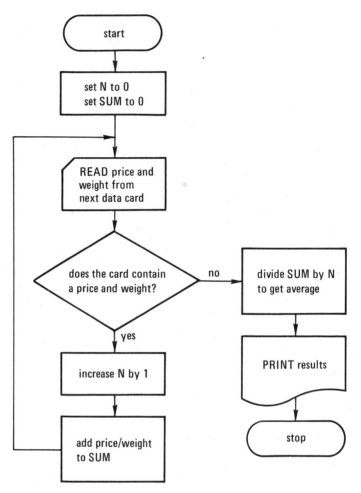

Figure 3 3 1   Computing the Average Price of a Laundry Detergent

How can the program know what is a price and weight and what isn't? The method we used in the check balancing program was to put a data card containing phony values after the data cards containing legitimate values and testing for the phony values in the program. We can do the same thing here. We know that no company is going to pay you to take their detergent, so no brand will have a negative price. Thus, we can put a data card indicating a negative price at the end of the cards with legitimate prices. Then, to see if the card we just READ was the last card, we simply test to see if the value we READ is less than zero.

One thing we need to point out here is that the numbers we will be dealing with (price per pound) will not be whole numbers; they will have fractional parts and will need to be written with decimal points. Therefore, we can't use INTEGER memory cells to store the numbers. We will talk about numbers with fractional parts at length in Chapter 4, but for now, we'll simply say that in WATFIV numbers with decimal points are called REAL numbers, are always written with decimal points in them, and that memory cells containing REAL numbers must be declared to be of type REAL (as opposed to type INTEGER or CHARACTER*n, the types with which you are already familiar).

Follow through this program and convince yourself that it does what we want.

```
COMMENT:  FIND THE AVERAGE COST OF LAUNDRY DETERGENT
          REAL SUM, PRICE, WGT, AVG
          INTEGER N
C
C         GET PRICES AND WEIGHTS, KEEPING TRACK OF TOTAL UNIT
C         COSTS AND NUMBER OF BRANDS SAMPLED.
          N = 0
          SUM = 0.00
   10     READ, PRICE, WGT
C            HERE'S WHERE WE TEST FOR THE TERMINATION CARD
             IF ( PRICE .LT. 0.00 )  GO TO 20
C            AVERAGE IN THIS BRAND
             SUM = SUM + (PRICE/WGT)
             N = N + 1
             GO TO 10
C
C         WE'VE GOT THE TOTAL UNIT COST.  NOW COMPUTE AVERAGE.
   20     AVG = SUM/N
          PRINT, 'THE AVERAGE PRICE PER POUND OF THE'
          PRINT, N, 'BRANDS IS', AVG
          STOP
          END
```

data

```
4.49  15.0
1.47   3.1
2.96   4.7
6.95  18.3
5.36  15.8
-1.0   0.00
```

output

```
THE AVERAGE PRICE PER POUND OF THE
        5 BRANDS IS    0.4244668E 00
```

> 0.4244668E 00 *means* 0.4244668
> 0.4379221E 03 *means* 437.9221
> 0.7311489E-01 *means* 0.07311489
>
> *It's a form of* **scientific notation**. *We'll discuss it in Chapter 4. You'll have to tolerate it in your output.*

Loops like the ones you have seen in the check balancing program and the detergent price program are an extremely important part of most computer programs. In fact, many programs would simply be impossible to write in WATFIV without using loops. The loops you have seen so far have been quite simple, and you have probably had little difficulty in understanding what they do, but loops can get complicated quickly. (We'll show you a more complicated loop in the next section.) For this reason, it is advisable to construct loops carefully in an attempt to keep the program as well organized and straightforward as possible. Some rules to follow in writing loops are outlined in the accompanying box. We think that if you will keep these rules in mind when you write WATFIV programs, you will be able to avoid many errors.

---

loop writing

one entry, one exit

In general, a loop should be entered only at the top. That is, there should not be any jump (GO TO) from outside the loop to a statement in the middle of a loop. One reason for this is that, when writing a loop, you will tend to make many assumptions about the values of the memory cells involved in the loop. A jump into the middle of the loop often makes these assumptions unjustified. Similarly, exits from the loop should be jumps to the first statement following the loop. Following this rule tends to keep the program more straightforward.

pre-test, post-test

In general there should be only one statement in a loop which can terminate the loop, and this statement should be either at the very beginning of the loop (**pre-test**) or at the very end (**post-test**). Jumps out of the middle of a loop, especially if there is more than one of them, can lead to erroneous assumptions about the memory cells involved in the loop. Although the test in our detergent program is not the first statement of the loop, it is an inherent part of the first operation in the loop, namely the operation of obtaining a new piece of legitimate data. In a sense, it is reasonable to think of the test for legitimate input as a part of the READ statement itself, the first statement in the loop. It is possible to convert such loops into versions which satisfy a strict interpretation of the *pre-test* (or *post-test*) concept. But the idea is to produce clear, simple constructs. Bending over backwards to suit some supposed ideal can cause clutter itself.

indentation

Loops are, conceptually, a single unit in a program and should be made to appear that way by formatting the program listing in some appropriate way. We do this by indenting each statement of the loop after the first. This simple practice makes a surprising difference in the readability of the programs.

1 Any value that could not possibly be a price for a detergent can be used to signal the end of the data cards. Rewrite the IF statement in the detergent price program so that the value 99999.99 is the last card signal.

2 Write a program that counts by fives, printing the successive counts as it goes. Terminate the count when it reaches 100.

3 (optional) Rewrite the detergent price program so that its loop is in post-test form.

4 (optional) Compare the version of the bank balance program in Section 3 2 with the version of Exercise 3 above. Which follows our loop writing suggestions? Which is better?

Section 3 4

Nested Loops

We have decided to provide a bank balance computing service for our friends. At the end of each month our friends will bring us a record of their checking account transactions in the form of a deck of punched cards. We could simply take the first deck, use the program in Section 3 2 to compute the new balance, then take the next deck, run it, etc. We would have to repeat this process until we had completed each of our friends' new balances; that is, until we had no decks left to run. We might be at the computer center all day.

Alternatively we could let the computer do more of the work by adding a few statements to the bank balance program so that it automatically starts the process over for each friend's account.

Let's consider what sorts of things we would need to do to convert our old program to this new, more useful form. First we would need some way of making the correspondence between the new account balances and the person who gave us those cards. A good way to do that would be to ask our friends to place a card which has their name on it (in single quotes so it is a legal CHARACTER*n constant) at the front of their deck. Other than that, they need make no changes—just as before, they put the old account balance on a card, follow it by their transactions for the month, and indicate the end of their deck by putting a card with a 0 on it at the end.

All we have to do now is add some statements to our program so that it repeats its computations once for each of our friends' accounts. It can tell when it is through with one deck by testing (just as before) for a 0 transaction card. But wait . . . how can it tell when it has done the last deck? After it completes the last deck, how is it to know that no deck follows?

So far we've imagined the program to have the form of Figure 3 4 1. After it has finished the last deck, it would just go back, expecting another name card. A

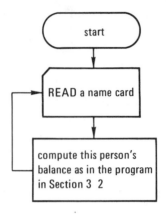

Figure 3 4 1

reasonable solution is for us to slap a special card at the end of the stack of our friends' decks—a card with the CHARACTER*11 constant 'END OF DATA' on it will do.

Our program now will have the form of Figure 3 4 2. It contains what is known as a **nested loop**; that is, a loop inside another loop. This structure is like that of the knitting algorithm in Section 1 3.

Our new program appears below. Although the general form of the program is familiar, some of the details are new. For example, it contains a new kind of IF statement. The statement to the right of the first IF statement is not

---

IF statement (restricted form)

form
    IF (*rel*) *s*

    rel is a relational expression
    s is an executable statement other than an IF (*s* is the **object** of
    the IF)

meaning
    perform *s* if *rel* is true

examples
```
IF ( A .LT. B )   STOP
IF ( G*Q .EQ. H )   A = 47*G + Q
IF ( 3*Z .GT. 96+H )   PRINT, Z
```

---

a GO TO statement as it has always been before. It is a STOP statement instead. In general any executable statement (READ, PRINT, assignment, or STOP) can be placed on the right of an IF. An exception is that an IF statement cannot be on the right of another IF. Of course, non-executable statements (*e.g.*, compiler instructions like INTEGER A, REAL B, or END) cannot be objects of IF statements because that would not make sense. In order to make sense of them, the compiler would have to check the value of the relational expression, but that can be done only when the controller executes the program.

There is one other new element in that same IF statement. The **relational**

                        WATFIV for Humans

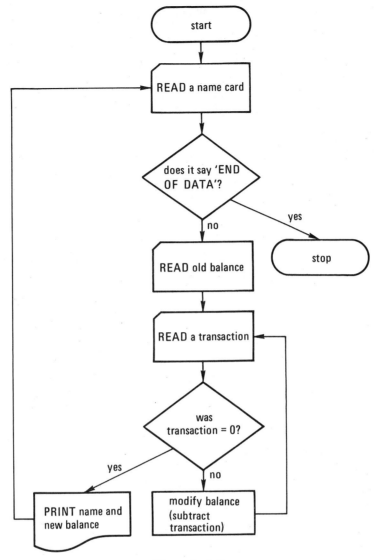

Figure 3 4 2

expression compares two CHARACTER*n strings instead of two numbers. Two strings are considered equal if they are the same except for extra trailing blanks.

---

character string equality

s .EQ. t is true if s and t are identical strings of the same length; if one is longer than the other, then it is true if they are identical up to trailing blanks on the longer one.

examples
'ABCD' .EQ. 'ABCD' is true
'ABCD' .EQ. 'ABC'   is false
'ABCD' .EQ. 'ABCD ' is true
'ABCD' .EQ. 'ABCD GOLDFISH' is false

```
COMMENT--THIS PROGRAM COMPUTES BANK BALANCES FOR ONE OR MORE
C           PERSONS.   THE DATA CARDS MUST BE ORGANIZED IN
C           GROUPS, EACH GROUP STARTING WITH A CARD CONTAINING
C           A CHARACTER STRING INDICATING THE NAME OF THE
C           PERSON WHOSE BALANCE IS TO BE COMPUTED.  THE SECOND
C           CARD MUST CONTAIN THE PERSON'S OLD BALANCE.  EACH
C           ADDITIONAL CARD MUST CONTAIN A TRANSACTION ON THE
C           ACCOUNT, POSITIVE NUMBERS FOR WITHDRAWALS AND
C           NEGATIVE NUMBERS FOR DEPOSITS.
C           EACH GROUP MUST TERMINATE WITH A CARD CONTAINING
C           A ZERO.  ALL AMOUNTS MUST BE IN PENNIES.
C           THE FINAL CARD FOLLOWING ALL THE GROUPS MUST
C           CONTAIN THE CHARACTER STRING 'END OF DATA'
      CHARACTER*78 NAME
      INTEGER BALNCE, TRANS
  100 READ, NAME
      IF ( NAME .EQ. 'END OF DATA' )  STOP
      READ, BALNCE
  150    READ, TRANS
         IF ( TRANS .EQ. 0 )  GO TO 160
         BALNCE = BALNCE - TRANS
         GO TO 150
  160    PRINT, ' '
      PRINT, NAME
      PRINT, BALNCE
      GO TO 100
      END
```

Data

```
'F. DAVID LESLEY'
 45632
  2298
  3354
-29155
  5439
  0000
'VERNOR VINGE'
 33252
  2203
-32941
  2211
  0000
'END OF DATA'
```

Output

```
    F. DAVID LESLEY
        63696

    VERNOR VINGE
        61779
```

EXERCISES 3 4

1   Why have we declared the memory cell NAME to be a string of length 78
    and not some other length?

2   Modify the program so that it prints a record of transactions as well as a balance for each person. If you can, have the program print each transaction as a positive number (even though deposits are READ as negative quantities) with the word DEPOSIT beside each deposit.

PROBLEMS 3

1   Write a WATFIV program to READ two numbers per card and PRINT these two numbers and their difference on one line; the last card will contain zeros.

2   Write a WATFIV program which will calculate the area of a right triangle given the lengths of the two legs. Each data card will contain two numbers representing the length of the legs. Assume that the last data dard will contain two zeros.

3   Write a program which computes the sum of the first N odd integers where the value of N comes from a data card.

4   Write a program which computes the product $1*2*3* \ldots *N$, where the value of N comes from a data card.

5   Write a program which computes the first perfect square larger than 84,123. A perfect square is an integer which is the square of another integer (perfect square = $n*n$). Use a loop in your program. (An easy technique is to square each integer, starting at 1 and going up until you find a square larger than 84,123.)

6   Bobby's mom gave him a new bike for his birthday. The gear ratios on his bike are

gear	ratio
1	3.3:1
2	2.02:1
3	1.52:1
4	1:1

and the speed of his bike is given by the formula

speed (miles per hour) = .02 * rpm/gear ratio

For example, his speed at 3300 rpm in low gear would be

.02 * 3300 * 1 / 3.3 = 20 mph

Write a program which reads in data cards giving the rpm's where he shifts. For each shift point, have your program print out his top speed in each gear. If an rpm value over 6500 rpm comes in, print the message

BOBBY'S BIKE EXPLODED

and then STOP.

Bobby's New Bike

4 EXPRESSIONS IN DETAIL

Section 4 1
Introduction

As you know, the computer's memory is made up of a number of cells and we can put values into these cells, make computations, and PRINT results. We have mentioned that the interpretation of these values is pretty much up to us. In WATFIV we can denote values of several different data types, and the system will automatically represent them as a pattern of 1's and 0's in memory cells. You're already familiar with the INTEGER, REAL and CHARACTER*n data types. In this chapter we'll discuss the remainder of the available data types and explain the rules for the evaluation of expressions.

Section 4 2
INTEGERs and REALs

Before jumping directly into the details of arithmetic expressions, we'd like to review the characteristics of their basic elements, numbers—REALs and INTE-GERs. An INTEGER is a signed or unsigned string of digits in the range −2147483648 to 2147483647. As you know, the finite range is a consequence of the fact that memory cells have a finite capacity.

INTEGER constant

form
> string of decimal digits which may be preceded by a + or − sign representing a number in the range −2147483648 to 2147483647

examples

(LEGAL)
> +1497
> −392
> −01124
> 33421

illegal forms

(ILLEGAL)
> +1,497   *no commas allowed*
> −392.0   *no decimal point allowed*
> 33,492.1

The Number of '54 Chevy's You've Seen
in Your Lifetime Is an INTEGER

For the same reason, REALs have a finite range. In practice, the limitations imposed by the finite range of REALs seldom comes into play, but their finite accuracy does. We didn't have the accuracy problem with INTEGERs because they are represented precisely. REAL numbers, on the other hand, are represented to about seven decimal digits of accuracy.

REALs are written as signed or unsigned strings of decimal digits containing a decimal point. For writing super big numbers like the national debt or super small numbers like the diameter of a chlorine atom, WATFIV provides a version of the widely used "scientific notation". This consists of writing a REAL constant in the usual form followed by a decimal point shift factor (which is an E followed by an INTEGER constant). The decimal point shift factor in a REAL constant indicates how far to move the decimal point in the number that precedes the E. Positive shifts indicate shifts to the right, negative shifts to the left.

REAL constants

form
  x
  $x\mathrm{E}s$

  x is a signed or unsigned string of up to 7 decimal digits containing a decimal point
  s is a one or two digit INTEGER constant
  $-78 \leqslant s \leqslant +75$

meaning
  the number indicated by x with its decimal point shifted s places (positive s indicates right shift; negative s, left shift)

If You Measure a Pizza, You Get a REAL Number

---

valid and invalid REALs

form   *meaning*
  1.00
  −7.7254
  +.000137
  .472E5   (LEGAL)   47200.
  +7.21E−2   .0721
  −1.22E−12   −.00000000000122
  +6.023E+23   Avogadro's Number
  .002E3   Avis's Number

  1,482.5   (ILLEGAL)   invalid, no comma allowed
  723   invalid, needs decimal point
  −4.18732E−.5   invalid, shift factor must be INTEGER

This E-notation for REALs is something like the way the numbers are represented in the computer. The 0's and 1's in a REAL valued memory cell are divided into two parts, the fraction or "mantissa" and the hexadecimal point shift or "exponent". If a computation results in a number with an exponent which is too large, an "overflow" occurs. On the other hand, computations may result in numbers whose exponent parts are too large in the negative direction to fit in the reserved space. Such a condition is called an "underflow" since the number is too small to be represented.

Overflows and underflows occasionally occur, but they don't cause nearly as many problems as the restricted (7 digit) accuracy in the mantissa. Limited accuracy makes it impossible to represent a number like

$$1./3. = .33333333333 \ldots$$

Any digits beyond those that fit into the memory word simply get lost. This can occasionally cause some embarrassing situations, because in WATFIV 1./3. + 1./3. + 1./3. doesn't quite equal 1.0! The errors due to this effect are called "roundoff errors". In certain applications roundoff errors, each one seemingly insignificant, can add up to make a final answer completely wrong. This is a serious problem, and numerical analysts have spent enormous effort trying to understand how to avoid getting such erroneous results.

EXERCISES 4 2

1 Which are legal INTEGER constants; which are not? If not, why not?

1	4*2
1.0	12.75
−12	−127.5
−134794	1275
12 + 2	−0

2 Which are legal REAL constants? If not, why not?

2	−22E+30
+2	5.67
+2.00	5.67E0
−2.01E3.2	300E30.
−2.1E3	−22.E+30
−2.22E−22	−.0000021

3 Look up the definitions of the terms real and rational in a math book. Which term do you think is closest to REAL numbers in WATFIV?

Section 4 3

Arithmetic Expressions

You have already seen many examples of arithmetic expressions. They were used as the value portion of assignment statements, as elements in PRINT lists and in relational expressions in IF statements. We purposely kept those expressions quite simple in order to defer a detailed explanation of the rules of evaluation until now.

Arithmetic expressions are formed of memory cell names and arithmetic constants separated by arithmetic operators (addition, subtraction, multiplication, division, exponentiation). In addition, parentheses may be used to force the controller to perform the operations in the desired order.

Consider the following examples of arithmetic expressions:

A+2   find the value of A and add it to 2

CAT−(DOG*18)   find the value of DOG, multiply it by 18 and sub-
                            tract the value of CAT

PI*(R**2)   raise the value of R to the power 2 (*i.e.,* square
                            R) and multiply the result by the value of PI

In each of these examples the meaning of the expression is quite clear, but
consider a more complicated expression like

```
SUMXSQ/(N-1.0)  -  SUMX**2/(N*(N-1.0))
```

In this case the expression appears ambiguous because it is not clear which operations should be performed first. Should we proceed left to right, right to left, or
by some other set of rules? Surely we should perform the operations grouped by
the parentheses first, but after that there is still ambiguity. Are we to raise SUMX
to the power 2 or to the power 2/[N*(N−1.0)]? Do we divide SUMXSQ by
(N−1.0) or by (N−1.0)−SUMX? The expression would be easier to interpret if we
could write it in normal algebraic notation, but we can't.

$$\text{in normal algebraic notation the expression is}$$
$$\frac{sumxsq}{n-1} - \frac{sumx^2}{n(n-1)}$$

In WATFIV the order of operations proceeds according to the following **rules
of precedence,** which are the same as those used in ordinary algebra.

( ) First	compute the expressions within parentheses
** Second	perform exponentiations
*, / Third	perform multiplications and divisions
+, − Fourth	perform additions and subtractions
→ Tiebreaker	perform adjacent additive operations (+, −) from left to right
	perform adjacent multiplicative operations (*, /) from left to right
	perform adjacent exponentiations (**) from right to left

Now no ambiguity remains. The expression is equivalent to

```
(SUMXSQ/(N-1.0))  -  ((SUMX**2)/(N*(N-1.0)))
```

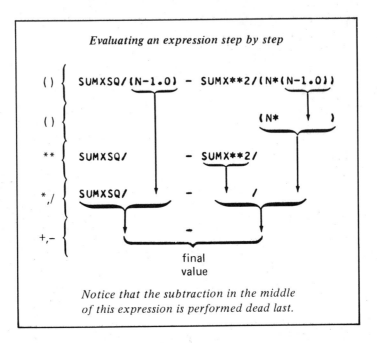

Evaluating an expression step by step

Notice that the subtraction in the middle of this expression is performed dead last.

The tiebreaker rule covers one further possible ambiguity which didn't arise in our example. Consider the expression

$$A/B * C - D + E$$

The rules of precedence tell us to perform multiplications and divisions before additions and subtractions. Therefore $A/B * C$ must be evaluated first. But does that mean $(A/B) * C$ or $A/(B * C)$? Using the tiebreaker rule, we see that $(A/B) * C$ is the WATFIV interpretation.

tiebreaker		
A – B + C	means	(A – B) + C
A/B * C	means	(A/B) * C
A**B**C	means	A**(B**C)

Arithmetic operators may be used with either INTEGERs or REALs, as both are numeric quantities, but there are fundamental differences in the ways in which these two data types are represented in memory as well as differences in the results of computations involving the different types. As you know, quotients of INTEGERs are always INTEGERs (the remainders are simply dropped), but quotients of REALs retain their fractional part. Therefore, it is quite important to be aware of the data types in arithmetic expressions involving different kinds of numbers. This is crucial to understanding why 10/4 * 6.0 evaluates to 12.0. The rule is this: when a +, –, *, or / operation involves a REAL and an INTEGER, the computation is performed as if both were REALs and the result is REAL. Thus, 10/4 * 6.0, which by the rules of precedence is equivalent to (10/4) * 6.0, is the product of the INTEGER 10/4 or 2 and the REAL 6.0. The result is the REAL 12.0.

Because INTEGERs and REALs are so different and because the rules for combining them arithmetically don't conform to our usual expectations, it is wise to keep the two types separate. We'll try to do this in the text. However, exponentiation operations are an exception to the rule. Here is one place where it is quite desirable to mix REAL and INTEGER in the same expression. For example, the expression 4.73**8 means to form a product containing eight factors, 4.73 times itself eight times. The result of this computation is quite naturally a REAL.

It is also possible to raise a REAL to a REAL power, but the computation which is performed is quite different. For example, 4.73**1.79256 clearly cannot mean to multiply 4.73 times itself 1.79256 times. In order to make this computation, the controller first computes the logarithm of the base in the exponentiation, multiplies that by the exponent, getting a product p and finally raises $e = 2.7182818\ldots$ to the power p. Since logarithms of negative numbers do not generally result in REAL values, *it is illegal to raise a negative number to a REAL power.* No logarithms are involved in raising a number to an INTEGER power, however, so there is nothing wrong with an expression like (−4.73)**8 even though the expression (−4.73)**8.0 would be illegal. Therefore, use INTEGERs for exponents whenever you can.

$$x^y = e^{y\,\log(x)}$$

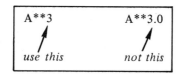

```
  A**3            A**3.0
   ↗               ↗
use this         not this
```

There is one other thing that can cause trouble. We told you that INTEGER constants could be numbers like −2 or 3 and we said that you could use an arithmetic operator between two constants; however, 3 * −2 is illegal in WATFIV. In addition to the rules for forming arithmetic expressions that you've seen so far, there is the rule that *no two operator symbols (*, /, +, −, **) may come in a row,* no matter what they're used for. The expression 3 * −2 can be written legally as 3 * (−2).

Now that we know how to create and interpret arithmetic expressions, let's return to the assignment statement—one place where we can use arithmetic expressions. Recall that an assignment statement is a memory cell name followed by the assignment operator (=) followed by an expression. The assignment statement tells the controller to evaluate the expression and store the result in the memory cell named to the left of the assignment operator. In this way the controller gives the cell a new value. For example, if we had made the declarations

```
INTEGER NUMB1, NUMB2, SUM, CENTS
REAL DOLARS
```

then these assignment statements

```
NUMB1 = 1
NUMB2 = 2
SUM = NUMB1 + NUMB2
CENTS = 125
DOLARS = 125./100.
```

would leave the assignees with these values:

NUMB1	1
NUMB2	2
SUM	3
CENTS	125
DOLARS	1.25

---

arithmetic expressions

form
> basic arithmetic elements (numeric memory cells, unsigned numeric constants, or parenthesized subexpressions) separated by arithmetic operators (+, −, *, /, or **) with an optional sign (+ or −) at the beginning of the expression

meaning
> the meaning is the value computed according to the rules of precedence and meaning of the arithmetic operators

examples
> X**(−2)
> Z * X + ((A/B−C) * 18.4)
> X**B + 10.4
> 3 + 14 * (Q + P)
> 4 * (−3)
> −4 * A

illegal forms
> X**−2
> 4 * −3
> A * −4

Everything was nice and easy—each expression on the right was of the same type as the memory cell named on the left, so it was obvious what to store. What if, however, a statement like

```
CENTS = DOLARS*100.0
```

had appeared? The memory cell named on the left is an INTEGER; the expression on the right is REAL. A very important rule about assignment statements takes care of this situation.

The rule is that *the expression to the right of* the replacement operator *is evaluated first* without any concern being given to the memory location named on the left. After the expression has been evaluated, a check is made to see if the type of the result agrees with the type of the memory cell where the result is to be stored. If it does not agree, then *the value stored in the memory cell is the value of the expression after being converted to the data type required by the memory cell.*

So, in the example above, first DOLARS * 100.0 is evaluated to get the REAL value 125.0, and then, since CENTS is declared to be an INTEGER, the corresponding INTEGER value 125 is stored in CENTS.

This is a very important rule to understand. Here are a few examples.

```
INTEGER DAF, FIAT, VW
REAL FORD, REBEL
DAF = 1
FIAT = 2
VW = DAF*3 + FIAT*2
```

leaves the memory cells with the values

DAF	FIAT	VW
1	2	7

Now, follow through these assignments.

```
FORD = (DAF + FIAT)*2
```

results in

FORD	6.0

```
REBEL = VW/2
```

results in

REBEL	3.0

The last result follows from the peculiar nature of the INTEGER division which occured *before* the result was changed to REAL to be stored in REBEL.

EXERCISES 4 3

1 Using the precedence rules, compute the value of the expression (−1**4).

2 Use parentheses to make the meaning of the following arithmetic expressions perfectly clear.

```
MOUSE + CAT*DOG**2
SEX + DRUGS - SKIN*FLICK + BUSTER**BROWN**SHOES
ROCK/ER/FELLOW
```

3 Suppose A has the value −3.7, then A**2 is legal, but A**2.0 isn't. Why?

4 In the following program, SNAFO takes on several different values at different times. What values are they?

```
INTEGER A, B, C
REAL SNAFO, R1, R2
R1 = 1
R2 = 2
A = 1
B = 4
C = 16
SNAFO = R1 * R2
SNAFO = A * R2
SNAFO = B/(A+B)
SNAFO = B
SNAFO = C/B
STOP
END
```

5 In algebraic notation we write the product of two terms like *a* and *b* as *ab*. Why isn't this allowed in WATFIV?

Section 4 4

Other Operators

Many people write programs which involve finding the logarithm of some value. Although not as many people use the logarithm operation as, say, addition, it still would be a terrible waste for each person to have to rediscover his own algorithm for computing logarithms. WATFIV provides a number of additional commonly used operators which may be used in expressions. This program uses two of these operators

```
REAL X, T, SQRT, ALOG
X = 144.0
PRINT, 'SQUARE ROOT OF 144=', SQRT(X)
T = ALOG(X/12.0)
PRINT, 'LOGARITHM OF 144/12=', T
STOP
END
```

```
SQUARE ROOT OF 144=     0.1200000E 02
LOGARITHM OF 144/12=    0.2484906E 01
```

Notice that the operators appear just before the expression we wish them to operate on, and that that expression is enclosed in parentheses. Also notice that we have declared that the operators will yield REAL values by listing their names in a type statement.

The quantity in parentheses after an operator is called its argument. Probably this term is familiar to you from mathematics. Some operators have more than one argument, and in that case the arguments are separated by commas. In fact, some operators may be given a different number of arguments at different times (MIN0, for example, which yields the minimum value of all its arguments, no matter how many there may be).

A number of commonly used operators (or built-in FUNCTIONs as they are commonly called) are shown in Figure 4 4 1. The rest of the built-in FUNCTIONs are described in the MiniManual.

Some useful built-in FUNCTIONs

The argument should be REAL valued if shown as *r* and INTEGER if shown as *i*.

FUNCTION	value computed	type of result
SQRT(r)	$\sqrt{r}$	REAL
ALOG10(r)	log to the base 10 of r	REAL
ALOG(r)	natural logarithm of r	REAL
EXP(r)	e^r, where e is the base of natural logarithms	REAL
SIN(r)	trigonometric sine of r radians	REAL
COS(r)	cosine of r radians	REAL
TAN(r)	tangent of r radians	REAL
ATAN(r)	the angle $\left(-\frac{\pi}{2} \text{ to } \frac{\pi}{2}\right)$ whose tangent is r	REAL
ABS(r)	the absolute value of r, $\lvert r \rvert$	REAL
IABS(i)	$\lvert i \rvert$	INTEGER
FLOAT(i)	REAL version of i FLOAT(2) is 2.0	REAL
INT(r)	INTEGER version of r INT(−3.7) is −3	INTEGER
MAX0($i_1, i_2, \ldots, i_n$)	largest value of $i_1, i_2, \ldots, i_n; n \geqslant 2$	INTEGER
MIN0($i_1, i_2, \ldots, i_n$)	smallest value of $i_1, i_2, \ldots, i_n, n \geqslant 2$	INTEGER
AMAX1($r_1, r_2, \ldots, r_n$)	largest value of $r_1, r_2, \ldots, r_n; n \geqslant 2$	REAL
AMIN1($r_1, r_2, \ldots, r_n$)	smallest value of $r_1, r_2, \ldots, r_n; n \geqslant 2$	REAL

Figure 4 4 1   Built-in FUNCTIONs

The compiler should be informed what type of result each FUNCTION you use will provide. Thus we would declare FLOAT to be REAL because that's the sort of result it gives.

EXERCISES 4 4

1 What is the value of

    IABS(MINO(-2,-3,149*79675/1888))

2 Rewrite this program by replacing the four statements between REAL ... and STOP with one statement which makes equivalent computations and prints the same results.

```
REAL AMAX1, ALOG, SQRT, SIN, LSOFAR
LSOFAR = ALOG(1.E+2)
IF ( LSOFAR .LT. SQRT(144.) )  LSOFAR = SQRT(144.)
IF ( LSOFAR .LT. SIN(3.14159) )  LSOFAR = SIN(3.14159)
PRINT, 'LARGEST VALUE=', LSOFAR
STOP
END
```

```
LARGEST VALUE=    0.1200000E 02
```

Section 4 5 *

Using Truncation

> This section may be skipped without loss of continuity.

You are probably wondering why WATFIV chooses to deal with two different kinds of numbers instead of sticking with one kind as we normally do in our hand computations. The answer probably lies in the fact that experience has shown that integers and numbers with fractional parts are used in basically different ways in most computations. It is also true that the difference allows for greater flexibility in our programs. For example, INTEGER division, with its truncation property, can often be used to advantage. The following question can be dealt with easily in WATFIV because INTEGER division drops the remainder.

Question: Is the INTEGER value stored in N evenly divisible by 2?

Answer: If (N/2) * 2 is equal to N, then yes, otherwise no.

Explanation: If N is evenly divisible by 2, then N/2 will not have any fractional part to lose, so (N/2) * 2 will equal N. If, however, N is not even, then the division will lose a fractional part and (N/2) * 2 will be different from N.

Examples: If N = 6, then
              (N/2) = 3 and 3*2 is equal to 6.
              If N = 7, then
              (N/2) = 3 and 3*2 is not equal to 7.

WATFIV for Humans

There are many other ways in which the differences between INTEGERs and REALs are useful. Our next example uses the fact that if an assignment statement has a REAL right hand side and an INTEGER memory cell on the left, an INTEGER version of the right hand side is stored in the cell. Another way of saying this is that the fractional part is *truncated* or *chopped* so that the value can be expressed as an INTEGER.

A bar graph is a popular way to summarize data. Figure 4 5 2 is a bar graph summarizing the data pictured in Figure 4 5 1.

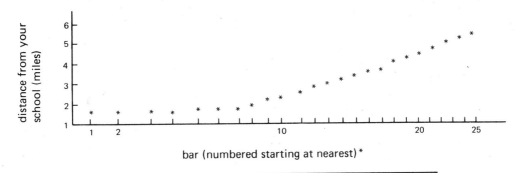

bar (numbered starting at nearest) *

Bars are numbered rather than named to avoid giving free publicity to the United Bar, Santa Cruz.

Figure 4 5 1

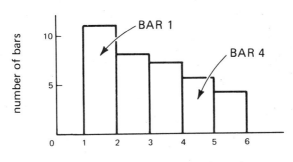

distance from your school (miles)

Figure 4 5 2

How might we convert our data from the first form to the second? Basically what our program will do is to read information about one bar at a time and decide which data summary, BAR0, BAR1, BAR2, BAR3, BAR4, or BAR5, the information should be added to. For example, if we find an establishment 3.27 miles from school, we would count it in BAR3, since the height of BAR3 indicates the number of establishments between 3.00 and 4.00 miles away. A flowchart for the program which organizes the data in this way is shown in Figure 4 5 3.

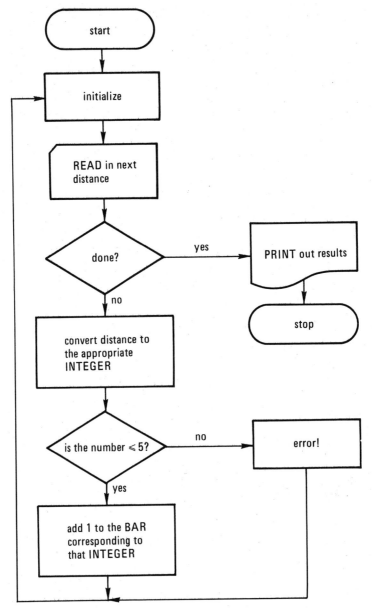

Figure 4 5 3

```
COMMENT--MAKE A BAR GRAPH FROM DISTANCE DATA.
        INTEGER BAR0, BAR1, BAR2, BAR3, BAR4, BAR5, NUMB
        REAL DIST
COMMENT--INITIALIZE BAR HEIGHTHS
        BAR0 = 0
        BAR1 = 0
        BAR2 = 0
        BAR3 = 0
        BAR4 = 0
        BAR5 = 0
COMMENT--READ IN A DISTANCE.  IF IT'S NEGATIVE, THEN
C          THERE ARE NO MORE DISTANCES IN THE DATA.
  10    READ, DIST
          IF ( DIST .LT. 0.0 )  GO TO 200
C         CONVERT THE DISTANCE INTO AN INTEGER. DROP FRACTION.
  18    NUMB = DIST
C         FIGURE OUT WHICH BAR IT FITS IN.
        IF ( NUMB .NE. 0 )  GO TO 20
           BAR0 = BAR0 + 1
           GO TO 10
  20    IF ( NUMB .NE. 1 )  GO TO 30
           BAR1 = BAR1 + BAR1
           GO TO 10
  30    IF ( NUMB .NE. 2 )  GO TO 40
           BAR2 = BAR2 + 1
           GO TO 10
  40    IF ( NUMB .NE. 3 )  GO TO 50
           BAR3 = BAR3 + 1
           GO TO 10
  50    IF ( NUMB .NE. 4 )  GO TO 60
           BAR4 = BAR4 + 1
           GO TO 10
  60    IF ( NUMB .NE. 5 )  GO TO 100
           BAR5 = BAR5 + 1
           GO TO 10
C         ERROR CONDITION.
 100    PRINT, 'DISTANCE', DIST, 'IS OUT OF RANGE.'
        GO TO 10
COMMENT--STOP READING CARDS.  WE'RE READY TO PRINT.
 200    PRINT, ' '
        PRINT, 'BAR          HEIGHT'
        PRINT, ' 0', BAR0
        PRINT, ' 1', BAR1
        PRINT, ' 2', BAR2
        PRINT, ' 3', BAR3
        PRINT, ' 4', BAR4
        PRINT, ' 5', BAR5
        STOP
        END
```

Statement number 18 is the heart of the program. Let's see how it works. Suppose READ statement number 10 gives DIST the value 1.275. Then, since NUMB is an INTEGER,

```
18    NUMB = DIST
```

will *convert* the value 1.275 to an INTEGER before storing it in NUMB. So, in this case, NUMB would be given the INTEGER value 1.

Given the data corresponding to Figure 4 5 1 such as

```
1.9
0.4
0.9
3.9
17.5
2.8
4.5
4.1
3.2
5.8
6.9
4.5
3.7
2.9
5.2
-1.0
```

our program would finally print out:

```
DISTANCE      0.1750000E 02 IS OUT OF RANGE.
DISTANCE      0.6900000E 01 IS OUT OF RANGE.

BAR           HEIGHT
 0               2
 1               0
 2               2
 3               3
 4               3
 5               2
```

From this, we could draw Figure 4 5 2.

Section 4 6*

DOUBLE PRECISION and COMPLEX Numbers

Skip this section
if you want to.

There are more types of WATFIV numbers than just INTEGERs and REALs. One type, DOUBLE PRECISION, makes it simple to handle numbers with a little more than twice the precision of ordinary REALs, about 16 decimal digits for DOUBLE PRECISION as compared to 7 for REAL. The range remains about the same. DOUBLE PRECISION constants are written like REALs except that they contain more digits, in general, and a "D" is used to separate the mantissa from the decimal point shift factor instead of the "E" used in REALs.

> **DOUBLE PRECISION** *constants*
>
> *examples*
>   129.748239
>   −49734004.88
>   1.00000000
>   −4.72D−8
>   .31415926535898D+01
>   2.7182818204590D0
>   5.77215664901D−01

DOUBLE PRECISION variables are declared using the usual form of a declaration statement with the *type* position occupied by the phrase DOUBLE PRECISION, as below.

```
DOUBLE PRECISION A, D, Z
```

Like INTEGERs and REALs, DOUBLE PRECISION values may be used in arithmetic operations involving numbers of any of the three types, INTEGER, REAL, and DOUBLE PRECISION. The result of an arithmetic operation involving a DOUBLE PRECISION value and an INTEGER or REAL value is a DOUBLE PRECISION number. As with REALs however, negative DOUBLE PRECISION numbers cannot be raised to non-INTEGER powers. Thus (−4.7D00)**0.5 is not legal.

Another kind of WATFIV number is COMPLEX. COMPLEX numbers have two parts, the real part and the imaginary part, and are written in the form (*r part*, *i part*) where *r part* (the real part) and *i part* (the imaginary part) are REAL constants.

> **COMPLEX** *constants*
>
> *examples*
> (1.0, 0.0)
> (0.0, 1.0)
> (1.0, −1.0)
> (4.93, 7.948)
> (−5.221, 6.14)

COMPLEX variables are declared in exactly the way you would expect.

`COMPLEX ZETA, MU, A`

As with the other types of numbers, COMPLEX values can be used in arithmetic expressions. Whenever an arithmetic operation involves a number of type COMPLEX the result of the operation is a COMPLEX value, no matter what the type of the other operand. There are two restrictions to be aware of: (1) the exponent in a ** operation can never be COMPLEX, and (2) if the base in a ** operation is COMPLEX, the exponent must be of type INTEGER.

> *number* **COMPLEX *is illegal*
> COMPLEX**INTEGER *is legal*
> COMPLEX**non-INTEGER *is illegal*

EXERCISES 4 6

1 What are the values of the following expressions?
   a 2.0 * (1.4 −3.7)
   b (0.0, 1.0)**2
   c A * (1.0, 0.0) + B * (0.0, 1.0) where A and B are REALs
   d ZETA * (1.0, −1.0) where ZETA is COMPLEX

2 Does the following statement make sense?

   `IF ( ZETA .GE. (1.4,3.72) ) STOP`

Section 4 7

CHARACTERs

The CHARACTER data type, one of the two non-numeric WATFIV data types, is extremely useful. People often fall into the trap of believing that computers deal only with numbers. Computers are *symbol* manipulators—there is a whole world of computing outside "number crunching". Of all the written symbols you've seen today, numbers probably comprise only a small part, so it is natural that computers are equipped to handle non-numerical data.

CHARACTER*n constants are strings of from 1 up to 255 characters (any character you can find on your keypunch should be OK) enclosed by single quotes. The quote marks are not considered part of the string, so the *length* of a string is the number of characters inside the quotes (except that two apostrophes in a row count as only one character, an apostrophe).

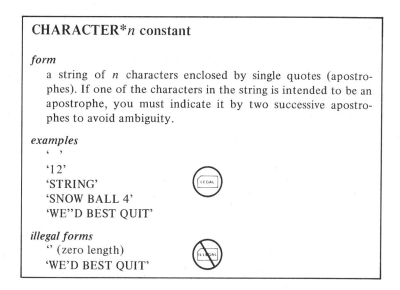

CHARACTER*n constant

form

a string of n characters enclosed by single quotes (apostrophes). If one of the characters in the string is intended to be an apostrophe, you must indicate it by two successive apostrophes to avoid ambiguity.

examples

' '
'12'
'STRING'
'SNOW BALL 4'
'WE''D BEST QUIT'

illegal forms

'' (zero length)
'WE'D BEST QUIT'

CHARACTER*n strings may be compared by using relational operators. For instance, if SONG is a CHARACTER*14 memory cell, then the statement

```
IF ( SONG .EQ. 'NORWEGIAN WOOD' ) STOP
```

performs a test which succeeds (and hence STOPs the program) only if the value in SONG is 'NORWEGIAN WOOD'. Two CHARACTER*n values which start out the same are still considered equal even if they have a different number of blanks at the end. For example, the test in

```
IF ( 'BEST' .EQ. 'BEST    ' ) STOP
```

succeeds, and the program stops.

CHARACTER*n strings have the pleasant feature that if one CHARACTER*n string comes before another in alphabetical order, then the first is .LT. the second. Thus, the test

'DAY TRIP' .LT. 'DRIVE MY CAR'

succeeds.

Although there are no operators which can alter CHARACTER*n values, it is possible to use the assignment statement to make limited alterations.

---

declaring CHARACTER memory cells

forms
> CHARACTER *list*
> CHARACTER*n *list*
>
> *n* is an unsigned INTEGER ($1 \leqslant n \leqslant 255$)
> *list* is a list of memory cell names. The first form is equivalent
> to the second with $n = 1$

meaning
> instructs the compiler to attach the names in *list* to memory
> cells which can contain CHARACTER strings of length *n*

---

conversion of CHARACTER *values*

given: A value of type CHARACTER*n to be stored in a mem-
> ory cell of type CHARACTER*m

rules: If **m = n**, no conversion is necessary.
> If **m > n**, add **m − n** blanks to the right of the value.
> If **m < n**, drop the rightmost **m − n** characters and issue a
> warning.

Suppose that we have made the type declaration

```
CHARACTER*4 ASSOCS
```

and we attempted this assignment;

```
ASSOCS = 'ONO'
```

Following the standard rules about assignment statements, the controller evaluates the expression on the right (since it's a constant there's nothing to do) and then converts the result to the type of the memory cell on the left before storing the value there. The value on the right is of type CHARACTER*3, the memory cell on the left is a CHARACTER*4, so the reasonable solution is to add a blank to the value on the right (making it 'ONO   ') and then storing it.

Suppose the assignment was

```
ASSOCS = 'VOORMAN'
```

Here the value is of type CHARACTER*7, which is too long for the memory cell. In this case, the value on the right is deprived of its rightmost 3 characters, making it

'VOOR'

which, at least, now fits in memory cell ASSOCS. Since you may have lost something you didn't want to lose, WATFIV issues a warning message.

EXERCISES 4 7

1 Which of these is a legal character constant?

‘ ’

‘147*SQRT(17.9)’
‘WENDOVER, NEVADA’
‘NORTHERN SONG’

2 Suppose that each of the constants above is to be assigned to a memory cell which is declared to be a CHARACTER*8. What form will each be converted to?

3 What is printed?

column 7

```
      CHARACTER*9 CLUB1, CLUB2, CLUB3, FIRST
      CLUB1 = 'ULTRADYNE'
      CLUB2 = 'PRODUCER'
      CLUB3 = 'CENTURION'
C
      FIRST = CLUB1
      IF ( CLUB2 .LT. FIRST )  FIRST = CLUB2
      IF ( CLUB3 .LT. FIRST )  FIRST = CLUB3
C
      PRINT, FIRST
      STOP
      END
```

Section 4 8

LOGICALs

Numbers and CHARACTERs are not the only sorts of information that we can conveniently represent in WATFIV. There is also a LOGICAL data type. There are only two LOGICAL values, written .TRUE. and .FALSE. In Chapter 3 you used tests like

```
IF ( X .GT. 2 )  STOP
```

The expression X .GT. 2 is a LOGICAL expression and its value is either .TRUE. or .FALSE.. The way an IF statement works is that when the LOGICAL expression in parentheses has the value .TRUE., the statement to the right is performed. Otherwise (*i.e.*, when the value is .FALSE.), the statement to the right is ignored.

To state that our program wants to use a memory cell named YES and have the values stored there treated as LOGICAL values, we would write

```
LOGICAL YES
```

After the assignment statement

    YES = .TRUE.

the memory cell called YES would have the .TRUE. value.

YES $\boxed{\text{.TRUE.}}$

> **LOGICAL**: *a built-in WATFIV data type which corresponds to Boolean (2-valued) logic*

As with other data types, WATFIV uses a pattern of 1's and 0's to represent LOGICAL values, but unlike the other data types there is no range problem with LOGICALs. Since there are only two LOGICAL values, any memory cell has the capacity to represent all (that is, both) of the possibilities.

Describing arithmetic expressions was pretty easy because most everybody is familiar with the arithmetic operator (+, −, *, /, and **). Similar to arithmetic expressions, LOGICAL expressions may also contain operators. Probably you tend to use LOGICAL operators when you speak and think without being too familiar with their formal definitions.

A LOGICAL expression is formed of a string of basic LOGICAL elements separated by LOGICAL operators (.AND., .OR., and .NOT.) and grouped by parentheses. **A basic LOGICAL element** can be one of three things:

1 a LOGICAL constant (.TRUE. or .FALSE.);

2 the name of a memory cell which has been declared to have type LOGICAL; or

3 a relational expression (like those you've seen in IF statements).

Before you read any further, we'd like to warn you that the concepts presented in this section are extremely simple. They are so simple that you can easily confuse yourself by looking for too deep a meaning. Try to keep firmly in your mind that a LOGICAL memory cell always has exactly one value (just as an INTEGER variable may have only one value at a time). That value is either .TRUE. or .FALSE.. There are no in betweens. No LOGICAL value is partly true and partly false. This isn't much like real life, and perhaps that makes it confusing, but LOGICAL expressions are used to tell the controller exactly what to do. WATFIV instructions are *precise,* not "maybe do this" or "maybe do that", so LOGICAL values are always either .TRUE. or .FALSE., never both.

Let's start by describing the LOGICAL operators .AND., .OR., and .NOT..

If P and Q are names of LOGICAL type memory cells, then P .AND. Q is a LOGICAL expression which has the value .TRUE. if both P *and* Q have the value .TRUE.; otherwise, the expression has the value .FALSE..

The expression P .OR. Q has the value .TRUE. if either P *or* Q (or both) has the value .TRUE.; otherwise, the expression has the value .FALSE..

The expression .NOT. P has a value just the opposite of P. That is, if P has the value .TRUE., then .NOT. P has the value .FALSE.; if P has the value .FALSE., then .NOT. P has the value .TRUE..

Examples

   .AND.

   "[It is raining] and [the sun is shining.]"
     A   B

The statement is true if both A *and* B are true.

   .OR.

   "[He is heavy] or [he's wearing a pillow around his waist.]"
     A   B

The statement is true if either A *or* B (or both) is true.

   .NOT.

       "She is not [pregnant]."
          A

The statement is true if A is not true.

The above examples are, of course, not WATFIV but English. The "basic logical elements" in the sentences are bracketed. Two of the logical operators, "and" and "or" are *conjunctions*; they connect two statements (or "basic logical elements", as we have called them). In WATFIV the LOGICAL operators .AND. and .OR. are also conjunctions in the sense that they connect two basic LOGICAL elements. The third LOGICAL operator, .NOT., is different. As you can see in the English example, the word "not" applies only to "pregnant" rather than to two parts of a sentence. Similarly, the WATFIV .NOT. operates on *one* basic LOGICAL element. For this reason .AND. and .OR. are called **binary operators** (operating on two things), and .NOT. is called a **unary operator** (operating on *one* thing).

Now that we've explained the three LOGICAL operators, let's discuss the basic LOGICAL elements, and then we'll be ready to make LOGICAL expressions.

The simplest basic LOGICAL element is a LOGICAL constant (either .TRUE. or .FALSE.). The second kind of basic LOGICAL element is a memory cell name which has been declared to be of type LOGICAL. For example, the statement

```
LOGICAL X, Y, Z
```

would declare X, Y, and Z to be memory cells to contain LOGICAL values. Any of them could then be basic LOGICAL elements in a LOGICAL expression.

The third type of basic LOGICAL element, the relational expression, states a relation between two arithmetic expressions. The value of a relational expression is .TRUE. if the stated relation is true.

As you may recall from Chapter 3, relations are stated using the six relational operators.

.EQ.	meaning equals
.NE.	meaning not equal to
.LT.	meaning less than
.LE.	meaning less than or equal to
.GE.	meaning greater than or equal to
.GT.	meaning greater than

The results of the comparisons (relational expressions) we used in Chapter 3, then, are LOGICAL values. For example, the relational expression

$$(A**2) + (B**2) \text{ .EQ. } C**2$$

has the value .TRUE. if the square of the value of C is the same as the sum of the squares of the values of A and B; otherwise, its value is .FALSE..

The six operators above are the *only* relational operators that are defined in WATFIV. Other natural relations like .EG. ("equal to or greater than") or .SGT. ("slightly greater than") will not be accepted. However, you can use LOGICAL operators to make combinations of relational expressions.

Notice the difference between *relations* (like .EQ. or .GT.) and LOGICAL *operators* (like .AND. or .NOT.). Relations compare two arithmetic expressions or two CHARACTER strings, and the result of the comparison is either .TRUE. or .FALSE.. LOGICAL operators operate on *LOGICAL* expressions, and again the result is .TRUE. or .FALSE.. Since a relational expression results in a LOGICAL value, it is a special case of the general class of LOGICAL expressions.

There are several ways in which LOGICAL expressions can be used in WATFIV programs. You have already seen their use in IF statements. Another use is as the right hand side of an assignment statement. For example, the program fragment below assigns a LOGICAL value to each of the three memory cells P, Q, and R, then tests to see if R has the value .TRUE. (in which case the program stops) or .FALSE. (in which case it goes on). For practice, determine which alternative would happen. Remember! a LOGICAL variable can take only one value at a time.

```
LOGICAL P, Q, R
P = 2+7 .EQ. 3+6
Q = 3+1 .EQ. 3-1
R = P .AND. Q
IF ( R ) STOP
    •
    •
    •
```

The most common use of LOGICAL expressions is in IF-statements. You already know how to write IF-tests like

```
IF ( I .GT. 2 ) PRINT, I
```

Now, using the LOGICAL operators, you can write all sorts of elaborate tests. For example,

```
IF ( (X .GT. 0.0) .AND. (X .LT. 10.0) ) STOP
```

which will cause the program to STOP if X lies between zero and ten.

A **LOGICAL** *expression is evaluated in this order:*

1 evaluate terms in parentheses
2 evaluate relational expressions
3 .NOT.
4 .AND.
5 .OR.

---

the IF statement

form

IF (*b*) *stmt*

b is a LOGICAL expression

stmt is an executable statement other than an IF or DO (DO statements are covered in Chapter 8)

meaning

If the expression *b* has the value .TRUE. then execute statement *stmt*. In any case, proceed from the next statement unless the execution of statement *stmt* transferred control to another part of the program (as in a GO TO).

examples

```
IF ( X .LE. 0.0 ) GO TO 27
IF ( A*B + 10.4 .GT. C**2 ) PRINT, C**2
IF ( Q1 .AND. (.NOT. Q2) ) A = B + 2
IF ( N .EQ. 0 .OR. Q ) STOP
```

The following program reads three numbers from a data card and tells us whether or not the first two can be the legs of a right triangle while the third is the hypotenuse.

```
COMMENT--PROGRAM PYTHAGORAS
        LOGICAL PYTHAG
        INTEGER A, B, C
COMMENT--GET LENGTHS OF SIDES OF TRIANGLE.
        READ, A, B, C
COMMENT--PYTHAG WILL BE .TRUE. IF THESE SIDES COULD MAKE A
C          RIGHT TRIANGLE
  200   PYTHAG = (A**2)+(B**2) .EQ. C**2
  220   IF ( PYTHAG )  GO TO 300
C       THEY COULDN'T
        PRINT, 'NO,', A, ',', B, 'AND', C,
        PRINT, 'COULDN''T BE THE SIDES OF A RIGHT TRIANGLE'
        STOP
C       THEY COULD
  300   PRINT, 'YES,', A, B, 'AND', C,
        PRINT, 'COULD BE THE SIDES OF A RIGHT TRIANGLE'
        STOP
        END
```

```
3    4    5
```

```
YES,             3              4 AND             5
COULD BE THE SIDES OF A RIGHT TRIANGLE
```

Statement number 200 is the key, for only if we have a right triangle will the sum of the squares of the first two sides equal the square of the third side. Therefore PYTHAG has the value .TRUE. if A, B, C is a right triangle and .FALSE. if it isn't.

There are two common errors that people tend to make when using LOGICAL expressions. First, people tend to write things like

```
IF ( A .GT. 0 .AND. .LT. 100 )  STOP
```

when they should have written

```
IF ( A .GT. 0 .AND. A .LT. 100 )  STOP
```

Remember that LOGICAL operators can operate only on LOGICAL values, and

.LT. 100

is not a LOGICAL value.

The other common error is writing a statement which tries to compare two LOGICAL values using a relational operator. A relational operator cannot compare LOGICAL values.

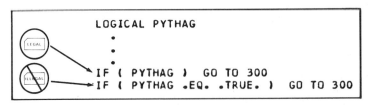

Like arithmetic operators, LOGICAL operators have a hierarchy of precedence: .NOT. is performed first, then .AND., and finally .OR. operations are performed. Of course, parentheses may be used to override this hierarchy.

EXERCISES 4 8

1 If

```
LOGICAL A, B, C
A = .TRUE.
B = .TRUE.
C = .FALSE.
```

then what values do these expressions have:

A .OR. B
.NOT. C
(A .OR. B) .AND. C
.TRUE. .OR. C
.TRUE. .AND. C
(.NOT. C) .OR. B

2 Write one IF-statement which will have the same effect as the statements below.

```
      IF ( X .GT. 0 )  GO TO 20
      GO TO 30
20    IF ( X .LT. 10 )  STOP
30    ...
```

3 Again, as in 2 above

```
      IF ( X .GT. 10 )  GO TO 20
      IF ( X .LT. 0  )  GO TO 20
      GO TO 30
20    STOP
30    ...
```

4 Write a LOGICAL expression involving two LOGICAL variables A and B, which has the value .TRUE. if only A is .TRUE. or if only B is .TRUE.; and is .FALSE. if both A and B are .TRUE. or both are .FALSE.. (This expression is called the **exclusive-or**.)

5 If you wanted to use program PYTHAGORAS to test REAL values you would need to make changes in two statements. Which ones, what changes, and why?

Section 4 9*

Alternate Length Memory Cells

We suggest you skip this section on a first reading.

Although you now know about all of the WATFIV data types (REAL, INTEGER, DOUBLE PRECISION, COMPLEX, LOGICAL, and CHARACTER), there are a few more options within these types. The options give you some choice of how large specific memory cells should be. You might want to use some smaller than normal memory cells if you were writing a program so large that you needed some conservation measures to fit it into your computer's memory. You might want to use larger than normal memory cells to gain greater accuracy in numeric computation.

The exact choices that you have and the WATFIV notations for these choices are probably best described as the result of historical accidents. WATFIV is a version of Fortran which was developed on IBM equipment, and the partially overlapping collection of choices below resulted.

---

length options in type statements

form
   type*len list
   *len is a length specifier consistent with *type*
   list is a list of memory cell names

meaning
   affix the names in *list* to memory cells *len* bytes in length and of data type *type*

examples
   INTEGER*2 A, BORK
   REAL*8 KLING,ON
   LOGICAL*4 GEEK

   Note: See MiniManual for more details. Length specifiers may also appear within *list,* for example.

---

byte: the internal unit of storage in IBM 360/370 machines (8 bits)

---

length specifier

form
   *len
   len is either 1, 2, 4, 8, or 16

meaning
   specifies one of the optional lengths (in bytes) of memory cells.

Legal Combinations

Normal Fortran type	length options	remarks
INTEGER	*2	−32768 ⩽ INTEGER*2 ⩽ 32767
	*4	default
REAL	*4	default
	*8	same as DOUBLE PRECISION
DOUBLE PRECISION	no options	same as REAL*8
COMPLEX	*8	default
	*16	
LOGICAL	*1	
	*4	default
CHARACTER	*n	default value is *1
		1 ⩽ n ⩽ 255

No particularly tricky cases arise in using optional length memory cells. If an expression involves a number of values of different lengths, WATFIV will convert each pair of values to the longest of the two before combining them. Consult the MiniManual for the exact details.

Section 4 10

Implicit Typing

Because WATFIV deals with different data types in vastly different ways, and because each memory cell has a single data type associated with it, it is extremely important to be aware of the data type of each memory cell you use. However, many people feel that having to name each memory cell in a declaration statement is too much of a burden and that programs are easier to read if the programmer uses a consistent set of rules for naming memory cells of the various types. For that reason WATFIV allows undeclared memory cell names to be used in programs. Of course, it must make some assumption about the types of the undeclared memory cells and the normal conventions are these: if the memory cell name begins with an I, J, K, L, M, or N, the variable is given the type INTEGER, otherwise REAL.

These standard assumptions can be augmented (or over-ridden) by placing an IMPLICIT statement at the beginning of the program. Such a statement associates certain letters with certain data types so that undeclared memory cells can be given types according to any desired scheme. It is important to remember that the IMPLICIT statement, if there is one, must be the first statement in the program.

Of course, explicit declarations of memory cell names over-ride these implicit assumptions. We feel that the importance of being explicitly aware of the types of memory cells, especially for beginning programmers, is so important that we always use explicit declarations in this text, but there are good arguments for using a set of standard naming conventions. One of the strongest arguments is that when a programmer is reading a large program, the types of variables named in standard ways can be determined without glancing up at the declarations. But this argument is far more relevant in the case of the advanced professional programmer working on a large staff than it is in the case of the novice.

Section 4 11

Compile-time Initialization

You already know two ways to put values in memory cells—with assignment statements and with READ statements. Both of these methods cause the controller to take action while performing the instructions in your program. The memory cells don't have values until the program begins to run.

It is possible to give values to memory cells before execution of the program begins by including these values in the memory cells' declaration statements. By doing this, you instruct the compiler to place a value in the memory cell being named and typed, a value which, of course, must be of the appropriate data type.

It is important to realize, however, that values given at execution-time wipe out any values given at compile-time (a memory cell can't have two values). For this reason it is usually best to use compile-time initialization only for memory cells which don't change values at execution-time. Such memory cells become named constants instead of variables, and this type of constant-naming idea can lead to programs which are more flexible than they would be otherwise. For example, if your program is designed to handle INTEGERs between 10 and 50, and you have a test to make sure all input values are in the right range, you might have an IF statement using those numbers in its test at several points in the program.

```
IF ( INPT .GE. 10  .AND.  INPT .LE. 50 )  GO TO 999
```

On the other hand, if you used IF statements with variables in place of the constants

```
IF (INPT .GE. MIN  .AND.  INPT .LE. MAX) GO TO 999
```

then the variables could be initialized at compile-time, right at the beginning of the program in a declaration statement. Then, if you needed to change the legal range to 14 to 67 to treat some other cases, you'd only need to change the one declaration statement instead of all the IF statements.

```
INTEGER MIN/10/, MAX/50/
```

Of course you could just as well have used MIN and MAX and given them values with assignment statements at the beginning of the program, but then you'd have to change two cards instead of one in order to change the range. Furthermore, those two cards would be imbedded more deeply in the program and might be more difficult to find.

---

declaration statements

form
$$type \ m_1/c_1/, \ m_2/c_2/, \ \ldots, \ m_n/c_n/$$
type is a WATFIV data type
m_i is an identifier
c_i is a constant whose data type is consistent with *type*
Note: Any c_i may be omitted, but then the surrounding slashes must also be omitted.

meaning
Attaches each name m_i to a memory cell whose data type is *type*. If c_i is present, puts c_i into m_i at compile-time.

examples
```
REAL X/1.7/, Y/3.2/, Z/-9.1/
CHARACTER*4 ATOM/'BONG'/, KUNG/'FLUE'/
COMPLEX ZETA/(1.0,1.0)/
```

PROBLEMS 4

1 A mechanical engineer has to compute points for plotting a curve. He needs to find the safe loading of a certain type of column as a function of the slimness ratio of the column. He has formulas as follows.

$$S = 17000 - 0.485\ R^2 \text{ when } R < 120$$
$$S = 18000/(1+R^2/18000) \text{ when } R \geqslant 120$$

where S = safe load, psi
and R = slimness ratio

The safe loading must be calculated for slimness ratios from 20 through 200, in steps of 5. For each value of R write out values of R and S. Label your output clearly. Do not use any READ statements.

2 Write a program to compute the square root of a number A between zero and one. READ the number from a data card, and use the following technique to compute the square root to six decimal places. Try to understand how the algorithm homes in on the square root.

INITIALIZE:	let X be 0
	let DX be 0.1
LOCATE:	let X increase by increments of DX until X**2 exceeds A (whose square root we want)
BACKUP:	reduce X by DX (so that X is now smaller than the square root of A)
REDUCE:	let DX be DX/10
REPEAT:	repeat from the LOCATE step if DX is still larger than .0000001
FINISH:	at this point X will be equal to the square root of A to six decimal places

3 You are given eight sets of three values each.

23.37	19.51	8.37
57.46	40.06	27.57
42.09	35.78	61.65
8.63	15.74	12.38
61.94	78.07	10.87
19.56	23.54	33.28
84.37	61.98	15.93
37.80	49.24	23.51

Write a program to determine whether or not the three values of a set could represent the lengths of the sides of a triangle. In a triangle the length of the longest side is less than the sum of the lengths of the other two. If the three sides could make a triangle, calculate its area and PRINT a message like:

WHEN AB = 3.00 AND BC = 4.00 AND CA = 5.00, THE AREA OF TRIANGLE ABC = 6.00.

The area may be calculated using the equation
$$\text{area} = \sqrt{s(s-a)(s-b)(s-c)}$$
where s is the half perimeter, and a, b, and c are the three side lengths.
If there is no triangle, print out a message like

DATA SET 23.37, 19.51, 9.37 DOES NOT REPRESENT A TRI-ANGLE.

4 (a) Write a program which READs INTEGERs, one from each card, and PRINTs the value of a LOGICAL variable which is .TRUE. if the latest number is bigger than the former one.

(b) Change the program you wrote so that, after it has READ all the cards, it PRINTs a LOGICAL value telling whether the numbers were in increasing order.

5 Using a series of PRINT statements, write a program which PRINTs a giant version of the letter of your choice in the middle of the page.

```
Z Z Z Z Z
Z Z Z Z Z
        Z Z
      Z Z
    Z Z
  Z Z
Z Z Z Z Z
Z Z Z Z Z
```

6 READ a CHARACTER*n value from a data card. PRINT the string unless it is your own name. In that case, PRINT an alias (to protect your real identity). Keep READing cards until you come to one with 'DONE' on it.

7 There are many infinite series whose sums are equal to π. Leibnitz's formula (1674) is one.
$$\pi = 4 - 4/3 + 4/5 - 4/7 + 4/9 - 4/11 + \ldots$$
When we stop with a positive term the estimate of π is too large; when we stop with a negative term, the estimate is too small. Thus we can get upper and lower bounds on π. Write a program to estimate π using Leibnitz's formula. Find the 99 term sum and 100 term sum. Your output should consist of the values of the 99 and 100 term sums properly labeled.

8 Find the number of half-dollars, quarters, dimes, nickels, and pennies to be returned in change for a one-dollar bill after the purchase of an item at a given price. READ a purchase price (from 001 to 100); first find the number of half-dollars, quarters, etc. to be returned in change. Continue until you come to a data card with a negative purchase.

9 Write a program which uses the trapezoidal rule to approximate the area under the curve $f(x) = x^3$ from $x = 0$ to $x = 1$. The formula is

$$\text{area} = (h/2)[f(0) + 2f(h) + 2f(2h) + \ldots + 2f(1 - h) + f(1)]$$

The stepsize h should be chosen so that $1/h$ is a whole number (integer). What this formula does is to divide the area into strips of width h, and sum up estimates of the area of each strip.

Optional: Use a loop to compute the area for several values of h, say .1, .01, and .001, and compare the results.

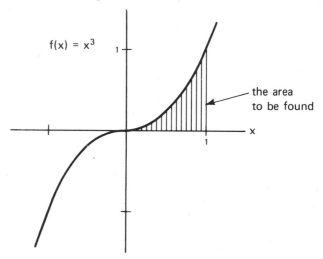

10 Write a program to compute the mean and variance of a set of numbers. READ the numbers from data cards one to a card. Design the READ statement and FORMAT so that each card contains two values, one REAL and one LOGICAL. The program can test for the LOGICAL value .TRUE. to determine when it has reached the last card. You will need a memory cell in which to accumulate the sum of the numbers, a second memory cell for the sum of the squares of the numbers, and a third to accumulate the number of terms in the sum. Compute the mean and variance by

$$\text{mean} = \text{sum of numbers}/n$$
$$\text{variance} = (\text{sum of squares}/n) - \text{mean}^2$$

where n is the number of terms in the sum

11 Write a program to make daily weather reports. Each data card should contain 9 INTEGER values giving the following information: current month, day, and year; high temperature for the day, low temperature for the day; year in which the record high for this day was set, record high temperature; year of record low, record low temperature. After READing a data card, PRINT a message of one of the following four types, depending on the data.

1.	10/23/73	HIGH TODAY	52
		LOW TODAY	23
2.	10/24/75	HIGH TODAY	71*
		LOW TODAY	38

*(BEATS RECORD OF 70 SET IN 1906)

3.	10/25/73	HIGH TODAY	73*
		LOW TODAY	−10**

*(BEATS RECORD OF 68 SET IN 1932)
**(BEATS RECORD OF −8 SET IN 1918)

4.	10/26/73	HIGH TODAY	22
		LOW TODAY	−18*

*(BEATS RECORD OF −12 SET IN 1892)

Stop READing data cards when you come to one whose month number is zero.

12 Design and write a program that simulates a population of fleas on a dog. Keep track of things like the number of fleas currently on the dog, how many scratches the dog has made so far, etc. Choose values for the number of fleas that are born each second, the number (proportion) of fleas that die of old age, how many seconds per minute the dog can scratch (he gets too tired to scratch all the time). Your program should print out a description of what happens each second.

5 DEBUGGING YOUR PROGRAMS

Section 5 1
Introduction

So far it must seem that we think if you read this book you'll be able to write programs that contain no errors. After all, all our examples have involved programs that work properly. Probably you are spending most of your time rewriting programs that *don't* work. As you know, the often laborious task of getting a program to run the way you want is called **debugging**. This chapter gives a few hints about how to proceed.

The best course, obviously, would be to avoid errors in the first place. By using flowcharts, verbal descriptions, and designing your program carefully before you write down anything in WATFIV, you can eliminate an amazing number of bugs. By using comment statements in your program you can make it much easier to follow the logic of the troublesome parts of your program. By taking your time and

> **debug:** *to remove the errors (bugs) from a program*

checking each card carefully after you punch it, you can eliminate a number of typing errors. Even if you do all these things, however, you will, no doubt, still have bugs in your programs. Everybody does, and everybody *will* for a long time, although some people think that new proof-based techniques of writing programs can be developed which will help enormously.

Let's assume that you've done all you can beforehand, you've run your program, and it doesn't work right. There are three main ways your program can fail. First, it might be that you have written some illegal statements and the compiler couldn't figure out what you meant. We'll call such errors **compile-time errors** because they are detected in the process of translating your WATFIV statements into machine language. Another possibility is that even though you've written a legal WATFIV program, it has illegal consequences; for example, it might wind up dividing by a variable which has the value zero. We'll call such errors **execution-time errors** because they are detected while the machine language instructions corresponding to your program are being performed (executed). The third possibility is that while your program produces results, the results are wrong. For example, if your program was supposed to compute the area of a basketball court and it gave a negative number as the answer, you'd know right away that something was wrong. We'll call these kinds of errors **logic errors** because they are caused by flaws in the way you wrote your program, errors in your logic. Often, logic errors cause execution-time· errors, and we'll tend to lump the two together for that reason.

Section 5 2

Compile-time Errors

Compile-time errors are easy to find—the compiler itself will carefully mark where they occur and will supply an error message that usually explains the problem. Keypunching mistakes often cause this sort of error. Things like accidentally leaving out the replacement operator (=), forgetting to mark column 6 on

> *If the* WATFIV *system you are using doesn't provide the full error message text, look in the MiniManual to decode the error number it gives you.*

continuation cards, leaving out a "*", using too many letters in a memory cell name, and not balancing parentheses are typical compile-time errors. If you're not absolutely certain of the form of a statement you want to use, look it up.

Sometimes one error can lead to lots of error messages. For example, an error in a type statement which was supposed to declare an array will result in an error

```
INTEGER A(200, B
```

message each time you try to assign a value to a spot in the array, as in A(1) = 0, because the compiler won't know A is an array. The mistake in your declaration causes this cascade of errors. Fortunately, it is likely that some error messages in this cascade caused by the erroneous declaration will suggest the possibility of an undeclared array, a good hint toward what went wrong.

> *error cascade: Each compile-time error leaves the compiler with less information than it needs to properly compile the program. Often this lack of information causes the compiler to flag errors in statements which are actually correct. This is an error cascade.*

Another thing to watch for is this: if you have *two* errors in one expression, *e.g.*,

```
AT = 2(1+(M + IFIX(B))
```

sometimes only the *first* error is discovered by the compiler. If you didn't look closely, you might correct the statement to read

```
AT = 2*(1+(M + IFIX(B))
```

and then find error PC-0 staring at you after your next run. You need another right parenthesis. Look over your statements carefully to find all the errors at once.

> *Because people tend to make errors in groups, it is quite common for one statement to have several errors. When this happens, the compiler often fails to catch the later ones. Therefore, you should check each erroneous statement carefully for multiple errors.*

Compile-time Errors

Section 5 3

Execution-time Errors

To correct an error you need to know (1) where in your program the error occurred, and (2) what caused it. Fortunately, the WATFIV compiler solves the first problem for you. It numbers the lines in your program, and when an error occurs, it identifies the offending statement.

The WATFIV compiler also helps you determine the cause of an error by providing a message which pin-points the error condition. Sometimes this tells you exactly what you need to know to correct the problem, but more often the precise error condition only hints at what went wrong. Then you must deduce how your program developed such an error. If the error is

```
KO-6     JOB-TIME EXCEEDED
```

then the immediate problem is that your program has run too long. But the root of the problem is probably that a loop has an incorrect stopping condition.

If the error is one of the arithmetic errors (KO-1, KO-2, KO-3, etc,), then some memory cell must be taking a value you didn't expect.

> *The precise nature of an execution-time error, that is, the error mentioned in the resulting error message, is often only the tip of the iceberg. You must deduce the underlying cause.*

Many errors result from bad logic in the program and ultimately make the instructions in your program impossible to perform, thus helping you detect the errors. However, some logic errors simply cause your program to produce incorrect results without asking the computer to perform impossible operations. These errors are often more difficult to fix—you simply may not notice that there is anything wrong. Just because something comes out of a computer doesn't mean it's right! It's a good idea to run a small test case in order to verify that your program really is working properly. If the small test doesn't work as you expect,

> *Test your program on simple data where you know the results before you assume it is producing correct results on more complicated data.*

you may be able to locate the trouble, or you may be forced to get more information by sprinkling your program with PRINT statements to give you partial results. Once the error is located and you know what caused it, alter the program and run it again. It is an *extremely* bad bet ever to assume that the error was a fluke and to run the program again hoping the error will go away!

> *Print partial results to trace the execution of the program and find errors.*

Once you get the hang of it, debugging is almost fun. There's a Sherlock Holmes flavor to it. To illustrate, we'll run through an actual case from our programming diary.

Debugging Example

Recall the program we wrote in Section 3 3 which computed the average cost of laundry detergents. Look at the flowchart in Figure 3 3 1 to refresh your memory about how the program was organized, but don't look at the program because here we're going to see it in a prior (un-debugged) form.

Here's what we started with after drawing a flowchart, converting it to WATFIV, punching up the deck, and removing the compile-time errors.

```
        REAL SUM, PRICE, WGT, AVG, N
COMMENT: THIS IS A PROGRAM TO FIND THE AVERAGE COST
C           OF LAUNDRY DETERGENT
        N = 0.0
        SUM = 0.0
C       READ PRICES AND WEIGHTS.
  10    READ, PRICE, WGT
C          ANOTHER BRAND TO AVERAGE IN
        N = N + 1.0
C          IF PRICE IS NEGATIVE, WE'RE DONE.
        IF ( PRICE .LE. 0.0 ) GO TO 20
C          ADD IN UNIT PRICE OF THIS BRAND
        SUM = SUM + PRICE/WGT
        GO TO 10
COMMENT: GOT THEM ALL--COMPUTE AVERAGE
  20    AVG = SUM/N
        PRINT, 'THE AVERAGE PRICE PER POUND IS', AVG
        STOP
        END
```

We made up some data cards with a few easily computed values on them to test our program before turning it loose on our real data.

```
2.00    2.0
10.00    5.0
-1.00
```

If our program had worked the way we wanted, it would have gotten the result $(2./2. + 10./5.)/2. = 1.5$. We ran it and instead of 1.5, we got

```
***ERROR***
UN-0     CONTROL CARD ENCOUNTERED ON UNIT 5 AT EXECUTION.
         PROBABLE CAUSE: MISSING DATA OR INCORRECT FORMAT.
```

Needless to say, we were a little disappointed. The error message seemed a little obscure, but we were also told that the error occurred while the controller was carrying out the READ statement (statement 10). This set us to thinking. . . The READ statement must not have found the value it needed on our cards and must have gone on past what we intended to be our last card, looking for another value. Of course! The statement

```
READ, PRICE, WGT
```

requires that *two* values be found on the cards, but since our last card has a different meaning from the others, we forgot about listing a value for WGT on it. We changed our last data card to

```
-1.0    0.0
```

and tossed our program in to be run again. This, by the way, is a *mistake*. You should *never* just correct one error and assume there aren't others. If we had taken a little more time to go over our program carefully, we could have avoided the next round of errors.

This time we got no error messages, but the result was

```
THE AVERAGE PRICE PER POUND IS    0.1000000E 01
```

"What?" we said. "We expected an average of 1.5!" We stared at the statements for a while but didn't see anything wrong. We looked at the data cards carefully to see if we had mispunched any (wishing all the time that we had placed a statement like

```
PRINT, 'PRICE=', PRICE, 'AND WEIGHT=', WGT
```

after the READ statement). Since we didn't find anything wrong, we began a time-honored process. We wrote down the names of all the memory cells we used in the program and drew a box beside each. Then we put one finger beside the first statement of the program, keeping one hand free to write values into the 'memory cells' as necessary. We analyzed the effect of the statement our finger

> *mirror printing:* It is usually a good idea, especially in the debugging state of writing a program, to print values obtained by READ statements immediately after READing. This is called mirror printing. It helps discover errors in the program which cause the data to be misinterpreted.

was on. If it altered a memory cell value, we crossed out any old value we had for that cell and wrote in the new one. If it was a control statement like

```
GO TO 10
```

we moved our finger appropriately. After a while we found the problem. By the time we got to statement 20, N had the value 3.0. even though there were only two brands of detergent in the data. Our program was counting the end-of-data card!

Tracking Down Errors

Now that our attention was drawn to it, we were embarrassed to discover that our loop wasn't even one of the recommended forms (pre-test or post-test). We made the loop a pre-test READ loop by moving the statement

```
N = N + 1.0
```

and its associated comment so that they appeared immediately *after* the IF test, not before. This had the twin benefits of making the loop into a pre-test form and of allowing 1.0 to be added to N only when the data represented a legitimate detergent price and weight.

We looked our program over carefully, decided to change the PRINT statement to

```
    PRINT, 'THE AVERAGE PRICE PER POUND OF THE',
   +        N, 'BRANDS SURVEYED IS', AVG
```

and run it again. Notice that if we'd been awake enough to use this more informative PRINT statement to begin with, we would have been able to find the problem more quickly.

The computer is a "great humbler". It seems that no matter how careful you are, there will always be bugs in your programs. Learning to avoid them requires great patience and great self-control. Like a master craftsman, a good programmer produces well thought out, finely finished work.

> *For a number of good ideas about how to improve your programs, make them more readable, more easily debugged, more efficient, and so forth, see the little book* **Elements of Programming Style** *by B. W. Kernighan and P. J. Plauger, McGraw-Hill, 1974.*

6 ARRAYS

Section 6 1

Using Arrays

You already have a repertoire of WATFIV instructions sufficient to describe all possible computations. Many computations, however, would require programs of unmanageable size if you used only your present stock of instructions. For this reason, all programming languages incorporate some way of referring to a large number of memory cells simply and concisely. In WATFIV **arrays** are provided for this purpose. The following problem is one in which the use of arrays leads to great simplification.

Let's suppose we have written to the governors of eleven western states inquiring about sales tax. While we are waiting for replies, we will prepare a program to analyze the data we hope to receive. Given eleven data cards, each of which contains the name of a state and its sales tax rate, we want our program to list those states where the sales tax is below average.

We can compute the average from the data easily enough. The problem arises from the necessity to print certain parts of the data after the average is computed and, therefore, after the data cards have all been read. Since there is no way to reread the cards, we must save the information in memory cells. Figure 6 1 1 describes our general strategy. Our program appears below.

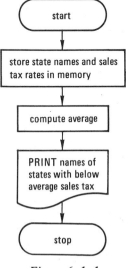

Figure 6 1 1

```
COMMENT--PROGRAM TO LIST THE WESTERN STATES WITH
C       BELOW AVERAGE SALES TAX RATES
        CHARACTER*10 S1,S2,S3,S4,S5,S6,S7,S8,S9,S10,S11
        REAL T1,T2,T3,T4,T5,T6,T7,T8,T9,T10,T11, AVE
C
C       STORE DATA
C       STORE DATA AND S
        READ, S1 , T1
        READ, S2 , T2
        READ, S3 , T3
        READ, S4 , T4
        READ, S5 , T5
        READ, S6 , T6
        READ, S7 , T7
        READ, S8 , T8
        READ, S9 , T9
        READ, S10, T10
        READ, S11, T11
C
        AVE = (T1+T2+T3+T4+T5+T6+T7+T8+T9+T10+T11)/11.0
C
        PRINT, 'STATES WITH BELOW AVERAGE SALES TAX'
        PRINT, ' '
        IF ( T1  .LE. AVE )   PRINT, S1
        IF ( T2  .LE. AVE )   PRINT, S2
        IF ( T3  .LE. AVE )   PRINT, S3
        IF ( T4  .LE. AVE )   PRINT, S4
        IF ( T5  .LE. AVE )   PRINT, S5
        IF ( T6  .LE. AVE )   PRINT, S6
        IF ( T7  .LE. AVE )   PRINT, S7
        IF ( T8  .LE. AVE )   PRINT, S8
        IF ( T9  .LE. AVE )   PRINT, S9
        IF ( T10 .LE. AVE )   PRINT, S10
        IF ( T11 .LE. AVE )   PRINT, S11
        STOP
        END
```

data

```
'WASHINGTON'    0.045
'IDAHO     '    0.03
'MONTANA   '    0.00
'OREGON    '    0.04
'WYOMING   '    0.03
'CALIFORNIA'    0.06
'NEVADA    '    0.03
'UTAH      '    0.04
'COLORADO  '    0.03
'ARIZONA   '    0.04
'NEW MEXICO'    0.04
```

output

```
STATES WITH BELOW AVERAGE SALES TAX

IDAHO
MONTANA
WYOMING
NEVADA
COLORADO
```

As you can see, the program's input section has eleven almost identical statements. So does the output section. Normally we'd like to make a loop out of such a section, but in this case we have no way of making the statements identical so that we can replace them with a loop. To do so, we'd have to refer to the same memory cells in each READ, and this would continually wipe out previously recorded information. We'd wind up with only one state's sales tax rate in memory. What we need is some way to change the memory cell used by the READ statement without changing the READ statement itself. We can do this by using arrays.

An **array** is a group of memory cells all of which have the same name. They are distinguished by a **subscript** or **index** which is associated with the name. In a program the name and the subscript are associated by enclosing the subscript in parentheses to the right of the name. In our example we will need two arrays, each of which is a group of eleven memory cells, one group for the names of the states, and the other for the taxes. Then, instead of dealing with the eleven separate memory cells S1, S2, S3, etc., we will use the array S and refer to S(1), S(2), S(3), and so on.

Of course, if our only option were to write S(5) instead of S5 or S(7) instead of S7, nothing would be gained. The advantage is that we can write the subscript as an *arithmetic expression* whose value can change from time to time as the program runs. Instead of writing

```
READ, S1, T1
```

we will write

```
READ, S(N), T(N)
```

where N is an INTEGER memory cell whose value will be 1 the first time the computer executes the READ statement, 2 the second time, and so on.

Arrays used in a program must be declared at the beginning. Like memory cell declarations, array declarations establish the name and the type of information the array will contain—INTEGER, REAL, or whatever. (An array may contain only one type of data; no single array can contain both INTEGER and REAL numbers, for example.) In addition, an array declaration must specify the number of memory cells in the array by placing that number in parentheses after the array name. This part of an array declaration is known as the **length declarator** and should not be confused with a subscript. A subscript designates a particular memory cell in an array. A length declarator establishes the *number* of memory cells in an array.

---

array declarator

form
> name (*len*)
>
> *name* is a WATFIV identifier (up to six characters)
> *len* is an unsigned INTEGER constant

meaning
> establishes an array named *name* with *len* memory cells

example
```
INTEGER A, B(12), ARA(103)
REAL QX(27), BAG, ROT
LOGICAL P, Q(33), G
```

These statements establish four arrays to contain various kinds of information. In addition, the types of five simple memory cells are established. Array declarators and memory cell declarators may be mixed in the same declaration statement.

Together, the name and length declarator make up an **array declarator**. Array declarators are placed in type statements (INTEGER statements, REAL statements, and the like) either interspersed with ordinary memory cell declarations or alone.

An **array element** (a memory cell in an array) is used in the same ways that other memory cells are used, but each reference to an array element must include both the array name and the subscript. The elements are always numbered starting from one. The last element's subscript, therefore, is the same as the number of elements in the array.

> *array element: a memory cell in an array*

---

array reference

form
> name (*e*)
>
> *name* is an array name
> *e* is an expression whose value is in the range 1 to *len* where *len* is the number of elements in *name*

meaning
> designates the *e*th element of *name*

examples
```
A(3) = 47.0*Q
PRINT, B(3*J-I)
IF ( 4.0*RT(L-2) .LT. T(3)+1 )  STOP
B(L) = B(L-1) + 5.7
A(I+2) = A(J) + A(I)
```

Using arrays, we can rewrite our sales tax program in a simpler way still following the plan of Figure 6 1 1

```
COMMENT--PROGRAM TO LIST THE WESTERN STATES WITH
C          BELOW AVERAGE SALES TAX RATES
       CHARACTER*10 S(11)
       REAL T(11), AVE
       INTEGER N
C
C      STORE DATA
       N = 1
  100  READ, S(N), T(N)
         N = N+1
         IF ( N .LE. 11 )  GO TO 100
C
       AVE = (T(1) + T(2) + T(3) + T(4) + T(5) + T(6) +
      +        T(7) + T(8) + T(9) + T(10) + T(11))/11.0
C
       PRINT, 'STATES WITH BELOW AVERAGE SALES TAX'
       PRINT, ' '
       N = 1
  300  IF ( T(N) .LE. AVE )  PRINT, S(N)
         N = N+1
         IF ( N .LE. 11 )  GO TO 300
       STOP
       END
```

data

```
       'WASHINGTON'    0.045
       'IDAHO      '    0.03
       'MONTANA    '    0.00
       'OREGON     '    0.04
       'WYOMING    '    0.03
       'CALIFORNIA'    0.06
       'NEVADA     '    0.03
       'UTAH       '    0.04
       'COLORADO   '    0.03
       'ARIZONA    '    0.04
       'NEW MEXICO'    0.04
```

output

```
       STATES WITH BELOW AVERAGE SALES TAX

       IDAHO
       MONTANA
       WYOMING
       NEVADA
       COLORADO
```

EXERCISES 6 1

1 Under what conditions would B(I) and B(J) refer to the same element of the array B?

2 What would the following program print?

```
       INTEGER A(10), I
       A(1) = 0
       A(2) = 1
       I = 3
100    A(I) = A(I-1) + A(I-2)
       I = I+1
       IF ( I .LE. 10)  GO TO 100
       PRINT, A(1), A(2), A(3), A(4), A(5)
       PRINT, A(6), A(7), A(8), A(9), A(10)
       STOP
       END
```

3 Assuming that B is an array of 10 elements and I and J are memory cells with the values 3 and 7 respectively, which of the following statements are legal? If not, why not?

```
B(3) = B(I)
B(I) = B(I-1)
B(J) = B(2*I)
B(4) = B(J-1) + B(I*J-21)
B(2*I) = B(J+4)
B(1.7) = 0
```

4 Suppose that, instead of wanting to list only the states whose sales tax is below average, we had wanted to make a list of the states and their sales taxes and print the average sales tax at the end of the listings. If the data provided were the same as that of this section, would we need to use arrays to write the program?

5 Which of the following are legal declarations?

```
REAL A(10)
INTEGER A(13-2)
INTEGER A(I)
REAL A(150), BOK(3472)
REAL X(15.0)
LOGICAL QS(23), PS(47)
```

Section 6 2

A More Useful Solution

We were probably not being realistic when we wrote the program of Section 1 because we assumed that all eleven governors would reply to our letter. A program which would still work with only a partial response would be more useful. Fortunately such a program is easy to write now that we know about arrays. (Without arrays the program becomes much more difficult—see the exercises).

With our new assumption that the data may be incomplete, we can no longer compute the average by summing and dividing by 11.0. The program itself will have to keep track of the number of responses so that it can divide the sum by the appropriate number. So the program can recognize the end of the input loop, we'll append a special data card containing the string 'END DATA'.

Figure 6 2 1 depicts the general plan of our revised program. With the exception that it keeps track of the number of data items, our new plan doesn't differ much from the old one in Figure 6 1 1.

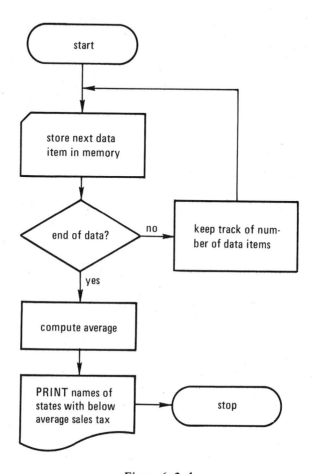

Figure 6 2 1

Study the new program carefully; it is typical of many that you will write in the future. An important point to notice is that the memory cell N is used to count the number of state governors who responded to our question. The computer performs the READ statement (statement 100) many times, but it is always true that just prior to a time when the READ statement is performed, the value of N is the number of governors' responses which have been read. In addition, since N is not increased until after the test for 'END DATA', the value of N when the computer reaches statement 200 is the total number of governors' responses. Thus the count N does not include the special 'END DATA' card; it counts only response cards. This section's exercises help explain other details of the program.

```
      COMMENT--PROGRAM TO LIST STATES WITH BELOW AVERAGE SALES TAX
            CHARACTER*10 S(12)
            REAL T(12), AVE, SUM
            INTEGER N, K
C
C        STORE DATA
            N = 0
  100   READ, S(N+1), T(N+1)
            IF ( S(N+1) .EQ. 'END DATA' )  GO TO 200
            N = N+1
            GO TO 100
C
C        COMPUTE AVERAGE
  200   SUM = 0.0
            K = 1
  210   SUM = SUM + T(K)
            K = K+1
            IF ( K .LE. N )  GO TO 210
            AVE = SUM/N
C
            PRINT, 'STATES WITH BELOW AVERAGE SALES TAX'
            PRINT, ' '
            K = 1
  310   IF ( T(K) .LE. AVE )  PRINT, S(K), T(K)
            K = K+1
            IF ( K .LE. N )  GO TO 310
            STOP
            END
```

data

```
    'WASHINGTON'    0.045
    'IDAHO     '    0.03
    'MONTANA   '    0.00
    'OREGON    '    0.04
    'WYOMING   '    0.03
    'CALIFORNIA'    0.06
    'NEVADA    '    0.03
    'UTAH      '    0.04
    'COLORADO  '    0.03
    'ARIZONA   '    0.04
    'NEW MEXICO'    0.04
    'END DATA  '    0.00
```

output

```
    STATES WITH BELOW AVERAGE SALES TAX

    IDAHO           0.3000000E-01
    MONTANA         0.0000000E 00
    WYOMING         0.3000000E-01
    NEVADA          0.3000000E-01
    COLORADO        0.3000000E-01
```

EXERCISES 6 2

1 Why did we allocate 12 memory cells to the arrays instead of 11?

2 Why does the 'END DATA' card also contain a number?

3 Show how the running sum could be incorporated into the input loop to avoid the loop in the section where the average is computed.

4 If none of the governors respond and we run our program with only the 'END DATA' card, something bad will happen. What?

5 Suppose, by some fluke, we give the program more than 11 response cards. What will happen? How can we change the program to avoid this problem? (This is a very important way of making the program more robust.)

> *robust:* a program is more robust if it functions properly given a wider range of input values

6 What changes need to be made in the program to allow all fifty states to be included in the data?

7 Write a program which does the same thing as the one in this section without using arrays.

8 Rewrite the program of Section 4 5 so that it uses an array in place of the memory cells BAR0, BAR1, BAR2, BAR3, BAR4, and BAR5.

Section 6 3*

Some Misconceptions to Avoid

This section may be skipped without loss of continuity.

Arrays confuse many novice programmers. The following list may help you avoid some common mistakes.

1 Don't confuse the subscript value with the array element value. The value of the element A(5) usually has nothing to do with the number 5.

	A
A(1)	−4.7
A(2)	192.1
A(3)	3.9
A(4)	485.3
A(5)	−19.1
A(6)	0.00

2 When a memory cell name is used in a subscript, it is only the *value* of that memory cell which is important; its name is irrelevant. At one point in a program, we may refer to A(I), and at another point in the same program we may refer to A(J). In each case we are dealing with the same array. In fact, we may even be referencing the same element of the array depending on what values I and J have at the times of the array references.

3 For the same reason, a program may reference both A(I) and B(I). That is, the same memory cell may be used as a subscript in referencing two (or more) different arrays. Again it is the value of the subscript which counts, not its name.

4 Don't use arrays when you don't need them. Profligate use often results in unclear, inefficient programs (see Exercise 6 1 4).

Deciding on an Array

5 In general, WATFIV can deal with only one element of an array at a time. For example if A is an array of ten elements, then the statement

```
IF ( A .NE. 0 )  GO TO 100
```

does not test all ten elements of A. In fact, it isn't even a legal statement. If the intention is to transfer to statement 100 in case some element of A is non-zero, then each element must be tested individually as in the loop below.

```
      I = 1
10    IF ( A(I) .NE. 0 )  GO TO 100
      I = I+1
      IF ( I .LE. 10 )  GO TO 10
```

WATFIV for Humans

6 Remember: in WATFIV, the number of memory cells in an array may not be changed by your program. If you don't know exactly how much room you will need (as we didn't in Section 6 2), you must declare the array larger than you will actually need, and let your program keep track of how many memory cells it is using.

Section 6 4

Arrays With Two Subscripts

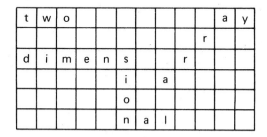

There are situations in which it would be convenient to have arrays with more than one subscript. For instance, imagine that you work for a politician and you want to analyze patterns of support for your candidate. You have block by block results of preliminary polls taken by your volunteers and would like to store your data in a convenient form. An array with two subscripts works beautifully here since you can let the value of the first subscript represent the north-south position of the block, the second subscript represent the east-west position, and the value stored in each memory cell be the percent of positive responses in that block (see Figure 6 4 1).

An array with two subscripts is usually called a **two-dimensional array**. The name of a memory cell in a two-dimensional array is simply the array name followed by a parenthesized list of two subscripts separated by a comma. The memory cells with the names POLL(2,4) and POLL(6,5) are indicated in Figure 6 4 1. As with one-dimensional arrays, dimensions must be given at the beginning of our program. The lowest legal value of a subscript is 1, so all we need in the declaration is the maximum subscript value. In our case the declaration

    REAL POLL(7,5)

would be appropriate since we want to be able to use all memory cells from POLL(1,1) (the top left memory cell in Figure 6 4 1) to POLL(7,5) (the bottom right memory cell). We'll give a precise summary of all types of array declarations in Section 6 5. Until then, we will make do with this informal description.

It is often convenient to think of a two-dimensional array as a grid of boxes arranged in rows and columns, as we have pictured the array POLL in Figure 6 4 1. The first subscript is customarily thought of as the row number and the

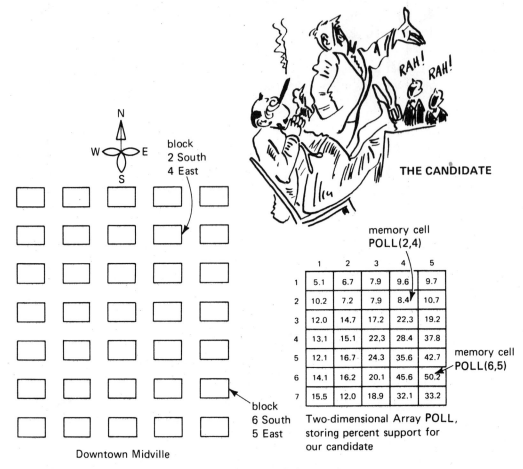

Figure 6 4 1

second as the column number. Thus the declaration says how many rows and columns the array has. (We should emphasize, however, that this is only a custom. You can think of subscripts in any arrangement you like.) Arrays in which the number of rows is the same as the number of columns are thought of as **square arrays.** Those like the one we're using here in our polling problem, in which the numbers of rows and columns are different, can be visualized as **rectangular arrays.**

Storing our poll data in a two-dimensional array makes it easy to analyze the data in a number of different ways. For instance, let's compute the average support for our candidate in the eastern blocks as opposed to his support in the west. This amounts to looking at the average of the numbers in each column of the array. To compute these averages, we will use a loop which cycles across the columns. For each column we have to sum the elements, and to do this we'll use another loop nested inside the column loop which scans down a column. Figure 6 4 2 shows the overall plan. We've left out the details of computing the sum for two reasons: it makes the plan easier to follow, and you are already familiar with the process of computing sums. The WATFIV program follows.

 If an array has ROW *rows and* COLUMN *columns, then the number of elements in each row is* COLUMN *and the number of elements in each column is* ROW.

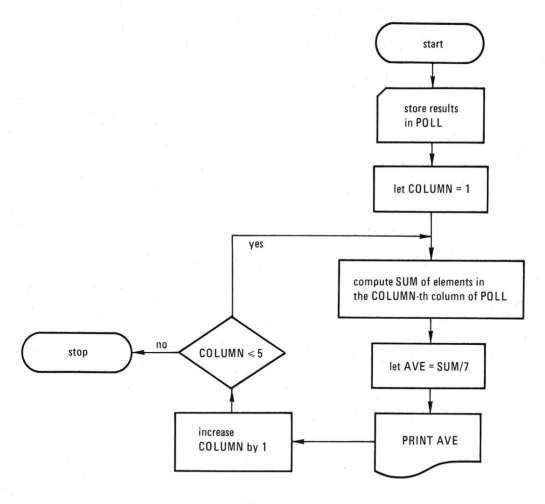

Figure 6 4 2

```
COMMENT--PROGRAM TO PRINT POLITICAL POLL SUMMARIES
        REAL POLL(7,5), AVERGE, SUM
        INTEGER COLUMN, ROW, I
C       STORE DATA
        I = 1
  100   READ, ROW, COLUMN, POLL(ROW,COLUMN)
          I = I+1
          IF ( I .LE. 35 )  GO TO 100
C
C       COMPUTE AVERAGE SUPPORT IN NORTH-SOUTH SLICES OF AREA
C
C       START WITH COLUMN 1 AND AVERAGE ONE COLUMN AT A TIME
        COLUMN = 1
  200   SUM = 0.0
          ROW = 1
  250     SUM = SUM + POLL(ROW,COLUMN)
            ROW = ROW + 1
            IF ( ROW .LE. 7 )  GO TO 250
C         FINISHED SUMMING COLUMN--COMPUTE AVERAGE
          AVERGE = SUM/7.0
          PRINT, 'THE AVERAGE SUPPORT IN SLICE',COLUMN
          PRINT, 'FROM THE WEST IS', AVERGE, 'PER CENT'
          PRINT, ' '
          COLUMN = COLUMN + 1
          IF ( COLUMN .LE. 5 )  GO TO 200
        STOP
        END
```

data

```
    1   1   21.0
    1   2   35.3
    1   3   27.4
    1   4   47.8
    1   5   35.2
    2   1   28.7
    2   2   34.5
    2   3   45.7
    2   4   45.3
    2   5   51.4
    3   1   38.7
    3   2   45.2
    3   3   48.7
    3   4   68.7
    3   5   57.5
    4   1   22.1
    4   2   35.8
    4   3   25.8
    4   4   22.1
    4   5   12.8
    5   1   18.9
    5   2   46.2
    5   3   14.3
    5   4   10.5
    5   5   08.3
    6   1   12.4
    6   2   14.8
    6   3   22.3
    6   4   34.1
    6   5   28.4
    7   1   16.8
    7   2   24.7
    7   3   27.5
    7   4   29.2
    7   5   19.7
```

WATFIV for Humans

output

```
THE AVERAGE SUPPORT IN SLICE            1
FROM THE WEST IS     0.2265714E 02 PER CENT

THE AVERAGE SUPPORT IN SLICE            2
FROM THE WEST IS     0.3378571E 02 PER CENT

THE AVERAGE SUPPORT IN SLICE            3
FROM THE WEST IS     0.3024284E 02 PER CENT

THE AVERAGE SUPPORT IN SLICE            4
FROM THE WEST IS     0.3681427E 02 PER CENT

THE AVERAGE SUPPORT IN SLICE            5
FROM THE WEST IS     0.3047142E 02 PER CENT
```

As you can see, the way the results are organized in the two-dimensional array POLL makes all kinds of regional analysis of the data easy.

EXERCISES 6 4

1 Add a section to the political poll analysis program which computes the average support for our candidate in each of the east-west slices across the region.

2 Add a section which computes the average support for our candidate in the southwest quarter of the region.

3 Change the input section of the poll analysis program so that it accepts raw data from the pollsters: each card will contain a north-south block number of 2100, 2200, 2300, . . . , or 2700, an east-west block number between 4800 and 5200, the number of votes for our candidate, and the number for the other candidate.

4 Which of the following are legal declarations?

```
INTEGER A(100,3), B(3,100),I
REAL QRT(3,49)
LOGICAL P(10), Q(4,2)
REAL X(N,100)
```

5 Assuming the declarations of exercises 4 have been made, mark the statements below which are not legal.

```
A(4,2) = 0
B(4,2) = 1
A(3,50) = 0
I = 10
Q(I/3,I-8) = .TRUE.
P(8) = Q(3,2)
```

Section 6 5

Arrays With More Than Two Subscripts

WATFIV arrays aren't restricted to one or two subscripts; they may have as many as seven. Problems where arrays with several subscripts are handy come up occasionally, but since you are already familiar with one- and two-dimensional arrays, you should have no problem applying your knowledge to arrays with higher dimensions. Just for fun, we include the following example where a three-dimensional array is useful.

Rumor has it that one agency of a large government kept careful records on the habits of some of its citizens during the decade of the sixties. The citizens of interest to this agency were those belonging to certain organizations which will remain unnamed. Many records were kept on each of these citizens, but the ones of greatest interest had to do with their age, political affiliation, and hair length.

---

array declarator

form

  a (*size*)

  a is an array name
  size is a list of up to seven unsigned INTEGER constants separated by commas. The declarator appears as an element in the list of a type statement.

meaning

  Used in a type statement, it declares an array a. The array will have as many subscripts as there are elements in the list *size*; each subscript will have a range starting at 1 and running up to the corresponding element of *size*.

examples

```
INTEGER A(4), B(10,40), C(22)
REAL X(4,10,8,7,2), Y(37)
LOGICAL P(2,2,2,2,2,2,2), Q(9,7,4)
```

Let's suppose the agency has hired us to organize the data in such a way as to make it easy to obtain facts like the number of organization members who have long hair and are Republicans, or the proportion who are between ages 20 and 25 and are neither Republicans nor Democrats.

The approach we will take is to produce a three-dimensional array of class counts. Each class will consist of those organization members of a given age, political affiliation, and hair length. The raw data consists of one punched card for each member containing his age (in the range 18 to 29), his political affiliation (Republican, Democrat, or other), and his hair length (long or short). Thus, one class is composed of those members who are age 18, Republican, and have long

hair; another class contains members who are age 28, Democrat, and have long hair, and a third class contains those who are age 21, Republican, and have short hair. There are 12*3*2 = 72 different classes because there are 12 possible ages, 3 possible political affiliations, and 2 possible hair lengths. Therefore, our array C of class counts will have three subscripts used as follows.

subscript 1 indicates age: 1 for age 18
                             2 for age 17

                         .
                         .
                         .

                      12 for age 29

subscript 2 indicates affiliation: 1 for Republican
                                  2 for Democrat
                                  3 for other

subscript 3 indicates hair length: 1 for short
                                  2 for long

After we organize the raw data, C(9,3,1) will contain the number of short haired 26 year olds who are neither Republicans nor Democrats. What will C(1,2,2) contain?

The following program organizes the raw data according to this scheme and computes the number of long-haired members of the organizations of interest who are between ages 21 and 26. The exercises at the end of this section involve adding other summary calculations to the program.

```
COMMENT--THIS PROGRAM ORGANIZES RAW DATA CONSISTING OF THE
C          AGES, POLITICAL AFFILIATIONS, AND HAIR LENGTHS
C          INTO A TABLE OF CLASS COUNTS
       INTEGER C(12,3,2)
       INTEGER AGE
       CHARACTER*10 AFIL
       CHARACTER*5  HAIR
       INTEGER AGECD, AFILCD, HAIRCD, S
C
C      INITIALIZE COUNTERS
       AGECD = 0
 100   AGECD = AGECD + 1
          C(AGECD,1,1) = 0
          C(AGECD,2,1) = 0
          C(AGECD,3,1) = 0
          C(AGECD,1,2) = 0
          C(AGECD,2,2) = 0
          C(AGECD,3,2) = 0
          IF ( AGECD .LT. 12 )  GO TO 100
C
C      GET DATA AND COMPUTE CLASS COUNTS
 200   READ, AGE, AFIL, HAIR
          IF ( AGE .EQ. 0 )  GO TO 300
          AGECD = AGE - 17
          AFILCD = 3
          IF ( AFIL .EQ. 'REPUBLICAN' )  AFILCD = 1
          IF ( AFIL .EQ. 'DEMOCRAT  ' )  AFILCD = 2
          HAIRCD = 1
          IF ( HAIR .EQ. 'LONG ' ) HAIRCD = 2
          C(AGECD,AFILCD,HAIRCD) = C(AGECD,AFILCD,HAIRCD) + 1
          GO TO 200
C
C      PRINT SUMMARY
 300   S = 0
       AGE = 21
 310   AGECD = AGE - 17
          S = S + C(AGECD,1,2)+C(AGECD,2,2)+C(AGECD,3,2)
          AGE = AGE + 1
          IF ( AGE .LE. 26 )  GO TO 310
C
       PRINT, 'THERE ARE', S, 'LONG HAIRED MEMBERS OF THE'
       PRINT, 'SUSPECT ORGANIZATIONS BETWEEN AGES 21 AND 26'
       STOP
       END


data
    18      'DEMOCRAT  '      'LONG '
    20      'OTHER     '      'LONG '
    26      'DEMOCRAT  '      'LONG '
    24      'DEMOCRAT  '      'LONG '
    21      'OTHER     '      'SHORT'
    21      'REPUBLICAN'      'LONG '
    27      'REPUBLICAN'      'SHORT'
    27      'DEMOCRAT  '      'SHORT'
    20      'OTHER     '      'LONG '
```

```
23       'DEMOCRAT   '      'LONG '
22       'OTHER      '      'LONG '
28       'DEMOCRAT   '      'LONG '
22       'DEMOCRAT   '      'SHORT'
27       'REPUBLICAN'      'SHORT'
18       'DEMOCRAT   '      'SHORT'
22       'DEMOCRAT   '      'SHORT'
29       'DEMOCRAT   '      'LONG '
25       'REPUBLICAN'      'LONG '
26       'OTHER      '      'SHORT'
24       'DEMOCRAT   '      'LONG '
18       'OTHER      '      'LONG '
29       'DEMOCRAT   '      'SHORT'
18       'DEMOCRAT   '      'SHORT'
29       'REPUBLICAN'      'LONG '
24       'DEMOCRAT   '      'LONG '
 0       '          '      '     '
```

output

```
THERE ARE              8 LONG HAIRED MEMBERS OF THE
SUSPECT ORGANIZATIONS BETWEEN AGES 21 AND 26
```

EXERCISES 6 5

1   The program, as written, does not check for illegitimate data and may get incorrect results. For example, if a 16-year-old is inadvertently included in the data, the subscript AGECD will be a negative and therefore not a legal subscript. Write the program so that it will reject illegitimate data. (This will make the program more **robust** in the sense that it will behave satisfactorily even on bad data.)

2   Add a section to the program which will compute the number of 29-year-old longhairs.

3   Add a section to the program which will compute the number of 21-year-olds.

Section 6 6

Input and Output of Arrays

By now you have had a fair amount of experience printing out arrays. Perhaps you have noticed that in each PRINT statement you had to know while writing the program exactly how many elements of an array you wanted to print. If the number of array elements you wanted to print depended on a computation in the program, you had to write a loop and print one element at a time until you had printed all the appropriate elements (as in the example in Section 6 2). This doesn't cause any particular problems if you want each element on a separate line, but if you want them on the same line, you're in for a lot of work. To eliminate this extra effort, there is an alternative form of the I/O list.

Previously we said that the list in a READ or PRINT statement must be made up of variable names separated by commas. Until now we haven't really needed anything else. However, the list can be slightly more complicated. In addition to variable names, it can also contain repetitive lists called **implied DO lists**.

An **implied DO list** is a list of variable names (possibly subscripted) followed by indexing information which specifies how many times to repeat the variables in the implied DO list (that is, how many times to "do" the list) and what values of the index to use in these repetitions. Before we describe the exact form of an implied DO list, let's look at an example or two.

Suppose we want to print out all the values in the array A from A(1) to A(N) where N is a memory cell containing some INTEGER. Instead of writing a loop,

```
      I = 1
50    PRINT, A(I)
      I = I+1
      IF ( I .LE. N )  GO TO 50
```

we can simply write

```
PRINT, (A(I), I=1,N)
```

This is not only shorter to write and easier to read but has the added benefit of commanding the computer to try to put all the values on one line. If there are too many to fit on one line, the computer will automatically go on to the next. In the case of the loop, each value goes on a separate line because each time the computer performs a PRINT statement, it begins on a new line.

An implied DO list doesn't have to be exactly like the one we have written above. The list section can contain more than one element and the indexing section doesn't have to start the index at one and increase by one each time; it can start at any positive INTEGER value and increase at each stage by any positive INTEGER value. What's more, these starting and increment values can be specified by variables instead of constants. For example, the following PRINT statement's implied DO list is legal.

```
PRINT, (L, A(L), B(L), L=M,N,K)
```

It says to set L equal to M, print out the value of L, then the value of A(L), then B(L), and then to increase L by K and print L, A(L), B(L), etc. It keeps repeating as long as L isn't larger than N. If we had known while writing the program that M would be 2, N would be 7, and K would be 3, we could have gotten the same result by writing

```
PRINT, 2, A(2), B(2), 5, A(5), B(5)
```

We should mention what happens if the upper bound in the indexing section is smaller than the starting value. This is a strange case, so perhaps it is not too odd that a strange thing happens: the list section is printed for the starting value of the index, and that is all. This is not a case you should worry about excessively, but it might happen and it pays to be vaguely aware of the consequences.

> **nesting:** *placing a certain program construct inside a program construct of the same form*

114

---

implied DO list

forms

($list, v = s, b$)

($list, v = s, b, i$)

list is any legal I/O list

v is an unsubscripted INTEGER memory cell name

s, *b*, and *i* are nonzero unsigned INTEGER constants or unsubscripted INTEGER memory cell names (with positive values).

meaning

describes an I/O list consisting of consecutive repetitions of *list* for each value of *v* starting at *s* and incrementing by *i* as long as *v* doesn't exceed *b* (the increment is one if *i* is omitted)

examples

```
READ, (A(I), I=1,10,3)
PRINT, (A(K-1), K=2,N)
PRINT, (NXT, A(NXT), FXD, NXT=L,M,INC)
```

---

array transmission: Entire arrays may be transmitted to output or filled from data cards by placing the array name alone, without subscripts, in an I/O list. The order of transmission is the order in which the array's memory cells are stored in the machine.

```
REAL A, B, C(3)
READ A, C, B
```

is equivalent to

```
REAL A, B, C(3)
READ A, C(1), C(2), C(3), B
```

Note that the general form allows *nesting* of implied DO lists. That is, one implied DO list can be inside another. The effect of nesting is to cause the inside implied DO list to be completely repeated with every repetition of the outside implied DO list. The following examples should help clarify the effects of this nesting.

1
```
PRINT, C, (B, (A, I=1,3), J=1,2), D
```
         is equivalent to
```
PRINT, C, B,A,A,A, B,A,A,A, D
```

2
```
PRINT, ((A(I,J),J=1,3),I=1,2)
```
         is equivalent to
```
PRINT, A(1,1),A(1,2),A(1,3), A(2,1),A(2,2),A(2,3)
```

As you can see in example 1, the list section of an implied DO list does not need to involve the index. It may or it may not, at your option.

Implied DO lists may also be used in READ statements. They order input variables in the same way that they order output variables. You will get a chance to use some implied DO lists in READ statements in the exercises.

Here's one last example of using implied DO lists.

One of our friends is an eccentric, perhaps even a bit deranged, poet. He has developed a poetic style which has two main phases. First he writes down a list of four-letter words. ("Why four?" we asked. He mumbled something about the quartering of the universe according to primordial principles which we didn't understand.) The second phase consists of rearranging the original list into a square shape. He insists that the order of the original list be preserved in the columns of the square. For example, if the original list consists of the nine character strings 'AAAA', 'BBBB', 'CCCC', . . . , 'IIII', his resultant poem looks like Figure 6 6 1 (a). He has grown tired of doing the rearranging and asked us to write a program to do it for him. We suspected that he had just hit upon a cheap way to see his poetry in print but agreed to go along.

We asked him how many words were in one of his poems. He cocked his head to the side a little and said, "It doesn't matter, of course." When we pointed out that there might not be enough words to make a complete square, he looked at us as if we had taken leave of our senses and said incredulously, "You think I don't know that? The blank lower right corners symbolize the emptiness of ratiocination! Idiots!"

We left, shaking our heads, but with an example of a poem made from five words [Figure 6 6 1 (b)].

AAAA DDCD GGGG   AAAA DDDD
BBBB EEEE HHHH   BBBB EEEE
CCCC FFFF IIII   CCCC

(a)   (b)

Figure 6 6 1

Our strategy is outlined in Figure 6 6 2. The program appears below. We have assumed that a special termination card containing the string '++++' will be inserted at the end of the data deck, and we've assumed that our poet friend will never think up more than 100 words for a poem. In order to compute the size of the square, the program simply searches for the first INTEGER s such that $s**2$ is larger than the number of input strings. Then, if we put s strings in each column of the output, there won't be more than s columns. In order to preserve the order of the input strings in the columns of the square, each row will consist of every sth string.

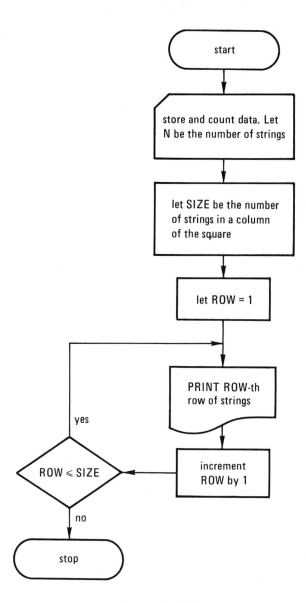

Figure 6 6 2

```
COMMENT--PROGRAM TO PRINT A SQUARE OF UP TO 100
C          FOUR CHARACTER STRINGS
        CHARACTER*4 STR(101)
        INTEGER N, SIZE, ROW, K
C
C       STORE AND COUNT DATA
        N = 0
  100   READ, STR(N+1)
           IF ( STR(N+1) .EQ. '++++' )  GO TO 200
           N = N+1
           GO TO 100
C
C       COMPUTE SIZE
  200   SIZE = 1
  210   IF ( SIZE**2 .GE. N )  GO TO 300
           SIZE = SIZE + 1
           GO TO 210
C
C       PRINT SQUARE
  300   ROW = 1
  310   PRINT, (STR(K), K=ROW,N,SIZE)
           ROW = ROW + 1
           IF ( ROW .LE. SIZE )  GO TO 310
        STOP
        END
```

data

```
'MASH'
'ACHH'
'BAM '
'OOOW'
'BASH'
'URCH'
'BAM '
'ACHH'
'BASH'
'OOOW'
'BAM '
'URCH'
'BASH'
'ACHH'
'POW '
'OOF '
'BASH'
'URCH'
'POW '
'ACHH'
'BASH'
'OOF '
'POW '
'URCH'
'WHAP'
'++++'
```

output

```
MASH URCH BAM  OOF  BASH
ACHH BAM  URCH BASH OOF
BAM  ACHH BASH URCH POW
OOOW BASH ACHH POW  URCH
BASH OOOW POW  ACHH WHAP
```

118

EXERCISES 6 6

1 Without using implied DO lists, write I/O statements equivalent to the following ones, assuming that M, N, and K have the values 4, 12, and 2 respectively.

```
READ, (A(J), J=1,4)
PRINT, (A(J), J=M,N,K)
PRINT, (A(J), J=K,N,M)
READ, ( (B(I,J),I=1,M), J=1,K )
PRINT, Q,R, (S, B(3,J), A(J), J=1,K), BC, (A(J),J=1,4)
```

2 Using implied DO lists, write I/O statements equivalent to the following ones.

```
PRINT, A(1), A(2), A(3), A(4), A(5)
PRINT, A(2), A(4), A(6), A(8), A(10)
PRINT, 1, A(1), 2, A(2), 3, A(3), 4, A(4)
READ, B(2,1), B(3,1), B(2,2), B(3,2), B(2,3), B(3,3)
```

3 What is illegal in the following I/O statements?

```
PRINT, (A(J), J=1,N-1)
READ, (J, A(J), J=1,N)
PRINT, (A(J), J=1,C(N))
```

4 How do we know that none of the lines printed by the poet's program will have more than SIZE strings on them?

5 Change the poet's program so that it centers its SIZE by SIZE square in an imaginary 12 by 12 square on the output page.

6 Change the poet's program so it encloses the square with asterisks; *i.e.,* the "poem" in Figure 6 6 1 (a) would be printed like this:

```
* * * * * * * *
* AAAA DDDD GGGG *
* BBBB EEEE HHHH *
* CCCC FFFF IIII *
* * * * * * * *
```

PROBLEMS 6

1 Write a program to compute the sales price of an automobile given its base price and the prices of its optional equipment, if any. The data cards for the program will be in groups. Each group will describe one car and will be organized as follows.

Typical group of cards describing a car:

card 1: car name (CHARACTER*40), base price (INTEGER)

0 to 25

more cards: name of option (CHARACTER*40), price (INTEGER)

termination

card: `'NO MORE OPTIONS'    0.00`

There may be from 0 to 25 option cards, making a group consisting of anywhere from 2 to 27 cards. Following all the groups of cards will be the termination card shown below.

'NO MORE CARS'   0.00

For each automobile described in the data cards, store the information about the car in memory, compute its total price by adding its base price, all its option prices, a $150 dealer preparation charge, and 6 per cent sales tax, and print the results in the following order:

line 1:   car name   base price   total price (including tax and dealer prep)

0 to 25 more lines: name of option   price

last line: blank

Your program should make *no* assumptions about the number of cars described in the data cards.

2 Write a program to produce a list of students, an honor roll, and a list of suspended students. Each data card will contain a student's name (CHARACTER*40) and his grade point on a scale from 0.000 to 4.000 (REAL). The terminating data card will be

'NO MORE STUDENTS'   0.000

Your program should print the heading CLASS ROLL followed by the list of all students, their grade points, the heading HONOR ROLL followed by a list of those students whose grade points exceed 3.299, and finally the heading SUSPENDED followed by a list of students whose grade points are less than 1.7. Your program may assume that there are no more than 100 students.

3 Write a program using the same data cards as those in problem 2 but which prints the list of students with an asterisk (*) beside each student whose grade point is above the average grade point for all the students. After the list, print the percentage of students whose grade point is above average.

4 Prepare data cards containing values for a 10 by 10 two dimensional array named VOLTS. These values represent the potentials induced on a 10 by 10 square sheet of polystyrene by the meditations of an aging guru.

Write a program to store the potentials in the array, compute and print the largest potential and the average potential on the sheet of polystyrene. If the largest is more than ten times the average, have the computer print the message "HE DID IT".

Aging Guru Radiates Potential

5 Write a program which prints out a multiplication table. The size of the table should be determined by an INTEGER between 2 and 9 written on a data card. Your program should print a table of products up to that number. For example, if the number is 3, your output should look like that below.

```
*       1       2       3
1       1       2       3
2       2       4       6
3       3       6       9
```

6

> **palindrome**: *a word or phrase which reads the same forward as backward.*
>
> A palindrome: "Madam, I'm Adam."
>
> Not a palindrome: "Able was I ere I saw Chicago."

Write a program which detects palindromes. Assume that there won't be more than 50 characters. Remember that blanks, punctuation marks, and CapiTaliZations don't count in determining palindromes, so don't enter anything but letters on your data cards. Print the input phrase on one line and follow it by the phrase "is palindromic" or "is not, in fact, palindromic" whichever is appropriate.

Sample input:

```
                    'R'
                    'A'
                    'D'
                    'A'
                    'R'
                    '*'            (marks end of data)
```

7 Write a program which prints beef price differences in a group of up to 100 cities. Each data card will contain the name of a city (CHARACTER*40) followed by the price of a pound of hamburger at a local supermarket. The last data card will be

'NO MORE CITIES'   0.00

Your program should compute the average price of hamburger over all the cities and print a table of cities, hamburger prices and the amounts above or below the average price. Thus, each line of the table should contain the name of a city, the price of hamburger there, and the difference between that price and the average price of hamburger (a positive number if the price is above average and a negative number if it's below average).

8 Add a section to the program of problem 7 to print the lowest and highest of the hamburger prices surveyed along with the corresponding cities.

9 For people who are familiar with matrices. Write a program which reads values for two matrices and prints the matrix product

$$A = (a_{ij}), B = (b_{jk}) , C = AB \qquad c_{ik} = \Sigma_j a_{ij} b_{jk}$$

10 Write a program which evaluates polynomials. The data should consist of two groups of cards. Group 1 describes the polynomial by giving the coefficients and corresponding powers. That is, each card in group 1 contains a coefficient (REAL) and a power (INTEGER). This group is followed by a termination card with coefficient 0.0 and power -1. The following group of data cards would describe the polynomial $3x^4 + 2x^2 + 4.7x + 1$

3.0	4
2.0	2
4.7	1
1.0	0
0.0	-1

You may assume that there are no more than 51 cards in group 1.

Group 2 is a list of points at which the polynomial is to be evaluated. That is, each card in group 2 will contain a REAL value for the independent variable in the polynomial. The termination card for group 2 will contain 999999.9 (which shouldn't be taken as a value at which to evaluate the polynomial). Your program should print a description of the polynomial and a table of values of the polynomial at the points listed in the group 2 data cards.

11 Horner's scheme for evaluating polynomials is quicker and more accurate than the straight-forward scheme. Write the program of Problem 10 so that it uses Horner's evaluation scheme.

Horner's scheme

$$a_n x^n + a_{n-1} x^{n-1} + \ldots . + a_1 x + a_0 =$$

$$(((a_n x + a_{n-1})x + a_{n-2})x + \ldots . + a_1)x + a_0$$

e.g., $3x^4 + 2x^2 + 4.7x + 1 = (((3x + 0)x + 2)x + 4.7)x + 1$

12 If you are familiar with vectors, write a program to convert a given vector to a unit vector in the same direction. Assume each card contains the dimension (*i.e.*, number of components) of the vector (INTEGER) followed by the components of the vector (REALs). You may assume the dimension is less than 100. The termination card will contain the vector 0.0 of dimension 1. (Don't try to convert it to a unit vector!)

The unit vector in the same direction as $(x_1, x_2, \ldots, x_n)$ is $(u_1, u_2, \ldots, u_n)$ where

$$u_k = x_k / r$$
and $r = \sqrt{(x_1{}^2 + x_2{}^2 + \ldots + x_n{}^2)}$

Print the vector and the corresponding unit vector.

13 Write a program to compute the cosine of the angle between two given vectors. Assume each data card will contain the dimension of the two vectors involved (INTEGER) followed by the components of the one, and finally the components of the other. As in Problem 12, assume the dimension is less than 100. The termination card will contain 1,0.0,0.0. If $(u_1, \ldots, u_n)$ and $(v_1, \ldots, v_n)$ are the unit vectors in the same direction as the given vectors x and y, respectively, then the cosine of the angle between the two given vectors is $u_1 v_1 + u_2 v_2 + \ldots + u_n v_n$. A formula in Problem 12 shows the relation between a given vector and the corresponding unit vector.

> *WARNING: The following problems are more challenging than the ones above.*

14 Write a program to do the matching for a computer dating service. The dating service's questionaires have twenty statements and the applicant indicates his degree of agreement with each question on a scale of one to five. Thus each data card will contain the name of an applicant (CHARACTER*30), sex ('M' or 'F'), and responses to the questionaire (20 INTEGERs). The last data card will contain the string 'NO MORE APPLICANTS' in place of the name. You may assume there are no more than 100 applicants.

Match each person with the two most compatible people of the opposite sex. As a measure of compatibility, use the cosine of the angle between their two response vectors, the larger the cosine, the more compatible the couple (see Problem 13 for a way to compute the cosine).

Your program's output should be a list of the applicants along with the names of their two guaranteed dates, *e.g.*,

```
JOHN DOE                                    DATES MARY SLATE
                                                  AND ALICE HILL

JANE FLUG                                   DATES ROGER WHIMSBY
                                                  AND JOE THORNTON
        •
        •
        •
```

15 Problem 14 has a feature which wouldn't be acceptable to a real computer dating service. If one person is particularly compatible, he or she will receive the names of two dates, but may be listed as a good date on *many* people's lists. The whole thing could get out of balance with almost everybody trying to date a few highly compatible people. Do Problem 14 so that no one person is listed for more than six other people. Print *all* the dates a person is involved in, not just his own two optimal matches as before. Now another problem arises. You may have to refund some participants' money because in some cases there may not be enough suitable matches to go around. Print a polite apology to those who come up short.

16 Dress up the input and output of Problem 14 or 15 to include addresses and phone numbers.

17 Write a program which, given a tic-tac-toe board situation, decides on a nonlosing next move, or, if there is none, prints a snide concession of defeat.

18 Write a program to compute unemployment statistics. Assume each data card contains the name of a city (CHARACTER*40) followed by the unemployment percentages (INTEGERs) for each month of the fiscal year, from July through the following June. The termination card will contain the string 'NO MORE STATISTICS'. For each month, print out the cities with the lowest and highest unemployment rates and the average unemployment rate for all the cities that month. At the end, print the average unemployment rate over all the cities for the entire year. You may assume that there are no more than 50 cities.

19 Suppose you own a travel service and your policy is to book your customers with a direct flight if possible. You have a stack of punched cards describing the direct flights for which you may schedule passengers. That is, each card contains a departure point and time, an arrival point and time, and the name of an airline; *e.g.*,

flight description card:

        'KANSAS CITY'   '10:00AM'   'DENVER'   '11:00AM'   'TWA'

You have a second stack of cards each of which contains the name of a customer, his point of departure and his destination; *e.g.*,

customer request card:

        'CLIFFORD TREASE'   'CHICAGO'   'SAN FRANCISCO'

You are to write a program which stores the flight descriptions in memory then tries to find a direct flight to fill each customer request. If the program finds a direct flight, it should print out the customer's name, departure point and time, arrival point and time, and airline. Otherwise print the customer's name and a message to the effect that there is no direct flight available for the customer between his requested departure and arrival points.

Your program may *not* assume that the cards have been counted, so you will need some sort of termination card at the end of each of the two stacks so that it can test to see when it has stored all the flight descriptions and when it has taken care of all the customers. You may assume that there are no more than 100 flight descriptions, but your program should not depend *in any way* upon the number of customers.

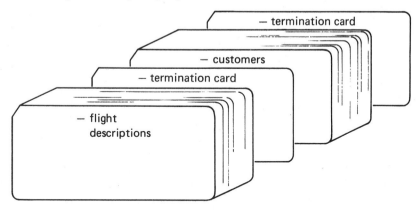

20 Write a program to make airline reservations. Assume that the airline you work for has seven flights with the number of seats given in the table below.

FLIGHT	SEATS AVAILABLE
101A	147
237G	83
208	6
505	21
A007	122
01A4	62
G27R	3

Your program should reserve seats on these flights on a first come, first serve basis. Each data card will contain a customer's name (CHARACTER*40) and the number of the flight he wants (CHARACTER*4). The termination card will contain the string 'NO MORE CUSTOMERS' in place of the name. Make no assumptions about the number of customers.

For each request, print the name of the customer and a message indicating whether or not his reservation is confirmed.

21 Write a program to solve a more general version of the previous problem. The program should first READ the flight information from data cards. Each flight description will be on a separate card with the flight number (CHARACTER*4) followed by the number of seats available (INTEGER). The termination card for the flight descriptions will be

'++++'   0

The rest of the data cards will be customer requests as in Problem 20. As before, make no assumptions about the number of customers, but assume that the airline has no more than 100 flights.

The advantage of this version is that the airline can still use the program if it adds or deletes flights or changes to planes of different capacities.

22 Dress up the input and output of the program in Problem 21 to include times and points of departure and arrival.

23 For people who really like factorials: Write a program that can compute $n! = n * (n-1) * (n-2) * \ldots * 2 * 1$ for values of n that are so large that the answer can't fit in a single INTEGER memory cell.

$$25! = 15, 511, 210, 043, 330, 985, 984, 000, 000$$

One way to do this is to use an array to store the answer (and partial results) using one memory cell in the array per digit. Thus, $12! = 479, 001, 600$ would be stored like this

	9	8	7	6	5	4	3	2	1
. . .	4	7	9	0	0	1	6	0	0

Now to find 13!, multiply each memory cell by 13 (taking care to move carries) to get

	11	10	9	8	7	6	5	4	3	2	1
. . .		6	2	2	7	0	2	0	8	0	0

24 Write a program to list all the prime numbers between 1 and 1000. To compute these numbers, use the algorithm below which is known as Eratosthenes' sieve.

1 Make a list of all the consecutive integers you are interested in, starting from 2.

2 Mark off all the multiples of 2 (they can't be primes).

3 Find the next integer remaining in the list beyond the one whose multiples you just marked off (they can't be primes).

4 Repeat step 3 unless the integer whose multiple you just marked off is the square root of the largest integer in the list; that is, the square root without its fractional part. (This termination condition depends on the fact that the two factors in a product can't both exceed the square root of the product.)

One way to keep track of which numbers are still on the list is to initialize a logical array of 1000 elements to .TRUE. (for "on the list") and cross the number n off the list by changing the nth element of the array to .FALSE.

7 FUNCTIONS AND SUBROUTINES

Section 7 1

Introduction

> "I'm learning to program."
> "What's that mean?"
> "I am learning to write instructions for computers."
> "Oh yeah? What's a computer?"
> "You're kidding."
> "No, what's a computer?"
> "A computer is, uh, a machine that manipulates symbols."
> "Oh yeah? What's a symbol?"
> "....."

All human languages encourage the use of short, simple words and phrases to refer to complex ideas. The meaning of a sentence depends on its words, many of whose meanings might be quite complicated and difficult to explain. Sometimes it's necessary to clarify the meaning of a sentence to the listener by defining some of its words or phrases. The definitions, of course, are given in other sentences whose words may be unfamiliar, and so on down the hierarchy of clarification until the meaning of the original sentence is couched in terms the listener understands. This process is time-consuming and difficult. We'd rather not do it at all, or at least keep the layers of definitions at a minimum. In fact many concepts are virtually impossible to explain in detail without assuming a considerable amount of specialized life experience on the part of the listener. Think, for example, of trying to explain to your friends about learning to program. You'd never get all the details across, but you could probably explain enough to leave them feeling that they had some idea what you're doing.

Writing a program is a problem in communication. It should come as no surprise that people have found that the most effective way to program is not to lay all the details out in linear order but to break the program up hierarchically, using simple expressions to refer to complex subparts which are specified elsewhere.

There are several convenient ways to give a sequence of statements a simple name in WATFIV. In fact, you've been using one of them all along! If you were asked to write a program which printed out a table of square roots, you would immediately recognize that somewhere in your program a reference to the built-in function SQRT would appear. You probably don't know, off hand, all the details

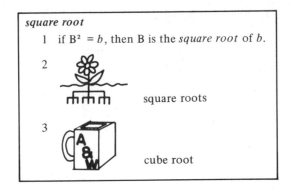

square root

   1   if $B^2 = b$, then B is the *square root* of b.

   2   square roots

   3   cube root

involved in computing a square root, and you certainly don't know all the details that your computer will go through to compute SQRT, but you *do* know what results to expect and that's enough to do the problem.

The MiniManual section on Built-in FUNCTIONs describes a variety of computations (subprograms) which you can invoke just by using their names. What you will learn in this chapter is how to define subprograms of your own, and how to use them to help make your programs more natural communications.

There are two kinds of WATFIV subprograms, the FUNCTION and the SUB-ROUTINE, and they are used in slightly different situations. FUNCTIONs are appropriate when a single value is returned from the subprogram (just as built-in FUNCTIONs like SQRT return a single value), and SUBROUTINEs are the choice when the subprogram returns a number of values each time it is referenced. We will deal with SUBROUTINEs first.

> *subprogram: a complete and separate program which may be referred to by another program*

> *program unit: the main program or a subprogram. Every WAT-FIV program has at least one program unit. All our programs up to now have had exactly one unit, the main program.*

Section 7 2

SUBROUTINEs

Using SUBROUTINEs can make complicated programs easier to write and easier to read. Even if you never plan to let anyone else see your program, you'll have to read it as you try to debug it, and every little bit helps! To demonstrate programming using SUBROUTINEs we'll go through an example showing both how SUBROUTINEs are written and how they are used in thinking out a solution.

Suppose you are asked to write a program which will convert integers written in our customary (arabic) notation into roman numerals. The first step in writing such a program is to remember how you did this in your grade school days. Take the number 7, for example. You may remember that the roman notation for 7 is VII, but in order to write a program to do this conversion, we need to analyze the conversion process carefully. To convert 7 to VII, you observe that there is one five in 7, with two ones left over. Thus the roman numeral consists of a V, the symbol for five, followed by two I's; that is, two one-symbols.

Let's look at another example, converting 29 to its roman notation. We observe that there are two tens in 29 with nine left over. Therefore, the first part of the roman numeral is two ten-symbols, XX. Now we have nine left to deal with. There is one five in nine, so the next part of the roman numeral is a five-symbol, and we get XXV. We still have four left over. Since there are four ones in four, the roman numeral for 29 is XXVIIII. For the time being we'll use this simple roman notation. Once we have figured out how to do the simpler notation, we'll be able to make a few changes which will implement the more sophisticated notation in which four identical symbols are always replaced by two. Thus, ultimately, we would like our program to return XXIX instead of XXVIIII. (Problem 7 11 has hints for improving the program in that way.)

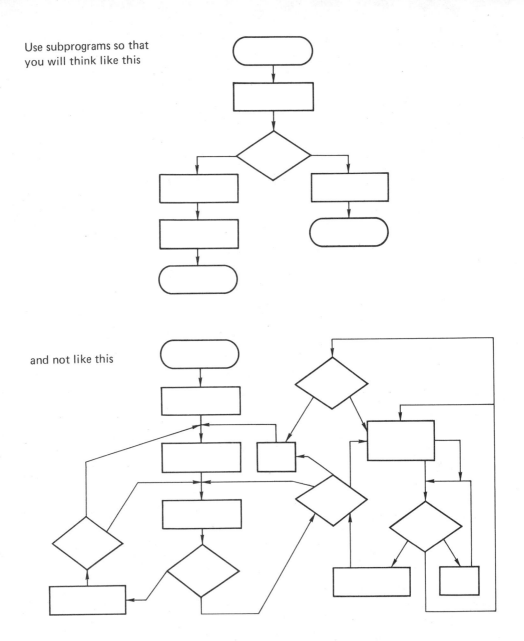

Use subprograms so that you will think like this

and not like this

Now that we have some ideas about the conversion process, let's think about the program. We must put some limit on the numbers our program can handle; let's say the limit is 4999. That way our program will be able to compute the roman numeral for any integer from 1 to 4999. The roman symbols we'll need are those for thousands, five hundreds, one hundreds, fifties, tens, fives, and ones; that is, M, D, C, L, X, V, and I, respectively.

As you can see from the examples, we convert a number to roman notation in stages. First we find out how many M's we need, that is, how many thousands are in the number, and how much is left over. Then we find out how many five hundreds are in the part left over and write down that many D's. In the part that remains after the five hundreds are subtracted, we see how many hundreds there are, and so on until none of the number remains. Figure 7 2 1 gives a specific example.

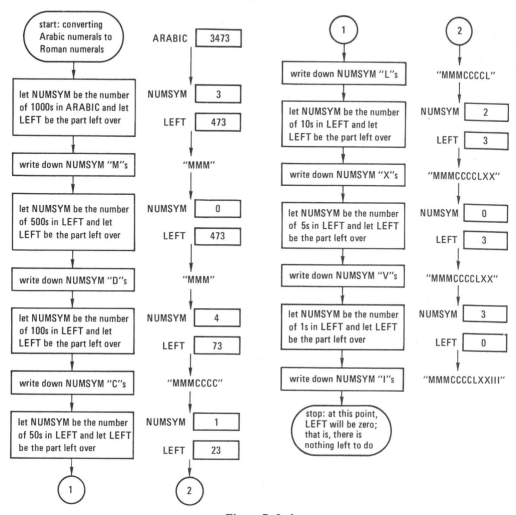

Figure 7 2 1

You will notice in the flowchart that two of the statements are frequently repeated: (1) let NUMSYM be the number of ___ s in LEFT and let LEFT be the part left over (the number in the blank changes from time to time) and (2) write down NUMSYM ___ 's (the letter in the blank changes from time to time). This gives us a perfect chance to use a SUBROUTINE to make programs easier to write. We will divide the programming task into pieces and solve each piece separately.

One piece in the solution will be a SUBROUTINE which, when invoked, will add a few characters to the roman numeral which we are building. In order to do this, the SUBROUTINE needs three items of information:

1 the symbol under consideration (I, V, etc.)
2 the meaning of the symbol (1, 5, etc.), and
3 the number under consideration.

When invoked, the SUBROUTINE must do two things: it must tell us how much of the number is left over, and it must add some symbols to the roman numeral. The statement which invokes the SUBROUTINE will specify, through a list of arguments, both the information the SUBROUTINE needs to make its computation and the names of some memory cells to store the results in.

A SUBROUTINE is invoked by a **CALL statement** which consists of the word CALL followed by the name of the SUBROUTINE, followed by a parenthesized list of values which can be constants, expressions, memory cell names, and/or array names. The elements of this list are the arguments to the SUBROUTINE. Some of them will be input arguments; that is, information the SUBROUTINE needs to make its computation. Others will be output arguments; that is, memory cells in which to store results. Some may be both input and output arguments. We'll see examples of all three.

CALL statement

forms

   CALL $s(a_1, a_2, \ldots, a_n)$

   CALL s

   s is a SUBROUTINE name
   a_1 is an argument (*i.e.*, a memory cell name, array name, constant, or expression).

meaning

   performs the computation described by SUBROUTINE s using the information and/or memory cells specified in the arguments.

examples

```
CALL SORT (NAMES, N)
CALL AVG(GRD, N, AV)
CALL PRMESS
CALL CMPT(A, 32.0*CAB+1.0, SQRT(C))
```

The argument list of the CALL statement is the only place in which information can be communicated to the SUBROUTINE. The values or memory cells named there are the only things the SUBROUTINE will know about the program which called it. Similarly, the only things the CALLing program will know about the SUBROUTINE will be the values the SUBROUTINE stores in memory cells named in the CALL statement. Occasionally the SUBROUTINE and calling program won't need to know anything about each other, and in those cases, the argument list is omitted from the CALL statement. In addition, there is a way of passing information implicitly, but we won't see that until Chapter 11.

Now that we have the general plan of the program and know something about invoking SUBROUTINEs, we must think about a few details. One important question in our roman numeral problem is what to do with the symbols of the roman numeral as it builds up. It would be nice if we could PRINT them as we go,

> *argument: an "input" to a computation. One very old meaning was related to the word "refashioning". We could say that in SQRT (2.0), the argument 2.0 is "refashioned" into 1.4142 ...*

but each new PRINT statement would start a new line, and we want the whole roman numeral on one line. Our other choice is to store it in memory until it is completed, then PRINT it all at once. Since there will be several symbols in the roman numeral, and since we won't know in advance exactly how many symbols it will have, it will be convenient to store the symbols in an array. We can use another memory cell to keep track of the number of roman symbols stored in the array as we go along so that, when it is completed, we will know how many symbols to PRINT. In order to declare the array we need to know how long it should be; that is, how many symbols are in the longest roman numeral. One way to answer the question is to notice that there are no more than four identical symbols in any roman numeral, and since we have only seven different symbols, M, D, C, L, X, V, I, no roman numeral can contain more than twenty-eight symbols. If we declare an array with twenty-eight memory cells, it will surely be long enough. A more careful analysis would show that we could get by with fewer, but it's hardly worth it with so few memory cells involved.

Let's go ahead and write the program, CALLing the SUBROUTINE whenever we want to add more symbols to the roman numeral. You have seen the general form of a CALL statement, but you haven't seen an example. A CALL to our SUBROUTINE will look like this:

```
CALL ROMSYM ('M', 1000, ARABIC, LEFT, ROMNUM, NUMSYM)
```

The name of our SUBROUTINE will be ROMSYM, pronounced "roman symbols". The first three arguments tell it information it needs to know; they are the three input arguments we described earlier. In the above CALL they are

    1   the symbol under consideration, 'M'
    2   the meaning of the symbol, 1000, and
    3   the number under consideration (stored in the memory cell ARABIC).

The next two arguments are the output arguments:

    4   the SUBROUTINE will use memory cell LEFT to store the number left over after the removal of the amount corresponding to the newly added symbols, and
    5   the SUBROUTINE will store the symbols added to the roman numeral (along with the part of the roman numeral assembled so far) in the array ROMNUM.

The sixth argument is both an input argument and an output argument. The SUBROUTINE finds out from the sixth argument how many symbols are already stored in the array containing the roman numeral (in this sense it is an input argument), and the SUBROUTINE increases its value when new symbols are added to the array (in this sense it is an output argument).

It is the *position of the arguments in the* CALL and *not their names or values* which determines their use in the SUBROUTINE. For example, in our program's CALLs to SUBROUTINE ROMSYM, the first argument must always be the symbol under consideration, the second argument must be an INTEGER indicating the meaning of the symbol, and so on.

Now we are finally ready to take a look at the main program. Later we'll write the SUBROUTINE.

```
COMMENT:  THIS PROGRAM CONVERTS AN INTEGER TO ROMAN NOTATION
          INTEGER ARABIC, I, LEFT, NUMBER, NUMSYM
          CHARACTER*1 ROMNUM(28)
C     GET AN INTEGER TO CONVERT.
 100  READ, ARABIC
C         TERMINATING DATA CARD CONTAINS NEGATIVE VALUE
          IF ( ARABIC .LE. 0 )   STOP
          IF ( ARABIC .LE. 4999 )   GO TO 200
             PRINT, 'SORRY, BUT', ARABIC, 'IS OUT OF MY RANGE'
             GO TO 100
C         INITIALLY, THERE ARE NO SYMBOLS IN 'ROMNUM'.
 200      NUMSYM = 0
C         PUT ONE 'M' IN 'ROMNUM' FOR EACH 1000 IN 'ARABIC'.
C         STORE THE REMAINDER OF 'ARABIC', AFTER SUBTRACTING
C         THE 1000'S, IN 'NUMBER'.
          CALL ROMSYM('M',1000,ARABIC, NUMBER, ROMNUM, NUMSYM)
C         PROCEED SIMILARLY FOR THE 500'S, 100'S, 50'S, 10'S,
C         5'S, AND 1'S IN 'NUMBER'
          CALL ROMSYM('D', 500, NUMBER, LEFT,  ROMNUM, NUMSYM)
          NUMBER = LEFT
          CALL ROMSYM('C', 100, NUMBER, LEFT,  ROMNUM, NUMSYM)
          NUMBER = LEFT
          CALL ROMSYM('L',  50, NUMBER, LEFT,  ROMNUM, NUMSYM)
          NUMBER = LEFT
          CALL ROMSYM('X',  10, NUMBER, LEFT,  ROMNUM, NUMSYM)
          NUMBER = LEFT
          CALL ROMSYM('V',   5, NUMBER, LEFT,  ROMNUM, NUMSYM)
          NUMBER = LEFT
          CALL ROMSYM('I',   1, NUMBER, LEFT,  ROMNUM, NUMSYM)
          PRINT, 'THE ROMAN NUMERAL FOR', ARABIC, 'IS',
     +                (ROMNUM(I), I=1,NUMSYM)
C     GO CHECK FOR MORE CONVERSIONS
          GO TO 100
      END
```

Now that the program is written, we need to think about the SUBROUTINE it uses. A SUBROUTINE is a complete and separate program itself. It has all the characteristics of a program, including declarations and an END statement, and may contain any statement that a program can use, including CALLs to other subprograms. In addition it contains two statements that a main program cannot use. The first is the **SUBROUTINE statement** which states the name of the SUBROUTINE and designates names for parameters. **Parameters** are place holders for the arguments which will be given to the SUBROUTINE in a CALL statement. The other new statement, the **RETURN statement** terminates the execution of the SUBROUTINE. When the SUBROUTINE is CALLed, the controller begins to execute its statements. When it comes to a RETURN statement, it leaves the SUBROUTINE and goes back to the statement immediately following the CALL statement which invoked the SUBROUTINE.

In addition to these two new statements, there are some declarations which take on an entirely new meaning even though their form is the same as that of declarations you've seen before. These are the parameter declarations. In the SUBROUTINE the parameters are merely used as *placeholders* for the values, memory cell names, or array names which will be arguments in the CALL statement. In the body of the SUBROUTINE the parameters show what will be done with the arguments when the SUBROUTINE is CALLed, but the parameters don't have values of their own until they get them from the arguments in a CALL statement. Therefore, the declarations of parameters do not give names to memory cells like normal declarations. They merely tell the SUBROUTINE what kind of value, memory cell, or array to expect in the corresponding argument when the SUBROUTINE is CALLed. Since parameter declarations are so different from memory cell declarations, it is wise to keep them separate. We make it a habit to put the parameter declarations immediately after the SUBROUTINE statement and then use separate declarations to declare memory cells needed in the SUB-ROUTINE.

Before we get bogged down in abstract explanations, let's write our roman numeral conversion SUBROUTINE.

```
      SUBROUTINE ROMSYM(SYMBOL, MEANIN, NUMBER, LEFT,
     +              ROMNUM, LENGTH)
      CHARACTER*1 SYMBOL, ROMNUM(28)
      INTEGER LEFT, LENGTH, MEANIN, NUMBER
COMMENT:  THIS SUBROUTINE DETERMINES HOW MANY TIMES 'SYMBOL'
C         OCCURS IN THE ROMAN NOTATION FOR 'NUMBER' AND
C         UPDATES 'ROMNUM' ACCORDINGLY.
C         'LENGTH' IS THE NUMBER OF SYMBOLS IN 'ROMNUM'.
C         'MEANIN' IS THE INTEGER MEANING OF 'SYMBOL'.
C         'LEFT' IS THE REMAINDER OF 'NUMBER' AFTER
C         DEDUCTING THE PORTION CONVERTED TO ROMAN NOTATION.
      INTEGER NUMADD
COMMENT:  SUBROUTINE 'DIV' COMPUTES 'NUMADD', THE NUMBER OF
C         'SYMBOL'S TO BE ADDED TO 'ROMNUM'.
      CALL DIV (NUMBER, MEANIN, NUMADD, LEFT)
COMMENT:  UPDATE 'ROMNUM'.
      LENGTH = LENGTH + NUMADD
  100 IF ( NUMADD .EQ. 0 )  RETURN
      ROMNUM(LENGTH-NUMADD+1) = SYMBOL
      NUMADD = NUMADD-1
      GO TO 100
      END
```

When we were writing SUBROUTINE ROMSYM, we decided that it would be easier for us to write it if we didn't have to worry about exactly how to figure out how many times to deduct MEANIN from NUMBER. So, we just made up a SUBROUTINE named DIV that does that. After we were satisfied with ROMSYM, we got around to thinking about how to write DIV. Here is what we came up with.

Note that this simple loop

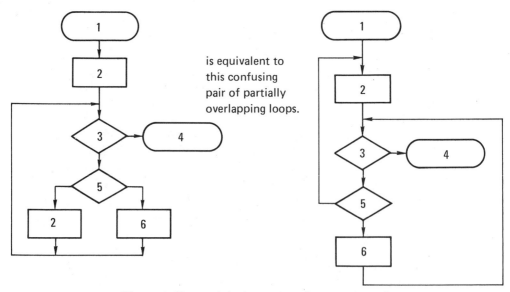

is equivalent to this confusing pair of partially overlapping loops.

Of course, if any of the boxes contain more than a few statements, you'll want to make them subprograms; especially 2, since it must be repeated to avoid the overlapping loops.

```
      SUBROUTINE DIV(DIVDND, DIVSOR, QUO, REM)
COMMENT:  THIS SUBROUTINE DOES GRADE SCHOOL DIVISION.
C         IT COMPUTES 'QUO' AND REM', THE QUOTIENT AND
C         REMAINDER WHEN DIVIDING 'DIVDND' BY 'DIVSOR'.
      INTEGER DIVDND, DIVSOR, QUO, REM
      QUO = DIVDND/DIVSOR
      REM = DIVDND-DIVSOR*QUO
      RETURN
      END
```

SUBROUTINE DIV computes quotients and remainders in the grade school style you learned years ago by taking advantage of the way WATFIV carries out INTEGER division.

$$\left.\begin{array}{r} 15 \\ 3566 \\ 788 \\ 97 \\ 10465 \\ -1 \end{array}\right\}$$ Data for the roman numeral program

Output

```
THE ROMAN NUMERAL FOR          15 IS X V
THE ROMAN NUMERAL FOR        3566 IS M M M D L X V I
THE ROMAN NUMERAL FOR         788 IS D C C L X X X V I I I
THE ROMAN NUMERAL FOR          97 IS L X X X X V I I
SORRY, BUT          10465 IS OUT OF MY RANGE
```

This is as far as we'll take the roman numeral problem. Problem 7 11 will help you carry it farther. You will see there that the way we've broken the problem up into parts is reasonable because the changes that remain involve just those parts of the developing roman numeral that are near by the part that SUBROUTINE ROMSYM works on. If the changes had to alter the entire roman numeral, that would be a sign that we had chosen a poor way to break the problem up.

> *subprograms help you break your program into smaller logical chunks. Then you can work on each chunk separately.*
>
>

The rest of this section concentrates on particular facts about SUBROUTINEs. Once again, note that it is the *order of the arguments* in the CALL statement rather than their names or values which determines how they will be used in the SUBROUTINE. The parameters in the SUBROUTINE statement are merely placeholders for these arguments, the first parameter holding a place for the first argument, the second parameter for the second argument, etc. You can think of it this way: when the SUBROUTINE is executed, the arguments in the CALL statement are temporarily renamed with the placeholder names.

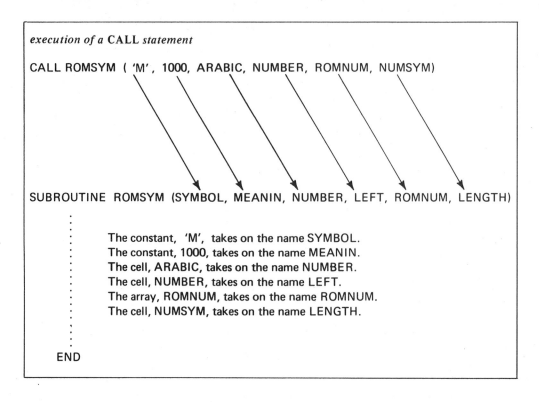

execution of a **CALL** *statement*

CALL ROMSYM ('M', 1000, ARABIC, NUMBER, ROMNUM, NUMSYM)

SUBROUTINE ROMSYM (SYMBOL, MEANIN, NUMBER, LEFT, ROMNUM, LENGTH)

The constant, 'M', takes on the name SYMBOL.
The constant, 1000, takes on the name MEANIN.
The cell, ARABIC, takes on the name NUMBER.
The cell, NUMBER, takes on the name LEFT.
The array, ROMNUM, takes on the name ROMNUM.
The cell, NUMSYM, takes on the name LENGTH.

END

You should also notice that both SUBROUTINE ROMSYM and the main program contain statements labeled 100. This causes no confusion because the two programs are entirely independent; statement labels within one program unit will not be confused with identical statement labels in other program units. The same goes for memory cell names. If two subprograms use memory cells with identical names, the two memory cells will have no relationship to one another. The only things one program or subprogram can know about another are those items of information given in the arguments of a CALL statement.

SUBROUTINEs (and FUNCTIONs, which are covered in the next section) are placed with your main program (see Figure 7 2 2). The compiler treats each

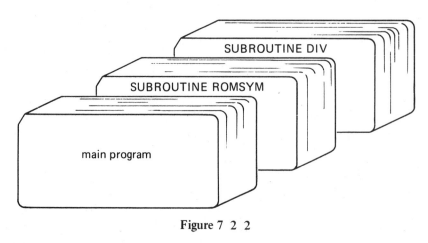

Figure 7 2 2

subprogram as if it were a new program. While compiling with one subprogram, the compiler completely ignores all other programs and subprograms. For this reason, subprograms are sometimes called **externals.** The consequences of this subprogram independence often confuse beginning programmers. Suppose, for example, that you write a SUBROUTINE XMPLE which declares a REAL parameter, but when you CALL XMPLE you accidentally use an INTEGER variable argument.

```
INTEGER KID
KID = 2
CALL XMPLE(KID)
   •
   •
   •
END

SUBROUTINE XMPLE(X)
REAL X
   •
   •
   •
END
```

This will cause an error when the computer tries to perform the CALL statement. The arguments in a CALL statement must match the corresponding parameter declaration.

WATFIV *subprograms are said to be* **externals.** *As a consequence of this organization, the compiler treats each program unit (i.e., your main program and your subprograms) independently. The END card, which must be the last card of every program unit, tells the compiler to stop compiling one program and to get ready to compile another.*

Things to remember about subprograms

Variable names and statement numbers are not confused between programs.

It is very easy to use subprograms written by someone else.

They can make your program more readable.

You cannot use variables from the calling program merely by making the names the same.

To illustrate this point further, let's consider another case. As you know, the arguments in CALL statements may be values (that is, arithmetic or LOGICAL expressions or constants), memory cell names, or array names. But you must be careful when you write CALL statements not to give the SUBROUTINE arguments that it will try to use in illegitimate ways. For example, the following CALL statement is inconsistent with the SUBROUTINE because it specifies a value as an argument where the SUBROUTINE expects to find a memory cell name. The statements say to change the value 10 to the value 5. This is, of course, nonsense.

```
CALL SUB(10)
      .
      .
      .
END

SUBROUTINE SUB(A)
INTEGER A
A = 5
RETURN
END
```

Similarly, if the SUBROUTINE expects an array in place of a parameter, the CALL statement must name an array. Anything else would be nonsense. Notice in Figure 7 2 3 (b) that A(2) names a single memory cell, and that is what the SUBROUTINE expects, as you can see from its parameter declaration. If we had wanted to list the entire array as an argument, we would have put A, which names the whole thing.

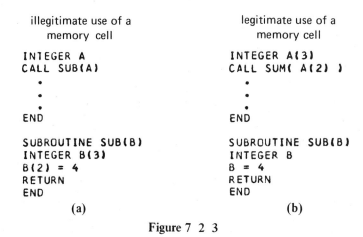

illegitimate use of a memory cell	legitimate use of a memory cell
`INTEGER A` `CALL SUB(A)`	`INTEGER A(3)` `CALL SUM( A(2) )`

```
INTEGER A              INTEGER A(3)
CALL SUB(A)            CALL SUM( A(2) )
      .                      .
      .                      .
      .                      .
END                    END

SUBROUTINE SUB(B)      SUBROUTINE SUB(B)
INTEGER B(3)           INTEGER B
B(2) = 4               B = 4
RETURN                 RETURN
END                    END
```

(a)   (b)

Figure 7 2 3

Over the years, people have written programs to do many things. Those which may be useful to others are often written in the form of SUBROUTINEs and saved. At your computer center, no doubt, there are a large number of SUB-ROUTINEs available for you to use. Since the means of access to them differs from place to place, you will have to consult a local expert. Once you have access, you can use the SUBROUTINEs simply by writing CALL statements with appropriate arguments. This alone is a good reason to learn how to use SUBROUTINEs.

EXERCISES 7 2

1 Which of the following are legal SUBROUTINE statements? If not, explain why not.

```
SUBROUTINE APPLE(RED,GREEN)
SUBROUTINE PEAR
SUBROUTINE POMEGRANATE(SEED)
SUBROUTINE PIZZA(SMALL, OR, LARGE(ONE))
```

2   Which of the following are legal CALL statements? If not, explain why not.

```
CALL APPLE(1,'RED')
CALL PEAR
CALL POMEG(RANATE)
CALL PIZZA(SMALL,OR,LARGE(ONE))
```

3   What would the following program print?

```
INTEGER A, B, C
CALL SQUARE(3,A)
CALL SQUARE(4,B)
CALL SQUARE(5,C)
PRINT, A, B, C
STOP
END

SUBROUTINE SQUARE (NUMBER,SQ)
INTEGER NUMBER, SQ
SQ = NUMBER*NUMBER
RETURN
END
```

4   What would the following program print?

```
CHARACTER*4 A(3)
A(1) = 'DOG '
A(2) = 'CAT '
A(3) = 'BAT '
CALL CHANGE(A,2)
PRINT, 'A=', A
STOP
END

SUBROUTINE CHANGE(ARRAY, INDEX)
CHARACTER*4 ARRAY(3)
INTEGER INDEX
ARRAY(INDEX) = 'NONE'
RETURN
END
```

5   What would the following program print?

```
REAL SIZE(3)
CHARACTER*4 TYPE(3)
INTEGER WHICH
SIZE(1) = 7.5
SIZE(2) = 12.0
SIZE(3) = 18.0
CALL NAMEIT('TINY', TYPE(1))
CALL NAMEIT('BIG ', TYPE(2))
CALL NAMEIT('HUGE', TYPE(3))
PRINT, 'SIZES:'
PRINT, '        ', TYPE(1), SIZE(1)
PRINT, '        ', TYPE(2), SIZE(2)
PRINT, '        ', TYPE(3), SIZE(3)
STOP
END

SUBROUTINE NAMEIT(A,B)
CHARACTER*4 A,B
B=A
RETURN
END
```

6 Change the roman numeral program to a SUBROUTINE with one input parameter: an INTEGER to be converted to roman notation; and two output parameters: (1) an array in which to store the characters of the roman numeral, and (2) a memory cell in which to store the number of characters in the roman numeral. (Note: your SUBROUTINE will be almost identical to our main program, but it won't need a READ statement.)

7 Rewrite the second assignment statement in SUBROUTINE DIV using the built-in FUNCTION MOD.

Section 7 3

FUNCTIONs

If you want to describe the warranty on your new car, you might say something like "it's good for 24,000 miles, 2 years, or when something goes wrong, *whichever comes first*." That is, the warranty period is equal to the minimum of the three time periods.

As you know, WATFIV gives us a way of using a simple word like "minimum" to refer to more detailed computations right in the midst of an expression. This clarifies the program by eliminating clutter. The built-in FUNCTION MIN0 is made to order for the problem of computing the actual warranty period of the car we were talking about. If it took us 57 weeks to drive 24,000 miles, and it took 7 weeks before something went wrong with our car, then these WATFIV statements tell us how long our warranty period was:

```
INTEGER WARPER
WARPER = MIN0(57,2*52, 7)
PRINT, 'WARRANTY LASTED', WARPER, 'WEEKS'
```

We are not limited to using just the built-in FUNCTIONs—we can define our own, suiting them to our exact needs. But before plunging into the details of defining our own, let's make clear where and how references to FUNCTIONs are used.

When we write MIN0(57, 2*52, 7) or SQRT(2.0) or ABS(−3.14159), we are referring to the FUNCTIONs MIN0, SQRT, and ABS, but more importantly, we are specifying numbers. For examples, MIN0(57, 2*52, 7) may be viewed as specifying the INTEGER value 7. Since FUNCTION references are values, you may use a FUNCTION reference anywhere that an expression may appear. Thus,

```
WARPER = MIN0(57, 2*52, 7)
```

contains a legitimate FUNCTION reference—it makes sense to assign the value of the FUNCTION reference to memory cell WARPER. However,

```
MIN0(57, 2*52, 7) = 7
```

is not legitimate—MIN0(57, 2*52, 7) is not a memory cell, it is a value.

```
FUNCTION-value
(FUNCTION reference)
```

form

$$f(e_1, e_2, \ldots, e_n)$$

f is the name of a FUNCTION taking n arguments ($n \geqslant 1$)

e is a constant, expression, memory cell, array, FUNCTION name, or SUBROUTINE name (Special arrangements are needed for the last two—see Chapter 11.)

meaning

A FUNCTION-value is a single value of numeric or LOGICAL type and may be used in any arithmetic or LOGICAL expression where a constant of that data type may be used.

examples

```
PRINT, ALOG(7.92)
X = F(Y**2)
J = LOCSM(A, N)  + 12
```

Notice that since a FUNCTION-value may be used in any expression, that one FUNCTION-value may appear as one of the arguments of another FUNCTION-value. Thus,

```
WARPER = MINO (MINO(24,57), MINO(104,48), 7)
```

is a legal form which, like the examples above, assigns the value 7 to memory cell WARPER.

In WATFIV, FUNCTION values may be LOGICAL or any of the numeric types. If you want a subprogram which computes a value of type CHARACTER, or one which computes more than one value, you should use a SUBROUTINE.

Now let's go through an example which shows why and how we might use a FUNCTION that's not built-in. Suppose you have written a program which uses factorials for several computations. To be more specific, let's suppose that part of your program has to compute the binomial coefficient $C(r, q)$; that is, the number of ways to choose q objects from a bagful of r different objects. You may recall that $C(r,q) = r!/(q!(r-q)!)$

Thus, if Lefty has six weapons and he wants to choose two of them (one for each of his two massive, scarcovered hands), there are

$$C(6, 2) = \frac{6!}{2!4!} = \frac{6*5*4*3*2*1}{(2*1) * (4*3*2*1)} = 15$$

different combinations of weapons that he may choose.

The following program is one way to describe the above computation.

```
      INTEGER R, Q, F, ANS, RFACT, QFACT, RQFACT
          •
          •
          •
COMMENT:  COMPUTE R FACTORIAL.
      RFACT = 1
      F = 2
 11   IF ( F .GT. R )  GO TO 20
          RFACT = RFACT * F
          F = F + 1
          GO TO 11
COMMENT:  COMPUTE Q FACTORIAL.
 20   QFACT = 1
      F = 2
 21   IF ( F .GT. Q )  GO TO 30
          QFACT = QFACT * F
          F = F + 1
          GO TO 21
COMMENT:  COMPUTE R-Q FACTORIAL.
 30   RQFACT = 1
      F = 2
 31   IF ( F .GT. R-Q )  GO TO 40
          RQFACT = RQFACT * F
          F = F + 1
          GO TO 31
 40   ANS = RFACT/(QFACT*RQFACT)
          •
          •
          •
```

> *42! is larger than the number of atomic particles on earth.*

Now, if only we could define our own FUNCTION FACT(*i*) which computed *i*!, we could make our program much easier to understand. In fact, we could do all of the above as follows:

```
      INTEGER R, Q, ANS
      INTEGER FACT
          •
          •
          •
COMMENT:  COMPUTE HOW MANY WAYS THERE ARE TO CHOOSE
C         Q OBJECTS FROM R OBJECTS.
 10   ANS = FACT(R)/(FACT(Q)*FACT(R-Q))
          •
          •
          •
```

A FUNCTION that will do the job is written below. Skim this FUNCTION definition, then we'll explain what the new ideas are.

```
      INTEGER FUNCTION FACT(N)
      INTEGER N
COMMENT:  COMPUTE N FACTORIAL.
      INTEGER F
COMMENT:  INITIALIZE PRODUCT ACCUMULATOR.
      FACT = 1
COMMENT:  SET FIRST FACTOR
      F = 2
COMMENT:  ACCUMULATE PRODUCT.
 10   IF ( F .GT. N )  RETURN
          FACT = FACT * F
          F = F + 1
          GO TO 10
      END
```

First of all, the FUNCTION has statements similar to the parts of the original program which computed factorials. The first statement

```
INTEGER FUNCTION FACT(N)
```

is new. It says a number of things. First, it says that the statements following it make up a FUNCTION; second, that the name of the FUNCTION is FACT; third, that the variable N will be treated in a special way (as a parameter); and finally, that the value that FACT produces will be of type INTEGER.

A FUNCTION will usually be an algorithm that you use a number of different places in your program. (We used the FUNCTION FACT in three places in our program.) To allow this, the FUNCTION needs to describe the algorithm with some generality. This generality is achieved by describing the algorithm we want the FUNCTION to compute but not saying (yet) what *values* we want it to use in the computation. Look back at the definition of FACT. You will see that the variable N is not given a value anywhere in the statements which define the FUNCTION. The name N appears, however, in parentheses in the first statement, the FUNCTION statement, and this means it is a **parameter**. Its value will be supplied from outside the FUNCTION definition. It is often called a **formal parameter** because it states only the *form* of the argument which will be used when the FUNCTION is evaluated. As in SUBROUTINEs, parameter declarations in FUNCTIONs are different from declarations of other variables in that they

---

FUNCTION statement

forms
    type FUNCTION $f(p_1, p_2, \ldots, p_n)$
    type FUNCTION $f*t(p_1, p_2, \ldots, p_n)$
        FUNCTION $f(p_1, p_2, \ldots, p_n)$

type is any data type except CHARACTER*n (*type* may not contain a data type length modifier)
f (the FUNCTION name) is an identifier
t, an unsigned INTEGER constant, is a data type length modifier consistent with *type*
$p_1, p_2, \ldots, p_n$ (the parameter names) are identifiers
The body of the FUNCTION, that is, the statements between the FUNCTION statement and the corresponding END, must assign a value to the name f and must contain at least one RETURN statement. There must be at least one parameter in the parentheses.
If *type* is omitted, implicit typing takes over.

meaning
    The value the FUNCTION computes when invoked is the value of its name when a RETURN statement is executed.

examples
```
REAL FUNCTION F(X)
INTEGER FUNCTION LOCSM(A,N)
FUNCTION G(X,Y,Z)
```

---

don't give you memory cells to work with; they say only that the FUNCTION will be given a value, memory cell, or array of a particular type to work with when the FUNCTION is invoked.

As you know, a FUNCTION like FACT is invoked by writing its name followed by parentheses which surround an arithmetic expression. Then, in the body of the FUNCTION FACT, the parameter N will take on the value of the arithmetic expression. For example, a statement like

$$Z = FACT (3)$$

assigns the value 6 to Z by using the algorithm described in the FUNCTION FACT with N taking the value 3.

Next, you may have noticed that the name of the FUNCTION FACT appears as a variable within the statements that make up the FUNCTION definition; that is, the body of the FUNCTION. Whatever value the variable FACT has when the controller reaches the statement RETURN is the value that the FUNCTION has computed.

Let's see how the FUNCTION FACT is used in our program. It is referred to three times in statement 10. If R had the value 6 and Q the value 2, then statement 10 would be carried out in the following way.
First,

```
10    ANS = FACT(R)/(FACT(2)*FACT(R-Q))
```
then (after the call to FACT to compute 2!)
```
10    ANS = FACT(R)/(  2    *FACT(R-Q))
```
then
```
10    ANS = FACT(R)/(  2    *FACT( 4 ))
```
then (after the second reference to FACT)
```
10    ANS = FACT(R)/(  2    *    24    )
```
then
```
10    ANS = FACT(R)/        48
```
then
```
10    ANS = FACT(6)/        48
```
then (after the third)
```
10    ANS =  720   /        48
```
and finally ANS gets the value 15.

Then on to the next statement. As you can see, the algorithm which the FUNCTION describes is executed three times using different values for the parameter N.

Since using a FUNCTION is like using a value, you must say what type of value it will be. You specify this type once in the FUNCTION definition. However, the compiler complies each program or subprogram independently. No program or subprogram which uses a FUNCTION knows automatically what kind of value that FUNCTION computes. This means that in each program or subprogram in which you use a FUNCTION value, you must say what type of value the FUNCTION computes by declaring it in a type statement exactly as if it were a variable.

In the program above which computed the number of ways Q things can be chosen from R things, we declared FACT to have INTEGER type.

You may define as many FUNCTIONs as you like, and a FUNCTION may be called from within the body of another subprogram. However, you may not refer to a FUNCTION within its *own* definition. It may seem odd that anyone would want to refer to a FUNCTION within its own definition, but consider the following definition of factorial.

$$\text{factorial }(n) = \begin{cases} 1 & \text{if } n \leqslant 1 \\ n*\text{factorial}(n-1), & \text{otherwise} \end{cases}$$

This type of definition is said to be **recursive**, and it is illegal in WATFIV.

FUNCTIONs and SUBROUTINEs share a number of characteristics. The last part of Section 7 2 which gives some details about SUBROUTINEs also applies to FUNCTIONs. For example, just as with SUBROUTINEs, the arguments specified in the reference to a FUNCTION will be matched up one by one in the same order with the parameters in the FUNCTION definition. Also, just as with SUBROUTINEs, the memory cell names, parameter names, and statements labels used in a FUNCTION definition are not confused with names or labels in other program units.

The type of a FUNCTION may be any data type except CHARACTER*n. Here is an example of a FUNCTION called TRIGHT which returns the LOGICAL value .TRUE. if its arguments could be the three sides of a right triangle. Incidentally, TRIGHT itself uses two other FUNCTIONs, one called RSS (Root of Sum Squares), and one called EQUAL, which makes a safe test for equality of two REAL numbers.

```
        LOGICAL FUNCTION TRIGHT (A, B, C)
        REAL A, B, C
        REAL RSS
        LOGICAL EQUAL
COMMENT:   MAYBE A IS THE HYPOTENUSE.
        IF ( EQUAL(A,RSS(B,C)) )  GO TO 20
COMMENT:   NO, BUT MAYBE B IS.
        IF ( EQUAL(B,RSS(A,C)) )  GO TO 20
COMMENT:   STILL NO LUCK...TRY C
        IF ( EQUAL(C,RSS(A,B)) )  GO TO 20
COMMENT:  NONE OF THESE.
        TRIGHT = .FALSE.
        RETURN
COMMENT:   YES, THE THREE LENGTHS COULD MAKE A RT TRIANGLE.
  20    TRIGHT = .TRUE.
        RETURN
        END
```

We can define the FUNCTION RSS as follows:

```
        REAL FUNCTION RSS (S1, S2)
        REAL S1, S2
        REAL SQRT
COMMENT:   COMPUTE THE SQRT OF THE SUM OF THE SQUARES.
        RSS = SQRT(S1**2 + S2**2)
        RETURN
        END
```

The FUNCTION RSS uses another FUNCTION, namely the built-in FUNCTION SQRT.

Finally, we write the FUNCTION EQUAL to test for equality of two REAL numbers

```
        LOGICAL FUNCTION EQUAL (X, Y)
        REAL X, Y
        REAL ABS
COMMENT:  TEST FOR EQUALITY TO THREE DECIMAL PLACES.
        EQUAL = ABS(X-Y) .LT. 0.5E-3
        RETURN
        END
```

We could use our FUNCTION by writing a program containing the following statements:

```
COMMENT:  PROGRAM USING FUNCTION TRIGHT
        LOGICAL TRIGHT
  10    IF ( TRIGHT(3.0, 4.0, 5.0) )
    +           PRINT, '3 4 5 IS A RIGHT TRIANGLE'
        IF ( .NOT. TRIGHT(3.0, 4.0, 5.0) )
    +           PRINT, '3 4 5 IS''NT A RIGHT TRIANGLE'
        STOP
        END
```

output

```
3 4 5 IS A RIGHT TRIANGLE
```

In the process of carrying out statement 10, the controller would execute our FUNCTION TRIGHT and would, in turn, perform the FUNCTIONs RSS and EQUAL three times. In addition, RSS calls upon SQRT and EQUAL calls ABS. Thus carrying out statement 10 involves performing a total of thirteen FUNCTION references.

Notice that in the above program we took care to declare that the values TRIGHT computes are LOGICAL.

As with SUBROUTINEs, FUNCTION definitions are placed after the main program. The END cards serve to separate one subprogram from another.

EXERCISES 7 3

1 Why did we write
    ```
    EQUAL = ABS(X-Y) .LT. 0.5E-3
    ```
    instead of
    ```
    EQUAL = X .EQ. Y
    ```
    in the definition of the FUNCTION EQUAL? What would be the effect of changing 0.5E-3 to 1.0E-2? What other considerations should we make in such an equality test?

2 What sequence of values will the REAL memory cell A be given by the following statements using built-in FUNCTIONs?
    ```
    A = ABS(1.0 - 2.0)
    A = ABS(A)*4.0
    A = SQRT(ABS(2.0-A)*2.0)/2.0
    ```

3 What is wrong with the following FUNCTION definition?

```
REAL FUNCTION R
R = 2.0
RETURN
END
```

4 What value does FUNCTION FACT return if its argument is less than 0?

5 Write a FUNCTION which duplicates the effect of the built-in FUNCTION ABS.

6 Write an INTEGER FUNCTION C with two INTEGER parameters, Q and R, which describes an algorithm to compute the binomial coefficient C(Q, R) using our FUNCTION FACT.

Section 7 4

Array Parameters with Variable Lengths

A marketing and sales research firm has asked us to help them out. Many customers come to them with lists of sales figures (usually either monthly or weekly) tabulated over several years. Normally the research firm begins by preparing a year by year listing of this data. For each year the sales figures are listed two ways. One is simply a month by month (or week by week) tabulation of the monthly (or weekly) sales amounts. The other lists the amounts in decreasing order, from the best sales period to the worst. In this way the research firm gets a picture of seasonal effects on the customer's sales.

The research firm's business has grown in recent years and its staff is no longer large enough to handle all of these tabulations. Consequently they have decided to turn it over to a computer. The sales figures will be punched on cards, one group of cards for each year. The first card of each yearly group will have the year and the sales period type (MONTHLY or WEEKLY) punched on it. The remaining cards of the group will have the sales figures (in whole dollars) punched on them. The firm wants us to write a program to print the tabulations in order to save the staff this tedious job.

If you think about it, you will see that it is a relatively simple programming task except for the business of listing the sales figures in order of decreasing sales period. Up to that point it is simply a matter of READing values and PRINTing them in the order in which they appeared (chronological). But in order to PRINT the sales figures in order of decreasing sales periods, we need to rearrange the data. One way to do that is to put the sales figures into an array, and to change the order in which they are stored when necessary. We will want the output from the program to look something like the sample below.

SALES TABULATION

1976
MONTHLY SALES FIGURES

CHRONOLOGICAL			BEST TO WORST	
MONTH	SALES		MONTH	SALES
1	6472		12	10428
2	4103		10	9342
3	2001		11	8497
4	2422		1	6472
5	3501		6	5402
6	5402		7	5117
7	5117		8	4322
8	4322		2	4103
9	2173		5	3501
10	9342		4	2422
11	8497		9	2173
12	10428		3	2001

1976
WEEKLY SALES FIGURES

CHRONOLOGICAL			BEST TO WORST	
WEEK	SALES		WEEK	SALES
1	1647		49	2544
2	1500		52	2544
3	1399		45	2422
4	1822		41	2411
5	1021		50	2144
6	1059		43	2134
7	987		44	2111
8	855		51	2066
9	502		48	2032
10	408		46	2031
11	201		40	2011
12	422		42	1955
13	385		47	1902
14	638		4	1822
15	655		1	1647
16	588		25	1621
17	574		24	1534
18	788		2	1500
19	698		23	1422
20	755		39	1422
21	802		3	1399
22	621		29	1354
23	1422		26	1308
24	1534		28	1307
25	1621		30	1238
26	1308		27	1205
27	1205		31	1104
28	1307		6	1059
29	1354		5	1021
30	1238		32	987
31	1104		7	987
32	987		33	855
33	855		8	855
34	445		21	802
35	655		18	768
36	521		20	755

37	411	19	698
38	322	15	655
39	1422	35	655
40	2011	14	638
41	2411	22	621
42	1955	16	588
43	2134	17	574
44	2111	36	521
45	2422	9	502
46	2031	34	445
47	1902	12	422
48	2032	37	411
49	2544	10	408
50	2144	13	385
51	2066	38	322
52	2544	11	201

Because the line printer can't back up to print the columns under BEST TO WORST SALES MONTH, we'll have to store the sales information twice, once in chronological order and once in order of decreasing sales. When we arrange the sales figures in decreasing order, we must also arrange the corresponding month numbers to be printed beside the sales figures. Thus, in addition to the array storing the sales figures in chronological order, we need a pair of arrays to store the month numbers and sales figures in decreasing order. We'll use a SUBROUTINE to arrange the data for the columns on the right. We'll call it SORT since it sorts data into a certain order. It will have three parameters: (1) the array containing the sales figures, (2) the array containing the corresponding month numbers, and (3) the number of elements in the arrays (12 or 52). The first two are both input and output parameters (when SORT is CALLed, the first two arguments will contain information in some order and SORT will rearrange the information) and the third is an input parameter.

Study the program below. We'll discuss the SORT subprogram once you understand its purpose.

```
COMMENT:  THIS PROGRAM MAKES SALES REPORT SUMMARIES
          INTEGER YEAR
          CHARACTER*1 PERIOD
C         PRINT HEADING
          PRINT, '                        SALES TABULATION'
C         GET YEAR AND SALES PERIOD FROM FIRST CARD OF GROUP
  100     READ, YEAR, PERIOD
          IF ( YEAR .EQ. 0 )  STOP
          PRINT, ' '
          PRINT, YEAR
C         CALL APPROPRIATE SUBROUTINE TO HANDLE
C         WEEKLY OR MONTHLY SALES PERIOD.
          IF ( PERIOD .EQ. 'M' )  GO TO 200
          CALL WEEKLY
          GO TO 100
  200     CALL MNTHLY
          GO TO 100
COMMENT:  THE SUBROUTINES 'WEEKLY' AND 'MNTHLY' NEED NO
C         INFORMATION FROM THIS PROGRAM. THEREFORE, THEY'VE
C         NO ARGUMENTS.  THEY GET THEIR INFORMATION
C         FROM DATA CARDS AND PRINT THEIR RESULTS.
C         HENCE,   THEY DON'T NEED TO COMMUNICATE VALUES TO
C         OF FROM THE CALLING PROGRAM.
          END
```

```
      SUBROUTINE MNTHLY
      INTEGER SALES(12), MN(12), MNSALE(12), I
COMMENT:  PRINT HEADINGS.
      PRINT,  'MONTHLY SALES FIGURES'
      PRINT, ' '
      PRINT, '                   CHRONOLOGICAL',
     &       '                          BEST TO WORST'
      PRINT, '         MONTH      SALES            ',
     &       'MONTH      SALES'
      READ, SALES
C     SAVE SALES FIGURES AND MAKE A LIST OF MONTH NUMBERS
      I = 1
 100  MN(I) = I
      MNSALE(I) = SALES(I)
      I = I + 1
      IF ( I .LE. 12 ) GO TO 100
C     SORT INFORMATION ACCORDING TO DECREASING SALES.
      CALL SORT (MNSALE, MN, 12)
C     PRINT REPORT
      I = 1
 200  PRINT, I, SALES(I), '       '  , MN(I), MNSALE(I)
      I = I + 1
      IF ( I .LE. 12 ) GO TO 200
      RETURN
      END


      SUBROUTINE WEEKLY
      INTEGER SALES(52), WK(52), WKSALE(52), I
COMMENT:  PRINT HEADINGS.
      PRINT,  'WEEKLY SALES FIGURES'
      PRINT, ' '
      PRINT, '                   CHRONOLOGICAL',
     &       '                          BEST TO WORST'
      PRINT, '          WEEK      SALES            ',
     &       'WEEK      SALES'
C     READ SALES FIGURES
      READ, SALES
C     SAVE SALES FIGURES AND MAKE A LIST OF  WEEK NUMBERS
      I = 1
 100  WK(I) = I
      WKSALE(I) = SALES(I)
      I = I + 1
      IF ( I .LE. 52 ) GO TO 100
C     SORT INFORMATION ACCORDING TO DECREASING SALES.
      CALL SORT (WKSALE, WK, 52)
C     PRINT REPORT
      I = 1
 200  PRINT, I, SALES(I), '       '  , WK(I), WKSALE(I)
      I = I + 1
      IF ( I .LE. 52 ) GO TO 200
      RETURN
      END
```

Both of the above SUBROUTINEs use the SORT subprogram, but the arguments in the two CALLs are different.

Now that the program is written, we must write the SUBROUTINE SORT. The problem of sorting numbers into decreasing order has been studied by many people and there are lots of solutions. Some are better than others. The method we describe here has at least two virtues: it is easy to understand, and it clearly demonstrates the uses of subprograms. We will have more to say about other methods later.

Briefly, the idea is to locate the largest of the numbers and put it on top of the list, then repeat the same process on the remaining unsorted numbers (from the second to the last). We keep repeating the process on shorter and shorter lists

until finally there are none left. The only tricky part of the process arises from the way in which the numbers are stored, which is in an array. When we find the largest number and want to put it on top of the unsorted portion of the list, we must find something to do with the number currently in the top position. It must go into the unsorted portion of the list, of course, and the natural place to put it is in the position vacated by the largest number. In order words, we interchange the largest number with the number on top of the unsorted portion of the list. Figure 7 4 1 illustrates the method.

The SUBROUTINE below uses a FUNCTION to locate the largest number in the unsorted part of the array, and a SUBROUTINE to interchange the largest with the top number. You have already seen techniques for locating the largest several times, so the FUNCTION should be easy to follow. You haven't seen a technique for switching the values in a pair of memory cells, however, and we'll get to that shortly.

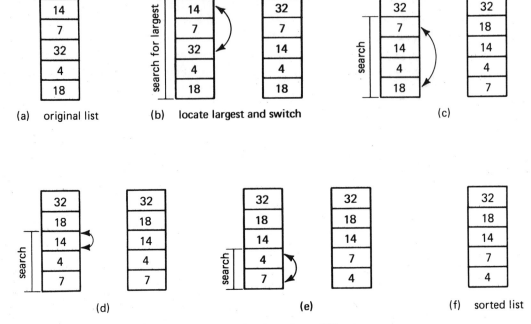

Figure 7 4 1   Sorting a List of Numbers

You will notice something unusual in the parameter declarations of the following subprograms. The array declarations have subprogram parameters for length declarators. This clearly illustrates the difference between parameter declarations and true declarations. Since parameter declarations describe already existing objects, the compiler is not required to reserve space for them. Consequently, the length of a subprogram parameter array may be specified by one of the variables in the parameter list. (If the array has more than one subscript, then the range of values for any one or all of the subscripts may be specified by variables in the

---

length declarator for parameter arrays

form
   t p(*list*)
   t is a WATFIV data type
   p (a parameter array name) is an identifier
   list is a list of INTEGER parameter names and/or unsigned INTEGER constants

meaning
   The array p, which is a parameter in the subprogram being defined, will have the dimensions specified in *list* and the type t.

examples
```
SUBROUTINE VARLEN (A, B, N, C, D, M)
INTEGER N, M, A(N)
REAL B(4,N), C(M, N)
```

---

parameter list.) It is important to realize that this does not mean that any existing array actually has a varying length. All actual array declarations must have a constant length declarator; only parameter array declarations may have variables for length declarators. Furthermore, the value(s) of the parameter(s) declaring the dimension(s) of the array should not be changed by the subprogram because this would imply a change in the length of the actual array given in the argument list in the subprogram reference. No such change is possible.

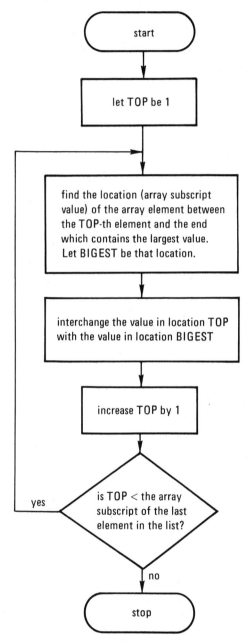

Figure 7 4 2 Flowchart for SUBROUTINE SORT

```
        SUBROUTINE SORT (KEYS, CTHER, N)
        INTEGER N, KEYS(N), OTHER(N)
COMMENT:  ARRANGE THE VALUES IN 'KEYS' AND 'OTHER' INTO
C            DECREASING ORDER ACCORDING TO 'KEYS'
        INTEGER TOP, BIGEST
        INTEGER LOCBIG
        TOP = 1
C       FIND LARGEST NUMBER IN 'KEYS' BETWEEN 'TOP' AND 'N'.
 100    BIGEST = LOCBIG(KEYS, TOP, N)
C          INTERCHANGE KEYS(TOP) WITH KEYS(BIGEST)
           CALL SWITCH (KEYS(TOP), KEYS(BIGEST))
C          TO AVOID MESSING UP THE CORRESPONDENCE BETWEEN
C          VALUES IN 'KEYS' AND VALUES IN 'OTHER', MAKE AN
C          IDENTICAL INTERCHANGE IN 'OTHER'.
           CALL SWITCH (OTHER(TOP), OTHER(BIGEST))
C          INCREMENT 'TOP' TO REFLECT NEW TOP OF UNSORTED
C          PORTION OF ARRAYS.
           TOP = TOP + 1
           IF ( TOP .LT. N )  GO TO 100
        RETURN
        END

        INTEGER FUNCTION LOCBIG (A, FROM, TO)
        INTEGER FROM, TO, A(TO)
COMMENT:  LOCATE THE LARGEST NUMBER IN 'A' BETWEEN A(FROM)
C            AND THE END OF THE ARRAY.
        INTEGER I
        LOCBIG = FROM
        I = FROM + 1
 100    IF ( I .GT. TO )  RETURN
        IF ( A(I) .GT. A(LOCBIG) )  LOCBIG = I
        I = I + 1
        GO TO 100
        END
```

The subprogram SWITCH which interchanges the values in a pair of memory cells requires a little explanation. It has three steps: (1) the value in the first cell is copied into a third cell so that it won't be lost in step 2, (2) the value of the second cell is copied into the first, and (3) the value in the third cell is copied into the second. If you think about it, you will realize that a two step process simply won't work.

```
        SUBROUTINE SWITCH (A,B)
        INTEGER A, B
        INTEGER COPYA
        COPYA = A
        A = B
        B = COPYA
        RETURN
        END
```

Please be sure that you understand how this sorting method works by following through a small example. We'll want to use it again.

When our completed program was run using the data cards below, it produced the sales report you saw at the beginning of this chapter.

```
1976   'M'
  6472   4103   2001   2422   3501   5402   5117   4322   2173   9342
  8497  10428
1976   'W'
  1647   1500   1399   1822   1021   1059    987    855    502    408
   201    422    385    638    655    588    574    788    698    755
   802    621   1422   1534   1621   1308   1205   1307   1354   1238
  1104    987    855    445    655    521    411    322   1422   2011
  2411   1955   2134   2111   2422   2031   1902   2032   2544   2144
  2066   2544
     0   '  '
```

EXERCISES 7 4

1 Which of the following parameter declarations is legal and which isn't? If not, explain why.

```
SUBROUTINE ONE(A, N, M)
INTEGER M, N, A(N,M)

SUBROUTINE TWO (A,N)
INTEGER N, A(10, N, 4)

SUBROUTINE THREE (A,N)
INTEGER N, A(LENGTH)
```

2 What is wrong with the following SUBROUTINE?

```
SUBROUTINE WRONG (A,N)
INTEGER N, A(N)
N = N + 1
A(N) = 0
RETURN
END
```

3 What would need to be changed in order to make our SUBROUTINE SORT arrange the numbers into increasing (rather than decreasing) order?

4 What would happen to INTEGER memory cells ONE and TWO if the statement CALL BADSWT (ONE, TWO) were executed?

```
SUBROUTINE BADSWT(A,B)
INTEGER A, B
A = B
B = A
RETURN
END
```

5 What is wrong with the statement CALL BADSWT (1, 2), given the above subprogram?

Section 7 5*

You know what the asterisk means by now.

Random Numbers

There are many situations in computing in which we need to have access to random numbers. For this reason, most computer centers provide a subprogram which generates a random number each time it is called. Actually, the numbers it generates are usually called "pseudorandom" because they are produced by a deterministic program; every time you start the program over, you get the same sequence of pseudorandom numbers. However, the numbers pass a large number of statistical tests for randomness so that we can say that they act very much like true random numbers, whatever those are.

Can you know if an event is really random?

The pseudorandom numbers are usually uniformly distributed REAL numbers in the range from 0.0 to 1.0 (end-points *not* included). In other words, the likelihood that a number will fall in a particular subinterval is the same as the likelihood that it will fall in any other subinterval of the same length. (A descriptive, albeit imprecise, way of saying this is: "all numbers between 0.0 and 1.0 are equally likely.") They are generated using the multiplicative congruential method: each new number is obtained from the last by multiplying it by a fixed multiplier and taking the last few digits of the product as the new random number.

It isn't our purpose to dwell on random numbers or random number generators here. We simply want to make sure that you have access to a random number generator since we will use them in later chapters. If you don't have one easily available, you can copy SUBROUTINE RANDOM which appears below. It has one parameter, an output parameter. When you CALL it, it will store a pseudorandom, uniformly distributed, REAL number in the memory cell you specify as its argument. This number will be greater than 0.0 and less than 1.0.

```
      SUBROUTINE RANDOM (X)
      REAL X
COMMENT:  THIS SUBROUTINE PRODUCES A SAMPLE 'X' FROM A
C         UNIFORM DISTRIBUTION ACROSS THE INTERVAL (0.0,1.0)
C         FOR INFORMATION ON HOW WELL THIS TYPE OF RANDOM
C         NUMBER GENERATOR WORKS, SEE 'THE ART OF COMPUTER
C         PROGRAMMING', VOL. 2, D. KNUTH, ADDISON-WESLEY.
      INTEGER MOD
      REAL FLOAT
      INTEGER A/19727/, MULT/25211/, BASE/32768/
      A = MOD(MULT*A,  BASE)
      X = FLOAT(A) / FLOAT(BASE)
      RETURN
      END
```

Often it is very useful to have a FUNCTION which generates a random INTEGER between 1 and some given upper limit, each possible value having the same likelihood. The FUNCTION CHOOSE does this. It uses our SUBROUTINE RANDOM, but it could just as well use any random number generator with similar properties.

```
      INTEGER FUNCTION CHOOSE (N)
      INTEGER N
COMMENT:   THIS FUNCTION CHOOSES, AT RANDOM, ONE OF THE
C          INTEGERS 1, 2, 3, ..., N .
      REAL U
      CALL RANDOM(U)
      CHOOSE = INT(FLOAT(N)*U) +1
      RETURN
      END
```

PROBLEMS 7

1   Write and test a SUBROUTINE which accepts a CHARACTER array of people's names and which returns the name which comes first alphabetically and the one which comes last.

2   Do a problem from Chapter 4 or 6, perhaps one you have already done, making use of FUNCTIONs and SUBROUTINEs and any other technique you can think of to make it more clearly organized.

3   Use the built-in FUNCTION ATAN to compute the value of π.

4   Write a LOGICAL FUNCTION called INHERE which has three parameters: (1) a CHARACTER*25 array of people's names, (2) the number of names in the array, and (3) a CHARACTER*25 variable which is the name of a customer. INHERE should return the value .TRUE. if the customer's name appears in the array, and .FALSE. otherwise.

5   Write a FUNCTION called LOG which has two parameters, BASE and X, and returns the largest INTEGER, LOG, such that BASE**LOG does not exceed X. For example, L = LOG(2, 10) would result in L having the value 3 since $2^3 \leqslant 10$ but $2^4 > 10$.

6   Write and test four FUNCTIONs called SINE, COSINE, ARCTAN and EXPT each of which takes a real argument, x, and returns the value of $\sin(x)$, $\cos(x)$, $\arctan(x)$, and e^x respectively. The values are computed by adding up enough terms of an infinite series expansion so that the change caused by adding in the next term is less than the accuracy desired (say 1.0E−6). Compare the values computed by your FUNCTIONs to the values returned by the built-in FUNCTIONs SIN, COS, ATAN, and EXP. (The built-in FUNCTIONs make use of a number of tricks to make the computation more rapid and more accurate.)

$$\text{sine}(x) \quad = \frac{x^3}{3!} + \frac{x^5}{5!} - \frac{x^7}{7!} \cdots$$

$$\text{cosine}(x) = 1 - \frac{x^2}{2!} + \frac{x^4}{4!} \cdots$$

$$\arctan(x) = \begin{cases} x - \dfrac{x^3}{3} + \dfrac{x^5}{5} - \dfrac{x^7}{7} + \ldots \text{ for } x^2 < 1 \\ \dfrac{\pi}{2} - \dfrac{1}{x} + \dfrac{1}{3x^3} - \dfrac{1}{5x^5} + \ldots \text{ for } x^2 > 1 \end{cases}$$

$$\exp(x) \quad = 1 + x + \frac{1}{2!} x^2 + \frac{1}{3!} x^3 + \frac{1}{4!} x^4 + \ldots$$

7 Suppose there are 20 cars driving at 70 m.p.h. in a single lane. Each car is *d* feet from the next. A small child wearing red shorts and Buster Brown shoes with shoe laces 6.0" long suddenly appears ahead. The first car slams on his brakes.

Write a program which computes the final position of each car after all have come to rest. Assume all cars' brakes work the same and bring a car to a stop within 280 feet *after they have been applied.* Assume that each driver's reaction time (the time to apply his brakes after seeing the brake lights of the car immediately in front) is a random variable uniformly distributed between .45 and .95 seconds; *i.e.,* each car's reaction time is given by

$$\text{reaction time} = .7 + (U - .5)/2. \text{ seconds}$$

where U comes from CALL RANDOM (U). Compute the stopping position of the *i*th car, then the $(i + 1)$th, etc. If the $(i + 1)$th car hits the *i*th, assume they both stop where the *i*th car was. Write out where each car stops and the number of collisions. Do this for $d = 70$ feet, $d = 90$ feet, and $d = 110$ feet.

8 Write a SUBROUTINE CONVERT whose input is an INTEGER and whose output is an array of INTEGERs representing that number in binary notation.

9 Rewrite CONVERT so that it has an additional input parameter, a base to which to convert the input INTEGER's representation.

10 A well-known dare-devil stunt man plans to jump a canyon on his motorcycle. Assuming that the air drag is proportional to his velocity (*k* is the proportionality constant), his position after *t* seconds is given by the equations below.

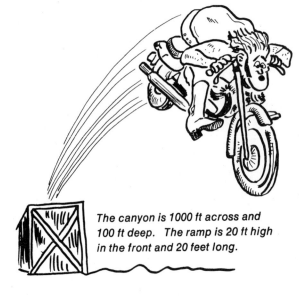

$$x = \frac{v_0 \cos\alpha}{k} (1 - e^{-kt})$$
$$= \text{distance}$$

$$y = \frac{-g}{k} t + \frac{1}{k}\left(v_0 \sin\alpha + \frac{g}{k}\right)(1 - e^{-kt})$$
$$= \text{height}$$

$g = 32.2 \text{ ft/sec}^2$
$\quad = \text{acceleration due to gravity}$

$v_0 = 330 \text{ ft/sec.} = \text{take-off speed}$

$\alpha = 45° = \text{angle of take-off}$

The canyon is 1000 ft across and 100 ft deep. The ramp is 20 ft high in the front and 20 feet long.

Write a program that writes out his path (x, y, and t) for the cases when k is .05, .15, and .25. Draw the trajectories your program predicts. If he lands on the other side, assume he stops immediately (in a heap).

11 Finish the roman numeral program by adding the ability to make the correct decision when SUBROUTINE DIV determines that we need four of the current SYMBOL. First of all, notice that to make the decision, the *two* symbols before SYMBOL are needed, for if the numeral so far is MCCCL and DIV says we need four X's, we must convert to MCCXC, but if the numeral was MCCC, we would simply add XL to have MCCCXL. Also convince yourself that we can never have more than one of the symbols D, L, or V in any roman numeral. The roman symbol for 5000 is $\overline{V}$. If it would make your program easier to write, include the ability to handle $\overline{V}$. (Call it W since $\overline{V}$ isn't a legal WATFIV character.) Good luck!

12 Undo the effects of the roman numeral program. Write a SUBROUTINE which, when sent a CHARACTER array containing a roman numeral, rips it apart symbol by symbol and returns the equivalent INTEGER. Do the problem in two phases: first figure out how to handle inputs in the simple roman notation, then upgrade it to handle the more sophisticated form.

13 Write a FUNCTION which computes the mean of a list of REAL numbers and one which computes the variance (see Problem 4 10). Use your FUNCTIONs to see how close our SUBROUTINE RANDOM (Section 7 5) actually comes to generating uniformly distributed numbers in the range from 0.0 to 1.0.

14 Suppose you were running a pizza parlor and you wanted to figure out how many waitresses/waiters you should hire. If you have too few, then customers will have to wait a long time to be served and you'll lose business, but if you have too many, then you'll lose money paying them. You decide to simulate the process. You estimate that every minute, the odds are 50/50 that a new customer will come in and that it takes three minutes of a waitress' time to serve each customer. Your program should simulate the arrival of 1000 customers and should print out the total amount of time customers spend waiting and the amount of time waitresses/waiters spend waiting. Try your program with one, two, and three waitresses/waiters to see how many it would be best to have.

Here are some hints about how you could write the program:

1 Have one main loop which corresponds to what happens each successive minute.
2 Have memory cells which keep track of the following things:
  □ How many customers are waiting: CWAIT
  □ How many waitresses/waiters are waiting: WWAIT
  □ How many waitresses/waiters have just started waiting on a customer: WWAIT0
  □ How many waiters/waitresses have been waiting on a customer for one minute: WWAIT1

☐ How many waiters/waitresses have been waiting on a customer for two minutes: WWAIT2
☐ How much (total) time customers have spent waiting: CTIME
☐ How much (total) time waitresses/waiters have spent waiting: WTIME

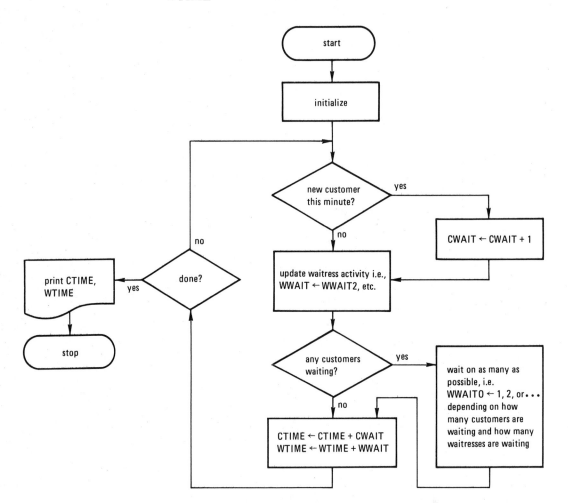

15 The motorcyclist in Problem 10 has a parachute to ease his fall, but the release mechanism is somewhat unstable. When the parachute releases, its effect is to increase the wind resistance factor k. Do Problem 10 using $k = .05$ in the equations before the parachute opens and $k = .5$ after. Print his path (x, y, and t) for these three cases:

case	parachute opens after
1	2 seconds
2	10 seconds
3	60 seconds

8 DO LOOPS

Section 8 1

The DO Statement

By now you have read enough programs to have noticed that GO TO statements make a program difficult to read because you have to hunt around for the statement label a GO TO transfers control to. In addition, GO TO statements used without discretion can lead to programs with extremely contorted logic. It would make programs easier to read if there were some way to write loops without using GO TO statements. WATFIV provides a little help in this direction with a GO TO-less, though highly restricted, loop construction known as the DO-loop. The DO-loop can be used whenever the looping is controlled by an INTEGER variable which increases by uniform increments on each pass through the loop and the loop terminates when the variable exceeds some upper bound. Such a loop may be called a **counting loop** since the control variable is counting from some initial value to some final value.

A surprisingly large proportion of program loops are counting loops. This makes the DO-loop very useful. However, many WATFIV programmers try to force their loops to fit this category even when they could be more clearly written in some other way. By this point, however, you should be familiar enough with looping in general that you will be able to choose the most appropriate construction.

HI FRIENDS! FRIENDLY FRANK THE STATEMENT SALESMAN HERE! HAVE I GOT A DEAL FOR YOU! TIRED OF USING COUNTERS AND HAVING TO INITIALIZE THEM? TIRED OF USING IF STATEMENTS TO STOP LOOPS? TRY THE NEW, IMPROVED, LEMON-FRESHENED DO STATEMENT.

Here is an example of a DO-loop in use.

```
        INTEGER N, TOP/10/
COMMENT:  PRINT THE SQUARES AND CUBES OF
C         THE FIRST 'TOP' NUMBERS
        PRINT, '        NUMBER      SQUARED        CUBED'
COMMENT:  HERE'S THE DO-LOOP .
        DO 10 N = 1,TOP,1
 10       PRINT, N, N**2, N**3
        STOP
        END
```

NUMBER	SQUARED	CUBED
1	1	1
2	4	8
3	9	27
4	16	64
5	25	125
6	36	216
7	49	343
8	64	512
9	81	729
10	100	1000

Probably you can tell what's going on just by staring at the program and the output for a while. There are a number of formal rules, however.

Each DO-loop starts with a statement called a **DO statement** which specifies five things:

1 the control variable or **index**
2 the **starting value** of the index,
3 the **upper bound** for the index,
4 the **increment** for the index,
5 the **range** of the DO-loop (that is, the statements which are part of the DO-loop).

The index must be an unsubscripted INTEGER variable. The starting value, upper bound, and increment must have positive INTEGER values. The **range** is specified by a statement label in the DO statement which indicates the last statement which is part of the loop. Thus the loop includes all the statements *following* the DO statement up to and including the terminal statement. It is important to realize that the DO statement itself is *not* part of the loop; it merely sets up the loop.

The statements in the range of the DO-loop are repeated once for each value of the index, starting at the starting value and increasing after each pass through the range by the specified increment, until the upper bound is exceeded.

Let's dissect the DO-loop in the example above to see how it fits the rules. While we're at it, we'll write out a program which does exactly the same thing but which doesn't use a DO-loop. That way you can always refer to the non-DO-loop form if you have a question about some detail of how DO-loops work.

```
          DO-loop form                          non DO-loop form

          DO 10 N = 1,TOP,1                      N = 1
   10          PRINT,N,N**2,N**3          10     PRINT,N,N**2,N**3
                                                 N = N+1
                                                 IF(N.LE.TOP) GOTO 10
```

```
          DO 10 N = 1 , TOP , 1
   10          PRINT, N, N**2, N**3
```

The DO statement comes first and specifies the number of times the loop will
be repeated, and the values the index will take. The statement label specifies the
range of the loop. In our example the range is all statements *after* the DO statement up to and including statement 10. The memory cell called N serves as the
index, and its value is changed on each pass through the loop. The index N is
initialized to the value 1 (the starting value) and is increased by 1 (the increment)
on each pass. The statements of the loop (here just the statement labeled 10) are
repeated as long as the index is less than or equal to the value of TOP (the upper
bound). Compare the DO-loop to the equivalent form using the conditional GO
TO again. You'll probably agree that the DO statement is easier to read, once you
understand the notation.

Let's look at another example. Suppose you want to compute an approximation to the infinite sum $1 + 1/4 + 1/9 + 1/16 + \ldots + 1/N^2 + \ldots$. To see how the
sum is progressing, you want to print it after every hundredth term has been
added. This is a perfect situation for a DO-loop; while you are adding terms, you
want to count to 100 over and over again and print out the sum each time you get
to 100. The following program does this computation. It stops adding terms when
they get very small.

```
COMMENT:   COMPUTE 1 + 1/4 + 1/9 + ... + 1/N**2 + ...
           REAL N, SUM
           INTEGER COUNT
COMMENT:   INITIALIZE SUM AND N
           SUM = 1.0
           N = 1.0
COMMENT:   ADD A HUNDRED TERMS
   10      DO 20 COUNT = 1,100,1
           N = N + 1.0
   20      SUM = SUM + 1.0/N**2
           PRINT, 'SUM SO FAR=', SUM
COMMENT:   REPEAT UNLESS THE LAST TERM WAS VERY SMALL
           IF ( 1.0/N**2 .GT. 1.0E-6 )  GO TO 10
           STOP
           END
```

output

```
SUM SO FAR=    0.1635036E 01
SUM SO FAR=    0.1639882E 01
SUM SO FAR=    0.1641480E 01
SUM SO FAR=    0.1642259E 01
SUM SO FAR=    0.1642710E 01
SUM SO FAR=    0.1642997E 01
SUM SO FAR=    0.1643188E 01
SUM SO FAR=    0.1643305E 01
SUM SO FAR=    0.1643400E 01
SUM SO FAR=    0.1643496E 01
```

Now that we've seen a couple of examples, let's look at a detailed description of the form and meaning of the DO statement.

There are lots of rules to remember about DO-loops.

1 The values of the DO-parameters (index, starting value, upper bound, and increment) may *not* be changed by any statement in the range.

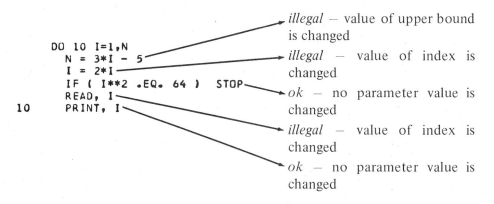

```
        DO 10 I=1,N
            N = 3*I - 5
            I = 2*I
            IF ( I**2 .EQ. 64 )  STOP
            READ, I
10          PRINT, I
```

illegal — value of upper bound is changed

illegal — value of index is changed

ok — no parameter value is changed

illegal — value of index is changed

ok — no parameter value is changed

2 No statement may cause a transfer into the range of a DO-loop from outside the range.

```
        GO TO 10
        DO 10 IN = 1,25
            IF ( (IN/2)*2 .EQ. NOW )  GO TO 20
10          PRINT, 'IN=', IN
20      ZOMBIE = 2.0*3.14159
```

illegal — transfers into DO-loop range

ok — transfers outside range

3 The index of a DO-loop may be assumed to have a value only within the range of the DO-loop. Once the loop terminates, the value is lost. The only exception is the case in which a transfer from inside the range to outside the range occurs before the loop is terminated.

```
        DO 100 IND = 1,25
            IF ( IND/3)*3 .EQ. NOW) GO TO 200
100         PRINT, 'IND=', IND
        PRINT, IND
        GO TO 300
200     PRINT, IND
```

illegal — the DO-loop has terminated so IND has no value

ok — transfer to this point occurs before DO-loop termination

4 DO-loops may be nested. That is, the range of one DO-loop may be wholly inside the range of another. However, the ranges of two DO-loops may not overlap in any other way.

LEGAL
```
      DO 20 KATZ = 1,142,2
         DO 10 LUMP=1,57
10          PRINT, KATZ*LUMP
20       PRINT, ' '
```

ILLEGAL
```
      DO 10 KATZ = 1,142,2
         DO 20 LUMP = 1,57
10          PRINT, KATZ*LUMP
20       PRINT, ' '
```

5 Nested DO-loops may have the same terminal statement, but if they do, then there cannot be a transfer of control to terminal statement except from the innermost loop.

LEGAL
```
      DO 10 KATZ = 1,142,2
         DO 10 LUMP = 1,57
            IF ( LUMP .EQ. KATZ )   GO TO 10
            PRINT, KATZ*LUMP
10          PRINT, ' '
```

ILLEGAL
```
      DO 10 KATZ = 1,142,2
         IF ( KATZ .EQ. 17 )   GO TO 10
         DO 10 LUMP=1,57
            PRINT, KATZ*LUMP
10          PRINT, ' '
```

6 The terminal statement of a DO-loop must be executable and must not be a GO TO, STOP or RETURN (*i.e.,* it can't be an unconditional transfer of control). It may be a CALL statement though.

There are two fairly common techniques associated with DO-loops that programmers use to improve the readability of their programs. One is to indent the statements in the range of the DO-loops. The other is to place a CONTINUE statement at the end of the range of every DO-loop so that the DO statement and the CONTINUE act as visual "brackets" for the DO-loop. The CONTINUE statement has no effect other than to act as a place to attach a statement label.

> **CONTINUE** *is an executable* WATFIV *statement. Its (rather unusual) meaning is to* do nothing. *It is often used as the terminal statement in the range of a* DO-*loop.*

EXERCISES 8 1

1 In the first DO-loop example program, what will be PRINTed if TOP has the value −1?

2 In what way would the output of the second example program be changed if its DO statement was changed to

```
DO 20 COUNT = 1,100
```

3 How many lines will this bizarre and possibly senseless program print?

```
         INTEGER OUTER, INNER, MIDDLE
COMMENT:  THIS PROGRAM IS BIZARRE AND POSSIBLY SENSELESS.
C         READ IT AT YOUR OWN RISK.
      DO 100 OUTER = 2,8,2
        DO 100 MIDDLE = OUTER,2,1
          DO 100 INNER = 1,4,2
 100        PRINT, 'LINE'
      STOP
      END
```

Section 8 2

DO-loops and Arrays: a great team

Commonly the values stored in an array are related and must be dealt with in a very similar way, but one at a time, of course. Such situations are great opportunities to use DO-loops, resulting in a more efficient program which is easier to read, hence easier to debug. Here's part of a program which locates the smallest value in an array of numbers. We assume that an earlier section of the program has succeeded in READing N values into array positions ROSE(1), ROSE(2), . . . , ROSE(N).

You have seen the algorithm before. Notice the use made of the CONTINUE

```
        INTEGER ROSE(1000), N, HERE, MINIM
             .
             .
             .
COMMENT:   FIND THE SMALLEST VALUE IN THE ARRAY 'ROSE', THUS
C             FINDING THE FEWEST NUMBER OF PETALS ANY ROSE HAS.
C          FIRST ELEMENT IS SMALLEST SO FAR
           MINIM = ROSE(1)
C          SEARCH THE OTHER ELEMENTS FOR SMALLER ONES
           DO 300  HERE = 2,N
              IF ( ROSE(HERE).GE.MINIM )  GO TO 300
C          HERE IS A SMALLER VALUE.  UPDATE
              MINIM = ROSE(HERE)
   300     CONTINUE
C          DONE
           PRINT, 'NO ROSE HAS LESS THAN', MINIM, 'PETALS'
           STOP
           END
```

statement in statement 300. It provides a convenient place to go when, under
certain conditions, you want to skip some part of the DO-loop range. In this case
we wanted to skip the statement

```
   MINIM = ROSE(HERE)
```

unless we had found a new minimum value.

A Chicago Peace has forty-five petals;   *an Austrian Copper has five.*

Nested DO-loops are convenient ways of dealing with two-dimensional arrays.
To illustrate this, let's look again at the program that we saw in the first part of
Section 6 4. That is where we first used two-dimensional arrays. We had an array
which stored the results of a poll taken for our political candidate. We used the
array

```
   REAL POLL(7,5)
```

and we wished to know the average value in each column. Using DO-loops our
program would look like the one below.

```
        REAL POLL(7,5), AVERGE, SUM
        INTEGER COLUMN, ROW
             .
             .
             .
        DO  200 COLUMN=1,5
           SUM = 0.0
           DO 100 ROW = 1,7
              SUM = SUM + POLL(ROW,COLUMN)
   100        CONTINUE
           AVERGE = SUM/7.0
           PRINT, 'THE AVERAGE SUPPORT IN COLUMN', COLUMN,
     +            'IS', AVERAGE, 'PERCENT'
   200     CONTINUE
        STOP
        END
```

Where they are appropriate, DO-loops help by providing a concise notation for a specific sort of loop. You already know how to write any sort of loop you want, so if the restrictions on DO-loops make them inappropriate to your problem, you know what to do.

EXERCISES 8 2

1 Look again at the examples in Chapters 3 and 6 and see which of the loops could be appropriately written as DO-loops and which of them couldn't.

2 Alter the example which computes the smallest value in ROSE so that it PRINTs the largest.

3 Alter the example which computes the smallest value in ROSE so that it also PRINTs the number of memory cells in ROSE which have the smallest value.

Section 8 3*

Fads

> Skip this section
> if you feel like it.

Let's look at a situation in which the DO-loop is useful. As you know, many people believe that fads spread faster when they start on one of the coasts than when they start in the middle of the country. If this is true there must be some reason for it. We will try to explain it by hypothesizing a fad spread mechanism and testing it on the computer to see if the results support the observation that fads spread faster from the coasts.

We will assume that fads spread by word of mouth and that a person's influence doesn't extend much beyond a small region around his home. (These assumptions can, of course, be criticized on many grounds, especially since we are long out of the nineteenth century, but let's forge ahead anyway.) Basically we are assuming that the percentage of people in a particular region who follow the fad on one day is changed (either up or down) by the percentages in neighboring regions. To be specific, let's divide the country up into a bunch of square regions by laying a 40 by 100 grid over the U.S. map. Each region has eight immediate neighbors: north, northeast, east, southeast, south, southwest, west, and northwest. The only exceptions are the border regions which are, of course, missing one or more neighbors. Let's say that fads spread by an averaging mechanism: if the percentage of people in a particular region who follow the fad is $r\%$ today, and the percentages in the neighboring regions are $n\%$, $ne\%$, $e\%$, $se\%$, $s\%$, $sw\%$, $w\%$, and $nw\%$, then the percentage in the region tomorrow will be $(r\% + n\% + ne\% + e\% + se\% + s\%, + sw\% + w\% + nw\%)/9$. If the region in question is on the border, then we leave the missing neighbors out of the average.

As a starting condition, we will assume that 100% of the people in a particular region, the home of the fad, decide to follow a fad on day 1 and that no one else knows about the fad until the next day, when it starts to spread according to our rules. We make a special case of the home of the fad: it stays at 100% at all times since the home town folks really love it. We'll let the simulation run for 60 days and then look at the results.

It will be easy to write the program. We can use a two dimensional array to store the percentages. However, since the United States isn't rectangular, we will have to initialize some points of the array to special values which indicate that they are not part of the United States. We can use negative values for this purpose since they are clearly not possible percentages. We can read the coordinates of these outside regions from cards. Then we initialize the starting region (read from a card) to 100% and the remaining regions to 0%. The heart of the program is the part which computes the next day's percentages for each region. On each of 60 days we must look at each region, compute its new percentage, and record it in another rectangular array. This is the only complex part of the program, and it's made complex because we have to worry about what to do on the boundary points. Suppose we want to update the percentage at the position whose east-west coordinate is stored in EAST and whose north-south coordinate is stored in NORTH. We want to sum up the values in the nine memory cells around (NORTH, EAST).

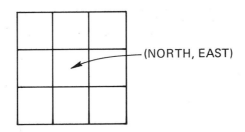
— (NORTH, EAST)

This means we'll need two nested loops, one to go from NORTH−1 up to NORTH+1 and one to go from EAST−1 up to EAST+1. Then, at each of the nine places we'll test to see if the stored value is negative (indicating a point outside the United States). If it is, we don't add its value in. Since this is such an important and basic part of the program, we've indented the statements that make it up.

The other important idea here is that when we compute the new percentage at a point, we can't just insert that new value back into the same array. If we did,

> *parallel process: a process which has subparts which function simultaneously.*
>
> *serial process: a process whose subparts function one at a time (sequentially).*
>
> *In the fad problem we are using a serial process (our WATFIV program running on our serial digital computer) to simulate a parallel process (the fad spread mechanism).*

then in trying to compute the new percentage for a neighboring point, one of the terms in the average would be wrong. That's why we need to use *two* arrays. The problem arises because this program is simulating a process that is going on simultaneously all over the country, *i.e.,* a parallel process. Since the program can do computations for only one part of the country at a time, it has to retain the old percentages until it has all the new ones computed.

At the end of sixty days we print the results in the form of a rectangular display of symbols, one for each region. Rather arbitrarily we decide on the use of symbols described in the table below.

Table of Symbols

Symbol	Meaning
—	outside U.S.
blank	0 – 10%
1	10 – 20%
2	20 – 30%
.	
.	
.	
9	90 – 100%
*	home of fad

The results shown in Figure 8 3 1 are from a program which is the same as the one below except for the PRINT statements. We used a type of PRINT statement (described thoroughly in Chapter 10) which gave us a little nicer looking map. With the PRINT statements shown here, the program will produce a map which is turned sidewise and sprawled across two pages. The exact output statements we used are shown in a box near Problem 10 14 in case you want to duplicate our map.

```
COMMENT:   PROGRAM TO TEST THE FAD THEORY.
C       TWO ARRAYS FOR PERCENTAGE OF SATURATION--ONE FOR
C       CURRENT DAY, THE OTHER FOR THE NEXT DAY
        REAL PCT(100,40), NXTPCT(100,40)
C       MEMORY CELLS FOR INPUT/OUTPUT
        CHARACTER*1 LINE(100)
        CHARACTER*1 SYMBOL(12)/'-',' ','1','2','3','4',
     +                 '5','6','7','8','9','*'/
C       MEMORY CELLS FOR COMPUTATION OF NEIGHBORHOOD AVERAGES
        REAL AVE
        INTEGER NEAR, N, E, NLESS1, NPLUS1, ELESS1, EPLUS1
C       OTHER USEFUL VARIABLES
        INTEGER NORTH,EAST,DAY,HOMEE,HOMEN,I
C
C       INITIALIZE ALL REGIONS TO ZERO PER CENT
        DO 10 NORTH = 1,40
           DO 10 EAST = 1,100
   10        PCT(EAST,NORTH) = 0.0
C
C       GET BOUNDARY COORDINATES FROM DATA CARDS.
   20   READ, EAST, NORTH
        IF ( NORTH .EQ. 0 )  GO TO 30
        PCT(EAST,NORTH) = -11.0
        GO TO 20
```

```
C
C       READ THE LOCATION OF THE HOME OF THE FAD.
  30    READ, HOMEE, HOMEN
C
C       FOR EACH OF 60 DAYS, UPDATE THE PERCENTAGES.
C
        DO 300 DAY = 1,60
C
C       COMPUTE NEW AVERAGE FOR EACH REGION (100*40=4000 AV'S)
        DO 100 NORTH = 1,40
          DO 100 EAST = 1,100
C           IF PCT(EAST,NORTH) IS LESS THAN 0.0, IT IS NOT IN
C           THE CONTINENTAL U.S. ITS PERCENTAGE WON'T CHANGE.
            IF ( PCT(EAST,NORTH) .GE. 0.0)  GO TO 40
              AVE = PCT(EAST,NORTH)
              GO TO 100
C           COUNT THE NUMBER OF NON-BORDER REGIONS AROUND
C           POSITION (EAST,NORTH) AND COMPUTE AVERAGE.
  40        NEAR = 0
            AVE = 0.0
            NLESS1 = MAXO(NORTH-1,1)
            NPLUS1 = MINO(NORTH+1,40)
            ELESS1 = MAXO(EAST-1,1)
            EPLUS1 = MINO(EAST+1,100)
            DO 60 N=NLESS1,NPLUS1
              DO 50 E=ELESS1,EPLUS1
C               TEST FOR BOUNDARY POINT
                IF ( PCT(E,N) .LT. 0.0 )  GO TO 50
C               ADD IN THIS NEIGHBOR.
                AVE = AVE + PCT(E,N)
                NEAR = NEAR + 1
  50          CONTINUE
  60        CONTINUE
C           FINISH BY TAKING NEW AVERAGE.
            AVE = AVE/NEAR
C           INSERT NEW VALUE.
  100       NXTPCT(EAST,NORTH) = AVE
C       NOW GET READY FOR THE NEXT DAY.
        DO 200 NORTH = 1,40
          DO 200 EAST = 1,100
  200       PCT(EAST,NORTH) = NXTPCT(EAST,NORTH)
C       REMEMBER--HOME PERCENTAGE STAYS AT 100.
        PCT(HOMEE,HOMEN) = 100.
  300   CONTINUE
C
C       PRINT THE RESULTS, ONE LINE AT A TIME.
        DO 500 EAST = 1,100
          DO 400 NORTH = 1,40
C           FIGURE OUT WHAT SYMBOL GOES HERE AND INSERT IT.
  400       LINE(41-NORTH)=SYMBOL(INT(PCT(EAST,NORTH)/10.0)+2)
C       PRINT PERCENTAGE SYMBOLS ON THIS LONGITUDE.
  500     PRINT, (LINE(I),I=1,40)
        STOP
        END
```

Figure 8 3 1 is the output of the program. As you can see, fads on the coast do *not* spread faster. Since the results of our model do not correspond to reality, we must not have understood the process. Perhaps the averaging mechanism we used to spread the fads is wrong. Perhaps people on the coasts are different from people in the middle of America. Perhaps both. Perhaps neither.

Central Fad

Coastal Fad

Figure 8 3 1 Output from the Fad Program

WATFIV for Humans

EXERCISES 8 3

1 Have a discussion with some friends about other ways to model the fad spread process.

PROBLEMS 8

1 Write a program which PRINTs a table of sines and cosines of the angles 0.00, 0.01, 0.02, . . . , 1.57 radians.

2 Rewrite a program from an earlier chapter which is appropriately done using DO-loops.

3 Write a program which READs values for N, and for each value computes

$$1 + 2 + 3 + \ldots + N \text{ and } 1^2 + 2^2 + 3^2 + \ldots + N^2.$$

4 Write a program which verifies (for N = 10, 20, . . . , 90, 100) that the sum of the first N odd numbers is N**2.

5 Using DO-loops, write a program which rearranges an array of REAL numbers until it is in descending order. Use the technique shown in Section 7 4.

6 The table shown below may be used for computing tax due for any person with income between $4500 and $5000 and no more than six exemptions. Also given is information regarding six individuals for whom the tax due is to be determined.

   Write a program which will READ the tax table and taxpayer information, select from the tax table the correct tax due for each person, then output all taxpayer information plus the tax due. Prepare the output so that it looks neat and provides all the input information plus the tax due.

TAX TABLE

Income		Exemptions					
		1	2	3	4	5	6
4500	4550	565	430	326	218	116	18
4550	4600	565	430	326	218	116	25
4600	4650	581	444	342	324	130	32
4650	4700	589	451	350	241	137	39
4700	4750	597	459	358	249	144	46
4750	4800	606	463	366	256	151	53
4800	4850	614	474	374	264	159	60
4850	4900	622	482	382	271	166	67
4900	4950	630	490	390	279	174	74
4950	5000	638	497	398	286	181	81

TAXPAYERS

Smith, William "Doc"
224 S. Loomis Street
Fort Collins, Colorado

Soc. Sec. No. 496-28-5293
exemptions: 5
income: $4,510

Walsingham, Louise M.
602 Encino Drive
Aptos, California

Soc. Sec. No. 216-70-4318
exemptions: 1
income: $4,700

Lesley, F. David
211 Cliff Street
Solana Beach, California

Soc. Sec. No. 511-46-8420
exemptions: 3
income: $4,580

Minda, Carl David
13402 Shawnee Run Road
Cincinnati, Ohio

Soc. Sec. No. 316-43-1124
exemptions: 2
income: $4,900

7   One of the methods used for analyzing a set of time series data for periodicity is to calculate an autocorrelation coefficient between values of the variate X_i and the same variate at a constant time-lag X_{i+p}. The autocorrelation coefficient for a particular time lag p is given by

$$r_p = \frac{\Sigma(x_i x_{i+p}) - \dfrac{\Sigma x_i \Sigma x_{i+p}}{N-p}}{\sqrt{\left[\Sigma x_i^2 - \dfrac{(\Sigma x_i)^2}{N-p}\right]\left[\Sigma x_{i+p}^2 - \dfrac{(\Sigma x_{i+p})^2}{N-p}\right]}}.$$

The summations extend over the range $i = 1$ to $i = N - p$. An examination of r calculated as a function of p indicates those lags or periods over which the data of the time series seem to be correlated. In other words, r will be large for time-lags p which are periods of the variate X_i.

Consider the following data, representing the monthly rainfall on a certain watershed between 1901 and 1920. Obtain the autocorrelation coefficients for time-lags of 1 to 25 months, printing each value as it is calculated.

RAINFALL IN INCHES

Year	Jan.	Feb.	Mar.	Apr.	May	June	July	Aug.	Sept.	Oct.	Nov.	Dec.
1901	0.14	1.04	1.61	1.63	1.45	1.41	0.01	0.13	0.01	0.05	0.19	0.45
1902	1.42	1.35	1.03	2.05	2.32	0.73	0.06	0.39	0.26	0.21	1.21	0.87
1903	1.31	1.14	1.76	1.85	1.76	1.32	0.11	0.24	0.09	0.37	0.29	1.59
1904	0.32	1.21	2.43	2.10	2.42	1.05	0.02	0.01	0.51	0.19	0.05	1.61
1905	1.07	0.47	1.82	1.92	3.17	1.04	0.03	0.13	0.27	0.26	1.07	0.92
1906	1.06	1.36	1.46	2.31	1.87	0.85	0.07	0.07	0.14	0.62	1.34	0.09
1907	2.04	1.13	2.64	0.95	2.17	1.93	0.09	0.32	0.36	0.32	0.42	1.42
1908	0.41	1.09	1.73	1.74	1.94	0.64	0.10	0.06	0.22	0.73	0.31	0.76
1909	1.71	0.87	1.93	1.42	3.03	1.52	0.00	0.23	0.08	0.93	0.59	1.21
1910	1.41	1.49	2.56	2.09	2.98	1.61	0.00	0.33	0.49	0.24	1.61	0.32
1911	1.33	1.20	0.42	1.67	2.55	1.06	0.13	0.15	0.36	0.15	0.16	1.05
1912	1.32	1.43	2.34	1.76	1.76	1.16	0.07	0.34	0.45	0.84	0.87	1.11
1913	0.95	1.18	1.34	2.04	3.21	1.24	0.10	0.23	0.13	1.01	0.54	0.69
1914	0.42	1.06	1.53	1.82	1.69	0.95	0.31	0.04	0.28	0.36	0.98	1.24
1915	2.61	0.64	1.75	1.94	2.63	1.13	0.05	0.33	0.22	0.09	0.04	0.92
1916	1.42	0.86	1.42	2.15	0.86	0.76	0.09	0.15	0.19	0.37	0.23	1.42
1917	1.17	1.24	2.03	0.61	2.42	0.84	0.13	0.33	0.42	0.19	0.75	0.76
1918	0.76	1.00	2.26	2.21	1.74	0.92	0.00	0.35	0.04	0.75	0.12	0.63
1919	1.61	0.34	1.72	2.20	1.74	1.70	0.21	0.25	0.34	0.27	0.39	1.32
1920	1.27	1.32	1.94	1.23	3.20	1.09	0.17	0.03	0.26	1.21	0.94	0.68

8 Suppose a zoologist comes to you with a collection of data. He had made a count of the number of prairie rattlesnakes (Crotalus viridis viridis) found on a square mile of land at various altitudes around Fort Collins, Colorado. The data he has gathered is summarized in the table below.

Altitude	Number of Snakes
5000'	30
5300'	28
5800'	20
6000'	14
6500'	10
7000'	3

He suspects that the number of snakes s at altitude a can be expressed as a linear function

$$s(a) = Da + M$$

He asks you to try to determine from his data what would be reasonable values to take for the coefficients D and M.

Naturally, you want to choose values for D and M so that the observed data deviates as little as possible from the values predicted by your coefficients D and M. In other words you want

$$s(5000) \text{ to be close to } 30$$
$$s(5300) \text{ to be close to } 28$$
$$s(5800) \text{ to be close to } 20$$

One technique that is often used in cases like this is to choose values for D and M which minimize the sum of the squares of the deviations from the observed values. In other words, so that

$$(s(5000) - 30)^2 + (s(5300) - 28)^2 + (s(5800) - 20)^2 + (s(6000)$$
$$- 14)^2 + (s(6500) - 10)^2 + (s(7000) - 3)^2$$

(where $s(a) = Da + M$)

is as small as possible.

Your job is to write a program which READs an integer n from a card, then READs n measurements a_i, s_i from the following n cards, then calculates values for D and M by solving the following pair of linear equations (which solve the least squares problem posed above).

$$\left(\sum_{i=1}^{n} a_i^2 \right) D + \left(\sum_{i=1}^{n} a_i \right) M = \sum_{i=1}^{n} a_i s_i$$

$$\left(\sum_{i=1}^{n} a_i \right) D + nM = \sum_{i=1}^{n} s_i$$

The output from your program should include the values of D and M as well as the value of the square deviation (for the computed values D and M) divided by n, that is

$$\frac{1}{n} \sum_{i=1}^{n} (Da_i - M - s_i)^2$$

9 We got this problem from Prof. Wm. M. McKeeman. Its basic structure is very similar to the fad program described in Section 8 3. We'll use a square two dimensional array of INTEGER memory cells to represent a patch of skin. Each element in the array is either *helathy, sick,* or *immune.* In order to operate, the program needs three numbers. The first, an INTEGER which we'll call SICK, tells how many time steps a skin spot remains sick once it has been infected. The second, an INTEGER called IMMUNE, tells how many time steps a skin spot remains immune after it is through being sick. The third is a REAL named RATE which tells the odds (probability) that a sick spot will infect a neighboring healthy spot during the current time step.

> *ringworm: a contagious disease caused by a fungus. Help end the heartbreak of ringworm. Do Problem 9.*

To represent a healthy spot of skin, store a 0 in the corresponding array location. To start things off, make the whole patch of skin healthy except for the spot in the very center. Store a 1 in the location representing a skin spot when that spot becomes sick. For each time step, sweep through the entire array. At each position with a non-zero value, add 1 to reflect the passage of one unit of time. Then check to see if the spot has completed both its sick and its immune phase (*i.e.,* if the value stored there is SICK + IMMUNE). If it is, restore that spot to the healthy state (0).

Next, still within the same time step, sweep through the array again. This time, stop at each spot that is sick and see if it infects any of its healthy neighbors.

If the fad program is clear to you, this program shouldn't be too hard. Just as in the fad program, you will need an auxiliary array so that the states of affairs at time step t and $t + 1$ don't get confused. Just as in the fad program you can convert INTEGERs into CHARACTERs to make the output nice. We suggest a blank for healthy spots, a "*" for sick spots and a "." for spots in the immune state.

By trying different values of the three numbers SICK, IMMUNE and RATE, you can observe a variety of "diseases," ringworm, blotches, measles, infestations that die out (cure themselves) and ones that continue re-infecting recovered skin.

Note: the computation time increases rapidly with the size of the array of cells. Write the program so that you can easily change the size of the array in case you have time limit problems. Start with a 20 by 20 patch of skin.

9 A BUNCH OF EXAMPLES (and a new statement)

Section 9 1

Craps and the Computed GO TO Statement

We've already come a long way on our strange journey through the intricacies and idiosyncrasies of programming. In this chapter we want to slow our mad dash past new statements and use the statements we already know to solve some interesting problems. There *is* one new statement here, but our main goal is using familiar statements in new contexts.

We are planning a trip to Las Vegas to gamble at the crap tables and wonder how much money we can expect to lose. If craps were a fair game, we would expect to come out about even. However, we know that it's not a fair game; there is a greater chance of losing than of winning, so we expect to come out a little behind. The question is, how far behind?

A quick way of making an estimate of how far behind we expect to be after a thousand games is to simulate the game on the computer (making use of the random number generator written in Chapter 7). To simulate the game, we need to know the rules; they are depicted by the flowchart below (Fig. 9 1 1).

In plain English, the rules are: roll the dice. If the sum of the spots is 7 or 11, you win immediately. If the sum of the spots is two ("snake eyes"), three ("craps"), or twelve ("box cars"), you lose immediately. Otherwise the number you rolled is called your **point**. You keep rolling until you get either (1) your point, in which case you win, or (2) a seven in which case you have "crapped out", and you lose.

We will use a SUBROUTINE ROLL which simulates the roll of the dice. In other words, when we call ROLL, it gives us the number (2, 3, 4, . . . , or 12) coming up on the dice. (ROLL will have one parameter, an output parameter.) To write this SUBROUTINE we can use the FUNCTION CHOOSE from Chapter 7. You will recall that CHOOSE needs one argument, a positive INTEGER. The number it computes is an INTEGER between one and the value of its argument. Each possible value of CHOOSE has the same likelihood of being chosen. Therefore CHOOSE(6) gives us a number between 1 and 6, like rolling a die.

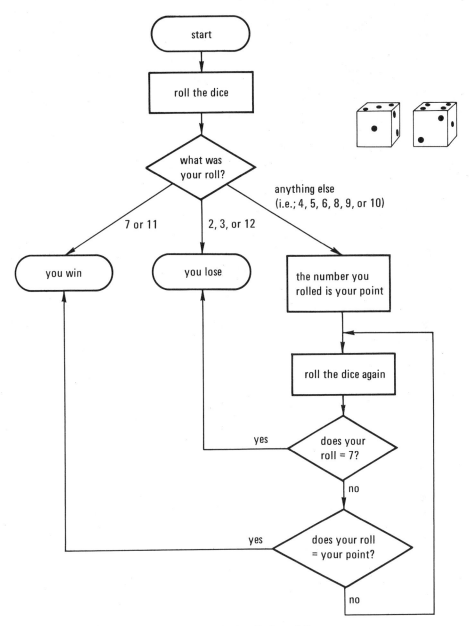

Figure 9 1 1 Rules of Craps

A philosophical question: The rules don't prohibit a game of craps from lasting forever. Should we worry about that in our program?

```
      SUBROUTINE ROLL (DICE)
      INTEGER DICE
      INTEGER CHOOSE
COMMENT:  'DICE' WILL BE SET TO A RANDOM VALUE 2, 3, ..., 12
C         LIKE ROLLING A PAIR OF DICE.
C         (FUNCTION CHOOSE IS FROM SECTION 7 5)
      DICE = CHOOSE(6) + CHOOSE(6)
      RETURN
      END
```

Note that it is crucial that we add together two random numbers uniformly chosen from 1 to 6 instead of just taking one number at random from 2 to 12. Look at the number of ways of getting the possible dice rolls. The table shows that the odds of getting a 7 are $6/36 = 1/6$. If we just used one random number uniformly chosen between 2 and 12, the odds would be $1/11$.

dice roll	number of ways of adding two numbers 1 to 6 to get the total	number of ways of getting 1 number 2 to 12
2	1	1
3	2	1
4	3	1
5	4 (i.e. 1+4, 2+3 3+2, 4+1)	1
6	5	1
7	6	1
8	5	1
9	4	1
10	3	1
11	2	1
12	1	1

---

computed GO TO statement

form

GO TO $(s_1, s_2, \ldots, s_n), v$

s_i is a statement label

v is an unsubscripted INTEGER memory cell name

meaning

Control is transferred to the vth statement in the list $s_1, s_2, \ldots, s_n$.

If $v < 1$ or if $v > n$ control passes to the next statement.

examples

```
INTEGER N, JMP, CASE
GOTO (85, 10, 100, 453), N
GOTO (465, 700, 25), JMP
GOTO (200, 100, 100, 200, 100, 400), CASE
```

182

In looking at the rules of the game, you probably noticed that after the initial dice roll, there is a fairly complicated series of tests which must be performed before deciding which of the three routes to take (win, lose, or roll again). We could make these tests using IF statements, but the situation is made to order for a special kind of statement that you don't know about yet: a multiple branch transfer of control called the **computed GO TO**. This GO TO statement, instead of specifying one place to go, specifies many possible destinations. One of them is selected based on the value of an INTEGER variable which is part of the statement. If the value of the variable is 1, then the program jumps to the first statement in the list; if it is 2, then to the second statement, and so on.

Here's our completed program for craps.

```
      COMMENT:  PLAY 1000 GAMES CF CRAPS KEEPING WIN-LOSS RECORD.
               INTEGER POINT, DICE, WINS, LOSSES
      C        INITIALIZE WIN-LOSS COUNTERS
               WINS = 0
               LOSSES = 0
      C        ROLL THE DICE.
       1       CALL ROLL (DICE)
      C        GO TO WIN(STATEMENT 20), LOSE(STATEMENT 30),
      C        ROLL AGAIN(STATEMENT 40), OR ERROR(STATEMENT 10).
               GOTO (10,30,30,40,40,40,20,40,40,40,20,30), DICE
      C        ERROR CASE
      10       PRINT, 'ERROR--DICE ROLL=',DICE
               STOP
      C
      C        WE WON
      20       WINS = WINS + 1
               GO TO 50
      C
      C        WE LOST ...
      30       LOSSES = LOSSES + 1
               GO TO 50
      C
      C        OUR ROLL BECOMES OUR POINT, AND WE GO ON.
      40       POINT = DICE
      45       CALL ROLL (DICE)
      C          TEST FOR POINT (WIN)
                 IF ( DICE .EQ. POINT )  GO TO 20
      C          TEST FOR UNLUCKY SEVEN (LOSE)
                 IF ( DICE .EQ. 7 )  GO TO 30
      C          NO DECISION ... ROLL AGAIN
                 GO TO 45
      C        GAME OVER.  IF WE HAVEN'T FINISHED 1000 GEMES YET,
      C        GO BACK AND PLAY SOME MORE.
      50       IF ( WINS + LOSSES .LT. 1000 )  GO TO 1
      C        PRINT RESULTS
               PRINT, 'OUT OF 1000 GAMES, WE WON', WINS,
              +        'AND LOST', LOSSES
               STOP
               END
```

output

```
OUT OF 1000 GAMES, WE WON          475 AND LOST          525
```

Please be sure you understand the computed GO TO in this program. We could have used a number of IF statements, for example

```
IF ( DICE .EQ. 2 )  GO TO 30
IF ( DICE .EQ. 3 )  GO TO 30
IF ( DICE .EQ. 4 )  GO TO 40
   .
   .
   .
IF ( DICE .EQ. 11 )  GO TO 20
IF ( DICE .EQ. 12 )  GO TO 30
```

but there is a big difference in efficiency between the two schemes. No matter what value memory cell DICE has, it takes just one step for the computed GO TO to direct control to the appropriate point. The sequence of IF statements technique, however, can take up to eleven steps (if DICE has the value 12). In general, the computed GO TO takes one step while the number of steps required by the IF statements is proportional to the number of choices to be made. This situation is analogous to the situation we saw in the bar graph example in Section 4 5 where we truncated the fractional part of a REAL and used the result directly as an array subscript to avoid having a number of IF tests to find its range.

> The odds of winning at craps are a little
> better than 49 out of 100.

EXERCISES 9 1

1   Write computed GO TO statements that do the same as

a
```
IF ( K .EQ. 1 )  GO TO 10
IF ( K .EQ. 2 )  GO TO 20
IF ( K .EQ. 3 )  GO TO 30
```

b
```
      IF ( I .GT. 2 .AND. I .LT. 5 )  GO TO 100
      IF ( I .LT. 6 )  GO TO 200
300   ...
```

Assume the value of I is positive.

2   How would you change the program to test the fairness of the game if the rule were that you lose if you get a 7 or 11 while going for your point?

Section 9 2

Sorting Several Arrays at Once

In Section 7 4 we discussed a problem in which a pair of arrays needed to be rearranged in a particular order. The arrangement was based on the values in only one of the arrays, but since elements in corresponding positions in the arrays were to be kept in corresponding positions, whenever we moved an element of one array, we had to make a similar change in the other array.

> *index:* a list of numbers telling us how to arrange another list in alphabetical order; the first entry in index tells us which element in the list goes first, the second index entry tells us which goes second, etc.

It is nearly always the case in a sorting problem that more than one array is involved, but often there are many more than two. We will see an example in this section where there are four such arrays, but the sorting subprogram we'll write will be useful for sorting any number of corresponding arrays. The sorting process will be the same as before, but instead of rearranging the arrays, we'll simply build an "index" which will tell us how they should be arranged. The first entry in the index will tell us where to find the array elements which come first in the ordering, the second entry says where to find the elements which should come second, and so on. Figure 9 2 1 pictures an index for some arrays containing the names, ages, weights, and heights of a group of children which we want to arrange in order from lightest to heaviest. The index tells us what order the elements should come in. Our subprogram won't rearrange the arrays at all so it won't need to know how many arrays are involved. It only needs to know what values are in the array containing the "keys"; that is, the values we want in increasing order. From that it can build the index which will tell us what order to take the array elements in. We'll use a technique that can be used in conjunction with almost any sorting algorithm.

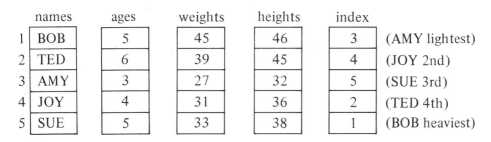

	names		ages		weights		heights		index	
1	BOB		5		45		46		3	(AMY lightest)
2	TED		6		39		45		4	(JOY 2nd)
3	AMY		3		27		32		5	(SUE 3rd)
4	JOY		4		31		36		2	(TED 4th)
5	SUE		5		33		38		1	(BOB heaviest)

Figure 9 2 1

> **keys:** *a list of values which we want to know how to arrange in some particular order (e.g., increasing order).*

In the beginning we set up the index as if the array were already in the correct order; that is, the index will have the entries 1, 2, 3, 4, etc. to begin with. Then we rearrange the index until it correctly orders the keys. The trick is that we always refer to the keys *through the index.* Instead of referring to the *i*th key, we refer to the key designated by the *i*th entry in the index. For example, if the keys array is called KEYS and the index array is called INDEX, then instead of referring to KEYS(I), we refer to KEYS(INDEX(I)). Whenever we want to interchange a pair of keys, we interchange the corresponding *index* entries (not the keys themselves). Since we are referring to the keys through the index anyway, it will be as if we had interchanged the pair of keys. Perhaps this is best explained by way of a flowchart and illustration, as in Figures 9 2 2 and 9 2 3.

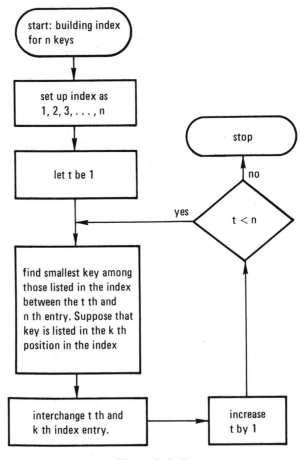

Figure 9 2 2

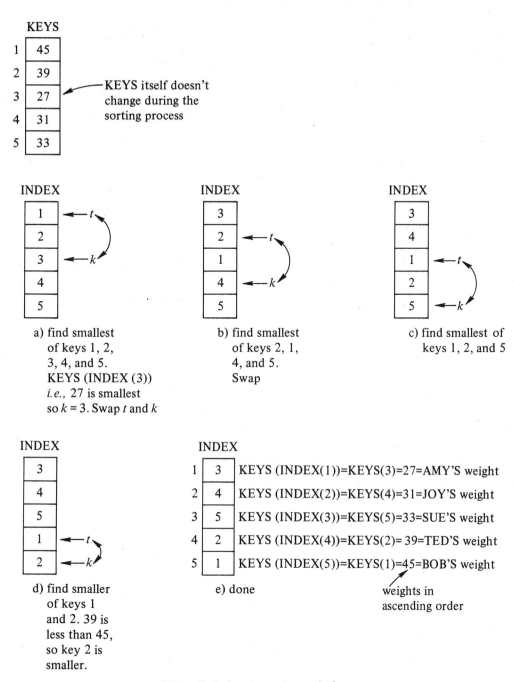

Figure 9 2 3 Arranging an Index

The subprogram below prepares an index for a list of keys in the way described by the flowchart of Figure 9 2 2. It has two input parameters: KEYS, an array of values we want to know how to arrange in increasing order, and N, the number of values in the array KEYS. It has one output parameter INDEX, an array which will tell us how to arrange the KEYS.

```
         SUBROUTINE INDSRT (KEYS, INDEX, N)
         INTEGER N, KEYS(N), INDEX(N)
COMMENT:   THIS SUBROUTINE PERFORMS AN INDEX SORT.
C          IT FILLS THE ARRAY 'INDEX' WITH VALUES WHICH TELL
C          US HOW TO ARRANGE THE ARRAY 'KEYS' IN INCREASING
C          ORDER.
         INTEGER TOP, SM, LOCSM
C        INITIALIZE INDEX
         TOP = 1
   50    INDEX(TOP) = TOP
            TOP = TOP + 1
            IF ( TOP .LE. N ) GO TO 50
COMMENT:   REARRANGE INDEX SO THAT KEYS(INDEX(I)),I=1,2,...,N
C          IS IN INCREASING ORDER.
C        INDEX(TOP), INDEX(TOP+1), ..., INDEX(N) WILL BE THE
C        PORTION OF INDEX YET TO BE ARRANGED.
         TOP = 1
C        LOCATE SMALLEST ELEMENT AMONG KEYS(INDEX(I)),I=TOP...N
  100    SM = LOCSM(KEYS, INDEX, TOP, N)
C          INTERCHANGE INDEX(TOP) WITH INDEX(SM) USING
C          SUBROUTINE 'SWITCH' OF SECTION 7 4.
            CALL SWITCH (INDEX(TOP), INDEX(SM))
C          NOW KEYS(INDEX(TOP)) IS THE SMALLEST OF THOSE LEFT
C          CONTINUE ARRANGING INDEX
            TOP = TOP + 1
            IF ( TOP .LE. N ) GOTO 100
         RETURN
         END


         INTEGER FUNCTION LOCSM(KEYS, INDEX, FROM, TO)
         INTEGER FROM, TO, KEYS(TO), INDEX(TO)
COMMENT:   ASSIGN LOCSM SO THAT
C          KEYS(INDEX(LOCSM)).LE.KEYS(INDEX(I)), I=FROM...TO
         INTEGER I
         LOCSM = FROM
         I = FROM + 1
  100    IF ( I .GT. TO ) RETURN
            IF (KEYS(INDEX(I)).LT.KEYS(INDEX(LOCSM))) LOCSM = I
            I = I+1
            GO TO 100
         END


         SUBROUTINE SWITCH (A,B)
         INTEGER A, B
         INTEGER COPYA
         COPYA = A
         A = B
         B = COPYA
         RETURN
         END
```

We can use this SUBROUTINE to solve the problem of printing our list of children's names (along with their ages and heights) in order of their weights. All we need to do, once the information is stored in the arrays, is CALL our SUBROUTINE, using the array that stores their weights as one argument, and providing an array to be used for an index. Then we will be able to PRINT the arrays in order by using the index. While we're at it, we may as well sort the arrays again so that we can also PRINT the lists in order of increasing age. That will just involve another CALL to the SUBROUTINE.

```
COMMENT:   THIS PROGRAM READS A LIST OF CHILDREN'S NAMES,
C          AGES, WEIGHTS, AND HEIGHTS FROM CARDS, THEN PRINTS
C          THE LIST TWICE.  ONCE IN THE ORDER OF INCREASING
C          WEIGHT, THEN ONCE IN ORDER OF INCREASING AGE.
       CHARACTER*4 NAME(100)
       INTEGER AGE(100), WGT(100), HGT(100)
       INTEGER N, I, X(100)
C      STORE THE DATA
       N = 0
 100   READ, NAME(N+1), AGE(N+1), WGT(N+1), HGT(N+1)
          IF ( NAME(N+1) .EQ. 'END ' )  GO TO 200
          N = N+1
          GO TO 100
COMMENT:  FIRST SORT ON WEIGHTS.
 200   CALL INDSRT(WGT,X,N)
       PRINT, 'CHILDREN BY INCREASING WEIGHT'
       PRINT, 'NAME            AGE          WEIGHT      HEIGHT'
       I = 1
 210   PRINT, NAME(X(I)), AGE(X(I)), WGT(X(I)), HGT(X(I))
          I = I+1
          IF ( I .LE. N )  GO TO 210
       PRINT, ' '
COMMENT:  NOW SORT ON AGES.
       CALL INDSRT(AGE,X,N)
       PRINT, 'CHILDREN BY INCREASING AGE'
       PRINT, 'NAME            AGE          WEIGHT      HEIGHT'
       I = 1
 310   PRINT, NAME(X(I)), AGE(X(I)), WGT(X(I)), HGT(X(I))
          I = I+1
          IF ( I .LE. N )  GO TO 310
       STOP
       END
```

data

```
'BOB '   5 45 46
'TED '   6 39 45
'AMY '   3 27 32
'JOY '   4 31 36
'SUE '   5 33 38
'END '   0 00 00
```

output

```
CHILDREN BY INCREASING WEIGHT
NAME            AGE          WEIGHT      HEIGHT
AMY             3            27          32
JOY             4            31          36
SUE             5            33          38
TED             6            39          45
BOB             5            45          46

CHILDREN BY INCREASING AGE
NAME            AGE          WEIGHT      HEIGHT
AMY             3            27          32
JOY             4            31          36
BOB             5            45          46
SUE             5            33          38
TED             6            39          45
```

EXERCISES 9 2

1 What statements would you add to the final program of this section to make it also print the lists in order of increasing height?

2 What statements could you add to the program to make certain it didn't try to READ more cards than it had room for in its arrays?

3 The arrays are declared to be of length 100 in the program. But the array parameters in INDSRT are declared to be of length N, where N is one of the parameters. When INDSRT is CALLed, the parameter indicating the length of the arrays won't have a value equal to the actual declared array length. Do you think this should cause an error? Do you think it will cause an error? Why or why not?

Section 9 3

Drag Race

This sample program makes use of the sorting SUBROUTINE we developed in Section 7 4 to keep track of the standings of cars at a drag race.

Suppose we have been hired by the founding fathers of Bleakwater Dragstrip to write a program which will be used to control their new all-weather electronic scoreboard. The scoreboard has two columns of lights, one which flashes a car's number, and another which shows the car's best elapsed time for the quarter mile. Each time a car runs, we are given a data card which has the car number and the elapsed time in seconds. For example, after Lefty "the Tooth" Snodgrass ran, we received a card with 3 and 6.782 punched on it. Each time the program READs a card, it should print out the standings of cars run so far. If, in the time slot of a card, we find a 100.0, this means that that car has been disqualified. We'll assume that there are five cars in the final race for lowest elapsed time and that each car gets two runs. After all ten runs, we'll want to print out the winner. Here are some sample things our program must be able to do:

Data card received: 1   8.202

The program should print:

STANDING	CAR	TIME
1	1	8.202

The pits go wild with excitement and the next data card is:

4   6.002.

Printout:

STANDING	CAR	TIME
1	4	6.002
2	1	8.202

Next data card:	72	100.0		
Printout:		STANDING	CAR	TIME
		1	4	6.002
		2	1	8.202
		3	72	DISQ.
Next data card:	4	7.220		
Printout:		STANDING	CAR	TIME
		1	4	6.002
		2	1	8.202
		3	72	DISQ.

(the *best* time is the one that counts)

Sample final output:	STANDING	CAR	TIME
	1	3	5.908
	2	4	6.002
	3	57	6.672
	4	72	7.996
	5	1	8.202

THE WINNER IS CAR NUMBER 3!

Think about how you might do this problem awhile before going on.

To store the information about the cars, we'll use two arrays (since there are two things we want to store—namely, the car number and its best time). Let's call the arrays CAR and TIME. After the first three cars have run, the arrays will look as below.

CAR(1)	4
CAR(2)	1
CAR(3)	72
CAR(4)	---
CAR(5)	---

TIME(1)	6.002
TIME(2)	8.202
TIME(3)	100.
TIME(4)	----
TIME(5)	----

So, the problem now is how to put data from new runs in the arrays, sort them, and print out the order.

The general flow of a program is described in Figure 9 3 1. Most of the flowchart is easily converted to WATFIV. Boxes 3 and 7 require a number of statements, however, so we'll use subprograms for them to avoid cluttering our main program with details. Box 7 is simply a matter of sorting a pair of arrays, putting the values of one in increasing order. Since that problem was solved in Section 7 4, we'll simply CALL SUBROUTINE SORT of that section to solve the problem of box 7. (Actually, the SUBROUTINE SORT of Section 7 4 puts numbers into decreasing order, but Exercise 7 4 3 describes a way to change the SUBROUTINE so that it puts numbers into increasing order.)

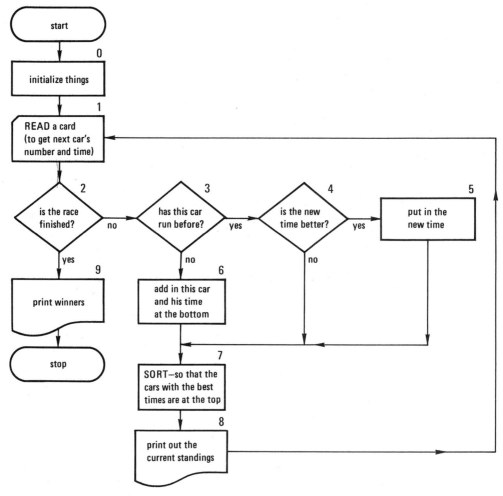

Figure 9 3 1

Box 3 is a matter of searching an array for a given value; if the value is in the array, we want to know where it is (so that we'll know which time to update). This will make a nice FUNCTION. For input the FUNCTION will need (1) the value we're looking for in the array, (2) the array, and (3) the length of the array. The value of the FUNCTION will be 0 if the item we're searching for isn't in the array; if the item is in the array, the FUNCTION's value will be the location of the item. This FUNCTION is written below.

```
            INTEGER FUNCTION LOCATE (ITEM, ARRAY, N)
            INTEGER ITEM, N, ARRAY(N)
COMMENT:  SET 'LOCATE' SO THAT ARRAY(LOCATE) .EQ. ITEM.
C             IF 'ITEM' IS NOT IN 'ARRAY', SET 'LOCATE' TO ZERO.
            LOCATE = 1
 100    IF ( ARRAY(LOCATE) .EQ. ITEM )  RETURN
            LOCATE = LOCATE + 1
            IF ( LOCATE .LE. N )  GO TO 100
            LOCATE = 0
            RETURN
            END
```

Now we're ready to write the program. We use an array CAR to store the car numbers, and an array TIME to store the corresponding time. In addition, we need a memory cell HOWMNY to keep track of the number of cars in the current standings.

```
COMMENT:  DRAG RACE SCOREBOARD
          INTEGER C, CAR(200), HOWMNY, L, LOCATE, RUN
          REAL T, TIME(200), AMIN1
C         IN THE BEGINNING, NO RUNS HAVE BEEN MADE, AND THERE
C         ARE NO CARS IN THE STANDINGS (UNLESS SOMEONE HAS PAID
C         OFF THE GUY WHO RUNS THE SCOREBOARD).
          RUN = 0
          HOWMNY = 0
C         GET INFO  ON NEXT HIGH EXCITEMENT, THRILL-A-MINUTE RUN
 100    READ, C, T
C         NEGATIVE CAR NUMBER INDICATES RACES ARE OVER.
          IF ( C .LT. 0 )  GO TO 500
          RUN = RUN + 1
C         HAS CAR NUMBER C RUN BEFORE?
          L = 0
          IF ( HOWMNY .GT. 0 )  L = LOCATE(C,CAR,HOWMNY)
          IF ( L .EQ. 0 )  GO TO 200
C            YES, IT HAS.  UPDATE ITS TIME.
             TIME(L) = AMIN1(T,TIME(L))
             GO TO 300
C            NO, IT HASN'T.  ADD IT IN.
 200       HOWMNY = HOWMNY + 1
           IF ( HOWMNY .LE. 200 )  GO TO 210
             PRINT, 'TOO MANY DRAG RACERS '
             STOP
 210       CAR (HOWMNY) = C
           TIME(HOWMNY) = T
```

```
C       ARRANGE CARS ACCORDING TO CURRENT STANDING
C         (USE SUBROUTINE 'SORT' OF SECTION 7 4, MODIFIED  TO
C         ARRANGE VALUES OF KEYS INTO  INCREASING ORDER.)
  300     CALL SORT (TIME,CAR,HOWMNY)
C         PRINT STANDINGS, CHECKING FOR DISQUALIFIED CARS.
          PRINT, ' '
          PRINT, '        STANDING     CAR              TIME'
          C = 1
  400     IF ( TIME(C) .LE. 99.0 )
     +                PRINT, C,CAR(C),'     ',TIME(C)
  410     IF ( TIME(C) .GT. 99.0 )  PRINT, C, CAR(C), 'DISQ.'
          C = C+1
          IF ( C .LE. HOWMNY )  GO TO 400
C         DEAL WITH THE NEXT THRILLING RUN
          GO TO 100
  500  PRINT, ' '
       PRINT, 'THE WINNER IS CAR', CAR(1)
       PRINT, 'ELAPSED TIME:', TIME(1)
       STOP
       END
```

data

```
11 99.9
92 99.9
83 1.0
92 1.1
21 1.3
83 1.4
64 99.9
64 99.9
55 5.0
55 1.0
-1 0.0
```

output

```
    STANDING        CAR              TIME
       1            11 DISQ.


    STANDING        CAR              TIME
       1            11 DISQ.
       2            92 DISQ.


    STANDING        CAR              TIME
       1            83           0.1000000E 01
       2            92 DISQ.
       3            11 DISQ.


    STANDING        CAR              TIME
       1            83           0.1000000E 01
       2            92           0.1100000E 01
       3            11 DISQ.


    STANDING        CAR              TIME
       1            83           0.1000000E 01
       2            92           0.1100000E 01
       3            21           0.1300000E 01
       4            11 DISQ.


    STANDING        CAR              TIME
       1            83           0.1000000E 01
       2            92           0.1100000E 01
       3            21           0.1300000E 01
       4            11 DISQ.
```

```
STANDING        CAR              TIME
    1            83        0.1000000E 01
    2            92        0.1100000E 01
    3            21        0.1300000E 01
    4            11 DISQ.
    5            64 DISQ.

STANDING        CAR              TIME
    1            83        0.1000000E 01
    2            92        0.1100000E 01
    3            21        0.1300000E 01
    4            11 DISQ.
    5            64 DISQ.

STANDING        CAR              TIME
    1            83        0.1000000E 01
    2            92        0.1100000E 01
    3            21        0.1300000E 01
    4            55        0.5000000E 01
    5            64 DISQ.
    6            11 DISQ.

STANDING        CAR              TIME
    1            83        0.1000000E 01
    2            55        0.1000000E 01
    3            92        0.1100000E 01
    4            21        0.1300000E 01
    5            64 DISQ.
    6            11 DISQ.

THE WINNER IS CAR            83
ELAPSED TIME:    0.1000000E 01
```

EXERCISES 9 3

1 Add in a test to see if there was a tie for first place—if there was, PRINT the cars that tied and their elapsed time.

2 What else would have to be done if, when a car has been disqualified, the time on his card was punched as 0 instead of 100.?

3 Look at statements 400 and 410 in the program. Is this a good or bad practice?

4 Improve the readability of the drag race program by replacing the sections of the program entitled "PRINT STANDINGS, CHECKING FOR DISQUALIFIED CARS" with a subprogram.

5 SUBROUTINE SORT of Section 7 4 was written for INTEGER values but we are sorting REALs here. What needs to be changed in the SUB-ROUTINE to make it applicable here?

Section 9 4

Permutations

There is a big demand these days for acronyms. Coming up with a good acronym is a lengthy process, so it would be nice if we could develop a computer program to do part of the work, preferably the most tedious and uninteresting part. Since an acronym is just some arrangement of letters or syllables each of which is the first part of a key word in the phrase you are trying to represent, it might be handy to have a list of all the different ways in which these letters or syllables can be written. While reading through such a list, you might come across a particularly appealing arrangement. Then you could check to see if the corresponding arrangement of the key words would make sense. If so, you have come up with a nice acronym.

> *acronym: a word formed from the initial letters or syllables of a compound term. For example, SOB is an acronym for Save Our Bay, a now defunct civic organization.*

The idea of the program is simple: its input would be a list of letters and/or syllables from the key words and its output should be all the possible orderings of the input list. If the input list is stored in an array, then we can identify each element of the list by a number, namely the subscript of the array element in which it is stored. All we need to do is write a program which rearranges these subscripts into all their possible orderings.

It is natural to write down the various orderings or **permutations** of integers in **lexical** or dictionary sequence. In this sequence, the permutation 1 2 4 5 3 would come before the permutation 1 2 5 3 4 because, although the first two digits are the same, the third digits differ and the third digit of the second permutation is larger than that of the first permutation. Our goal is to write a SUBROUTINE whose input is a list of INTEGERs in some order and whose output is that same list in a rearranged order. The rearrangement is to be made so that the output list is the next permutation in the lexical sequence from the input list. Once we have this SUBROUTINE, our acronym generating program will be easy to write.

The question is, given a certain permutation, how do you rearrange it so that it becomes the next permutation in the lexical sequence? This is not a trivial question, but if you think carefully, you will notice that what you want to change is the tail end (suffix) of the permutation because changes in digits at the upper (left-hand) end of a permutation make larger changes in its lexical sequence than changes at the right-hand end. Therefore, to make the smallest increase in the lexical sequence, we must rearrange the shortest suffix in which it is possible to make a lexical increase. It is not possible to make a lexical increase in a suffix in

·

which the digits are already in decreasing order because the only thing we can do to change a suffix is to interchange some of the integers that make it up, and any change would decrease that suffix's lexical position. Hence, we want to pick the shortest suffix in which the digits are *not* in decreasing order.

For example, consider the permutation 1 2 3 5 4. The suffix 5 4 is already in decreasing order and therefore the suffix can't be increased. However, the suffix 3 5 4 isn't in decreasing order so we can increase it. How do we increase it so as to make the smallest possible increase (the next larger suffix)? The answer is, we interchange its first digit with the next larger digit in the suffix and arrange the remainder of the suffix in increasing order. Thus the suffix 3 5 4 would be changed to 4 3 5: first 3 is exchanged with 4, the next larger digit in the suffix, and then the remainder 5 3 is arranged in increasing order, 4 3 5. Therefore 1 2 4 3 5 is the next permutation after 1 2 3 5 4.

Now we see how to write the SUBROUTINE. It simply examines the input permutation from right to left until it finds a digit which is smaller than the one to its right. Then it interchanges that digit with the next larger one to its right and rearranges the digits to the right of its original location into increasing order.

The following SUBROUTINE and associated subprograms accomplish this task. There is one additional output parameter which is .TRUE. if a new permutation was generated and .FALSE. if the input permutation could not be increased.

```
        SUBROUTINE PERM (LIST, N, NEW PRM)
        INTEGER N, LIST(N)
        LOGICAL NEW PRM
COMMENT:  THE N-DIGIT PERMUTATION STORED IN THE ARRAY 'LIST'
C         WILL BE REARRANGED INTO THE NEXT PERMUTATION IN THE
C         LEXICAL SEQUENCE.  IF THIS IS NOT POSSIBLE, THEN
C         'NEW PRM' WILL BE ASSIGNED THE VALUE .FALSE.
C
        INTEGER SUFFIX
        INTEGER NXTLGR
        INTEGER K, L, H
        NEWPRM = .FALSE.
        K = SUFFIX (LIST,N)
        IF(K.LE.0)RETURN
        NEW PRM = .TRUE.
        L=NXTLGR(K,LIST,N)
        H=LIST(K)
        LIST(K) = LIST(L)
        LIST(L) = H
        CALL REVRSE(K+1, LIST, N)
        RETURN
        END

        INTEGER FUNCTION SUFFIX (LIST,N)
        INTEGER N, LIST(N)
COMMENT:  THE FUNCTION 'SUFFIX' COMPUTES THE SUBSCRIPT
C         POINTING TO THE LONGEST DECREASING SUFFIX OF LIST
        SUFFIX = N-1
10      IF ( SUFFIX .LE. 0) RETURN
        IF (LIST(SUFFIX) .LT. LIST(SUFFIX+1))RETURN
          SUFFIX = SUFFIX-1
          GO TO 10
        END
```

```
      INTEGER FUNCTION NXTLGR(SX,LIST,N)
      INTEGER SX,N,LIST(N)
      NXTLGR = SX+1
10    IF(NXTLGR .GE.N) RETURN
      IF(LIST(NXTLGR+1) .LT. LIST(SX)) RETURN
        NXTLGR = NXTLGR +1
        GO TO 10
      END

      SUBROUTINE REVRSE(SX,LIST,N)
      INTEGER SX,N,LIST(N)
      INTEGER MIDDLE, H, K
      MIDDLE = (SX+N)/2
      K = SX
      L=N
10    H = LIST(SX)
      LIST(SX ) = LIST(L)
      LIST(L) = H
      K = K+1
      L = L-1
      IF ( K .LE. MIDDLE )  GO TO 10
      RETURN
      END
```

Now that we have the permutation generator, we can write our program to
make a list of all possible acronyms on a given set of symbols.

```
COMMENT:  'LTRSYL' WILL BE USED TO STORE THE LETTERS AND
C           SYLLABLES TO BE USED IN THE ACRONYM.
C           'P' WILL BE USED TO STORE THE PERMUTATIONS OF
C           SUBSCRIPTS OF 'LTRSYL'.
      CHARACTER*4 LTRSYL(20)
      INTEGER P(20), LEN, I
      LOGICAL ANOTHR
C     GET SYLLABLES FROM DATA CARDS
      LEN = 0
10    READ, LTRSYL(LEN+1)
        IF ( LTRSYL(LEN+1) .EQ. '    ' )  GOTO 20
        LEN = LEN + 1
        P(LEN) = LEN
        GO TO 10
C     GENERATE ACRONYMS, ONE PERMUTATION AFTER ANOTHER
20    PRINT, (LTRSYL(P(I)), I=1,LEN)
      CALL PERM (P,LEN,ANOTHR)
        IF ( ANOTHR )  GO TO 20
      STOP
      END
```

data

```
'TRAN'
'FORM'
'WATE'
'    '
```

output

```
TRAN FORM WATE
TRAN WATE FORM
FORM TRAN WATE
FORM WATE TRAN
WATE TRAN FORM
WATE FORM TRAN
```

We ran this program trying to find an acronym for a translator devised at Waterloo, Canada which takes mathematical formulas and changes them to a form which makes sense to a computer. We decided the appropriate key word syllables would be TRAN for translator, FORM for formula, and WATE for Waterloo. You can see the results in the output from the program.

EXERCISES 9 4

1 List these permutations of the numbers from 1 to 5 in increasing lexical order.

1	2	3	4	5
2	3	5	4	1
5	4	2	3	1
5	4	3	1	2
3	2	5	4	1

2 By listing all the permutations of three numbers, verify that all possible acronyms based on WATE, TRAN and FORM are listed above.

PROBLEMS 9

1 READ a value for *m* (the number of grades for each student); READ in *m* grades for each student, compute each student's average, and store the average grades in a one-dimensional array; arrange the array of average grades in descending order and write out the ordered array; calculate and PRINT (with appropriate labeling) the number of average scores which fall in each percentile, 0 to 10, 10 to 20, . . . , 90 to 100.

2 Compare the sorting method of Section 7 4 with the bubble sort (described below) by generating 100 random numbers, sorting them each way, and counting how many times the routines compare pairs of numbers.

The bubble sort works like this: go through the array one spot at a time, comparing the current element with the next and reversing their order if the first is larger than the second. Keep doing this until you have gone completely through the array. Now go through the array again. Keep making passes through the array until you make one complete pass which requires no reversals. At that point you're finished—the array is in order.

PRINT the original numbers, the sorted numbers, and the number of comparisons made by the two different sorting methods. Each sorting method should be a SUBROUTINE.

3 Write a program which assigns grades. The input will be a bunch of cards each one of which contains a student's name and five scores. Your program should compute each student's average score and PRINT his name, grades, average score, and letter grade. Compute the letter grade by the time-honored formula

$$90 - 100 = A$$
$$80 - 89 \ = B$$
$$70 - 79 \ = C$$
$$60 - 69 \ = D$$
$$\text{lower} \quad = F$$

4 Suppose that we have several sets of data from laboratory experiments. Each set of data is composed of n_1 measurements on each of n_2 animals where n_1 and n_2 may vary from one data set to another. Our task is to process each set of data, finding the average measurement for each animal, and writing out the averages in descending order in a form similar to that shown here:

DATA SET 1
5 ANIMALS
6 MEASUREMENTS PER ANIMAL

AVERAGES IN DESCENDING ORDER	ANIMAL NUMBER
43.5	4
39.3	5
30.5	2
30.3	3
26.6	1

DATA SET 2
8 ANIMALS
9 MEASUREMENTS PER ANIMAL

.
.
.

etc.

Make up your own experiments and collect your own data. Write the program in such a way that the data cards are not hard to prepare.

5 A certain company rents time on five of its machines. Each time a customer uses a machine, he turns in a time card. At the first of each month the company sends out bills for the use of the machines for the past month.

The rates on the machines are different for different customers and for different time periods during the day. Therefore, your first input will be 10 price cards, each card specifying a price code (00–09) and the cost per hour for the price code.

You are to compute a bill for each customer to include the following information:

> customer number
> machine number
> total hours and total cost for each machine used by the customer
> total cost for the customer

The time cards for the month are sorted by customer number but not by machine and contain the following information:

> customer number (xxxxxxx)
> price code (xx)
> machine number (1, 2, 3, 4, or 5)
> time in (xx. xx)
> time out (xx.xx)

Assume the time is given to the nearest hundredth of an hour on the 24 hour clock (*e.g.*, 20.25 means 8:15 p.m.)

6   Bicycle Registration

You are a programmer for a progressive college town which has a great deal of bicycle thievery. The town council decides to require everyone to register his or her bicycle so that there will be some chance of restoring captured stolen bikes to their original owners. Your job, should you decide to accept it, is to write a program which maintains and searches the data on bicycles. Your program must accept data cards of two different types:

new registrations

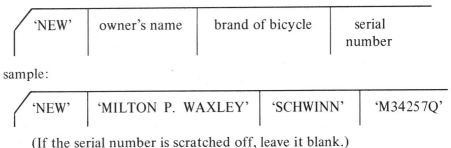

sample:

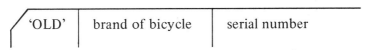

(If the serial number is scratched off, leave it blank.)

found bicycles

| 'OLD' | brand of bicycle | serial number |

Obviously, if a 'NEW' card comes in, you just add the information in. If an 'OLD' card comes in, there are two different situations: first, if the serial number of the recovered bike is known, you search the data and if such a bike has been registered, print the owner's name (so he can be notified). If the serial number was scratched off, your program should print the names of everyone who owns that type of bike so they can be asked if the recovered bike is theirs.

7   Each of the following data cards has three pieces of information; the name of a football player, his number and his weight. Write a program to read and print the arrays in four different orders. First in the original order, second in alphabetical order using the player's last names, third in order of their numbers, and fourth in order of their weights.

Data:

SQUARE, JOHNNY	27	170
DUDA, PAUL	31	200
JULIANA, PAT	9	180
BLACKFORD, BOB	5	183
WILSON, MIKE	25	197
CASWELL, GERALD	95	240
DRISCOLL, MARK	8	175
BABICH, FRED	80	220
BATTLE, GREG	46	195
MONTGOMERY, CHARLES	63	255
ST. CLAIR, STEVE	87	195
STEWART, GUY	18	170
MOSS, JESSE	19	190
O'ROURKE, DAN	22	190

8   Bank Accounts

Your program will create and keep track of bank accounts for up to 20 people. For each person you will keep track of (1) the person's name, (2) the balance in his account, and (3) the number of withdrawals or deposits. A person making a deposit will correspond to a data card such as

'MARY MOONY'   +303.02

and a withdrawal will correspond to a card like

'CAPT. BEEFHEART'   −2.00

Each time your program reads a card, you must check to see if there is an account for that person, and if not, create a new entry. If there already is an account, add or subtract the deposit or withdrawal and add one to the number of transactions. After there are no more data cards to read, your program should print the information it has compiled about each account.

Data:

FRANK FEEBLES	+ 100.00
RALPH WILLIAMS	+1901.74
RALPH WILLIAMS	+2794.25
BETTY FURNACE	+ 3.01
RALPH WILLIAMS	+ 470.00
HARRY IGNAZ	+ 25.00
FRANK FEEBLES	− 35.00
JESS UNRUH	+ 11.00
WAYNE ASPINALL	+ 342.00
RALPH WILLIAMS	− 400.00
JESS UNRUH	−5243.00
MINNEY MOOS	+ 35.75
RALPH WILLIAMS	+7500.20
WAYNE ASPINALL	− .06
BETTY FURNACE	+ 3.01

HINT: Use three arrays to keep track of the accounts so that after the first 3 cards have been read, the arrays look like the following:

	NAME	BAL	TRANS
1	'FRANK FEEBLES'	100.00	1
2	'RALPH WILLIAMS'	4695.99	2
3			
4			

9 a Write a LOGICAL FUNCTION which takes the value .TRUE. if its INTEGER argument is a perfect square. (A number n is a perfect square if there is some other number k such that $n = k^2$).

b Using nested loops (and the FUNCTION of part a), write a program which PRINTs all the Pythagorean triples a, b, c, with a and b between 1 and 50. (A Pythagorean triple is three integers a, b, and c such that $a^2 + b^2 = c^2$.)

c Write a program which PRINTs out all of the (rare) Fermatean triples a, b, c, with a and b between 1 and 50. (A Fermatean triple is three integers a, b, and c such that $a^3 + b^3 = c^3$.)

10 Write a program which READs the coefficients of a linear system of equations and solves the system by Gaussian elimination. (Almost any numerical analysis book in the library will describe Gaussian elimination.)

10 I/O WITH FORMAT

Section 10 1

Describing PRINTed Lines

A PRINT statement, as you know, tells the computer what values to print. Until now we have been depending on the computer to decide how to represent these values—that is, how many spaces to use, whether or not to use scientific notation for REALs, and so on. You probably haven't been particularly concerned about this slight lack of control over your output, but as you progress, you will find it increasingly annoying to find your REAL output always printed in scientific notation, disturbing to be able to fit only a dozen INTEGERs on one line, even though they're only one digit each, and extremely vexing always to find spaces between adjacent CHARACTER constants that you wanted to bump together on the printed line. It is at this point, when the lack of control really starts to bug you, that you'll want to learn about FORMATs.

A FORMAT statement is used in conjunction with a PRINT statement to describe the details of the line to be printed. The PRINT statement specifies what values to put on the line and the FORMAT describes where to put them. Let's look at an example.

```
      INTEGER A/27/
      REAL B/729.2/
      LOGICAL C/.TRUE./
      PRINT 1000, A,B,C
 1000 FORMAT(' ', G5.0, G10.3, G2.0)
      STOP
      END
```

output

*bbb*27*bb*729.*bbbbb*T

Fortran Charlie prepare[s]
to learn FORMATs (It'[s]
a whole 'nother languag[e])

> *b means blank*

As you see in the example, a PRINT statement which uses a FORMAT designates the label of that FORMAT immediately after the word PRINT. All FORMAT statements must have labels so that the corresponding I/O statement can refer to them. This is necessary because the FORMAT may appear *anywhere* in the program; it doesn't have to be right next to the I/O statement which uses it.

The FORMAT describes a line to be printed by a parenthesized list of **FORMAT descriptors.** Each element in the PRINT list is matched with a corresponding entry, called a **data descriptor**, in the FORMAT. In our example above the first data descriptor, G5.0, is matched with memory cell A in the PRINT list, the second, G10.3, with B, and the third, G2.0, with C. These data descriptors tell the computer how much room on the line to use for printing the value.

FORMATted PRINT statement

forms
> PRINT *s, list*
> PRINT *s*
> *s* is the statement label of a FORMAT statement
> *list* consists of one or more constants, memory cell names, or expressions, separated by commas (*i.e., list* is an output list)

meaning
> Print the values from *list* using the FORMAT *s*. If *list* is omitted, the FORMAT normally contains only literal descriptors to be printed; all descriptors beyond the first data descriptor will be ignored if *list* is omitted.

warning
> There is not a comma between PRINT and *s*. If one were allowed, there would be no way for the compiler to tell whether PRINT, 1000, 2 meant "PRINT the value 1000 followed by the value 2 according to the FORMAT-free conventions" or "PRINT the value 2 according to the FORMAT with label 1000". If you mean the latter, use PRINT 1000, 2.

examples
```
PRINT 1000, A, B, C
PRINT 2000
PRINT 3000, A+B, 37.2, T, BETA
```

In our example we have told the computer to use 17 spaces in all. For the first value, A, it is to use 5 spaces on the line, for the second, B, 10 spaces, and for the third, C, 2 spaces. Of course, the value of A has only two digits, not five. Therefore, the computer needs only two of the spaces indicated in the data descriptor; the other three are left blank. The spaces the computer uses to print an INTEGER value (like A) are *always* the *rightmost* spaces. That is, the value is *right justified* in the field specified by the data descriptor. Thus, the first part of the line printed in this case consists of three blanks, then 27. The second value in the PRINT list, B, corresponds to the second data descriptor, G10.3, and is a REAL. This is where the part of the data descriptor beyond the decimal point comes into play. In this case, it says to print REALs rounded to 3 significant digits. In general, a G data

---

significant digits: The number 1001.70 has six significant digits. The numbers 00147.2 and 00.001570 have four significant digits. Rounded to two significant digits, these numbers are 1000., 150., and .0016 respectively. Rounding a number to n significant digits amounts to finding the closest approximation with n or fewer nonzero digits.

---

descriptor takes the form G*w.d* where *w* is the number of spaces to be used to print the corresponding value in the PRINT list and *d* is the number of significant digits desired if the value is a REAL. The rightmost four spaces in a REAL data field are reserved for a decimal point shift factor if one is necessary to make the number fit into *w* spaces. Thus, scientific notation is used for REALs only if it is needed.

The third valué in the PRINT list, the LOGICAL memory cell C, corresponds to the data descriptor G2.0. As with INTEGERs, the part of the descriptor beyond the decimal point isn't needed and the value, represented by T for .TRUE. or F for .FALSE., is right justified in the field. Putting this all together, you can see why the line printed has three blanks, then 27, then two blanks and 729., followed by four blanks, one more blank, and finally a T.

But what about the mysterious CHARACTER*1 constant ' ' at the beginning of the FORMAT? It is there because the FORMAT must not only describe the line to be printed, it must also say where to put the line on the page. There are five choices:

' ' (blank) single space from previous line
'0' (zero) double space from previous line
'1' skip to the top of the next page
'+' overprint previous line
'−' triple space from previous line

Our example uses the single space option. The character at the beginning of the FORMAT is known as the **carriage control** character because of its meaning for the line printer. It is important to understand the process in some detail in order to interpret results in case you forget the carriage control character. What happens is this: the computer sends an entire line of characters to the printer. In our example the computer sends the line *bbbb27bb729.bbbbbT* (*b* stands for blank) which includes the blank character at the beginning as specified by the carriage control character in the FORMAT. No matter where the first character on the line came from, the printer removes it and uses it to decide how far to move the paper before printing. The printer never prints the first character on the line sent to it. This is why the line printed in our example begins with three instead of four blanks. It's possible, of course, to specify a blank carriage control character implicitly, simply by putting an extra space in the field described by the first data descriptor. In our example this would amount to leaving off the ' ' and changing the first data descriptor from G5.0 to G6.0. But we feel that it is much wiser to make all carriage control *explicit* in the FORMAT. Your program will be clearer, your thinking will be straighter, and you'll get fewer surprises in your output.

> *b*   *In picturing printed lines or punched cards where spacing is critical, we'll use the symbol b for the blank character.*

The most important thing to remember from this section about formatted output is that the FORMAT describes the layout of the line to be printed, first

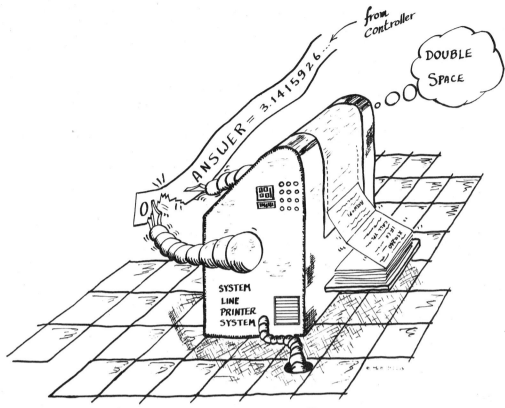

The printer rips off the first character on each line sent by the controller and uses it to decide how far to move the paper before printing.

with the carriage control character which says where on the page to put the line, and then with the data descriptors which say how many spaces to use to print the values on the line.

The second most important thing to remember is that each value in the PRINT list is matched with a data descriptor in the FORMAT. The matching proceeds left to right across the PRINT list and the list of data descriptors in the FORMAT.

The third most important thing to remember is the $Gw.d$ data descriptor. It can be used for any kind of numeric value and for LOGICAL values. It can't be used with CHARACTER values though. You'll see a data descriptor for them in Section 10 3.

EXERCISES 10 1

1 Describe precisely, including blanks, the line printed by the following PRINT statement

```
      PRINT 1001, 14, 37*2, 12*4-9*6
 1001 FORMAT (' ', G5.0, G3.0, G8.0)
```

2 Precisely what would be printed by the following program fragment?

```
      INTEGER A/10/, SQA, E
      SQA = A**2
      E = (A-SQA)*(-A)
      PRINT 1000, SQA, E, E/SQA, A-10
1000 FORMAT (' ', G4.0, G4.0, G5.0, G3.0)
      PRINT 2000, A
2000 FORMAT ('0',G10.0)
```

3 Write a PRINT statement and FORMAT which will print the line

$$bbbb47bbbbb102$$

at the top of a page.

4 What do you think the following PRINT statement would print?

```
      PRINT 3000, 4037, 10009428, 98
3000 FORMAT (' ', G6.0, G6.0, G6.0)
```

5 What would the following PRINT statement print?

```
      PRINT 4000, 4.9793E2, 42+9, 0.7932E-6
4000 FORMAT (' ', G11.2, G3.1, G11.4)
```

Section 10 2

Describing Data Cards

As you no doubt suspect, there are formatted READs as well as formatted PRINTs. The FORMAT used by a READ statement describes a data card rather than a printed line, but the idea is much the same. The FORMAT again says how much room the values on the card will take. There is no carriage control to worry

---

FORMATted READ statement

form
    READ *f, list*

    f is the statement label of a FORMAT statement
    list is a list of memory cell names separated by commas (*i.e.,* an input list)

meaning
    Values on data cards described by the FORMAT *f* are placed into the memory cells in *list*

warning
    There is no comma between READ and *f*.

---

about; each time the computer performs a READ statement, it automatically starts on a new data card. In the example below,

```
      INTEGER A, B, C, D
      READ 1000, A,B,C,D
1000 FORMAT (G1.0, G3.0, G2.0, G5.0)
```

data

$7b13b9b-492$

the READ statement takes four values from the data card. According to the FORMAT the first value must be in column 1 (A corresponds to G1.0) the second in the next three columns, columns 2 to 4 (B corresponds to G3.0), the third in columns 5 and 6, (C corresponds to G2.0), and the fourth in the next five columns, columns 7 to 11, (D corresponds to G5.0). The values store; in the memory cells are pictured below.

A [7]   B [13]   C [9]   D [−492]

It is important to notice that the values on the data card are right justified in the fields specified by the data descriptors in the FORMAT. Since the memory cells in the READ list are INTEGERs, the corresponding fields on the data card are known as **numeric fields.** In a numeric field a blank is interpreted as the digit zero. If the numbers aren't right justified, we come up with bigger numbers than we expected. For example, if the data card for the above READ had been $713bb9b$ -492, then memory cell B would have been given the value 130 instead of 13 because columns 2 to 4 contain $13b$ and the blank would be interpreted as a zero.

When the Gw.d descriptor is used in an input FORMAT, the .d part is ignored unless the decimal point in a REAL value on the card is omitted. What happens in this bizarre circumstance will be described in Section 3. Until then always include the decimal point in REAL constants on data cards. The Gw.d descriptor may be associated with numeric and LOGICAL memory cells only, not CHARACTER memory cells. With INTEGER and LOGICAL memory cells, the .d part is ignored.

> *numeric data field: a field on a data card corresponding to a numeric data descriptor in the* FORMAT. *In numeric fields blanks are interpreted as zeros.*

EXERCISES 10 2

1 Write a FORMAT to describe a data card which contains INTEGERs in columns 1–10, columns 11–25, and columns 26–30.

2 Make up a data card which would give the values 14, 137, 4963, and −192 to G, A, S, and P respectively if read by the following program fragment.

```
      READ 1000, G, A, S, P
1000 FORMAT (G3.0, G3.0, G5.0, G5.0)
```

3 What values would be placed in A, B, and C respectively if the following program fragment read a data card containing 1b34b927.1 starting in column 1?

```
      REAL C
      INTEGER A, B
      READ 3000, A, B, C
3000 FORMAT (G1.0,G3.0,G6.0)
```

4 What values would A, B, and C above get if the FORMAT were as below?

```
3000 FORMAT (G3.0,G4.0,G7.0)
```

5 What values would D, E, and F get if the following program fragment read a data card containing

$$bbb349.7bb4.7E-2bb9.3E4b$$

starting in column 1?

```
      READ 1000, D,E,F
1000 FORMAT (G8.0,G8.0,G8.0)
```

Section 10 3

Data Descriptors

So far we have seen only one data descriptor, the G$w.d$ descriptor. It is a fairly forgiving, fairly general descriptor. Using it gives you more control than using the format-free input/output that WATFIV provides. In this section we go the last step to complete control.

There are eight different data descriptors which can be used in FORMATs. This provides a considerable amount of freedom in the choice of input and output forms. As you have seen earlier in this chapter, data descriptors in the FORMAT are matched one by one with elements of the I/O list. With an input list, the data descriptor tells the computer how to interpret the characters on the data card; with output, it determines the form of the character string which will represent the corresponding value in the output list. In either case the data descriptor directs a conversion between an *external* character string and an *internal* computer representation of data.

Each data descriptor is associated with only one data type. (The primary exception is the G descriptor you've already seen which may be associated with INTEGER, REAL, DOUBLE PRECISION, or LOGICAL data.) Therefore, in the left to right matching of I/O list elements with data descriptors, the type of each element must correspond to the respective data descriptor in the FORMAT. Otherwise an error occurs.

In what follows, w stands for an unsigned INTEGER constant and denotes the field width associated with a data descriptor (that is, the number of characters to be included in the conversion between external and internal forms); d is also an unsigned INTEGER constant which has different meanings in different contexts but usually has to do with the number of decimal places in the external representation of the data value.

Iw (INTEGER)

input

An external string of w or fewer digits which may include a preceding sign (+ or −) to be converted to as an INTEGER constant. As such it should contain no characters other than digits, although the first non-blank character in the field may be a + or − sign. Any blanks in the field will be interpreted as zero digits.

external	I6	internal
bb1042		1042
bbb−27		−27
−27bbb		−27000
bb+bb6		6
−3bb4b		−30040
bbbbbb		0
b−3+44		illegal
bb3.14		illegal

> The descriptor Iw has exactly the same effect that Gw.d does when it is dealing with INTEGERs.

output

An internal INTEGER value is converted to a string of w characters. If the value is negative, the digits will be preceded by a minus sign. If the value does not use up all w characters in the field, the number is right justified in the field with blank fill to the left. If the value is too large to fit in a field of width w, the field is filled instead with asterisks. If the value involves a memory cell which has not yet been given a value, the field is filled with U's.

internal	I6	external
1042		bb1042
−27		bbb−27
−27000		−27000
6		bbbbb6
−30040		−30040
0		bbbbb0
−300400		******
3.14		illegal

Fw.d   (REAL or DOUBLE PRECISION)

input

The external character string in the field of width w is interpreted as a REAL or DOUBLE PRECISION constant. As such it may be preceded by a + or − sign and contain a decimal point. If the decimal point is not present, it is assumed to precede the d rightmost characters in the field (d must be smaller than w). The number may be written in scientific notation (E− or D− notation). All blank characters are interpreted as zeros.

external	F 6.2	internal
bb3.14		3.14
b−2.79		−2.79
+b90.1		90.1
0.1234		0.1234
bbb372		3.72
bb372b		37.20
9001+1		900.1
2.1E−3		0.0021

> The descriptor **Fw.d** has a different effect on output than does **Gw.d** operating on REALs. **Fw.d** produces a number with d digits to the right of the decimal, **Gw.d** produces a number with d significant digits.

output

An internal REAL value is converted to a character string of length w. The value is rounded (not truncated) to d decimal places (digits beyond the decimal point). If the external value has fewer than w characters, including the decimal point and a possible minus sign, then the number is right justified and the field is blank filled to the left. If the number is too large to fit into w character positions, the field is filled with asterisks. The field is filled with U's if the value involves a memory cell which hasn't been given a value.

internal	F 6.2	external
3.14		bb3.14
−2.79		b−2.79
90.1		b90.10
$49.2*10^{-3}$		bb0.05
$49.2*10^{-6}$		bb0.00
0.0000		bb0.00
$49.2*10^{6}$		******
3927		illegal

Ew.d   (REAL)

input

The effect is the same as F$w.d$ if the external value isn't written in scientific notation. If it is written in scientific notation, then the decimal point shift factor must be right justified in the field; otherwise, the blanks following it will be interpreted as zeros, thus increasing the shift by factors of ten. If a sign is included with the decimal point shift factors, as in 1.7E−6, and 4.932E+8, then the E may be omitted to save room in the data field In addition, the decimal point may be omitted from the number, but, if so, it is implicitly placed d places to the left of the decimal point shift factor. The following examples should clarify the myriad cases.

external	E7.2	internal
bb3.141		3.141
bbb3.14		3.14
$bbbb$314		3.14
3.14E00		3.14
3.14E−2		.0314
b314E−2		.0314
bb314−2		.0314
314b+2b		$31.40*10^{20}$

output

The REAL value in the corresponding memory cell is output in scientific notation, rounded to d significant digits. The rightmost four spaces in the output field of width w are used for the decimal point shift factor printed in the form Ebxx or E–xx where each x is a single digit, and b is a blank. The number is printed in the $d+3$ spaces to the left of the decimal point shift factor in the form $b0.f$ or −$0.f$ where f is a d digit unsigned INTEGER. The leftmost $w−(d+7)$ spaces are left blank. As you can see, w should be at least as large as $d+7$ to allow enough room for the number. As usual U's fill the field if the value is undefined.

internal	E10.2	external
3.168		bb0.32Eb01
$492.1*10^{-23}$		bb0.49E−21
−3987.12		b−0.40Eb04
3749		illegal

FORMAT Fatigue Sets In

Dw.d   (DOUBLE PRECISION)

input

The input field is interpreted as in the E data descriptor except that E's in the data field must be D's instead, and the corresponding memory cell in the input list should be of type DOUBLE PRECISION (REAL*8).

external	D16.9	internal
1.7*bbbbbbbbbbbbb*		1.700000000000000
1.23456789012345		1.234567890123450
*bbbbbbbb*4.92D–3		.004920000000000000
*bbbbb*5123456789		5.123456789000000

output

The output form of a DOUBLE PRECISION value under a D data descriptor is like that of a REAL under an E descriptor except that a D instead of an E separates the number from the decimal point shift factor.

COMPLEX

There is no data descriptor specifically for COMPLEX values. A COMPLEX or COMPLEX*16 memory cell is treated, in FORMATs, as if it were two REAL or DOUBLE PRECISION memory cells respectively. That is, a COMPLEX memory cell in an I/O list is matched with *two* corresponding data descriptors in the FORMAT. In the program fragment below, the real part of ZETA is input under the F10.3 descriptor, and the imaginary part is matched with the E10.3 descriptor.

```
      INTEGER A, B
      COMPLEX ZETA
      READ 1000, A, ZETA, B
 1000 FORMAT (I10, F10.3, E10.3, I4)
```

data

*bbbbbbbb*10*bbbbbbbb*0.0*bbbbbbbb*1.0*bbbbbbbb*20

Lw   (LOGICAL)

input

The corresponding LOGICAL memory cell in the input list is given the value .TRUE. if the first non-blank character in the data field is a T. If the first non-blank character in the field is F, or if the entire field is blank, the cell is given the value .FALSE.

external	L6	internal
*bb*T*bbb*		.TRUE.
TURF*bb*		.TRUE.
*bbbbb*F		.FALSE.
F*bbbbb*		.FALSE.
*b*TRUE*b*		.TRUE.
bbbbbb		.FALSE.

output

The letter T or F is right justified with blank fill to the left if the value of the corresponding memory cell in the output list is .TRUE. or .FALSE. respectively. The field is filled with U's if the value is undefined. A right justified J is placed in the field if the value isn't a LOGICAL value. Rumor has it that the J stands for JUNK.

> The descriptor **Lw** *has exactly the same effect as the* **Gw.d** *descriptor when it is used with* LOGICAL*s.*

internal	**L6**	*external*
.TRUE.		*bbbbb*T
.FALSE.		*bbbbb*F
3.14		*bbbbb*J

Gw.d   (generalized INTEGER, REAL, DOUBLE PRECISION, or LOGICAL)

Most data descriptors can be used with only one data type. We have seen one exception, F, which can be used with both REAL and DOUBLE PRECISION data. The G data descriptor is another exception. It can be used to describe INTEGER, REAL, DOUBLE PRECISION, or LOGICAL values.

input

If the corresponding memory cell in the input list is REAL, then the G*w.d* descriptor acts like an F*w.d* descriptor; if DOUBLE PRECISION, then like D*w.d*; if INTEGER, then like I*w* (the *.d* is ignored and may be omitted); and if LOGICAL, then like L*w* (again, *.d* is ignored and may be omitted).

output

If the corresponding memory cell in the output list is INTEGER or LOGICAL, then the G*w.d* descriptor acts like the I*w* or L*w* descriptor respectively (the *.d* is ignored). If the memory cell is REAL or DOUBLE PRECISION, then the rightmost four spaces in the field of width *w* are reserved for a decimal point shift of the form E*bxx* or E–*xx* for REAL or D*bxx* or D–*xx* for DOUBLE PRECISION (each *x* is a single digit). If the number rounded to *d* significant digits will fit in the remaining *w*–4 leftmost spaces in the field, then the rightmost four spaces are left blank. On the other hand, if the number won't fit into *w*–4 spaces, then it is written with a decimal point shift factor (E or D notation, as appropriate). In this case the number itself is rounded to *d* significant digits and written in the form *bx.ys* or –*x.ys* where *x* is a single digit, *y* is *d*–1 digits, and *s* is the decimal point shift factor.

internal	**G11.4**	*external*
–1.7526843		*b*–1.753*bbbb*
–175268.43		*b*–1.753D*b*05
3.1416		*bb*3.142*bbbb*
0.000031416		*bb*3.142E–05
–1234567		*bbb*–1234567
.TRUE.		*bbbbbbbbbb*T

Aw (CHARACTER)

The **A** here stands for **alphameric**, another name for character strings. Normally this data descriptor is used only with the CHARACTER data type, but it may be used in connection with any type of memory cell. The result is that the value in the cell is interpreted as if it were a character string. For different types of cells, this amounts to different numbers of characters. A field on a data card corresponding to an A descriptor is a character field no matter what the data type of the corresponding input list element.

type	number of characters
CHARACTER	1
LOGICAL*1	1
INTEGER*2	2
INTEGER	4
REAL	4
LOGICAL	4
REAL*8	8
COMPLEX	8
COMPLEX*16	16
CHARACTER*n	n where $1 \leqslant n \leqslant 255$

> *In character fields blanks are legitimate characters and stand for blanks, not zeros.*

input

The w characters in the data field are placed into the corresponding memory cell in the input list. All characters in the field, blanks and single quotes included, are part of the character string placed into the cell. If the cell isn't large enough to hold all w characters, then only the rightmost w characters in the data field are placed in the cell. On the other hand, if the cell is large enough to hold more than w characters, then the w characters are placed into the leftmost part of the cell and blank characters are put into the remainder of the cell.

external	A2	internal		
		CHARACTER*2	*1	*3
AB		'AB'	'B'	'AB*b*'
b+		'*b*+'	'+'	'*b*+*b*'
X*b*		'X*b*'	'*b*'	'X*bb*'
12		'12'	'2'	'12*b*'

output

The w characters in the corresponding memory cell in the output list are written in the w space output field. If the memory cell has more than w characters, then only the leftmost w characters in the cell are written in the output field.

On the other hand, if the cell has fewer than *w* characters, then its characters are right justified in the output field with blank fill to the left. The field is filled with U's if the value is undefined.

internal	A5	external
'ABCDE'		ABCDE
'ABC'		*bb*ABC
'ABCDEFGH'		ABCDE
'12'		*bbb*12
'*bbbb*12'		*bbbbb*
'*bbbb*123'		*bbbb*1

Z*w* (hexadecimal)

Each value stored in the computer is actually represented as a string of *hexadecimal digits*. We denote the sixteen hexadecimal digits by the symbols 0123456789ABCDEF. We won't concern ourselves with the way the computer actually represents these hexadecimal digits. The important thing to understand is that every value, REAL, INTEGER, LOGICAL or whatever, is represented internally as some string of hexadecimal digits. Different data types have different numbers of digits in the internal representations. For example, INTEGER, REAL, and LOGICAL values are represented by eight hexadecimal digits, CHARACTER*n values by 2*n* hexadecimal digits, and COMPLEX and DOUBLE PRECISION (REAL*8) values by sixteen hexadecimal digits. The Z data descriptor is used when you want to communicate with the computer in terms of its internal hexadecimal representations. The external value will be written in terms of hexadecimal digits possibly preceded by blanks, but with no signs or other symbols.

input

The external value with *w* hexadecimal digits (blanks interpreted as zero digits) is placed into the corresponding memory cell in the input list. If *w* is smaller than the number of hexadecimal digits in the memory cell, the leftmost digits in the cell are set to zeros.

output

The hexadecimal digits in the corresponding memory cell are put into the *w* spaces in the output field. If *w* exceeds the number of digits in the memory cell, the leftmost spaces in the field are skipped. If *w* is smaller than the number of digits in the cell, then only the rightmost digits of the cell are output.

*s*P (scaling factor)

s is an unsigned INTEGER constant or a negative INTEGER constant.

The P scaling factor is not really a data descriptor in the sense we have been using the term. Instead of matching with an element of the I/O list and serving to describe the corresponding data item, it changes the effect of all succeeding REAL and DOUBLE PRECISION data descriptors in the FORMAT (that is, it alters the effect of F, E, D, and G data descriptors).

A P scaling factor is written immediately before an F, E, G, or D data descriptor (with no comma), *e.g.,* −2PF10.1 or 3PD11.3. If the data descriptor is modified by a replication factor (see Section 10 6), the P scaling factor must precede the replication factor. To remove the effects of a previous P scaling factor in a FORMAT, a new scaling factor can be included. The scaling factor 0P returns REAL and DOUBLE PRECISION data descriptors to their normal meanings.

input

REAL or DOUBLE PRECISION numbers written in an input field without decimal point shift factors (*i.e.,* without E or D) are rescaled by a factor of 10^{-s}. Thus, the relationship between the number in the data field and the stored value is

$$\text{internal value} = 10^{-s} * \text{external value}.$$

Numbers written in the input field *with* decimal point shift factors are not affected.

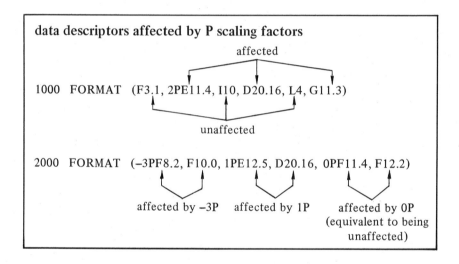

external	−2P	internal
1.952		195.2
397489.55		39748955.00000000
0.47		47.
3.72E−2		0.0372
4.951D01		49.51000000000000

external	2P	internal
492.1		4.921
3.72E−4		0.000372
4.951D01		49.51000000000000
397489.55		3974.895500000000

output

The *s*P scaling factor affects the meanings of different data descriptors in different ways.

effect on F: *external value = 10^s * internal value*

internal	3PF8.2	external
1.9873		b1987.30
−0.00314		bbb−3.14

effect on E and D: the decimal point is shifted *s* places (right for positive *s*, left for negative *s*) and the decimal point shift factor is reduced by *s*.

internal	2PE10.3	external
1.9873		bb19.9E−01
−0.00314		b−31.4E−04

effect on G: no effect unless the number must be written with a decimal point shift factor in which case the result is like that with E or D output.

Section 10 4

Literal Descriptors

Suppose you wanted to print a heading at the top of a page for, say, a checking account program. One way to do it would be as follows.

```
    PRINT 1000, 'CHECKING ACCOUNT SUMMARY'
1000 FORMAT ('1',A24)
```

Another way to do it is to place the heading directly in the FORMAT in the form of a **literal descriptor** as shown below.

```
    PRINT 1000
1000 FORMAT ('1', 'CHECKING ACCOUNT SUMMARY')
```

No doubt you can see a similarity between the notation for the carriage control character and the notation for the literal descriptor. This is no coincidence, of course. A literal descriptor is simply a character string whose contents are to be literally copied onto the printed line. Since the carriage control character is simply the first character on the line sent to the printer, it can be written conveniently as a literal descriptor in the FORMAT. Literal descriptors may be used at any point in a FORMAT to dress up the printed line. They don't correspond to any memory cell in the output list, but they do take up space on the printed line; thus they move the fields associated with succeeding data descriptors.

```
      REAL MILES/316.0/, GALLON/12.4/
      CHARACTER*20 BRAND/'VOLVO 244DL'/

COMMENT:  EQUIVALENT PRINT STATEMENTS

      PRINT 1000,'GAS MILEAGE',MILES/GALLON,' CAR ',BRAND
 1000 FORMAT(' ', A11, G10.3, A5, A20)

      PRINT 2000, MILES/GALLON, BRAND
 2000 FORMAT(' ', 'GAS MILEAGE', G10.3, ' CAR ', A20)

      PRINT 3000, MILES/GALLON, BRAND
 3000 FORMAT (' GAS MILEAGE', G10.3, ' CAR ', A20)

      STOP
      END



GAS MILEAGE  25.5     CAR VOLVO 244DL
GAS MILEAGE  25.5     CAR VOLVO 244DL
GAS MILEAGE  25.5     CAR VOLVO 244DL
```

EXERCISES 10 4

1 Describe precisely the printed line produced by each of the following PRINT statements.

```
      PRINT 1001
 1001 FORMAT ('1','SOME COMPUTATIONS')
      PRINT 2001, 493, 846, 493*846
 2001 FORMAT ('0', 'THE PRODUCT OF',I4,' AND',I4,' IS',I8)
      PRINT 3001, '493', '846', '493*846'
 3001 FORMAT (' ', 'THE PRODUCT OF',A4,' AND',A4,' IS',A8)
      PRINT 4001, 4392,'+',6947,'=', 4392+6947
 4001 FORMAT ('0THE SUM',I5,A1,I4,A1,I5)
      STOP
      END
```

2 Write a PRINT statement (with FORMAT) which will print the values of the REAL memory cells A and B along with a message indicating the values involved and the sum of the values, double spaced from the previous line.

Section 10 5

Spacing Descriptors

If you want to leave spaces on a printed line, you already know at least two ways to do it. You can put blank CHARACTER constants in the PRINT list or blank literal descriptors in the FORMAT. To avoid punching long strings of blanks, you can include an X descriptor in the FORMAT instead. It simply consists of an X preceded by an unsigned INTEGER constant indicating the number of blanks desired. For example, 10X means to leave ten spaces on the printed line. Like literal descriptors, X descriptors aren't matched with values in the PRINT list.

X descriptors may also be used in input FORMATs to cause the READ statement to ignore certain fields on the card.

---

nX

    n is an unsigned INTEGER constant

input

    The next n spaces on the data card are ignored.

```
        INTEGER A,B
        READ 1000, A, B
   1000  FORMAT(5X,G2.0,5X,G3.0)
```

    data card

        HT*bbb*72*bb*WT*b*185
        ignored ignored

    results

    A [72]   B [185]

output

    The next n spaces on the line are left blank.

```
        PRINT 2000, A, B
   2000 FORMAT(1X,3X,G2.0,5X,G3.0)
```

    results

        *bbb*72*bbbbb*185

    note that the first blank on the line corresponding to the 1X descriptor is used as carriage control

---

In printing tabulated output where the results are to be lined up in columns starting at certain points in the line, it is sometimes convenient to use the Tn descriptor. Here, n is an unsigned INTEGER constant indicating the line position (column) at which the next field in the FORMAT is to start. The use of the T descriptor requires some care because it may cause backward positioning on the line, thus causing some previously output characters to be wiped out.

Input FORMATs may also contain the T descriptor to indicate the beginning card column of the next FORMAT descriptor. As in output, it's possible for this to cause backward positioning on the card, thus causing some characters to be read again.

T*n*

> *n* is an unsigned INTEGER constant

input

> The next field in the FORMAT following the T*n* descriptor starts in column *n* on the card.

```
      INTEGER A,B
      REAL C
      READ 1000, A,B,C
 1000 FORMAT(T2,G2.0,T5,G2.0,T1,G6.0)
```

data

> *b*47.52

results

A   47   B   52   C   47.52

output

> The next field in the FORMAT following the T*n* descriptor starts in position *n* on the line. Since position 1 is the carriage control character, position *n* actually corresponds to the *n*-1th character on the printed line.

```
      PRINT 2000, A,B,C
 2000 FORMAT (' ',T5,I2,T10,I2,T16,F5.2)
```

results

> *bbb*47*bbb*52*bbbbb*47.52

EXERCISES 10 5

1   What gets printed by the following statements?

```
      PRINT 1001, 15/5, 18+12
 1001 FORMAT(' ',5X,I2,3X,I2)
      PRINT 1002, 45/15, 2*10
 1002 FORMAT(' ', T7, I2, T12, I2)
```

2   What values do DOLARS and CENTS have after the READ statement is performed?

```
      INTEGER DOLARS, CENTS
      READ 2000, DOLARS, CENTS
 2000 FORMAT(I3, 1X, I2)
```

data:

> *b*49.07

3   How about this one (same data)?

```
      READ 3000, DOLARS, CENTS
 3000 FORMAT(T5,I2,T2,I2)
```

WATFIV for Humans

Section 10 6

Repeat Specifications and Groups

Formatted records, whether they are lines or cards, often have a very regular structure. That is, they often have several identical data descriptors in a row. For example, a data card may contain ten numbers in fields of width eight. One way to describe the card is with FORMAT 1000 below.

```
1000 FORMAT(G8.0, G8.0, G8.0, G8.0, G8.0,
     &       G8.0, G8.0, G8.0, G8.0, G8.0)
```

Fortunately, we don't need to write so many identical descriptors. Instead, we can place repeat specification in front of one descriptor. The effect is then the same as if the descriptor is repeated the number of times indicated by the repeat specification. Thus, FORMAT 2000 below is equivalent to FORMAT 1000 above.

```
2000 FORMAT(10G8.0)
```

The repeat specification is an unsigned INTEGER constant r which appears in front of a FORMAT descriptor.

> *repeat specification: an unsigned* INTEGER *constant r between 1 and 255 placed in front of a data descriptor or group to indicate that the group is to be repeated r times*

If the same pattern of FORMAT descriptors is repeated several times, as in FORMAT 3000 below, then that *pattern* may be grouped by parentheses and a repeat specification placed in front of the group, as in the equivalent FORMAT 4000 below.

```
3000 FORMAT(' ', G11.4, ' AND', I10, 20X,
     &            G11.4, ' AND', I10, 20X, I15)

4000 FORMAT(' ', 2(G11.4, ' AND', I10, 20X), I15)
```

> *group: A group is a parenthesized sublist of* FORMAT *descriptors. It may be preceded by an explicit repeat specification. Groups may be nested to a depth of two.*

Any list of FORMAT descriptors can become a group, and groups may be nested two deep, but no deeper. Usually a group is preceded by a repeat specification, but it doesn't have to be. If the repeat specification is omitted, it is taken to be one. Even a group with no explicit repeat factor affects the meaning of a

FORMAT in the aberrant (but legal) case when a READ or PRINT list includes more values than the FORMAT appears equipped to handle. We'll ignore that possibility for a while. Then these two FORMATs are equivalent.

```
5000 FORMAT(A5, A5, I3, I3, 1X, A1, 1X, A1,
     &              I3, I3, 1X, A1, 1X, A1,
     &              I3, I3, 1X, A1, 1X, A1, A8, A8, A8)

6000 FORMAT(2A5, 3(2I3,2(1X,A1)), 3A8)
```

EXERCISES 10 6

1 Which pairs of FORMATs below are equivalent?

```
1000 FORMAT(' ', I3, I3, I3, G12.2, G12.2, G12.2)
1001 FORMAT(' ', 3(I3,G12.2))

2000 FORMAT(I3, I3, A2, I3, I3, A2)
2001 FORMAT( 2(I3,I3,A2) )

3000 FORMAT(13(' '), I10)
3001 FORMAT(13X,I10)


4000 FORMAT(A1, A2, A2, A1, A2, A2, A1,
     &        A1, A2, A2, A1, A2, A2, A1,
     &        A1, A2, A1, A2, A1, A2)
4001 FORMAT( 2(A1, 2(2A2,A1)), 3(A1,A2) )
```

Section 10 7

Multiple Records

Most FORMATs described a single line or a single card. In other words, they describe one I/O *record*. The length of a formatted I/O record is measured in characters. For example, the length of a record for the card reader is 80 characters. No FORMAT should describe a record longer than the record length for the

> *record: The basic unit of I/O is the **record**. Different I/O devices have different types of records. The card reader record is one **card**, 80 characters. The printer record is one **line**. Different printers have different line lengths; 132 is the line length for many printers.*

intended I/O device. However, it is possible for a FORMAT to describe more than one record. For example, the following PRINT statement prints two records (*i.e.,* two lines) as a heading on a page.

```
     PRINT 1000
1000 FORMAT('1', 3X, 'SCREWS'/ ' ', 'SIZE', 4X, 'PRICE')
```

The slash (/) in the FORMAT separates the descriptions of the two records. (Note that each record, being a printed line, has a carriage control character.) In general, a FORMAT may describe many records with each record separated from the next by a slash. For example, the following READ statement will read three cards. Two values will be taken from the first card, one value from the second, and two from the third.

```
    READ 2000, A, B, C, D, E
2000 FORMAT(2G20.0/ G30.0/ 2G15.0)
```

Two consecutive slashes imply a blank record in between. The printer will skip a line because the implied blank line includes a blank character for carriage control. The reader will skip a card when given a // specification.

An I/O statement may process several records even if the FORMAT describes only one. Here's how that can happen. The PRINT statement below has more values in its list than there are data descriptors in the FORMAT. The computer must print all the values listed, so it simply uses the FORMAT over again, starting a new record when it comes to the end of the specification.

```
    INTEGER A/10/, B/50/, C/100/
    PRINT 1000, A+C, A+B, C*A-B, B*A
1000 FORMAT(' ', 2G6.0)
```

results

    *bbb*110*bbbb*60

    *bbb*950*bbb*500

In general, if an I/O statement is not completed when it runs out of data descriptors in the FORMAT, it starts a new record and uses the FORMAT over again. This is a relatively simple and useful idea. It lets you describe one record or even several records that you're thinking of as one logical unit and use that description over and over to input or output several sets of data. The following FORMAT describes a pair of data cards, one containing a CHARACTER*10 value and the other a REAL and an INTEGER. The READ statement READs three pairs of cards, using the FORMAT three times.

```
    CHARACTER*10 C1, C2, C3
    REAL P1, P2, P3
    INTEGER M1, M2, M3
    READ 1000, C1,P1,M1, C2,P2,M2, C3,P3,M3
1000 FORMAT(A10/ 2G7.0)
```

data

    RABBIT*bbbb*

    3300.00*bbbbb*41

    FOX*bbbbbbb*

    5000.00*bbbbb*37

    DASHER*bbbbb*

    4500.00*bbbbb*38

The repeated use of the FORMAT gets a little more complicated if the FORMAT contains groups of descriptors. In this case, the repetition starts from the last top level group or from the repeat factor preceding it, if it has one. The following PRINT statement illustrates this feature. It assumes the memory cells have the values they were given by the READ statement above.

```
      PRINT 2000, C1,P1,M1, C2,P2,M2, C3,P3,M3
 2000 FORMAT('1', ' CAR', 7X, 'PRICE', 3X, 'EPA MILEAGE'//
     &        (' ', A10, F7.2, I8) )


      STOP
      END
```

data

```
   RABBIT
   3300.00     41
   FOX
   5000.00     37
   DASHER
   4500.00     38
```

output

```
    CAR        PRICE    EPA MILEAGE

   RABBIT     3300.00      41
   FOX        5000.00      37
   DASHER     4500.00      38
```

Now you know what happens if an I/O statement list includes more memory cell names than the associated FORMAT has data descriptors. There is yet another possibility.

What if there are fewer memory cells to be dealt with than there are data descriptors left in the FORMAT? Perhaps the answer "the remaining data descriptors are ignored" is obvious. But what's *not* obvious is what happens if there is a slash or a literal after the last data descriptor that was used but before a data descriptor which is not needed. Do we ignore those too, or not? Well, it's not hard to imagine cases in which you would want them to be used, nor is it difficult to imagine cases in which you wouldn't want them. Verbosity won out, as illustrated below.

```
      INTEGER X
      CHARACTER*8 WN
      X = 2
      WN = 'MILLER'
      PRINT 120, X, WN
      X = 0
      WN = 'PALMER'
      PRINT 120, X
  120 FORMAT(' ', 'THERE WERE', I2, ' PRIZE WINNERS   ',
     &        A8, ' CAME IN FIRST')
      STOP
      END
```

output
```
THERE WERE 2 PRIZE WINNERS   MILLER    CAME IN FIRST
THERE WERE 0 PRIZE WINNERS
```

> *last top level group: the group in a FORMAT which is terminated by the first right parenthesis to the left of the right parenthesis which closes the FORMAT*

The second PRINT statement doesn't have a list element to match with the A8 data descriptor. Hence, all the literal descriptors in the FORMAT, up to the A8 data descriptor, are printed; the remaining descriptors are ignored.

Believe it or not, we've exhausted the details of FORMAT specifications. There may be a few more details about specific I/O equipment that is available at your computer center, but if you've been able to maintain through this chapter, you have complete control over every aspect of data card layout and every nuance of placing symbols on the printed page.

FORMAT

form
    FORMAT (*spec*)

    spec is a list of FORMAT descriptors (*i.e.,* data descriptors, literal descriptors, spacing descriptors, slashes, or groups of these) separated by commas. Slashes serve as delimiters, so commas should be omitted around slashes. Commas may also be omitted if it doesn't cause ambiguity. Every FORMAT must have a statement label.

meaning
    A FORMAT describes the layout of an I/O record or records.

examples
```
1000 FORMAT(I10,A20,G11.4)
2000 FORMAT(5G10.0)
3000 FORMAT(' ',20('****',F5.2))
4000 FORMAT('1', 3F4.2// ' ',6(3F5.2,I5))
```

> *group: A group of FORMAT descriptors is a parenthesized sublist of descriptors in **spec**. It may be preceded by an explicit repeat specification. FORMAT 4000 above contains the group 6(3F5.2,I5).*

EXERCISES 10 7

1 What is wrong with the following FORMAT?

```
      READ 1000, A, B, C, D, E, F
 1000 FORMAT(6G15.0)
```

2 How should the data be punched on cards for the following READ statement?

```
      READ 2000, A, B, C, D, E , F
 2000 FORMAT(2G10.0)
```

3 What is printed by the following?

```
      CHARACTER*2 C1/'OF'/, C2/'AL'/, C3/'TA'/, C4/'SB'/
      CHARACTER*4 N1/'FRED'/, N2/'JUNE'/
      CHARACTER*4 N3/'JANE'/, N4/'TED '/
      PRINT 1000, N1,C1, N2,C2, N3,C3, N4,C4
 1000 FORMAT('1', 'NAME',6X, 'CODE'//2(' ',A4,'****'))
      STOP
      END
```

4 Write a FORMAT describing a pair of cards with the following layout.

card 1:	col 1–10, CHARACTER*10
	col 21–30, REAL
	col 41–50, REAL
	col 61–70, REAL
card 2:	col 1–5, REAL
	col 6–10, INTEGER
	col 11–15, INTEGER
	col 16–20, INTEGER

5 Write a formatted PRINT statement which will write the line

FORMAT IS A TRICKY LANGUAGE

one hundred times, starting at the top of a page.

6 What will be PRINTed by

```
      INTEGER X
      CHARACTER*8 WN1, WN2
      X = 2
      WN1 = 'BARBER'
      WN2 = 'MOODY'
      PRINT 135, WN1, X, WN2
 135  FORMAT('0', 'IN FIRST PLACE WAS ', A8/
     &         ' ', 'THERE WERE', I2, ' TIED FOR IT')
      STOP
      END
```

Section 10 8*

Variable FORMATs

> This section should be skipped unless you have read Chapter 6. And maybe even if you have.

Sometimes it is impossible to devise the FORMAT of a printed line or data card until the program has made some computations. For example, you may want to PRINT from one to ten numbers on a line in fields of width five so that if there are fewer than ten numbers, they appear to the righthand side of the line. Suppose there is a memory cell N whose value is the number of numbers you want to PRINT on the line and that the numbers are stored in an array A. It would be nice if you could simply put variables in the FORMAT itself. Unfortunately, this is illegal, but with a little more effort we can get the desired effect.

```
      PRINT 1000, (A(I),I=1,N)
1000 FORMAT (1X, (11-N) (5X) , N I5)
```

This FORMAT contains illegal uses of variables as repeat specifications.

A **variable FORMAT** is an array containing a character string. That string must be a legal FORMAT specification. That is, it must be a string which could appear after the word FORMAT in a FORMAT statement, including the parentheses. The I/O statement using the variable FORMAT is exactly the same as if it had used a normal FORMAT except that the name of the array containing the variable FORMAT now replaces the usual FORMAT label.

---

variable FORMAT I/O statements

form
    READ *f, list*
    PRINT *f, list*
    PRINT *f*
    f is the name of an array containing a character string of FORMAT specifications surrounded by parentheses.

meaning
    same as with constant FORMAT

To get back to the problem at hand, recall that we wanted a FORMAT like this:

$$(1X, \boxed{} \qquad (5X), \boxed{} \qquad I5)$$

where the boxes represent character strings which will change from time to time. For example, if the first box contains the character '1', then the second should contain the characters '10'. In order to be able to assign one of the necessary character strings to those parts of the FORMAT, we set up an array DIGIT containing them. For the FORMAT itself, we set up an array SKIP containing the parts of the FORMAT which are fixed and leave spaces in which to insert the variable portions. As you can see in the program fragment, before PRINTing, we assign character strings to those variable parts of SKIP using the array DIGIT.

```
        INTEGER A(10) /1,2,3,4,5,6,7,8,9,10/
        INTEGER N/6/, I
COMMENT:  INITIALIZE CONSTANT PARTS OF VARIABLE FORMAT,
C         LEAVING BLANKS IN THE VARIABLE PORTIONS
        CHARACTER*4 SKIP(6)/'(1X,', '    ', '( 5X', '),', ',
      &                '    ', 'I5 )'/
COMMENT:  INITIALIZE ARRAY CONTAINING STRINGS TO BE INSERTED
        CHARACTER*2 DIGIT(10)/'1 ', '2 ', '3 ', '4 ', '5 ',
      &                '6 ', '7 ', '8 ', '9 ', '10'/
        SKIP(2) = DIGIT(11-N)
        SKIP(5) = DIGIT(N)
        PRINT SKIP, (A(I),I=1,N)
        STOP
        END
```

output

          1   2   3   4   5   6

Section 10 9*

Plotting

> Skip this section unless you have read Chapters 6 and 7.

It wasn't long after the first printed pages came zooming out of computer line printers that people, perhaps initially attracted by the moving, shifting patterns of program listings, began writing programs which produce two dimensional patterns for their own sake. One example of the sorts of patterns that can be produced fairly easily is the map of the United States that the fad program (Section 8 3) printed out. Practitioners of computer graphics have developed elaborate techniques and can produce a fantastic range of visual effects.

Using formatted PRINT statements gives you enough control of your program's output to produce a wide range of interesting pictures, limited, really, only by your imagination.

In this section we'll point out a few of the mechanics of plotting, specifically, how to go from an internally stored or generated image to a properly scaled image on the printed page. There are numerous ways of creating images to plot. For the fad program we simply punched a card for each position not on the continental U.S. land mass. Other ideas include generating lines and boxes with random orientations, generating random subpatterns and sprinkling them around, storing subpatterns (circles, squares, whatever) and expanding or shrinking and shifting copies of them. It is also fairly simple to write subprograms which will make mirror images of already created subpatterns.

Your computer center may well have more elaborate devices for plotting which will make it possible to create more elaborate, more finely detailed drawings. Fancy gadgetry is no substitute for imagination, though.

The basic idea we will use to draw pictures on the line printer is **discretization,** which means representing something which is continuously, smoothly changing in terms of a small number of specific values. This is necessary because the printer can't print symbols just anywhere on the page; it is neatly organized to print in columns and rows. We must convert any other sort of image into one which has symbols in column and row positions. Conceptually we lay a grid over our image and let each grid square correspond to a character position on the printed page (*i.e.,* some specific row and column). Then we place a symbol on the page for each grid which covers any dark part of the image. Figure 10 9 1 shows a continuous image and three discrete versions of it at different levels of discretization.

a continuous image

a gross discretization

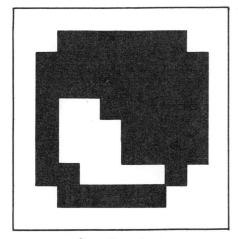

a finer discretization

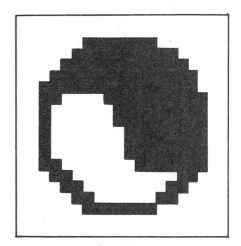

an even finer discretization

Figure 10 9 1   Discretization

Probably the most convenient way to deal with the print grid is to use a two dimensional array. If the image grid has H rows and W columns, then we use a W by H two dimensional CHARACTER*1 array to represent the printed page. To begin, we fill the array with blanks. Then we store nonblank symbols (*e.g.,* asterisks) in array positions which correspond to dark spots in the image. The hard part is setting up this correspondence between the image plane and the two dimensional array. What we need is a way to convert a pair of REAL coordinates (X,Y) in the image plane to a pair of INTEGER subscripts (I,J) in the ranges I to H and I to W respectively.

First we'll convert X to I. If the left boundary of the image plane corresponds to $X = XMIN$ and the right boundary to $X = XMAX$, then $(X - XMIN)/(XMAX - XMIN)$ is a number between 0.0 and 1.0. Consequently, INT $(W*(X - XMIN)/(XMAX - XMIN)) + 1$ is an INTEGER between 1 and W. This is the conversion formula we wanted. Essentially it divides the image plane into W vertical strips of equal width and takes the value I when X is in the Ith strip. Similarly we convert Y to INT $(H*(Y - YMIN)/(YMAX - YMIN)) + 1$ where YMIN and YMAX correspond to the bottom and top boundaries of the image plane. Actually, if an image point lies exactly on the top or right boundary, we'll have problems, so we won't allow image points on the top or right boundary. This is easy to do—if there are any troublesome points, just shift the grid a tiny amount by increasing XMAX and YMAX.

We will write three SUBROUTINEs to help plot pictures. One will put blanks in the two dimensional plotting array; another will put a symbol into the array at a point corresponding to a given point in the image plane; and the third will print the contents of the array. Thus, plotting a picture amounts to CALLing the blank-out routine, then CALLing the point-plotting routine once for each dark spot in the image, and finally, CALLing the printing routine. These SUBROUTINEs are written below. The only tricky part is the discretization, that is, converting X to I and Y to J, which we've already discussed.

```
        SUBROUTINE BLKOUT (GRAPH, W, H)
        INTEGER W, H
        CHARACTER*1 GRAPH(W,H)
COMMENT:  THIS SUBROUTINE FILLS THE PLOTTING ARRAY "GRAPH"
C            WITH BLANKS
        INTEGER I, J
        J = H
100     I = 1
200        GRAPH(I,J) = ' '
           I = I+1
           IF ( I .LE. W ) GO TO 200
        J = J-1
        IF ( J .GE. 1 ) GO TO 100
        RETURN
        END
```

```
      SUBROUTINE PLOT (X,Y, XMIN,XMAX,YMIN,YMAX,
     &                 SYMBOL, GRAPH,W,H)
      REAL X,Y, XMIN,XMAX, YMIN,YMAX
      INTEGER W,H
      CHARACTER*1 SYMBOL, GRAPH(W,H)
COMMENT:   THIS SUBROUTINE PUTS "SYMBOL" INTO THE PLOTTING
C          ARRAY "GRAPH" AT A POINT CORRESPONDING TO
C          (X,Y) IN THE IMAGE PLANE
C          THE RANGE OF COORDINATES IS ASSUMED TO BE
C           (XMIN TO XMAX   ,   YMIN TO YMAX)
C          COORDINATES OUTSIDE THIS RANGE WILL NOT BE PLOTTED
      INTEGER I,J
C      DISCRETIZE X AND Y
      I = INT( ((X-XMIN)/(XMAX-XMIN)) * FLOAT(W) ) +1
      J = INT( ((Y-YMIN)/(YMAX-YMIN)) * FLOAT(H) ) +1
C      PUT (X,Y) INTO "GRAPH" (IF IN RANGE)
      IF ( I .GE. 1 .AND.
     &      I .LE. W .AND.
     &      J .GE. 1 .AND.
     &      J .LE. H      ) GRAPH(I,J) = SYMBOL
      RETURN
      END


      SUBROUTINE PRGRPH (GRAPH,W,H)
      INTEGER W,H
      CHARACTER*1 GRAPH(W,H)
COMMENT:   THIS SUBROUTINE PRINTS THE PLOTTING ARRAY "GRAPH"
      INTEGER I,J
      J = H
 100  PRINT 1000, (GRAPH(I,J), I=1,W)
      J = J-1
      IF ( J .GE. 1 )  GO TO 100
      RETURN
 1000 FORMAT(' ', 120A1)
      END


COMMENT:  PLOT THE EXPONENTIAL CURVE
      REAL X, EXP
      CHARACTER*1 G(25,15)
      CALL BLKOUT (G,25,15)
      X = -1.0
 100  CALL PLOT (X,EXP(X), -1.0,1.0, 0.0,2.0 , '*',G,25,15)
      X = X + 0.05
      IF ( X .LE. 1.0 )  GO TO 100
      CALL PRGRPH (G,25,15)
      STOP
      END
```

```
                                *
                                *
                              **
                             **
                            *
                          **
                         **
                       ***
                      **
                    ***
                 ***
              ****
             *
```

When plotting with the line printer, you will get better results if you keep in mind that the distance between characters on a line is less than the distance between lines. That is, the plotting device you are using has sharper resolution in the horizontal direction than in the vertical direction. The ratio of these resolutions is about five to three for most line printers. Therefore, in order to avoid distorting your picture, you should divide the image plane into about five parts in the horizontal direction for every three parts in the vertical direction. In other words, the ratio W/H of the width to the height of your plotting array should be about 5/3.

Some of the problems at the end of this chapter will give you a chance to use this plotting package we have developed. In addition, Problem 10 2 illustrates a way to plot a single line at a time without using a big two dimensional array. This technique saves memory at the expense of time.

PROBLEMS 10

1   Do some problems from the other chapters you have read, but use formatted I/O instead of format-free I/O.

2   Write a program which computes weekly wages for the employees of the ZAPPO shampoo factory. Each worker is required to turn in a time card containing the following information.

        col 1–15   name (alphameric)
        col 16–20   hourly wage (REAL)
        col 21–30   hours worked Monday (REAL)
        col 31–40   hours worked Tuesday (REAL)

          .
          .
          .

        col 71–80   hours worked Saturday (REAL)

Each of the "hours worked" figures is a REAL number giving the number of hours worked that day to the nearest tenth of an hour.

Have the program print a list of wage totals for the workers. If your program is able to detect that a worker is female, compute her wages at $2.25 per hour. All other workers receive $5.50 an hour.

3   Write a program to count the votes in an election. There are three candidates, Milton P. Waxley (incumbent), Patricia Rhoder (progressive liveral), Frederick "Red" Kemmeny (a reluctant candidate who filed at the last minute). Each voter makes his vote by punching a card with a digit in the first column—1 for Waxley, 2 for Rhoder, or 3 for Kemmeny.

At 7:30 p.m. an election official places a card with an "X" in column 80 at the end of all the ballot cards in the box and submits them as data for your program. Your program should print the election results. (Note: be sure to reject all mismarked ballots.)

This man has supported Milton P. Waxley
in the last seventeen elections

4 Do Problem 3 and include the number of mismarked ballots in the output. Also print a brief victory statement by the winner which includes the names of his or her worthy opponents.

5 Write a program to prepare a table of squares, square roots, cubes, and cube roots of numbers from 0.0 to 10.0 at intervals of 0.1.

Use formatted PRINTs to make the output readable. If you are ambitious, divide the various columns with lines of I's (to look like vertical lines) and put a horizontal row of −'s every tenth row to separate 0.9 from 1.0, 1.9 from 2.0, etc.

All of the following problems require a knowledge of arrays (Chapter 6).

6 Write a program to READ a card containing a sentence. Assume that no punctuation is used other than blanks and commas in the sentence and a period at the end of the sentence.

Your program should print the sentence, then compute and print the number of words in the sentence. To do this, you'll have to READ the card in 80A1 FORMAT so that you can examine each character separately to look for symbols like ',' which indicate separations between words.

7 Write a program to read a word up to ten characters long from one card, and a sentence from the next card (up to 80 characters, including blanks and other punctuation), then print the word, the sentence, and the number of occurrences of the word in the sentence. You may assume that there is no punctuation other than blanks and commas, with a period at the end.

8   Do Problem 7, but replace each occurrence of the word in the sentence by a row of asterisks the same length as the word; then print this censored version of the sentence.

9   (No arrays needed, but implied DO list is needed) Use the line printer to make a graph of the function $\sin(x)/x$ from $x = 0$ to $x = 10$ stepping at intervals of 0.1. (Note: $\sin(x)/x = 1$ when $x = 0$, and all values of $\sin(x)/x$ are in the range -1 to 1.)

   In plotting graphs like this, it is easier to orient the x-axis down the page rather than across. That way, the program can compute one value of the function, plot it on the current line across the page, and then step to the next value and plot it on the next line, etc.

   The only tricky part might be translating values of the function (which lie between -1 and 1) to positions on the line to be printed (which typically run from column 1 to column 132). To figure out how far across the line to plot a particular value of $\sin(x)/x$, use the discretization formula

$$I = INT(100.0*(Y + 1.0)/2.0) + 1$$

   where Y is a value of $\sin(x)/x$. Then I will be in the range 1 to 101 and you can plot Y with a statement like

```
      PRINT 1000, (' ', K=1,I), '*'
 1000 FORMAT(' ', 102A1)
```

   which puts an asterisk in the appropriate position across the page.

10 In Problem 9 the discretization formula gives the value I if Y is in the range $-1.00 + (I - 1) * 0.01$ to $-1.00 + I*0.01$. Use this fact to draw and label the axes of your plot.

11 Draw graphs of other functions using the techniques of Problem 9 and 10. The discretization formula will continue to divide the range of values of the function into 100 equally spaced parts if you change the $(Y + 1.0)/2.0$ expression to $(Y - YMIN)/(YMAX - YMIN)$ where YMIN and YMAX are the smallest and largest values your function can take on.

   Note that you can shrink the plot of your function by making YMAX larger than the maximum value of the function and YMIN smaller than the minimum.

12 Typesetting

   After months of searching, you find a job as a programmer for an ad agency. Your first assignment (given to you by your boss who wears two foot wide ties, smokes mentholated cigars, and keeps calling you "baby") is to write a program which arranges ad copy. Your program READs in the paragraph from cards and PRINTs it out in the desired form. Desired forms are:

   rectangle: fit as well as possible within margins n columns wide (run your program with $n = 50, 25,$ and 12)

   triangle: Fit as well as possible in a triangle shape with base at the bottom of the ad.

Here is some ad copy to use, written in the triangle form.

YOUR
EYES? YOU
SAY. HOW COULD
YOU HAVE – EYE ODOR?
WELL, YOUR EYES ARE SO
CLOSE TO YOUR NOSE THAT YOU
GET USED TO THEIR SMELL. BUT DON'T
TAKE THE RISK OF OFFENDING OTHERS! USE
EYERON-F, THE GENTLE EYE FRESHENER AND
DEODORIZER. AVAILABLE IN THREE SIZES, GIANT,
JUMBO, AND FAMILY. (NOW LEMON-FRESHENED FOR
EVEN MORE PROTECTION.) GET SOME TODAY!

Your boss has changed his mind. He now wants the base of the triangle on the top. Write a new program. (Thanks to Raymond Langsford for this problem.)

13 The 57th Street Whiz Kids (a tough gang) have found it necessary to send messages to one another in secret code. In order to write a message in this secret code, a member must write down the message on a piece of scrap paper. Then under each character (including spaces and punctuation marks), he places an integer between 0 and 42 according to the following scheme: 0 through 25 for A through Z respectively; 26 through 42 for the characters blank . , – ( ) ' 0 1 2 3 4 5 6 7 8 9 respectively. Then he adds each pair of numbers and writes the result below the pair with the convention that if the sum is 43 or more, he subtracts 43 from it before writing it down, so that each number written will be between 0 and 42. He then decodes the numbers into characters, again using the above scheme.

Example:

1	written message:	MEET JIM 10 P.M.							
2	integers:	12	04	04	19	26	09	08	12
		26	34	33	26	15	27	12	27
3	added integers:	16	08	23	02	35	17	20	38
		17	24	16	41	42	39	39	
4	coded message:	QIXC2RU5RYQ8966							

Note that the coded message has only 15 characters, whereas the original message has 16. It will always be the case with this code system that the original message has one more character than the coded message. To make it possible to decode their message, the Whiz Kids made an agreement that the original message should always end with a period.

Write a program which will read coded messages from cards in the FORMAT 80A1 and PRINT out the decoded message. You may assume the coded message has fewer than 500 characters and that the end of the coded message will be marked with a slash(/). The slash will be used for no other purpose than to mark the end of the coded message and therefore should not be used in decoding the message. You may use the above message to test your program or code your own.

14 Do the ringworm problem (Problem 9, Chapter 8), making the output look good with proper FORMATing.

---

confession: The output scheme we actually used in the fad program of Section 8 2 is shown below. If we had used a format-free PRINT, there would have been spaces between the characters.

```
     PRINT 4000, (LINE(I), I=1,100)
4000 FORMAT(10X, 100A1)
```

All of the following problems assume a knowledge of subprograms (Chapter 7).

15 The 100 members of the Alpha Nu fraternity need a secret handshake by which they can identify each other. One night in a dream the spirit of Alpha Nu reveals a keen secret handshake to Joe College, ace football player, BMOC, and loyal Alpha Nudist. As Alpha Nudists go from class to class on campus, they meet each other at random. Whenever two randomly selected Alpha Nudists meet, if one knows the handshake, he teaches it to the other.

After each 10 random meetings, count how many Alpha Nudists know the secret handshake and PRINT that count. Stop after 600 random meetings have occurred. Your output should resemble a histogram.

```
10X
20XX
30XX
40XXXX
     .  .

     .  .


     .  .
590XXXXXXX
600XXXXXXX
```

Note: An implied do list of the form ('X', I = 1, N) is useful in printing the individual lines of this output. (We thank Gary Sager for this problem.)

The following problems are substantially more difficult than the previous ones.

16 Do Problem 6 23 on computing large factorials, but dress up the output so that the numbers are written in the usual form for large numbers (*i.e.,* with commas or spaces separating every group of three digits, starting from the rightmost digit).

17 As you know, in Morse code each letter is coded into a group of dots and dashes. To represent a Morse code message on data cards, we can use periods (.) for dots and minus signs (–) for dashes. The letters in the coded message can be separated by one space and the words by two spaces. The end of the message can be a message containing two words:

$$...b - - - b...bb...b.b-/$$

The cards may be considered contiguous. That is, words or letter codes may be continued from one card to the next.

Write a program which READs a coded message from cards and PRINTs it out in letters. (The message should be written in International Morse Code—see any encyclopedia or Boy Scout Manual for a description of it.) Try to write the program in such a way that it makes *no* assumptions about the length of the message. To do this you will probably find the following subprograms helpful. One of them delivers the next character in the coded message, no matter what card or where on the card the character comes from. The other "prints" the message, one character at a time. Actually it saves its input characters until it has a whole line and prints them all at once. For this reason, it has two arguments. The second argument should be .FALSE. until the last CALL. Then it should be .TRUE. to tell the routine to print the characters it's been saving even if the whole line isn't full. This is necessary to avoid losing the contents of a partially filled last line.

> *buffering: The technique of saving parts of an output record in memory until a whole record is accumulated is known as buffering the output. The array used to save the partial records is called a buffer. Input can be handled similarly when partial records are needed in sequence. The SUBROUTINEs GETCH and PRNCH are input and output buffering routines.*

```
      SUBROUTINE GETCH(CH)
COMMENT:  CH
      CHARACTER*1 CH
COMMENT:  "CH" IS ASSIGNED THE VALUE OF THE NEXT CHARACTER
C          IN THE INPUT STREAM
      CHARACTER*1 CARD(80)
      INTEGER CURSOR/0/
C
C     GET NEXT RECORD IF BUFFER IS EMPTY
      IF ( CURSOR .NE. 0 )  GO TO 200
         READ 1000, CARD
 1000    FORMAT(80A1)
         CURSOR = 1
C     PUT NEXT CHARACTER IN "CH" AND INCREMENT "CURSOR"
  200 CH = CARD(CURSOR)
      CURSOR = MOD(CURSOR+1,80)
      RETURN
      END
```

```
            SUBROUTINE PRNCH(CH, DUMP)
            CHARACTER*1 CH
            LOGICAL DUMP
    COMMENT:    "CH" IS PLACED IN THE LINE TO BE EVENTUALLY
    C           PRINTED.  THE LINE IS PRINTED IF IT IS FULL AND WE
    C           ARE AT A WORD BOUNDARY (SPACE).
    C              IF "DUMP" IS .TRUE., LINE IS PRINTED REGARDLESS.
            CHARACTER*1 LINE(100)
            INTEGER CURSOR/0/, I
    C       PUT "CH" IN "LINE"
            CURSOR = CURSOR +1
            LINE(CURSOR) = CH
    C       PRINT LINE IF LONG ENOUGH AND WE'RE AT A WORD BOUNDARY
    C       OR IF WE'VE BEEN ORDERED TO DUMP THE BUFFER
            IF (.NOT. ((CURSOR.GE.60 .AND.LINE(CURSOR).EQ.' ')
          &           .OR. DUMP)                     ) GO TO 200
               PRINT 1000, (LINE(I),I=1,CURSOR)
               CURSOR = 0
               RETURN
    C       PRINT LINE WITH HYPHEN IF WE JUST CAN'T HOLD ANY MORE
      200   IF ( CURSOR .LT. 100 )  RETURN
               PRINT 1000, LINE, '-'
               CURSOR = 0
               RETURN
     1000   FORMAT(' ',101A1)
            END
```

The following problems depend on Section 10 9.

18 Improve the output from the motorcyclist problem of Chapter 7 by plotting his trajectory instead of just printing a numerical summary of his
flight. If you feel ambitious, include a cross section of the canyon and a
puff of dust where he lands in the picture. You could plot different
symbols for the canyon boundary (perhaps '+'), trajectory (perhaps '–'),
and dust (perhaps '*').

19 Rewrite the PLOT routine so that instead of plotting only one point per
CALL, its input contains all the points to be plotted in the picture in a
pair of coordinate arrays. Plot the points line by line rather than all at
once. In other words, let your plotting array be one dimensional to
represent one line. Start at the top of the image, and look through all the
points to be plotted. Whenever you find one to be plotted, put a symbol
at the corresponding horizontal position in your array. When you've
cycled through all the coordinates to find those on the top line, print the
line, and repeat the process for the next line down, and so on.

20 Spiral of primes

Compute all the prime numbers less than 59^2 (see Problem 6 24 for an
algorithm to use). Then plot the primes in the following way. Number a
59 by 59 grid of squares from the center out in a spiral. To figure the
appropriate (I, J) subscript in the 59 by 59 array given a number N, use
SUBROUTINE COORD below.

22	21	20	19	18	
23	8	7	6	17	
24	9	1	5	16	
25	2	3	4	15	
10	11	12	13	14	

etc.

```
      SUBROUTINE COORD(N,I,J)
      INTEGER N, I, J
COMMENT:  THIS ROUTINE COMPUTES THE ARRAY SUBSCRIPT (I,J)
C            CORRESPONDING TO THE NUMBER N IN THE SPIRAL
C            NUMBERING OF A 59 BY 59 TWO DIMENSIONAL ARRAY.
      INTEGER OFFSET/30/
      INTEGER SQRTN, R, CNR, RES, RESRES, QUAD, SR
      INTEGER RSGN(4)/-1, +1, +1, -1/, ISIGN
      INTEGER DSGN(4)/+1, +1, -1, -1/
COMMENT:  CENTER WHEN N IS ONE
      IF ( N .GT. 1 )  GO TO 100
         I = OFFSET
         J = OFFSET
         RETURN
COMMENT:  COMPUTE SMALLEST INTEGER .GE. SQRT(N)
 100  SQRTN = INT(SQRT(FLOAT(N))) +1
      IF ( (SQRTN-1)**2 .EQ. N )  SQRTN = SQRTN -1
COMMENT:  COMPUTE RADIUS
      R = SQRTN/2
COMMENT:  FIND LOW CORNER NUMBER
      CNR = (2*R-1)**2 +1
COMMENT:  FIND DISTANCE ALONG PERIMETER
      RES = N-CNR
COMMENT:  FIND QUADRANT AND SIGNED RADIUS
      QUAD = RES/(2*R)
      SR = ISIGN(R, RSGN(QUAD+1))
COMMENT:  FIND SIGNED DISTANCE ALONG EDGE
      RESRES = DSGN(QUAD+1)*(MOD(RES,2*R) - R)
COMMENT:  COMPUTE COORDINATE
      IF ( MOD(QUAD,2) .EQ. 0 )  GO TO 200
         I = OFFSET + SR
         J = OFFSET + RESRES
         RETURN
 200     I = OFFSET + RESRES
         J = OFFSET + SR
         RETURN
      END
```

21 The year is 1811 and the fame of the pirate Lafitte has spread throughout the islands of the Caribbean and the Gulf. In Havana there resides a wealthy soldier of fortune, Captain Hawkbill, who owns a fast gunship and can hire a large crew of tough sailors. He reasons that he can make a fortune if he can capture Lafitte and take his loot. His enterprise would bring him both fortune and favor because Lafitte is universally hated by honest, law-abiding people.

The Captain sails his ship into the Gulf of Mexico to a point 5 nautical miles south and 5 nautical miles east of New Orleans. Then, from his position, he sees Lafitte's ship 5 nautical miles due west. Fortunately for Hawkbill, Lafitte's crew has just finished robbing a large cargo of

> *knot: a measure of speed, one nautical mile per hour*

gold and furs from a British ship. Lafitte's ship is sailing straight north toward New Orleans at 9 knots. Hawkbill gives chase immediately. In today's wind his ship can travel at 13 knots, and he orders his crew to keep the ship at top speed and pointed directly at Lafitte's ship.

Write a program which computes each ship's position at one minute intervals in terms of nautical miles south and east of New Orleans. Assume that the chase is ended if Lafitte reaches New Orleans or is overtaken by Captain Hawkbill. Print out on the line printer a graphic display of the chase in a format similar to the following:

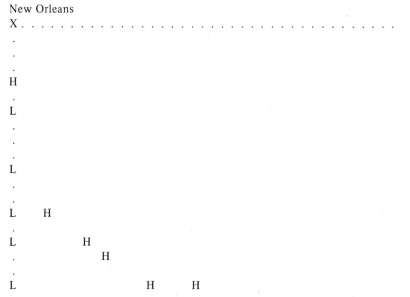

Note that the chase is over if either Hawkbill's distance east of New Orleans or Lafitte's distance south of New Orleans becomes negative.

22 Use the subprograms of Section 10 9 to create a work of art that will live forever.

11 ADDITIONAL STATEMENTS

Section 11 1

Introduction

You can do an enormous amount of programming without ever needing any of the features discussed in this chapter. In fact, some of the features are included in WATFIV primarily to improve compatibility with other dialects of Fortran and are just alternate notations for features you've already learned to use. Other features mentioned here are new and are useful in special circumstances.

We suggest that you skim the chapter to get a feeling for what's available. Don't try to remember all the details on the first pass. When you're writing a program and you think one of the features could be useful, read the details and try it out.

Section 11 2

Statement Functions

If there is an expression which appears repeatedly in your program, it may improve the clarity of your program to define a function which computes that expression. To do that, there is a simple notation you can use—the **statement function.**

Perhaps you are saying "but I thought we already... isn't that what a FUNCTION is for?" Ah yes, but there's a difference here. The difference is not a conceptual one but a matter of implementation. There are differences in how FUNCTIONs and statement functions are declared; one consequence is that a statement function is available only within the program or subprogram where it is declared. Also, a statement function can compute just a single expression whereas a FUNCTION can compute any sort of algorithm you wish to write.

Statement functions are defined by writing the name of the function followed by its parameters in parentheses, an assignment operator, and finally the expression which the function is to compute. For example, if we wished to do a true rounding division of INTEGERs, we could define the statement function RNDDIV

```
RNDDIV(I1,I2) = INT(FLOAT(I1)/FLOAT(I2)+0.5)
```

Since we want RNDDIV to return an INTEGER value, we would have to put the declaration

```
INTEGER RNDDIV
```

before the definition.

The definition of a statement function looks similar to an assignment statement, but the compiler can tell it's not since the function name is not declared as the name of an array (the only other possibility for a statement of this form is an array element assignment statement). In addition, statement function definitions must be placed *after* all relevant declaration statements and *before* any executable statements.

A statement function reference is identical to a FUNCTION reference: write its name followed by the arguments you want it to use in its computation. For example, the following assignment statement contains a reference to the statement function RNDDIV.

```
M = RNDDIV(2,3)
```

As a result, M would be given the value 1.

The identifiers which appear as parameters in the definition of a statement function (I1 and I2 in our example above) are not memory cell names—they are there only to indicate what *types* of values (both INTEGER in the case of RNDDIV) the statement function will receive as arguments when it is referenced.

---

statement function definition

form

$$f(a_1, a_2, \ldots, a_n) = e$$

f is an identifier (the function name)
each a_i is an identifier (the parameter names)
e is an expression.
There must be at least one parameter.

meaning

Defines a statement function *f* which may be referenced anywhere in the program unit. A reference to the function is like placing the expression *e*, with all occurrences of the parameters replaced by the corresponding arguments in the reference, in the place where the function reference occurs. Each actual argument in the reference must be of the type indicated by the corresponding parameter name in the definition. The type of the identifier *f* determines the type of the function. CHARACTER type functions are not allowed.

examples

```
STDG(X) = EXP(-0.5*X**2)/SQRT(8.0*ATAN(1.0))
G(X,U,S) = STDG( (X-U)/S ) /S
```

It is legal (although it may make the meaning of the function reference obscure) to include memory cell names as well as the parameters in the expression that defines a statement function. To see what effect that will have, you may imagine that when a statement function is referenced, the values given for the parameters replace each appearance of them in the expression and then the resulting rewritten expression *replaces* the function reference. For instance, if we make these declarations

```
REAL A, B, F, X, Z
```

and define this statement function,

```
F(X) = A*X + B
```

then, if later in the program we had,

```
A = 1.0
B = 5.0
Z = F(2.0)
```

the result would be the same as

```
A = 1.0
B = 5.0
Z = A*2.0 + B
```

so Z would get the value 7.0.

The expression which defines a statement function may contain references to FUNCTIONs and to *previously defined* statement functions. This last rule prevents mind bogglers like

```
F(X) = G(X)
G(X) = F(X)
```

It is important to remember that statement function definitions are local to the program unit where they occur. They cannot be used in other program units without being redefined.

> Please see the box at the beginning of Section 11·10.

EXERCISES 11·2

1 Write a statement function called EX OR which returns the LOGICAL value .TRUE. if one (and only one) of its two arguments has the value .TRUE..

2 Write a statement function called SDIST which computes the distance between two points (x_1, y_1) and (x_2, y_2) using the square root of the sum of the squares distance measure.

3 Write a statement function called ADIST which computes the distance between (x_1, y_1) and (x_2, y_2) using the sum of the absolute values of the differences between x_1, x_2 and y_1, y_2 as the distance measure.

4 Write a statement function called TRNCD which takes two REAL parameters R1 and R2 and computes a REAL value equal to the truncated division of R1 by R2. For instance,
```
TRNCD(3.25,2.7999)
```
should yield the value 1.00.

5 Statement function RNDDIV works only when I1 and I2 have the same sign. Alter it so that it will work in all cases.

Section 11 3

Subprograms as Arguments to Subprograms

On occasion you may wish to define a FUNCTION or SUBROUTINE which accepts yet another subprogram as one of its arguments. One very common use of this sort of thing is in subprograms which accept a FUNCTION from your program and then do something useful for you with it. Typical tasks are (1) plotting out its values over some range, (2) finding where your FUNCTION has maxima and minima, and (3) computing the area under your FUNCTION. Subprograms which do these things are no doubt available at your computer center.

Perhaps you recall from Chapter 7 that FUNCTIONs and SUBROUTINEs are said to be **external** subprograms because their definitions lie wholly without the program from which they are called, and because they are compiled separately and independently from the main program and from each other. This means that when the compiler is dealing with one program unit, it cannot look at other program units to decide if a particular identifier refers to a memory cell or to another program unit.

Let's examine the problem carefully. Suppose we have a SUBROUTINE called PLOT which accepts as arguments F (the FUNCTION whose values we want plotted), LIMI and LIM2 (describing the range over which values are to be plotted), and DELTA (the stepsize).

```
       SUBROUTINE PLOT (F, LIM1, LIM2, DELTA)
       REAL F, LIM1, LIM2, DELTA
       REAL STEP, Y
       INTEGER POINT, I
       STEP = LIM1
 100   Y = F(STEP)
       POINT = MAX0(1, MIN0(118,INT(10.*Y)+49))
       PRINT 1000, (' ',I=1,POINT), '*'
 1000  FORMAT(' ', 119A1)
       STEP = STEP + DELTA
       IF ( STEP .LE. LIM2 )  GO TO 100
       RETURN
       END
```

Look at statement 100. The form of the expression F(STEP) indicates that F is either an array or a FUNCTION. It can't be an array; if it were, there would be a declaration to that effect. Therefore, F must be a FUNCTION, and when SUB-ROUTINE PLOT is called, it will be informed of the FUNCTION's name. No problem here.

Now let's go to another program unit and look at a statement which CALLs SUBROUTINE PLOT. Suppose we want to plot out the values taken by the built-in FUNCTION ALOG10. We might write

```
CALL PLOT (ALOG10,1.0,10.0,1.0)
```

and hope that that would do the trick. However, "ALOG10" looks as if it could be a memory cell name. The only way for the compiler to tell that it is supposed to be a FUNCTION name is to look into SUBROUTINE PLOT and see how it uses its third argument. But the compiler cannot look at SUBROUTINE PLOT while it is compiling the program containing the CALL. To solve the dilemma we must inform the compiler that ALOG10 stands for the FUNCTION called ALOG10, not a memory cell of that name. An EXTERNAL statement gives the compiler this information.

```
EXTERNAL ALOG10
```

If our main program makes several references to SUBROUTINE PLOT, say

```
EXTERNAL ALOG10, EXP, SIN
REAL      ALOG10, EXP, SIN
CALL PLOT (ALOG10,1.0,10.0,1.0)
CALL PLOT (SIN, -3.0, 3.0, 0.5)
CALL PLOT (EXP, -1.0, 0.0, 0.1)
STOP
END
```

output

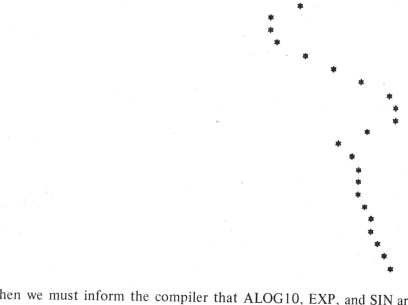

then we must inform the compiler that ALOG10, EXP, and SIN are all names of external FUNCTIONs.

```
EXTERNAL ALOG10, EXP, SIN
```

We've seen an example where a FUNCTION name was an argument for a SUBROUTINE. Other combinations (*e.g.*, a SUBROUTINE name as an argument for a FUNCTION) follow the same rules. Here's an example where a FUNCTION receives the name of another FUNCTION as an argument.

Suppose we have a number of FUNCTIONs we're trying out and we know (since we're going to divide by the result) that if any of our FUNCTIONs return the value 0, we're in trouble. For added safety we could define another FUNCTION called ZERCHK ("ZERo CHecK") to protect us. Our main program is outlined below.

```
        •
        •
        •
      INTEGER FN1, FN2, FN3, X, Y, ZERCHK
      EXTERNAL FN1, FN2, FN3
        •
        •
        •
COMMENT:  TRY FN1, BUT BE CAREFUL.
      Y1= 100/ZERCHK(X,FN1)
COMMENT:  TRY FN2, BUT BE CAREFUL.
      Y2= 100/ZERCHK(X,FN2)
COMMENT:  TRY FN3, BUT BE CAREFUL.
      Y3= 100/ZERCHK(X,FN3)
        •
        •
        •
      END
```

We want ZERCHK to try out the FUNCTION and test the result to protect us from zero.

```
      INTEGER FUNCTION ZERCHK (ARG, FUNCT)
      INTEGER ARG, FUNCT
COMMENT:  CARRY OUT THE FUNCTION WE'VE BEEN SENT
      ZERCHK = FUNCT(ARG)
COMMENT:  TEST FOR ZERO
      IF ( ZERCHK .NE. 0 ) RETURN
COMMENT:  IT WAS ZERO, NOTIFY AND SAVE THE DAY
      PRINT, 'WITH THE ARGUMENT', ARG,
    +       'THIS FUNCTION''S VALUE IS 0--BEWARE '
      ZERCHK = 1
      RETURN
      END
```

EXERCISES 11 3

1 Where must the EXTERNAL statement appear?
   a in the subprogram to warn it that one of its arguments is another subprogram.
   b in your job control cards so that the compiler can figure out the necessary communication among subprograms.
   c in your left ear.

Section 11 4*

Communication of Subprogram Arguments

A subprogram reference, that is, a CALL statement or FUNCTION reference, is performed as a special kind of transfer of control. Before transferring to the first instruction in the subprogram, the address of the calling program's next instruction is placed in a special register (fast memory location) and the address of the argument list is placed in another special register. The argument list is a group of contiguous memory cells each of which contains the address of an argument. After making the transfer to the subprogram, the machine uses the special register which contains the address of the argument list to look up the argument values. It then copies these argument values in the subprogram's parameter memory cells. Finally, it can begin carrying out the instructions in the subprogram. Once the machine has completed the computations in the subprogram, it again uses the special register containing the argument list to look up the memory cells which contained the original argument values. It replaces the values of these memory cells with the final values of the subprogram's parameter memory cells. Finally the machine uses the special register containing the address of the next instruction in the calling program to transfer back to the appropriate spot. The boxes below chart the process in a step by step way.

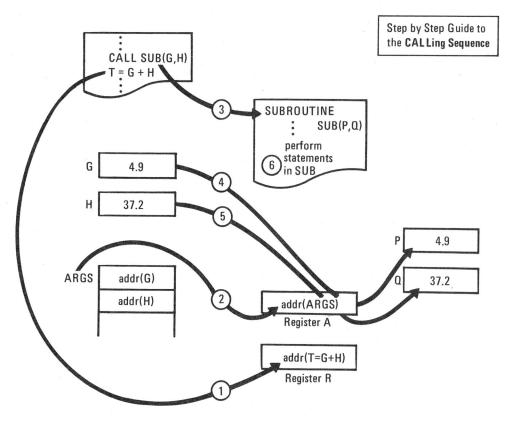

Step by Step Guide to the **CALLing Sequence**

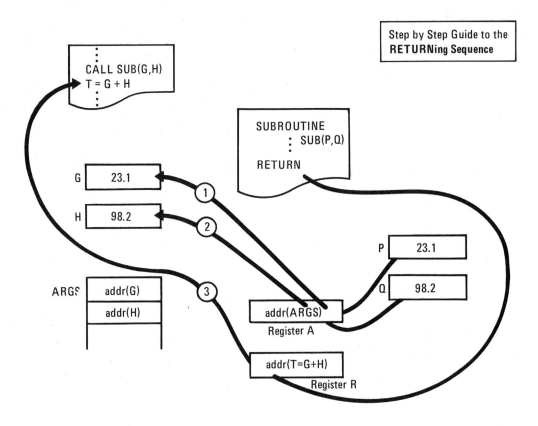

Step by Step Guide to the
RETURNing Sequence

This is the usual way that arguments are communicated between the calling program and the subprogram. However, there is another argument communication mechanism that changes results in certain cases. This other argument passing mechanism is known as **call by location** (also **call by name** and **call by reference** in some of the literature on computing). Using this mechanism, the compiler doesn't physically associate a memory cell with the parameter names in the subprogram. Instead, at each point in the subprogram where there is a reference to a parameter, the compiler leaves spaces for attaching the location of the argument memory cell in the calling program. The subprogram is called in the same way as before; that is, the argument list address and return address are stored in the special registers, but when the subprogram is entered, it first fills up these spaces left for the argument bindings. In other words, parameters called by location are attached to the actual argument locations before the subprogram computation starts. In this way, each time a parameter is referenced in the subprogram, the machine is actually dealing with a memory cell back in the calling program. Therefore, any changes to that memory cell are made directly in the subprogram's computation. The RETURN sequence is simplified—there is no need to take values from the subprogram parameter locations and put them into the actual argument memory cells. Indeed, there are no parameter locations in the subprogram, and, in any case, the actual arguments have been modified directly by the subprogram's instructions.

This call by location mechanism is always used in communicating arrays between the calling program and the subprogram. Otherwise, the subprogram would need space for a complete entire copy of the argument array. This could amount to a lot of wasted space. Worse yet, how would the compiler know how much space to leave for the copy of the argument array if the array parameter

---

call by location

form
SUBROUTINE n (... /f/ ...)
type FUNCTION n (... /f/ ...)

meaning
the parameter f is called by location

examples
```
SUBROUTINE EXT(A, /B/, C)
SUBROUTINE PZR(/T/, L, Q, /H/)
```

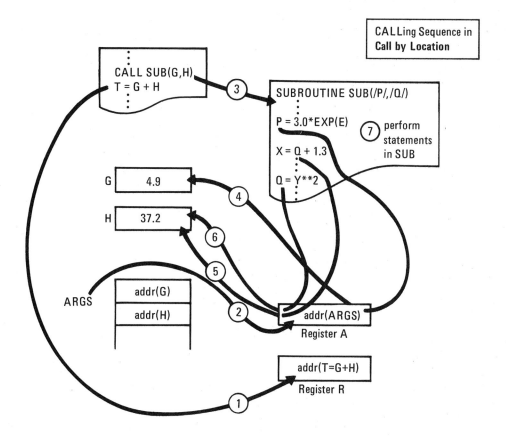

CALLing Sequence in **Call by Location**

---

declaration contained a variable length? The variable length couldn't be known at compile-time.

If you want to specify call by location for parameters which are not arrays, you simply place slashes around their names in the parameter list part of the sub-program header card. For a more graphic illustration, see the boxes on the CALLing and RETURNing sequence for call by location.

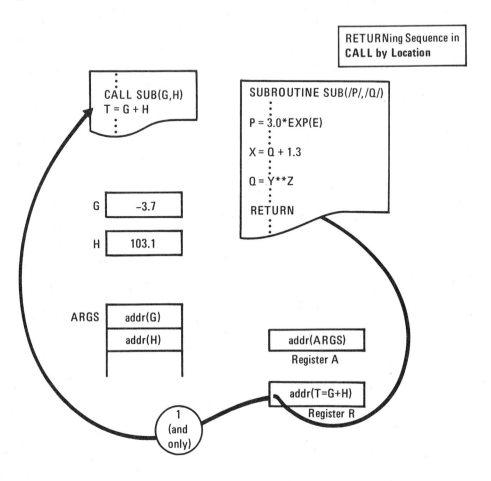

EXERCISES 11 4

1 Give an example of a situation in which call by location gives results different from those of the usual argument communication mechanism.

Please see box near Exercises 11 2.

Section 11 5

Multiple Returns and Entries

When a SUBROUTINE makes computations in which troublesome error conditions may arise, it is wise to provide a way of informing the CALLing program when these errors occur. One way to do this is to include an extra output parameter of LOGICAL type in the SUBROUTINE definition. When an error condition arises, we set the output parameter to .TRUE.; otherwise we leave it .FALSE. Then, after each CALL, we test this error flag and take appropriate action in case of an error.

```
time honored way to detect errors
          LOGICAL ERROR
          .
          .
          .
          CALL SUB (X,Y, ERROR)
          IF ( ERROR )  GO TO 999
          .
          .
          .
          CALL SUB (Z,Q, ERROR)
          IF ( ERROR )  GO TO 999
          .
          .
          .
    999   PRINT, 'BAD THINGS HAPPENNED'
          STOP
          END

          SUBROUTINE SUB (A,B; ERROR)
          LOGICAL ERROR
          ERROR = .FALSE.
          .
          .
          .
    COMMENT:  ERROR
    500   ERROR = .TRUE.
          RETURN
          END
```

The main disadvantage of this method of error detection is that the CALLing program gets cluttered with IF statements testing for the error condition. (Each CALL to the SUBROUTINE must be followed by an error check.) It is for situations like this that WATFIV provides the multiple returns feature. Using multiple returns, we can use the argument list in the CALL to designate a place to go in case an error occurs. Then the SUBROUTINE can return directly to the error handling part of the CALLing program and the cluttering IF statements can be omitted.

```
┌─────────────────────────────────────────────────────────┐
│  multiple return way to detect errors                   │
│                    •                                    │
│                    •                                    │
│                    •                                    │
│          CALL  SUB  (X,Y,  &999)                        │
│                    •                                    │
│                    •                                    │
│                    •                                    │
│          CALL  SUB  (Z,Q,  &999)                        │
│                    •                                    │
│                    •                                    │
│     999   PRINT,  'BAD  THINGS  HAPPENNED'              │
│           STOP                                          │
│           END                                          │
│                                                        │
│          SUBROUTINE  SUB  (A,B,  *)                     │
│                    •                                    │
│                    •                                    │
│                    •                                    │
│  COMMENT:   ERROR                                      │
│     500   RETURN  1                                    │
│           END                                          │
└─────────────────────────────────────────────────────────┘
```

For illustration, consider the random number generator in Section 7 5. There is a serious error which will occur if SUBROUTINE RANDOM is called too many times. It will start delivering the same 'random' numbers over again. If you give it some thought, you will see that the sequence must cycle eventually because all the values of A lie between 0 and 32767. It turns out that it cycles sooner than you might think (after about 8000 CALLs). We should put a test for cycling in the routine. We can do this by keeping track of the initial value, 19727. If A gets back to that value, the sequence has started over. (It is by no means obvious that this is a foolproof test for cycling. The eventual cycle might not include the starting value. But at least it's a precaution. See *The Art of Computer Programming, Vol. 2, Seminumerical Algorithms,* by D. Knuth and references therein for details on why this is a safe cycling test for this generator.) If A has not yet returned to its original value, we make a normal RETURN from the SUBROUTINE; otherwise, an error RETURN.

```
        •
        •
        •
CALL  RANDOM  (U,  &937)
        •
        •
        •
CALL  RANDOM  (U,  &982)
        •
        •
        •
END
```

```
      SUBROUTINE RANDOM (X, *)
      REAL X
      REAL FLOAT
      INTEGER A/19727/, MULT/25211/, BASE/32768/, MOD
      INTEGER CYCVAL/19727/
      A = MOD(MULT*A,  BASE)
C     ERROR RETURN IF GENERATOR HAS CYCLED
      IF ( A .EQ. CYCVAL )  RETURN 1
C     NO CYCLE YET--PROCEED AS USUAL
      X = FLOAT(A) / FLOAT(BASE)
      RETURN
      END
```

The error return is designated by an asterisk (*) in the parameter list of the SUBROUTINE definition. The corresponding argument in the CALL statement must be a statement label constant; that is, a statement label preceded by an ampersand (&). A SUBROUTINE definition may indicate several returns in the parameter list, one by an asterisk, and they can occur at any point in the list. Of course, CALLs to the SUBROUTINE must designate a destination for each of the returns by including a statement label constant at the appropriate point in the argument list. If there is more than one of these asterisks in the subprogram

---

statement label constant

form
&s
s is a statement label

meaning
used only in argument list to indicate destinations of multiple returns

examples
```
CALL STARK (A, &90, &472, B, &904)
CALL NAKED (&50, A, B, C)
CALL CITY  (A, &983)
```

---

multiple RETURN parameters

form
SUBROUTINE *name* (. . . , *, . . . , *, . . .)
name is an identifier
(There may be one or several * parameters at any point in the parameter list.)

meaning
Each * sets up a special return from the subprogram. Such a return is invoked by a RETURN *i* statement.

examples
```
SUBROUTINE STARK (A, *,*, B, *)
SUBROUTINE NAKED (*, A,B,C)
SUBROUTINE CITY  (A,*)
```

---

definition, then the statement RETURN 1 indicates a return to the statement label in the argument corresponding to the first asterisk. RETURN 2 refers to the second, and so on. Of course, the normal return to the statement after the CALL is still made using an ordinary RETURN statement.

RETURN *i* statements

form
   RETURN *i*
   i is an INTEGER constant between 1 and *n*,
   n is the number of asterisks in the SUBROUTINE parameter list

meaning
   RETURN to the statement in the CALLing program designated by the argument in the CALL corresponding to the *i*th * in the parameter list of the SUBROUTINE definition.

examples
   RETURN 1
   RETURN 2
   RETURN 3

In addition to having many returns, it is possible for a subprogram to be invoked at several different points of entry under different names with possibly different parameter lists.

There are many possible misuses of this feature. One not too unreasonable use is to initialize some local memory cells in a subprogram with a call to one point of entry. Then subsequent calls to the other point of entry won't need a bulky list of arguments to specify all of the values necessary in the computation. We don't particularly encourage the use of this feature, but the example below illustrates the point. It is a routine which delivers random numbers from a Gaussian (*i.e.*, normal) distribution. Upon entry at entry point INITG, the SUBROUTINE sets up the mean and variance and also delivers the first random number. Subsequent CALLs to the entry point GAUSS will deliver a random number from a Gaussian distribution with the mean and variance set by the (most recent) CALL to INITG. To make the program more robust, we have included an error exit in the INITG entry in case the variance argument is negative.

```
          SUBROUTINE INITG(X, MEAN, VAR, *)
          REAL X, MEAN, VAR
COMMENT:  "INITG" SETS UP MEAN AND STANDARD DEVIATION TO BE
C            USED IN GENERATING GAUSSIAN DEVIATES.
C            AN ERROR EXIT INDICATES AN INVALID VARIANCE.
C
          REAL MU, SIGMA, Y, S
          LOGICAL HAVEIT
          IF ( VAR .LT. 0 )  RETURN 1
          MU = MEAN
          SIGMA = SQRT(VAR)
          HAVEIT = .FALSE.
C
          ENTRY GAUSS(X)
COMMENT:  DELIVER "X", A SAMPLE FROM A GAUSSIAN DISTRIBUTION
C            WITH MEAN AND VARIANCE SET UP BY THE MOST RECENT
C            CALL TO THE ENTRY "INITG"
C         USE BOX-MULLER TECHNIQUE TO PRODUCE A SAMPLE
          IF ( HAVEIT )  GO TO 200
             HAVEIT = .TRUE.
   10        CALL RANDOM(X)
             CALL RANDOM(Y)
             X = 2.0*X-1.0
             Y = 2.0*Y-1.0
             S = X*X+Y*Y
             IF ( S .GE. 1.0 )  GO TO 10
             X = X*S*SIGMA + MU
             Y = Y*S*SIGMA + MU
             RETURN
  200        HAVEIT = .FALSE.
             X = Y
             RETURN
          END
COMMENT:  GENERATE THREE SAMPLES FROM THE GAUSSIAN
C            DISTRIBUTION WITH MEAN 100 AND VARIANCE 1000.
          REAL G1, G2, G3, G4
          CALL INITG (G1, 100.0, 1000.0, &999)
          CALL GAUSS(G2)
          CALL GAUSS(G3)
COMMENT:  GENERATE A SAMPLE FROM THE GAUSSIAN DISTRIBUTION
C            WITH MEAN -3.7 AND VARIANCE EQUAL TO THE LAST
C            SAMPLE CHOSEN ABOVE.
          CALL INITG (G4, -3.7, G3, &999)
          PRINT, G1, G2, G3
          PRINT, G4
          STOP
  999     PRINT, 'ERROR... VARIANCE CAN''T BE NEGATIVE'
          STOP
          END


output
      0.1150215E 03      0.9446729E 02      0.1202035E 03
     -0.3707346E 01
```

ENTRY Statement

form

 ENTRY *name* (*param*)
 ENTRY *name*

 name is the ENTRY name (an identifier)
 param is a parameter list (as in subprogram header statements).

meaning

 If a CALL or FUNCTION reference to name is made from outside the subprogram containing the ENTRY, control is transferred to the statement following the ENTRY statement. The parameter list may include some or all of the parameters in the subprogram header statement (main entry) or they may be entirely different. Any which are the same must agree in type, form, and parameter passing mechanism (see Section 11 4) to those in other ENTRYs and the main entry.

examples

```
SUBROUTINE S(A, /B/, C)
   .
   .
   .
ENTRY T(A,X)
   .
   .
   .
ENTRY U(Y,X,C,A)
   .
   .
   .
ENTRY V(/B/)
   .
   .
   .
ENTRY W
   .
   .
   .
END
```

Section 11 6

Additional I/O Statements

The I/O devices we have been principally concerned with have been the card reader and the line printer. However, there are many other kinds of I/O equipment (*e.g.,* punch, paper tape, magnetic tape, disk, drum, etc.). Each device has different advantages in terms of speed and convenience which we'll not dwell on here. Because of this great variety of I/O devices, some or all of which may be present at any particular computer center, it would be difficult for a language to

> *peripheral device:* any piece of hardware (other than the controller or memory) which is connected to a computer

provide a different I/O statement for each device. To communicate with these devices we use a more general form of I/O statement. In a WATFIV program we refer to each device by a different number called a unit number. The I/O statements specify the unit number of the I/O device to be used. Unit numbers are associated with I/O devices by a mechanism outside the program itself (job control cards). The exact details of associating I/O devices with unit numbers change from one computer center to the next and sometimes from one month to the next, so it would be of no service to delve into that topic here. See a local expert (*i.e.,* somebody walking around with a large deck of cards and tape reels) if you need to know. Usually unit number 5 is the card reader, unit 6 is the line printer and unit 7 is the card punch, but your system may have different conventions.

There are several options associated with the generalized input statement. It can be formatted or format-free (indicated by an * in place of the FORMAT). If it is formatted, it may have a fixed or variable FORMAT. In addition, the statement can specify what to do in case one of two abnormal conditions arises, an error in transmission on the READ unit or an end of file condition.

An error in transmission may occur if the equipment or storage medium is in bad repair or if someone has sneezed recently near the tape drives. An end of file condition occurs when the READ unit detects a special mark (EOF) on the storage medium. EOF marks are normally placed at the end of the data to assure that the READ unit won't go past the end without warning. The READ statement may designate places in your program to go to in case one of these conditions arises.

```
generalized READ statement

forms
    list directed forms
        READ (u, f) list
        READ (u, f, END = s) list
        READ (u, f, END = s, ERR = t) list
        READ (u, f, ERR = t) list
        READ (u, f, ERR = t, END = s) list
            u, the unit number, is an unsigned INTEGER * 4 constant
            or memory cell name
            f, the FORMAT, is a FORMAT statement label, an array
            name, or an asterisk (*)
            list is an input list (may be omitted)

    NAMELIST form
        READ (u, q)
            u is as above
            q is the name of a NAMELIST

    core-to-core form
        READ (c, f) list
            c is a CHARACTER * n array or memory cell name (sub-
            scripted or unsubscripted)
            f and list are as above
```

```
generalized READ

meanings
    list directed meaning
        Values from unit u are placed sequentially into the memory
        cells in list according to FORMAT f.
        If f is an asterisk, the format-free facility is used.
        If list is omitted, one record on u is skipped.
        If END = s is present, control transfers to statement s in
        case the READ encounters an end of file.
        If ERR = t is present, control transfers to statement t in
        case of an error in transmission.

    NAMELIST meaning
        see Section 11 7

    core-to-core meaning
        Values are placed into the memory cells in list. They are
        taken from the character in c, interpreted as records of
        length n according to FORMAT f.
```

```
┌─────────────────────────────────────────────────────────────┐
│                                                               │
│  generalized READ                                             │
│                                                               │
│  examples                                                     │
│     list directed examples                                    │
│         READ (5,1000) A,B,C                                   │
│         READ (5,FMT,END=450) (T(I),I=1,N)                     │
│         READ (LT,1000,ERR=310) X,Y                            │
│         READ (LT,FMT, ERR=450,END=310) Z,Q,R                  │
│         READ (5, *  ,END=890,ERR=999) Q,T                     │
│                                                               │
│     NAMELIST examples                                         │
│         READ (5,PARAM)                                        │
│         READ (LT,TERMS)                                       │
│                                                               │
│     core-to-core examples                                     │
│         CHARACTER*24 REC,RECS(10)                             │
│              •                                                │
│              •                                                │
│              •                                                │
│         READ (REC,1000) A,B,C                                 │
│         READ (RECS,FMT) (T(I),I=1,N)                          │
│         READ (RECS(3),1000) X,Y,Z                             │
│         READ (RECS(K),FMT) Q,ESP                              │
│                                                               │
└─────────────────────────────────────────────────────────────┘
```

In addition to the usual list directed input, the generalized READ also works with the NAMELIST feature discussed in Section 11 7. Thus NAMELIST input can also be read from devices other than the card reader.

These features of the generalized READ are not substantially different from those of the formatted READ you have been using. However, there is an important extension to the formatted READ known as **core-to-core READ**. This feature is used to convert CHARACTER strings stored in memory into other internal data types according to a FORMAT. The conversion rules are the same as the ones you know already. The only differences are in the record size and the place where the characters are obtained.

For the core-to-core READ, the unit number is replaced by a CHARACTER*n array name or memory cell name (possibly subscripted). The **record size** (see Section 10 7) for a CHARACTER*n unit is n, and the FORMAT should take this into account. If the "unit" in a core-to-core READ is a memory cell name, then there is only one record available; if it is an array of length k then there are k records available. Your core-to-core READ should not attempt to read more records than it has available.

One important use of the core-to-core READ is for data verification. To do this a card image is read into a CHARACTER*80 memory cell. It can then be read again from that cell into another under various FORMATs to find out whether all data is in the proper form. Finally, if verification shows it to be in the proper form, it can be read under the appropriate FORMAT, again from the CHARAC-

TER*80 memory cell to other cells in memory. The program below READs a card and checks to make sure columns 12–20 contain an unsigned INTEGER constant before making the final storing of the data in an INTEGER memory cell. Thus if the data field contains some invalid characters, the card can be rejected.

```
      INTEGER N
      CHARACTER*80 CARD
      CHARACTER*1 IFIELD(9)
      LOGICAL INTEGR
 100  READ (5,1000) CARD
 1000 FORMAT(A80)
COMMENT:  PUT CONTENTS  OF COLUMNS 12 TO 20 INTO "IFIELD"
      READ (CARD,2000) IFIELD
 2000 FORMAT(11X,9A1)
COMMENT:  MAKE SURE THE FIELD CONTAINS AN UNSIGNED INTEGER
      IF ( INTEGR(IFIELD) )  GO TO 400
         PRINT 3000, IFIELD
 3000    FORMAT (' ', 'INVALID DATA:', 9A1)
         STOP
COMMENT:  DATA OK... PROCEED
 400  READ (CARD,4000) N
      PRINT, 'UNSIGNED INTEGER:', N
 4000 FORMAT (11X,I9)
C        .
C        .
C        .
      GO TO 100
      END

      LOGICAL FUNCTION INTEGR (IFIELD)
      CHARACTER*1 IFIELD(9)
COMM  T:  THIS FUNCTION DECIDES WHETHER OR NOT THE CONTENTS
C         OF "IFIELD" IS AN UNSIGNED INTEGER.  THEREFORE,
C         ITS VALUE IS .TRUE. IF EVERY CHARACTER IN "IFIELD"
C         IS EITHER A DIGIT OR A BLANK. OTHERWISE, .FALSE.
      LOGICAL DIGIT
      INTEGER I
      DO 100 I=1,9
         IF ( .NOT. DIGIT(IFIELD(I)) )  GOTO 200
 100     CONTINUE
      INTEGR = .TRUE.
      RETURN
 200  INTEGR = .FALSE.
      RETURN
      END

      LOGICAL FUNCTION DIGIT (K)
      CHARACTER*1 K
COMMENT:  THIS FUNCTION TAKES THE VALUE .TRUE. IF  "K" IS A
C         DIGIT OR A BLANK. OTHERWISE, .FALSE.
      CHARACTER*1 LEGIT(11) /' ', '0', '1', '2', '3', '4',
     +                       '5', '6', '7', '8', '9'/
      DIGIT = .FALSE.
      DO 100 I=1,11
         IF ( K .EQ. LEGIT(I) )  DIGIT = .TRUE.
 100     CONTINUE
      RETURN
      END
```

data
```
   OK ...        4032
   BAD DATA...   +7033
```

output

```
    UNSIGNED INTEGER:          4032
    INVALID DATA:      +7033
```

As you no doubt suspect, there is also a generalized form of output statement (WRITE) so that a variety of output devices can be used. Its form is similar to the generalized READ and is described in the boxes below. There is also a core-to-core WRITE which converts values from internal representations in memory to character strings and stores them in CHARACTER*n variables. As with the core-to-core READ, the record length for such conversions of information is n when the "unit" is of CHARACTER*n type. One important use of the core-to-core WRITE feature is to convert numbers needed in computed (variable) FORMATs to the required character strings. Exercise 1 at the end of this section deals with this problem.

---

generalized WRITE statement

forms
  list directed form
      WRITE (u, f) *list*
      WRITE (u, f)
      u, the unit number, is an INTEGER constant or an INTE-
      GER*4 memory cell name.
      f is a FORMAT statement label, an array name, or an
      asterisk (*)
      list is an output list

  NAMELIST form
      WRITE (u, q)
      u is as above and
      q is the name of a NAMELIST

  core-to-core form
      WRITE (c, f) *list*
      WRITE (c, f)
      c is a CHARACTER*n array or memory cell name (sub-
      scripted or unsubscripted) and
      f and *list* are as above

---

generalized WRITE

meanings
  list directed meaning
      Write values in *list* sequentially onto unit u according to
      FORMAT f. If f is an asterisk, use the format-free facility.

  NAMELIST meaning
      See Section 11 7

  core-to-core meaning
      Write values in *list* sequentially into c according to
      FORMAT f in records of length n.

In addition to the generalized WRITE, there is a specialized output statement for use with the card punch. It is like the PRINT statement you are familiar with except that the word PRINT is changed to PUNCH. Like the card reader, the card punch has no carriage control. Each PUNCH statement automatically starts on a new card.

The I/O we have been dealing with has always involved a *conversion*. As we have used them so far, input statements convert character strings (taken from our data cards) into INTEGERs, REALs, or whatever type is specified in the FORMAT. An output statement performs the reverse conversion from a representation of data in memory to a character string (normally printed on paper).

    WATFIV for Humans

The I/O device stores the information in a form very different from the way it would be stored in memory cells. This is quite natural, of course, because we have been using I/O devices primarily as a means of communication between human and computer.

However, I/O devices can be used as an extension of the computer's memory as well as a means of communication. When an I/O device is used for this purpose, the information on the I/O device might just as well be stored in essentially the same form as it would be stored in memory cells since that would avoid the conversion process. This is the reason for *unformatted I/O* statements. We use the word "unformatted" to mean that the form in which the data is stored on the I/O device is left up to the computing system being used, hence is not specified by a FORMAT statement. Most computing systems choose a form essentially like the one used in representing data in memory cells so that the I/O process involves very little computation. Don't confuse this with format-free I/O which we use as a means of communication with the computer. Format-free I/O makes the conversion between character strings and internal representations according to a compiler supplied format.

Since unformatted I/O statements are used primarily to extend the computer's memory, the unit designated by an unformatted output statement should make records which can be read by some input device. The line printer, for example, would be an inappropriate unit for an unformatted I/O statement because the computer couldn't read the values back into its memory and the output would be wasted.

---

unformatted READ statement

form
>   READ (*u*) *list*
>   READ (*u*, END = *s*) *list*
>   READ (*u*, END = *s*, ERR = *t*) *list*
>   READ (*u*, ERR = *t*) *list*
>   READ (*u*, ERR = *t*, END = *s*) *list*
>
>   *u*, the unit number, is an INTEGER constant or unsigned INTEGER*4 memory cell name
>   *list* is an input list which may be omitted
>   *s* and *t* are statement labels

meaning
>   Place values into the cells in *list* from the next (unformatted) record on unit *u*. If there are more values in the record than there are cells in *list*, ignore the leftovers. If the *list* has more elements than the record has values, the leftover *list* elements don't get values. If an end-of-file is detected and the END = *s* option is used, transfer to statement *s*. If an error in transmission occurs and the ERR = *t* option is used, transfer to statement *t*.

examples
```
READ (10) X, (T(I),I=1,N), Y
READ (N) X,Y
READ (10)
```

unformatted WRITE

form
>   WRITE (*u*) *list*
>
>   *u* and *list* are as in the unformatted READ

meaning
>   Put the values from the memory cells in *list* sequentially onto
>   unit *u* in one (unformatted) record.

examples
```
WRITE (10)  (T(I),I=1,N),  X
WRITE (N)   X,  Y,  (T(I),I=1,N)
```

In order to use I/O devices as extended memory, you must be able to position the I/O device (*e.g.*, at the beginning of the information or back one record). For this reason the REWIND and BACKSPACE statements are provided. The REWIND statement positions the I/O device at the beginning of the first *record* written on the device. An unformatted *record* is a set of values written by a single unformatted WRITE statement. You already know the definition of a formatted record (Section 10 7). The BACKSPACE statement positions the I/O device at the beginning of the record just previous to the one at which it is currently positioned. An I/O device, when stopped, is always positioned at the beginning of a record and a READ statement must READ a whole record, even if some of the values in the record are not put into memory.

unit positioning statements

form
>   REWIND *u*

meaning
>   position unit *u* at beginning of first record

form
>   BACKSPACE *u*

meaning
>   position unit *u* at beginning of the immediately previous
>   record.

form
>   ENDFILE *u*

meaning
>   place an end-of-file mark on unit *u* at the current position

examples
```
BACKSPACE 10
BACKSPACE N
REWIND 10
REWIND N
ENDFILE 10
ENDFILE N
```

There is one further I/O statement we'll mention, the ENDFILE statement. It puts a special mark, called an **end-of-file,** on the I/O device specified. It is used to terminate a series of records written on the device. Since an end-of-file can be detected by a READ statement with the END = s option, it provides a way to insure that your program does not try to READ data which you haven't written on the I/O device. End-of-file marks are often used to separate logical blocks of information on I/O devices.

EXERCISES 11 6

1 Rewrite the program in Section 10 8 on variable FORMATs so that it uses core-to-core WRITE to convert INTEGERs to the CHARACTER strings needed in the FORMAT SKIP.

2 Find out about the different kinds of peripheral equipment you have available at your computer center. Perhaps some of it would be of great use to you.

Section 11 7

NAMELIST and DUMPLIST

The NAMELIST statement is used to describe I/O data groups. An I/O statement using the NAMELIST feature does not require a FORMAT. The information on the data cards or printed output looks like a series of assignment statements associating each value with a memory cell. Thus, the matching of memory cells with values is done in the I/O record itself rather than by the usual sequential pairing of data with elements of the I/O list. This allows random ordering of the input values which is not possible with other input statements.

A NAMELIST is a group of memory cells associated with a NAMELIST identifier. A NAMELIST may contain one or many memory cells and arrays, and a particular memory cell or array may be a member of several different NAMELISTs. A NAMELIST group is declared in a NAMELIST statement in the declaration section of a program unit. All memory cell names or array names in a NAMELIST statement should be previously declared; otherwise default data types will be established which may not be changed by later declarations.

One advantage of the NAMELIST form of input is that you don't have to be careful when punching the data cards; the values may be placed almost anywhere. There is another, more subtle, advantage. The data cards need not give a value for each memory cell in the NAMELIST. Those not given values remain unchanged. Thus, if your program depends on several variables, any of which might need to be changed from one run to another, but most of which will usually take on certain default values, you can put these variables in a NAMELIST, initialize them to their default values, then READ the NAMELIST group. The data cards need mention values only for those variables needing to be changed for the run at hand.

NAMELIST statement

form

NAMELIST/*name*/*list*/*name*/*list*/ . . . /*name*/*list*

each *name* is an identifier for the NAMELIST and
each *list* is a list of unsubscripted memory cell names or array names

meaning

declares NAMELISTs to be used for I/O purposes.

examples

```
NAMELIST /GRP/ A,B,C   /BUNCH/ A,Q,STP,GRAF
NAMELIST /GRPA/ G,C,B,HTS
```

An I/O statement using a NAMELIST has the same form as a normal I/O statement except that the FORMAT name is changed to the NAMELIST name and the list of memory cell names is deleted. When a READ statement using a NAMELIST is executed, the data cards are searched until one is found which contains an ampersand (&) in column 2 followed immediately by the NAMELIST name. After the NAMELIST name, values are specified for some or all of the variables in the NAMELIST. The specification of each value takes the form

memory cell name = constant

or

array name = list of constants separated by commas

If the memory cell name is subscripted, the subscript must be a constant. Neither constants nor names may contain imbedded blanks. The list of constants following an array name may contain repeat factors. A constant should be of the same data type as the corresponding memory cell. Every value specification must be followed by a comma, including the last one. Trailing blanks (before the comma) are treated as zeros. Each data card must have a blank in the first column. To terminate input, the symbol &END follows the last value specification.

Example

```
REAL AMT /1000.00/, INTRST(3) /.09, .12, .18/
LOGICAL PRNT(4) /4*.FALSE./
INTEGER DEPRC(3) /3, 5, 10/
REAL DWNPMT(4) /4*100.00/
NAMELSIT /TERMS/ AMT, INTRST, DWNPMT, DEPRC, PRNT
READ TERMS
    .
    .
    .
```

data cards:

```
&PARAM  AMT=20000.00,   INTRST=3*.085,
        PRNT(2)=.TRUE.,     &END
```

The READ statement in this example will give new values to AMT, INTRST(1), INTRST(2), INTRST(3), and PRNT(2). The remaining variables in the NAME-LIST, DWNPMT(1), DWNPMT(2), DWNPMT(3), DWNPMT(4), DEPRC(1), DEPRC(2), DEPRC(3), PRNT(1), and PRNT(3), keep the values given them by the compiler.

---

replication factor

form
    $r*$
    r is an unsigned INTEGER constant

meaning
    precedes a constant in a value specification on a NAMELIST
    data card and has the effect of repeating the constant r times

examples
    3*4.2 means 4.2, 4.2, 4.2
    5*0 means 0,0,0,0,0
    2*.TRUE. means .TRUE., .TRUE.
    3*'NO' means 'NO', 'NO', 'NO'

If a NAMELIST is used by an output statement, the output produced will include all the values and names of the variables in the NAMELIST in a form like that required for NAMELIST input. This can be valuable in debugging when you want to print the contents of a number of critical memory cells at several points in your program.

Another feature often useful in debugging is the DUMPLIST. Like a NAME-LIST, a DUMPLIST is a group of memory cells. In fact, DUMPLIST groups are declared in the same way as NAMELIST groups except for the keyword in the declaration (DUMPLIST replaces NAMELIST, of course). Unlike NAMELISTs, however, DUMPLISTs are not used in I/O statements. Instead, if your program terminates abnormally (*i.e.,* with some error condition), each DUMPLIST group is printed. The form of the output is similar to that of the NAMELIST so that values of key variables are easy to find in the listing.

Section 11 8

Direct Access I/O

The **direct access I/O** feature can be thought of as an implementation of **structured arrays**. Each element in a structured array, instead of being one of the standard data types, is a (fixed size) group of characters whose layout is described by a single record FORMAT. The elements of these structured arrays lie on an I/O device rather than in memory. Since an I/O device typically has a much greater storage capacity than the computer memory, these arrays can be considerably larger than the usual memory-residing arrays.

Elements of structured arrays are established on the I/O device by a special WRITE statement, the **direct access WRITE** which designates the name of the array, the subscript, and the structure (FORMAT) of the element. The name of a structured array, instead of being an identifier as with memory-residing arrays, is a positive INTEGER number usually referred to as the **data set reference number** in other literature on the direct access I/O feature. The subscript is also a positive INTEGER number which indicates the relative position of the structured array element in the array. In this sense structured array subscripts are like the subscripts of memory-residing arrays.

Structured array elements are recalled to memory in a similar way; the statement used is a **direct access READ** which specifies the array name, a subscript, and structure (FORMAT).

To declare a structured array, we use a DEFINE FILE statement which gives the array name and length like a memory-residing array declaration. In addition, it states the size of (*i.e.,* number of characters in) the array elements, and the mode of storage. The mode of storage may be formatted or unformatted. (So far, we have only been discussing structured arrays in the formatted form.) There is one other option; the structured array can be designed to operate in both modes with elements optionally formatted or unformatted according to the mode of the direct access WRITE statement which created them.

There is one other object associated with structured arrays that has no parallel in the WATFIV notation for memory-residing arrays—the **associated variable**. It can be thought of as a cursor indicating the current position of the read/write head which transmits the array values. Knowledge of this cursor's value makes it possible to speed processing by transmitting array elements to and from memory in a way that minimizes time-consuming repositioning of the read/write head.

So that repositioning of the head can be overlapped with other computer operations, there is another direct access I/O statement, the **FIND statement,** which locates a particular array element (without transmitting it) while the computer performs the computations following the FIND statement.

These direct access I/O statements are described more precisely in the boxes below. What is not described is the method of setting up an I/O unit to use for a direct access file. This procedure will depend on the particular system used at your computer center, and you'll have to check with local experts for details.

structured array declarator

form

a *(len, size, mode, cursor)*

a, the array name, is an unsigned INTEGER constant corresponding to the unit number (**data set reference number**) established for the structured array.

len, the array length, is an unsigned INTEGER constant specifying the number of elements in the array.

mode is E, U, or L depending on whether the array elements are to be stored in a formatted form, unformatted form, or a mixture of the two, respectively.

size is an unsigned INTEGER constant specifying the size of an array element. Size is specified in characters in modes E and L and in words (four-character storage units) if the mode is U.

cursor is an unsubscripted INTEGER memory cell name which will be used to store the current position of the read/write head.

Local Expert

DEFINE FILE statement

form

DEFINE FILE *list*

list is a list of structured array declarators separated by commas

meanings

Set up one structured array for each declarator in *list* according to the specifications in the declarator.

examples

```
INTEGER CARD,LINE,EXPNO,FILENO
DEFINE FILE 9(1000,80,E,CARD),   3(200,133,E,LINE)
DEFINE FILE 9(8000,20,U,EXPNO)
DEFINE FILE 9(2936,160,L,FILENO)
```

direct access WRITE statement

forms

WRITE (*a's, f*) *list*
WRITE (*a's, f*)
WRITE (*a's*) *list*

a, the array name, is an unsigned INTEGER constant or unsubscripted INTEGER*4 memory cell name.

s, the subscript, is a positive INTEGER valued expression.

f, the FORMAT, is a FORMAT statement label or the name of an array containing a FORMAT

list is an output list.

direct access WRITE

meaning

A value is stored in the *s*th element of the structured array *a*. The value is constructed sequentially from the values in *list* according to FORMAT *f* if *f* is present (formatted array element) or in an internal form if *f* is omitted (unformatted array element). If *list* is omitted, then the FORMAT *f* should contain literal descriptors (Section 10 4) for the array element. If the FORMAT *f* contains slashes, they will affect the position of the read/write head (before transmission if they are leading slashes). The cursor for *a* is updated to indicate that the read/ write head is positioned on element *s*+1 after the WRITE.

examples

```
      WRITE (9'694,1000) A,B,C
 1000 FORMAT('BEAM DOWN A BEER, SCOTTY', 3F10,2)
      WRITE (3'I+1 , 2000)
 2000 FORMAT ('THUS SPAKE ZARATHUSTRA')
      WRITE (N'3*I+J)  (T(I),I=1,20)
```

direct access READ statement

forms

READ (*a's, f*) *list*
READ (*a's, f*, ERR = *t*) *list*
READ (*a's*) *list*
READ (*a's*, ERR = *t*) *list*

a, s, f, and *list* are as in the direct access WRITE.
t is a statement label.

meaning

Bring the *s*th element of the structured array *a* sequentially into the memory cells in *list* according to FORMAT *f*, if present, or directly in internal form if *f* is omitted. The cursor for *a* is updated to indicate that the read/ write head is positioned on element *s* + 1 after the READ.

examples

```
      READ (9'694 , 3000) (T(I),I=1,8)
 3000 FORMAT(8I10)
      READ (3'K**2 , FMT) A,B,C
      READ (N'3*I+J) (T(I),I=1,20)
```

```
┌─────────────────────────────────────────────────────────┐
│  FIND statement                                          │
│                                                          │
│  form                                                    │
│      FIND (a's)                                          │
│      a and s are as in the direct access WRITE.          │
│                                                          │
│  meaning                                                 │
│      Move the read/write head to the sth element of a.   │
│      The cursor for a is updated to indicate that the    │
│      read/write head is posi-tioned on element s.        │
│                                                          │
│  examples                                                │
│      FIND (9'694)                                        │
│      FIND (3'K**3-I)                                     │
│      FIND (N'3*J+K)                                      │
│                                                          │
└─────────────────────────────────────────────────────────┘
```

Section 11 9

The DATA Statement

You have learned three ways to put values into memory cells: initialization in type declaration statements, the assignment statement, and READ statements. The assignment statement computes a value and places the result in a memory cell. The READ statement takes values from data cards outside the program itself and places them into memory cells. Both of these statements are executable; that is, they cause the controller to take some action.

Initialization in type declaration statements, however, is done at compile-time. The **DATA statement** is essentially another notation for compile-time initialization. The DATA statement is *not* executable. It is an instruction to the compiler rather than to the controller. When the compiler converts your program into machine language, it puts values in the memory cells that you have initialized in type declaration statements. In the same way, the DATA statement instructs the compiler to put initial values into memory cells. Until now we haven't made a big point of this, but you might find an example of an advantageous use of a DATA statement interesting at this point.

Normally compile-time initialization is used only when the memory cells being initialized don't change values during execution. Such use amounts to a constant naming device which helps to make programs more readable and more easily modifiable. However, there are times when it is advantageous to use compile-time initialization for memory cells whose values will later be changed. One situation in which this is useful is when a subprogram contains a computation which should be done only once during a computer run, even though the subprogram may be called several times.

DATA statement

form

DATA $list_1$ /c_1 /,$list_2$ /c_2 /, . . . ,$list_n$/c_n/

$list_k$ is a list of (possibly subscripted) memory cell names, array names, or implied do lists, separated by commas. Non-constant subscripts or parameters in implied do lists must have been previously initialized in the compilation.

c_k is a list of constants separated by commas. Any of these constants may be preceded by a replication factor $r*$, where r is an unsigned INTEGER constant. The replication factor $r*$ has the same effect that repeating the constant following it r times would have. The list c_k must have the same number of elements as $list_k$.

meaning

The compiler places the constant values from c_k into the memory cells in $list_k$, the first constant into the first memory cell, the second into the second, etc. Each constant must match the data type of the corresponding memory cell.

restriction

DATA statements must come after relevant declarations, but they may appear anywhere else in the program, even though they affect the program *only* at compile-time.

example

```
INTEGER I, J, MOD3AD(3,3), POPUS, P2(5)
REAL E,NHALFP(4)
DATA E, NHALFP /2.718282, 1.570796, 3.141593,
&                         4.712386, 6.283185/
DATA (MOD3AD(I,J),I=1,3), J=1,3) /1,3,1,3,1,2,1,2,3/,
&     P2/2,4,8,16,32/,    POPUS/203 235 298/
```

For example, if we need a FUNCTION which computes the area of a circle given its radius, the FUNCTION will compute the product of π and the square of the radius. Therefore, the FUNCTION will need to know the value of π. Of course, we can simply write the value to seven decimal places in the expression which computes the area, but then we'll have to go look up the value in a table. That's not so bad, even though it takes time we'd rather spend on something else,

$\pi = 3.14159265$
35897932
$3846 \ldots$

but there is another disadvantage: if we give our FUNCTION to someone else whose computer carries a different accuracy in its REALs, he'll have to change the number in the program. Therefore, we decide to let the computer compute π for us to whatever accuracy it's capable of. To do this, we use the fact that $\pi/4$ = arctan (1). We compute PI using the assignment statement PI = ATAN (1.0) * 4.0. If we put the above assignment statement first in the FUNCTION it will compute a value for PI every time it is called. To avoid this unnecessary computation, we use a DATA statement to place the value .FALSE. in a LOGICAL memory cell. The first statement of the FUNCTION tests this memory cell. If it has the value .FALSE., its value is changed to .TRUE. and PI is assigned the value ATAN (1.0) * 4.0. If its value is .TRUE. (which it will be on every call to the FUNCTION except the first) then that assignment statement is skipped. Instead of having to compute π every time, the FUNCTION only has to perform a simple test and transfer.

```
      REAL FUNCTION AREA (RADIUS)
      REAL RADIUS
      REAL PI
      LOGICAL NOT1ST
      DATA NOT1ST /.FALSE./
      IF (NOT1ST) GO TO 10
         NOT1ST = .TRUE.
         PI = ATAN(1.0)*4.0
 10   AREA = PI*RADIUS**2
      RETURN
      END
```

EXERCISES 11 9

1 Which of the following are legal DATA statements? For those that are, say what values the memory cells would contain if the program were compiled. For those that aren't, say why. Assume the following declarations have been made and that the program contains only one of the DATA statements so that there is no problem with reinitialization.

```
      INTEGER A, B, C(3)
      REAL D, E, F(4)
      DATA A,B /18,1/
      DATA A,C,D /1, 3*7, 4.0/
      DATA A/3/, E,F/5*5.0/
      DATA C/1,2*3/, E/2/, D/1.0/
      DATA C(2) /2/
      DATA A, C(A) /2,3/
```

Section 11 10

The COMMON Statement

In Chapter 7, the chapter on subprograms, you were told that statements in one program or subprogram could not affect the memory cells in another unless the memory cells in question were given to the subprogram as arguments. In other words, the only way two subprograms could have access to the same memory cells would be for one subprogram to call the other and use some of its memory cells as arguments. That wasn't the whole story.

| Please look at the box near Exercises 11 4. |

There are times when it is handy for several subprograms to use some of the same memory cells without having to put them in the arguments. For example,

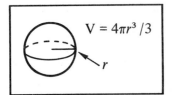

suppose we want to write three FUNCTIONs, one to compute the volume of a sphere, given its radius, another to compute the volume of a cylinder, given its radius and height, and a third to compute the volume of a cone, given its radius and height. Each of these FUNCTIONs needs to use the value of PI. It would be nice to be able to put that value into some memory cell in the computer and use that memory cell in each of the FUNCTIONs. Of course, we could do this by adding an extra argument to each FUNCTION and supplying the value to the FUNCTION through that argument. The problem with this approach is that including the argument PI in every FUNCTION reference is a nuisance. What we need is an alternative way to allow subprograms to share memory cells.

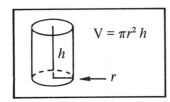
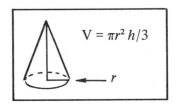

```
COMMENT:  A CLUMSY WAY TO COMMUNICATE PI TO THREE FUNCTIONS
          REAL PI /3.14159/
          REAL SPHERE, CONE, CYL
          PRINT,'VOLUME OF SPHERE OF RADIUS 1 =',SPHERE(1.0,PI)
          PRINT,'VOLUME OF CONE OF RADIUS 1, HT 2 =',
       &                                CONE(1.0, 2.0, PI)
          PRINT,'VOLUME OF CYLINDER OF RADIUS 1, HT 2 =',
       &                                CYL (1.0, 2.0, PI)
        STOP
        END
```

The COMMON statement provides that alternative. Using a COMMON statement, we can set up a part of memory which can be used by any subprogram or program.

Before things get too involved, let's look at the example at hand. We want the three FUNCTIONs, SPHERE, CONE, and CYL to be able to use a single memory cell whose value is PI. To make this possible, we place a COMMON statement in each of the FUNCTIONs. We name this region with a unique identifier which, as usual, is a string of six or fewer letters or digits beginning with a letter. We chose the name CONST in this example, as you see below. It is also possible to set up a COMMON region which is nameless; that is, its name may be blank. (We discuss several examples using blank COMMON in Chapter 13, but there is no real difference between blank and labeled COMMON other than the names, so we'll stick with labeled COMMON examples here.)

```
REAL FUNCTION SPHERE (RADIUS)
REAL RADIUS
REAL PI
COMMON /CONST/ PI
SPHERE = (4.0/3.0)*PI*RADIUS**3
RETURN
END
```

```
REAL FUNCTION CONE (RADIUS, HEIGHT)
REAL RADIUS, HEIGHT
REAL PI
COMMON /CONST/ PI
CONE = HEIGHT*PI*RADIUS**2 /3.0
RETURN
END

REAL FUNCTION CYL (RADIUS, HEIGHT)
REAL RADIUS, HEIGHT
REAL PI
COMMON /CONST/ PI
CYL = HEIGHT*PI*RADIUS**2
RETURN
END
```

COMMON statement

form

COMMON$/a_1/list_1/a_2/list_2/ \ldots /a_n/list_n$

a_k is an identifier or blank.

$list_k$ is a list of unsubscripted memory cell names or array names separated by commas.

If a_1 is blank, the first two slashes may be omitted.

An array name in $list_k$ may be followed by a length declarator if its length is not declared elsewhere.

meaning

COMMON storage regions with labels a_k are set up, one area for each distinct label. Within the program unit in which this statement appears, the memory cells in region a_k are given the names in $list_k$ in the order specified by the list. If an array name appears in the list, all of its memory cells are included in the COMMON region. If two of the area names are identical, the effect is the same as if the elements in the second list were placed on the end of the first list.

restriction

A COMMON statement must follow declarations and precede compile-time initializations of the memory cells involved.

example

```
REAL A(3), B(5), C
INTEGER X(3), Y(2), Z
COMMON /AREA1/ A,X,C  /AREA2/ Y,B,Z
```

sets up regions as follows

AREA 1		AREA 2	
	A(1)		Y(1)
	A(2)		Y(2)
	A(3)		B(1)
	X(1)		B(2)
	X(2)		B(3)
	X(3)		B(4)
	C		B(5)
			Z

As you can see, the COMMON statement labels a COMMON region in memory, the label being surrounded by slashes; then it names the memory cells to be included in the COMMON area. It is important to remember that the *label* is the only thing which can be communicated from one subprogram to another. The names of the individual memory cells within the COMMON area are local to the subprogram and *may* differ from one to another, although people usually choose to make them the same in all subprograms.

> **COMMON** *names: Each subprogram (or main program) which uses a* COMMON *region must declare the region with a* COMMON *statement. A* COMMON *region is a collection of contiguous storage units. The names referring to these storage units may be different in different subprograms. It is the* order *of the memory cell and array names in the* COMMON *statement which determines which names will be associated with which storage units.*

> **COMMON** *safety: To be safe, for each* COMMON *region, punch a "COMMON deck" of memory cell and array declarations and a single* COMMON *statement. Duplicate the deck for each program unit that uses the* COMMON *region.*

In our example of three FUNCTIONs using the COMMON area CONST. we did not include any statements giving PI a value. Of course, it would have to be given a value before any of the FUNCTIONs could be used. This could be accomplished in many ways. We will look at three ways. The first two are essentially different; the third is an embellishment of the second.

The first method is to assign PI a value in the main program before the FUNCTIONs are called.

```
REAL SPHERE, CONE, CYL
REAL PI
COMMON /CONST/ PI
PI=3.14159
PRINT,'VOLUME OF SPHERE OF RADIUS 1 =',SPHERE(1.0)
PRINT,'VOLUME OF CONE OF RADIUS 1, HT 2 =',
&                                CONE(1.0, 2.0)
PRINT,'VOLUME OF CYLINDER OF RADIUS 1, HT 2 =',
&                                CYL (1.0, 2.0)
STOP
END
```

```
VOLUME OF SPHERE OF RADIUS 1 =     0.4188786E 01
VOLUME OF CONE OF RADIUS 1, HT 2 =     0.2094393E 01
VOLUME OF CYLINDER OF RADIUS 1, HT 2 =     0.6283180E 01
```

The disadvantage of assigning PI a value in the main program is that the main program doesn't have any use for the value of PI, so it seems an inappropriate place to even have the memory cell PI around, let alone assign a value to it.

278   *WATFIV for Humans*

A nicer way is to simply include an initialization

`DATA PI /3.14159/`

after the COMMON statement in one of the FUNCTIONs. If it offends your sense of organization to put the initialization in only one FUNCTION and not the others (you must do so to avoid error messages) there is another feature of WATFIV which you can use to make the organization more symmetric.

We can instruct the compiler to give values to memory cells located in COMMON areas by using a BLOCK DATA subprogram. Actually, "subprogram" is a misnomer here since a BLOCK DATA subprogram contains *no* executable statements and, therefore, isn't a program at all. A BLOCK DATA subprogram may contain only DATA statements and declarations of memory cells, arrays, and COMMON areas. No executable statements are allowed. (It can also contain EQUIVALENCE statements; see Section 11 11). Its purpose is to instruct the compiler to put values into COMMON areas.

BLOCK DATA subprogram

form
    BLOCK DATA
    (declarations of memory cells, arrays, and COMMON areas;
    EQUIVALENCE statements)
    (DATA statements)
    END

purpose
    to instruct the compiler to put values into COMMON areas

example
```
BLOCK DATA
REAL PI
COMMON /CONST/ PI
DATA PI /3.14159/
END
```

In the present example, the BLOCK DATA subprogram would look like the one in the box above. If we put this BLOCK DATA subprogram together with the three FUNCTIONs, SPHERE, CONE, and CYL, the main program no longer needs the COMMON statement because PI is given its value by the BLOCK DATA subprogram.

The third technique that we'll discuss computes a value for PI in the same way as the example in Section 11 9 on the DATA statement. If you have trouble understanding the scheme of the subprograms below, read Section 11 9 again. Note that, no matter which of the three FUNCTIONs is called first, the value for PI is computed and assigned exactly once.

```
      REAL FUNCTION SPHERE (RADIUS)
      REAL RADIUS
      REAL PI
      LOGICAL NOT1ST
      COMMON /CONST/ PI, NOT1ST
      IF (NOT1ST)  GO TO 10
        NOT1ST = .TRUE.
        PI = 4.0*ATAN(1.0)
10    SPHERE = (4.0/3.0)*PI*RADIUS**3
      RETURN
      END

      REAL FUNCTION CONE (RADIUS, HEIGHT)
      REAL RADIUS, HEIGHT
      REAL PI
      LOGICAL NOT1ST
      COMMON /CONST/ PI, NOT1ST
      IF (NOT1ST)  GO TO 10
        NOT1ST = .TRUE.
        PI = 4.0*ATAN(1.0)
10    CONE = HEIGHT*PI*RADIUS**2 /3.0
      RETURN
      END

      REAL FUNCTION CYL (RADIUS, HEIGHT)
      REAL RADIUS, HEIGHT
      REAL PI
      LOGICAL NOT1ST
      COMMON /CONST/ PI, NOT1ST
      IF (NOT1ST)  GO TO 10
        NOT1ST = .TRUE.
        PI = 4.0*ATAN(1.0)
10    CYL = HEIGHT*PI*RADIUS**2
      RETURN
      END

      BLOCK DATA
      REAL PI
      LOGICAL NOT1ST
      COMMON /CONST/ PI, NOT1ST
      DATA    NOT1ST /.FALSE./
      END

      REAL SPHERE, CONE, CYL
      PRINT,'VOLUME OF SPHERE OF RADIUS 1 =',SPHERE(1.0)
      PRINT,'VOLUME OF CONE OF RADIUS 1, HT 2 =',
     &                        CONE(1.0, 2.0)
      PRINT,'VOLUME OF CYLINDER OF RADIUS 1, HT 2 =',
     &                        CYL (1.0, 2.0)
      STOP
      END
```

```
VOLUME OF SPHERE OF RADIUS 1 =    0.4188787E 01
VOLUME OF CONE OF RADIUS 1, HT 2 =    0.2094395E 01
VOLUME OF CYLINDER OF RADIUS 1, HT 2 =    0.6283184E 01
```

There are a few other things you should know about COMMON areas. The first is that the total number of memory cells in a particular COMMON area must be the same in all subprograms in which is it declared. The names of the memory cells in the COMMON area don't have to be the same from one subprogram to the next, but the total length of a COMMON area should be the same from one program unit to another. If they're not, the total length of the area is the maximum of its sizes in the various program units where it is declared. However, if the same COMMON area has different lengths in different program units, it's likely that you've made a mistake in typing the cards. For this reason, the compiler writes a message to warn you when it detects two declarations of the same COMMON area with differing lengths.

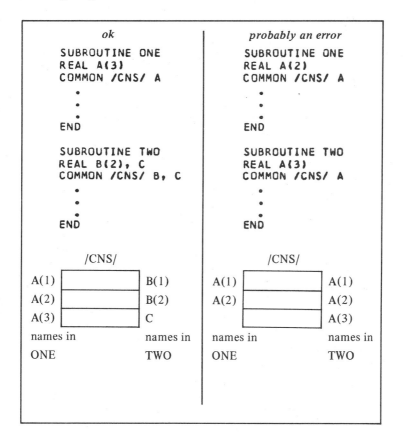

Although COMMON areas are usually used to communicate values from one subprogram to another, they are occasionally used to save memory space. To use them for this purpose is tricky, however, and should be left to the accomplished programmer.

1 Describe the correspondence between memory cells in the following SUB-ROUTINEs.

```
SUBROUTINE ONE
REAL A(3), B, C(2)
COMMON /BLK1/A, B     /BLK2/C
A(2) = 1.0
C(1) = 1.0
RETURN
END

SUBROUTINE TWO
REAL B(3) , C , D(2)
COMMON /BLK1/ C,B     /BLK2/ D
B(2) = 2.0
C = 2.0
RETURN
END

SUBROUTINE THREE
REAL Q(4), R, S
COMMON /BLK1/Q     /BLK2/ R, S
Q(1) = 3.0
Q(2) = 3.0
Q(3) = 3.0
Q(4) = 3.0
R     = 3.0
S     = 3.0
RETURN
END
```

2 The following program calls the SUBROUTINEs of Exercise 1. What does it print?

```
REAL A,B,C,D,E,F
COMMON /BLK1/A,B,C,D     /BLK2/E,F
CALL THREE
CALL TWO
CALL ONE
PRINT, A, B, C, D
PRINT, E, F
STOP
END
```

Section 11.11

The EQUIVALENCE Statement

The effect of the EQUIVALENCE statement is to allow the programmer to refer to a memory cell by more than one name. It is used to conserve memory, allowing a region of memory to be used for different purposes in one program without sacrificing the practice of giving memory cells names indicative of their use. The EQUIVALENCE statement must precede all executable statements, but should follow all relevant declarations and precede all relevant compile-time initializations.

> *Novice programmers who use the* EQUIVALENCE *statement are inviting trouble in the form of bugs which defy discovery.*

An EQUIVALENCE statement can increase the length of a COMMON area in the forward direction. That is, it can add memory cells onto the end of the COMMON area, but an EQUIVALENCE statement which implies a change in the beginning of a COMMON area is illegal.

> *Programmers with detailed knowledge of the internal representation of the various* WATFIV *data types, and a pressing need to do so, can use the* EQUIVALENCE *statement to rip values apart to manipulate their internal constituent parts. For instance, the 8 bytes of a REAL*8 constant can be examined by probing the elements of array BYTES.*
>
> ```
>         LOGICAL*1 BYTES(8)
>         REAL*8 VICTIM
>         EQUIVALENCE (BYTES,VICTIM)
> ```

ok EQUIVALENCE *extends* COMMON *region in* *forward direction*	*illegal* EQUIVALENCE *implies* *new origin for* COMMON *region*

`REAL A(3), B(4), C(2)`
`COMMON /AREA/ A`
`EQUIVALENCE (A(2),B(2),C)`
	`REAL A(3), B(3)`
	`COMMON /AREA/ A`
	`EQUIVALENCE (A(1),B(2))`

/AREA/

	A(1), B(1)
	A(2), B(2), C(1)
	A(3), B(3), C(2)
	B(4)

/AREA/

	B(1)
	B(2), A(1)
	B(3), A(2)
	A(3)

EXERCISES 11 11

1   Write all the names which can be used for memory cell A below in a list; similarly, write the alias groups for B, C(1), and C(2).

```
INTEGER A, B, C(2)
REAL X, Y(3)
EQUIVALENCE (A, Y(1), X), (C(1), Y(3)), (B, Y(2))
```

Section 11 12

The DIMENSION Statement

The DIMENSION statement provides an additional way to declare arrays. Its primary use is in conjunction with implicit typing since it declares an array without naming its type. The type may be given in an earlier declaration, however.

```
┌─────────────────────────────────────────────────────────┐
│  DIMENSION statement                                      │
│                                                           │
│  form                                                     │
│      DIMENSION list                                       │
│      list is a list of array declarators like those which │
│      may be used in type statements.                      │
│                                                           │
│  meaning                                                  │
│      Establishes array with names and lengths declared in │
│      list. Implicit types are assumed unless they have    │
│      been established by previous declaration.            │
│                                                           │
│  restriction                                              │
│      Array length declarators can't appear more than once │
│      in a program unit.                                   │
│                                                           │
│  examples                                                 │
│      DIMENSION AB(10), C(10,3,4), P(12)                   │
│      DIMENSION Q(37)                                      │
└─────────────────────────────────────────────────────────┘
```

There are three ways arrays may be declared:

1   in a type statement, *e.g.,* REAL A (10)
2   in a DIMENSION statement, *e.g.,* DIMENSION A (10)
3   in a COMMON statement, *e.g.,* COMMON A (10)

However, an array may be declared only *once* in a program.

```
┌───────────────────────┐      ┌───────────────────────┐
│ ok:                   │      │ ok:                   │
│ REAL A(10)            │      │ REAL A                │
│ COMMON A              │      │ DIMENSION A(10)       │
│                       │      │ COMMON A              │
└───────────────────────┘      └───────────────────────┘


┌───────────────────────┐      ┌───────────────────────┐
│ ok:                   │      │ ok:                   │
│ DIMENSION A(10)       │      │ COMMON A(10)          │
│ COMMON A              │      │                       │
└───────────────────────┘      └───────────────────────┘


┌───────────────────────┐      ┌───────────────────────┐
│ illegal:              │      │ illegal:              │
│ REAL A(10)            │      │ DIMENSION A(10)       │
│ COMMON A(10)          │      │ COMMON A(10)          │
└───────────────────────┘      └───────────────────────┘
```

Section 11 13

Other Branching Statements

There are two transfer of control statements we haven't yet discussed: the ASSIGNed GO TO and the arithmetic IF.

The ASSIGNed GO TO is a slightly restricted and rearranged form of the computed GO TO discussed in Section 9 1. It is included in the language because, in many implementations, it can be performed faster than the computed GO TO. Like the computed GO TO, it is a multiple branching instruction, and its branching destination is determined by the value of an unsubscripted INTEGER memory cell (not INTEGER*2). However, in the case of the assigned GO TO, the value of the INTEGER variable is actually a statement label rather than an INTEGER. The statement label value is given to the INTEGER variable by an ASSIGN statement. We describe the form of the ASSIGNed GO TO primarily for the sake of completeness.

There are many situations in which the computed GO TO is more convenient to use than the assigned GO TO, but no legitimate situations in which the assigned GO TO is more convenient. Its only advantages are a small saving in execution time and memory cells (generally, an assigned GO TO instruction requires less memory than the computed GO TO).

---

assigned GO TO statement

form
GO TO i, $(s_1, s_2, \ldots, s_n)$
$n \geqslant 1$
s_k is a statement label and
i is an unsubscripted INTEGER*4 memory cell name

meaning
transfer control to the statement whose label is stored in i.

restrictions
i must not be INTEGER*2 and must have been given one of the values s_k by an ASSIGN statement

example
```
INTEGER CASE
   .
   .
   .
ASSIGN 360 TO CASE
   .
   .
   .
GO TO CASE, (420,360,890,940)
   .
   .
   .
```

WATFIV for Humans

ASSIGN statement

form

ASSIGN s TO i

s is a statement label and
i is an unsubscripted INTEGER memory cell name

meaning

put the label s into the cell i

example

see ASSIGNED GO TO above

The arithmetic IF is a three-branch transfer of control. The choice of one of the three branches depends on whether the value of its arithmetic expression is positive, negative, or zero.

arithmetic IF

form

IF (e) s_{neg}, s_{zero}, s_{pos}

e is an arithmetic expression
s_{neg}, s_{zero}, and s_{pos} are statement labels

meaning

compute e and transfer to s_{neg} if e is negative, s_{zero} if e is zero, and s_{pos} if e is positive.

examples

```
IF ( A )   30,10,49
IF ( X-EXP(Y*T) )   189,200,18
```

12 SEARCHING AND SORTING

Section 12 1

Introduction

Some problems occur so often that people have spent a great deal of time inventing and comparing alternative algorithms which solve them. In this chapter we'll look at two such problems in detail to give you some ideas about how to compare different algorithms. Both problems are seemingly simple, but in fact people are still learning a lot from trying to find ever-better solutions. The first problem is that of *searching, i.e.,* looking in an array for a particular stored value. The second is *sorting, i.e.,* given an array of values, how can the array be manipulated so that the values wind up in order. You've seen solutions to both of these problems in the first part of the book; here you will see some solutions which are generally better.

Section 12 2

Searching

Our problem here is, how should you store numbers in an array if you are going to have to look up specific ones later?

One place the problem arises is in assembling, maintaining, and using files of information about people (data banks). In Section 9 2 we saw a way of using several arrays, one for each type of information. There we let the subscripts link the various pieces of information together—for example, letting the ith memory cell in each array correspond to the information stored about the ith person. For example, suppose we want a file of information to help prepare paychecks. For each person, we'd need to record (1) a social security number, (2) an hourly wage, (3) the number of income tax deductions claimed, and (4) whether or not they've elected to have company health insurance. If there are not more than 2000 employees, we'd declare the arrays:

```
INTEGER SOCSEC(2000), HRWAGE(2000), DEDUCS(2000)
LOGICAL INSURE(2000)
```

and the first part of our "data bank" might look like Figure 12 2 1.

	SOCSEC		HRWAGE		DEDUCS		INSURE
1	275307041	1	375	1	2	1	.FALSE.
2	444226810	2	425	2	1	2	.TRUE.
3	721337726	3	326	3	5	3	.TRUE.
	⋮		⋮	4	⋮		⋮

Figure 12 2 1

The information stored about the second person is that her social security number is 444226810, her hourly wage is \$4.25, she has claimed one deduction, and it is .TRUE. that she has the company health insurance. (Note that we've stored wages as INTEGERs instead of REALs so that we don't have to worry about round-off errors.)

Now when the records showing how many hours each person worked this week come in, we must find the information stored about that person to be able to compute his pay for the week. Suppose one such record is

soc-sec-no = 721337726 hrs worked = 36.5

As we have things set up, we would have to search in the SOCSEC array until we found an entry with the value 721337726. We would find it in SOCSEC(3), so we would know that the information about this person is stored in HRWAGE(3), DEDUCS(3), and INSURE(3). In this case, that wouldn't take much effort, but on the average we would have to look through about half of the employees before we found the one we wanted. There is a much faster way. Suppose that we stored things so that the person's social security number *was the array subscript value of the memory cells where his records were stored.* Then if memory cell ID contained a particular person's social security number, the cells

HRWAGE(ID), DEDUCS(ID) and INSURE(ID)

would contain the information we want. This way, no matter who we're looking for, once we know his social security number, we can immediately find the desired information.

No doubt you can see the trouble with our scheme. It requires that the arrays be as long as the largest possible social security number! If we had only 2000 employees, we'd still need 999999999 memory cells in each array, even though 999997999 of them wouldn't be used for anything. Inserting new records and retrieving old ones is very fast and easy, but the memory requirements are simply unacceptable.

"Aha!" you may say. Why not just give each employee a number between 1 and 2000? Then we could use the same technique but need only 2000 spaces in each array.

That solution is also unacceptable because it would mean that each employee would have to learn his employee number (and a number for his bank, his savings and loan, and every organization that wanted to use this efficient and convenient—for the computer—way of storing information). That's just the sort of thing that makes people say that computers are dehumanizing.

Ralph Zandworthy   Cynthia Sizemore   Bill Farr   Momma Kachunsteiner   Chester P. Thread

1282   470   992   729   12

The only acceptable way of utilizing a data bank such as we're describing is a combination of the techniques we've described: give each person a small number, but never let him know it. Instead, store an array which makes the correspondence between his social security number (or, even better, his name) and the number you want to use internally. To find a person's records, first locate his social security number, then use the corresponding element in the internal number array to retrieve his records. If you turn back a few pages, you'll see that this is equivalent to the way we started! Thus, no matter how much information you want to store about each person, the only acceptable ways of accessing that information involve looking up a number (or name) in an array.

Now that we've resigned ourselves to the fact that we must look in an array to locate the information we want, let's concentrate on that problem. The most obvious way is the simple one we already mentioned. Look at the contents of the first memory cell and see if that's the one we want. If so, then we're done. If not, we'll look at the second, and so on. We'll call this **sequential search**. Figure 12 2 2 describes the process, assuming the array we're searching is named PEOPLE and the value we're looking for is PERSON.

This algorithm will work fine as long as PERSON really is in the array PEOPLE somewhere. If there's been a typing error, or PERSON represents a new employee, then the algorithm gets into trouble because it doesn't check to make sure it doesn't keep going past the end of the array. As long as we're going to fix *that*, let's change it so that if PERSON doesn't appear in the array, we'll make a new entry. Let the memory cell NENTRY store the number of entries (people's names or numbers) stored in the array.

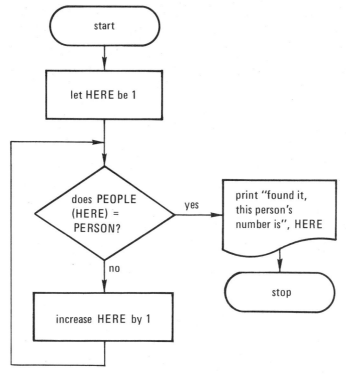

Figure 12 2 2

So, making a new entry is very easy. We just add one to NENTRY since there's now one more person stored and then stick in PERSON (see Figure 12 2 3). If there are NENTRY people, then finding a PERSON takes NENTRY/2 steps on the average. If the PERSON isn't in the array, it takes NENTRY steps to discover that fact. Sequential search is very easy, but it can take a long time even on a very fast computer. For instance, if there are 10,000 people on a company's payroll, it would take

$$\underbrace{10,000}_{\substack{\text{number of} \\ \text{searches}}} \quad * \quad \underbrace{10,000/2}_{\substack{\text{average steps} \\ \text{per search}}} = 50,000,000 \text{ steps}$$

to find the information needed to compute all the paychecks.

There is a situation that we're all familiar with that is very similar to the one we're facing. Suppose you are given someone's name and a phone book and are asked to find that person's phone number. If the phone book listings were in no particular order, you'd have to carry out the sequential search algorithm to find the name you're looking for! Except in a very small town, that would be a horrendous task. Fortunately, the phone company has had the good sense to put the listings in alphabetical order so that you have some hope of finding the name

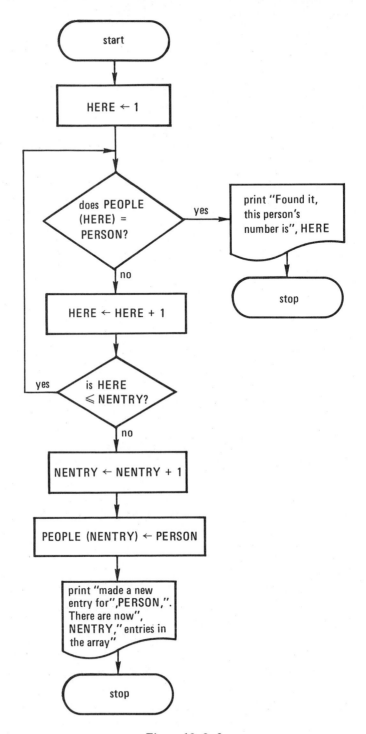

Figure 12 2 3

you want (or discovering that it's not listed) before your eyes fall out. Obviously, it would be faster to find an entry in an array if the array were arranged in a nice order. If the array is in increasing order, we can use the following algorithm, which is related to the way you look up a number in a phone book.

We'll use two variables, one called LOW which stores an array index value that we know is lower than the place we want, and a memory cell HIGH which is higher than the place we want. Before we look anywhere, we know that 0 is lower than the place we want, and the NENTRY + 1 must be higher than the place we want. Then we'll start looking. Since we don't yet know anything except that the place we want is somewhere in between LOW and HIGH, we might as well look in the *middle*, guessing that the place we want is just as likely to be in the first half of the array as the last half. The middle value is, of course, PEOPLE ((LOW + HIGH)/2. Maybe that's the value we wanted. If so, we've finished. If *not*, then we can tell if the value we wanted is before the middle or after the middle just by comparing the value PERSON to the value PEOPLE ((LOW + HIGH)/2). If PERSON is not equal to PEOPLE ((LOW + HIGH)/2) then we know that if PERSON appears at all, it (a) lies *above* the middle or (b) lies *below* the middle. In either case we continue the process, changing the value of LOW in case (a) or HIGH in

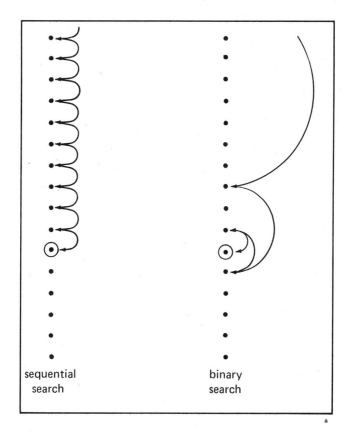

sequential
search

binary
search

case (b). If LOW and HIGH ever get so close together that there are no entries between them, we know that PERSON wasn't in the array at all! We call this kind of search *binary search* because at each step we eliminate about one half of the alternatives. The flowchart in Figure 12 2 4 describes the search more precisely.

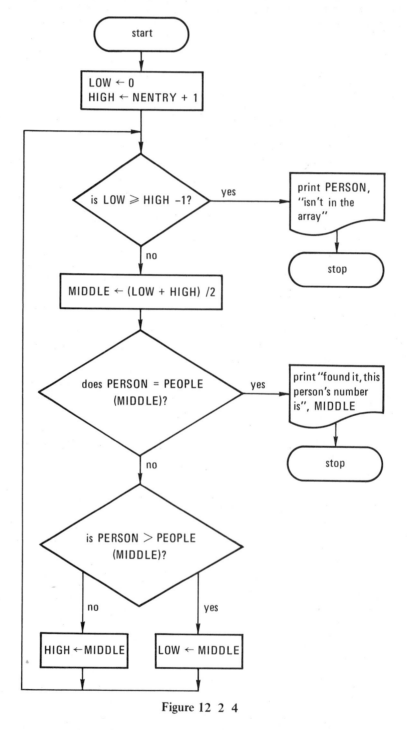

Figure 12 2 4

WATFIV for Humans

Since each time around the loop we eliminate about half of the alternatives, after 1 time there are NENTRY/2 alternatives left, after two times there are NENTRY/(2*2) left, after three times there are NENTRY/(2*2*2) left, and after n times there are NENTRY/2^n left. We stop if there can't be more than one alternative left, that is when NENTRY/$2^n \leqslant 1$. Solving for n, we find that the most steps it could ever take is $n = \log_2$ (NENTRY). Now to look up the information to compute the payroll for our company of 10,000, it takes no more than

$$
\begin{array}{ccccc}
10,000 & * & \log_2 (10,000) & = & 133,000 \text{ steps} \\
\text{number of} & & \text{maximum time} & & \\
\text{searches} & & \text{per search} & &
\end{array}
$$

which is many, many fewer than the number required by the sequential method.

While the binary search method is much better for looking things *up* than the sequential method, it's a little worse when we have to put a new person into the array. In the sequential scheme, to put in a new person, we just stick the number (or name) in at the bottom. In the binary scheme we must insert the new person in the right place so that the array stays in order.

If you look at the binary search flowchart, you'll see that when we discover that PERSON doesn't appear in the array, we at least know where it should be—it should be at position LOW + 1. All we need to do then is to slide all entries after LOW down one position and then stick in PERSON. On the average, that will take NENTRY/2 steps. Here's a complete binary search routine. It takes an array called PEOPLE as an argument along with a PERSON to look for, and it returns the position of PERSON in the array if it found it, or the position of PERSON after PERSON was inserted.

There are yet more algorithms for searching an array. One very common technique involves **hash coding**. Here the idea is a compromise between speed and the amount of memory you are willing to allow your program to use. It is a take-off on a storage method we briefly passed over earlier in this chapter. Recall that we noted that it would be very convenient to do insertions and retrievals if we just let the person's social security number be the array subscript associated with his records, but that it required an absurd amount of memory. We can get some of the same effect by just taking (say) the last three digits of the social security number and using that as an array subscript. Now we need only 999 memory cells instead of 999,999,999. However, it is likely that two people's social security numbers will have the same last three digits. This means that the numbers we get are not unique and there must be some way of telling which specific person we are looking for. There have been many, many algorithms proposed and used to do this. Since bad luck (what if the last three digits of the social security numbers of all your employees are the same!) can make hash coding degenerate into sequential search, and good luck (what if they are all different?) can make hash coding extremely fast, statistical studies are needed to recommend one technique over another.

Yet another technique for searching arrays is of value when items must often be deleted (during depressions, for example). This technique (using **AVL trees**) requires an even more elaborate structuring of the array than does binary search.

```
      SUBROUTINE BINARY(PERSON,PEOPLE,NENTRY,HERE)
      INTEGER PERSON, NENTRY, PEOPLE(100), HERE
COMMENT:   BINARY SEARCH ALGORITHM TO  FIND "PERSON" IN THE
C          ARRAY "PEOPLE" .
C             IF "PERSON" IS NOT FOUND, IT IS INSERTED.
      INTEGER LOW, HIGH, MIDDLE, SHIFT
C     IF "PERSON" IS IN THE ARRAY, IT MUST BE BETWEEN
C     THE FIRST AND LAST POSITION IN THE ARRAY.
      LOW = 0
      HIGH = NENTRY + 1
C     ARE "LOW" AND "HIGH" TOO CLOSE TOGETHER?
   10 IF ( LOW .GE. HIGH-1 ) GO TO 200
C        LOOK IN THE MIDDLE
         MIDDLE = (LOW+HIGH)/2
C        EXIT IF FOUND
         IF ( PERSON .EQ. PEOPLE(MIDDLE) ) GO TO 100
C        PROCEED IN TOP OR BOTTOM HALF OF ARRAY
         IF ( PERSON .GT. PEOPLE(MIDDLE) ) GO TO 20
         HIGH = MIDDLE
         GO TO 10
   20    LOW = MIDDLE
         GO TO 10
C
C     FOUND IT...RETURN ITS POSITION
  100 HERE = MIDDLE
      RETURN
C
C     NOT PRESENT.. INSERT IT
  200 SHIFT = NENTRY
  210 PEOPLE(SHIFT+1) = PEOPLE(SHIFT)
         SHIFT = SHIFT - 1
         IF ( SHIFT .GE. LOW+1 ) GO TO 210
      NENTRY = NENTRY + 1
      PEOPLE(LOW+1) = PERSON
      HERE = LOW +1
      RETURN
      END
```

If you are interested in hash coding or AVL trees, Problem 12 1 lists some references for further study.

There is no doubt some absolute limit to how good an algorithm can be for searching and inserting values in arrays on current digital computers. As parallel computers become more common, probably a new crop of commonly occuring problems will become the focal point of the race to find the fastest, most efficient algorithms.

EXERCISE 12 2

1 Try the following game to convince yourself of the speed of the binary search strategy. Pick a number between 1 and 1000. See how many guesses a friend makes before he gets the number if after each guess, you tell him whether his guess was "high" or "low". The binary search algorithm guarantees that you will find the answer in ten guesses or fewer.

Section 12 3

Sorting

The binary search algorithm made use of an array which we maintained in a particular order. In this section we'll see a sorting algorithm which uses another way of ordering an array to cut down on the amount of work that must be done. The sorting technique we used in Section 7 4 and Section 9 2 is slow; it takes an amount of time proportional to the square of the number of items to be sorted. In this Section we'll see a sorting method which sorts a list in an amount of time proportional to the number of entries times the logarithm of the number of entries. This seemingly small difference, multiplying the number of entries by itself as opposed to multiplying by its logarithm, can be amazingly large.

n	n^2	$n\log_{10} n$
10	100	10
100	10,000	200
1,000	1,000,000	3,000
10,000	100,000,000	40,000
.	.	.
.	.	.
.	.	.

The main idea is to organize the array of numbers to be sorted into a **tree** structure. Up to now we have tended to think of an array as providing a sequential, linear structure: array position i comes *before* position $i + 1$ and *after* $i - 1$. Here we'll organize things so that an element in the array is associated with one position that comes before it, called its **predecessor**; and two that come after it, called its **successors**, specifically, its **left successor** and its **right successor**. Since each array element has *two* successors, our trees are **binary trees**. One particularly easy way of effecting this structure is to let array position 1 be the **root** of our tree (a root is a position which has no predecessor—it's the *first* position) and to let positions 2 and 3 be its successors. In general, if we are at position i, then the left successor will be the array element at position $2*i$, the right successor will be at position $2*i + 1$, and the predecessor will be at position $i/2$ (recall that division of INTEGERs loses any fractional part so that the predecessor of positions 2 and and 3 is the same, namely the array element at position 1). Figure 12 3 1 shows the organization implied by our scheme.

Notice that (depending on how many memory cells we have in the array) some positions have no successors, and one position might have just one successor (as does position 5 here). If there are N ENTRY (for Number of ENTRies) elements

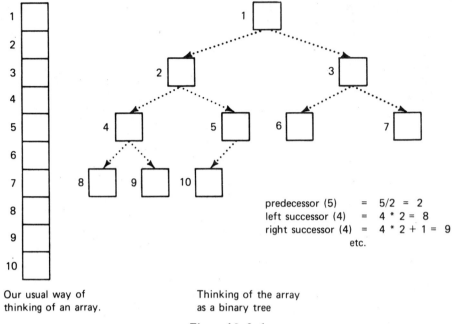

predecessor (5)   =   5/2 = 2
left successor (4)   =   4 * 2 = 8
right successor (4)   =   4 * 2 + 1 = 9
                                   etc.

Our usual way of
thinking of an array.

Thinking of the array
as a binary tree

Figure 12 3 1

in the array, then we can tell if position *i* has any successors by testing whether or
not 2**i* is less than or equal to N ENTRY.

It is this conceptual structure which will let us create the efficient algorithm
we've promised. This algorithm (due to Floyd* although our version is based
mainly on Stone's** presentation) is divided into two phases.

In Phase I we will take the unsorted array and rearrange it until we have a binary
tree with certain special properties. In Phase II we will produce the sorted array
by repeatedly removing the largest value from the binary tree and then patching
the tree up.

The binary tree we'll produce in Phase I consists of a partially sorted version of
the original array. The tree will have the property that the value stored at each
position is larger than the value stored at any successor position. We've said that
this tree is *partially* sorted because if you follow any path in the tree from the
root down through the successors, the values stored at those positions will be in
decreasing order. Such a tree automatically has the property (which we'll use in
Phase II) that the largest value of all is stored at the root node. Figure 12 3 2
illustrates the states the array to be sorted will go through. Notice that all the
properties we said the binary tree would have do, in fact, hold in the tree we've
drawn.

It probably seems odd to you that a tree structure like this could be of any

---

*R. W. Floyd, "Algorithm 245," *Comm. ACM,* vol. 7, no. 12 (1964), p. 701.

**H. S. Stone, *Introduction to Computer Organization and Data Structures,* (McGraw-Hill,
1972), pp. 257–263.

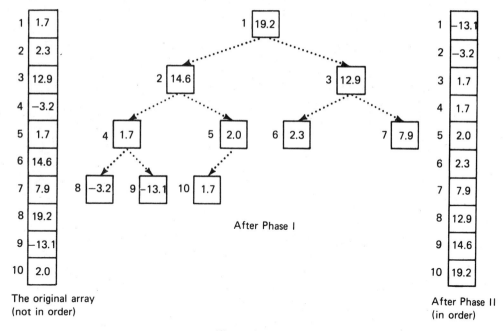

The original array
(not in order)

After Phase I

After Phase II
(in order)

Figure 12 3 2

help in sorting an array. If so, think of it this way: suppose you have in your possession a bunch of bags of gold which you want to number according to increasing weight. You also have a very accurate, but difficult to operate, scale which will compare the weights of two bags of gold. That is, at each weighing you can determine which of two bags is heavier. Since it takes so long to make a weighing, you want to retain as much information from each weighing as possible in the hope of doing as few weighings as possible.

Let's take an example with four bags and see how you might proceed. You don't have any choice in the beginning but to weigh some pair of bags, so let's say you start with bag A and bag B, and suppose A turns out to be heavier. You don't want to forget anything, so you write down an "A" above a "B" (with a line between them) indicating that bag A is heavier than bag B. Now let's say you weigh bag A and bag C and that bag A is again heavier. Now you know that bag A is the heaviest of the three bags A, B, and C, (but you don't know which of B and C is heavier) so you draw a diagram containing an "A" on the top level, and "B" and "C" on a lower level with lines extending down from "A" to "B" and to "C" to indicate that bag A is heavier than bag B and heavier than bag C. Now you want to see where bag D fits into the scheme, so you weigh bag D and bag B. Let's say bag D is heavier. Now you don't know quite how to draw the diagram. You know "D" should go above "B", but you don't know if it should also be above "A". Therefore, you weigh bag A and bag D. Let's say D is again heavier. Then "D" should go on the top level with "A" on the second level (lines from "D" to "A" indicate that bag D is heavier than bag A). "B" and "C" should go on the bottom level (connected to "A" by a line indicating that bag A is heavier than bag B, and bag A is heavier than bag C).

© rich didday

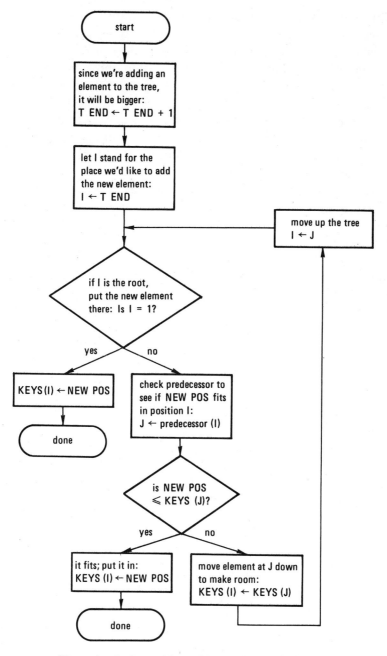

Figure 12 3 3 Adding a New Value to the Tree

Now you know bag D is the heaviest and bag A is the next heaviest. The only question left is the relation between bag B and bag C. (The diagram clearly shows this since "B" and "C" are on the same level. Therefore, you weigh bag B and bag C, finding that, say, "C" is heavier, and put the bags into increasing order by weight.

This is, of course, a special case; we have only four bags. Nevertheless, you can see that our diagrams, which looked like the trees we talked about earlier, helped us decide what weighings to make. Sorting values in WATFIV is a similar problem. You can compare only two values at a time and you don't want to make any extra comparisons if you can help it. Perhaps it is not surprising, then, that the idea of thinking of the array to be sorted as a tree helps. In the case of four objects our previous method (Sections 7 4 and 9 2) would need six comparisons, whereas we needed only five using the tree notation. Try a similar approach with five bags of gold and see how well you can do. Our old technique would need ten comparisons.

The flowchart in Figure 12 3 3 describes an algorithm for adding the next element to a partially completed binary tree in Phase I. In the flowchart we are to add the value NEW POS into the tree made up of positions 1 through T END (Tree END) of the array KEYS. The algorithm starts by trying to add NEW POS at the very bottom of the tree. If it doesn't belong there, then the value from the predecessor of the bottom spot is moved to the bottom and the process repeats. NEW VAL moves up the tree until it finds a place where it fits properly.

To create the original binary tree, we'll use our algorithm to insert one value at a time until they're all in the tree. After the tree is formed, we're through with Phase I. We are then assured that the largest value of all is in the root position.

In Phase II we collapse the tree one value at a time and build the sorted list of numbers from the bottom of the array up. Each time we take the value from the root node, we'll put it in the proper place at the bottom (since it is the largest remaining value). At the end of Phase II, the entire array will be in increasing order.

Each time we remove the largest remaining value in the tree (the value at the root), we will have to manipulate the rest of the tree so that it again has the properties we desire. Let's follow this at the point when the tree looks like this:

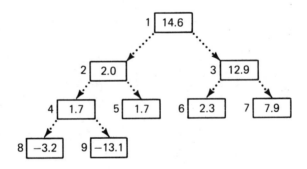

We remove the root value (14.6), and we must alter the remaining tree so that each element exceeds its successors. Thus we want to alter it by repeatedly moving up the larger value from the emptied spot's successors.

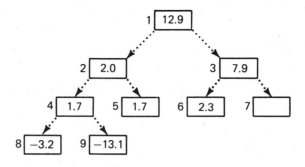

We see that everything is fine and that we no longer need position 7 since the value there was moved up in the process of patching up the tree. The only hitch is that we are supposed to put the largest element on the *bottom*, that is, position 9 rather than position 7. Fortunately that isn't any harder than the process we just described. After having removed the root, we know that we must fix up the remaining tree by inserting the value from position 9 somewhere. We'll just start at the top. Either the value from position 9 should go there, or else one of the values from the two successors of the top position goes there. We can tell which by choosing the largest of the three. If it was one of the successors, we move it up, leaving an empty position there. Then we repeat the process on the part of the tree below the empty position. Eventually we will find a legitimate place to put the value from position 9. Once it is in place, we put the largest value (14.6 in this case) into position 9 and go on to the next step of Phase II. In the next step, the tree will be smaller (in this case T END would decrease to 8). The step we just described corresponds to the changes shown in Figure 12 3 4.

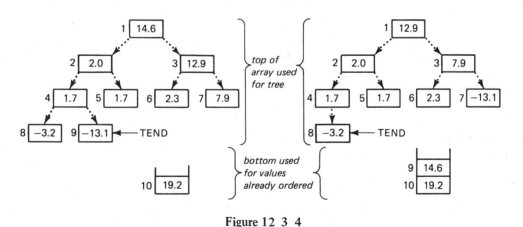

Figure 12 3 4

Figure 12 3 5 is a flowchart for a step of Phase II. In it, BOT POS is the value we want to remove from the bottom of the array to make room for the largest value.

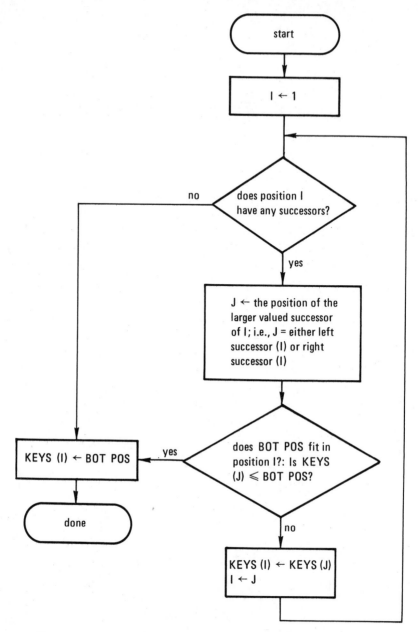

Figure 12 3 5 Repositioning the Largest Remaining Value After
Having Removed the Root

A program for the sorting algorithm we've been discussing follows. Each step of
Phase I (the flowchart of Figure 12 3 3) is performed by SUBROUTINE
CREATE; each step of Phase II (the flowchart of Figure 12 3 5) is performed by
SUBROUTINE FIXUP. The sorting program, SUBROUTINE T SORT (for Tree
SORT), can be used to sort an array of REALs.

```
        SUBROUTINE  T SORT (KEYS, NKEYS)
        INTEGER NKEYS
        REAL KEYS(NKEYS)
COMMENT:  THIS SUBROUTINE CARRIES OUT AN EFFICIENT SORTING
C         ALGORITHM BASED ON THE 'TREESORT' TECHNIQUE OF
C         R. FLOYD.  IT CONSISTS OF TWO PHASES.  PHASE I
C         CONSTRUCTS A PARTICULAR BINARY TREE.  PHASE II
C         TEARS THAT TREE APART, ONE VALUE AT A TIME, TO
C         PRODUCE A REARRANGEMENT OF "KEYS" INTO INCREASING
C         ORDER.
        INTEGER I, T END
        REAL BOT POS, NEW POS
C
COMMENT:  FIRST PUT THE VALUES INTO THE DESIRED BINARY TREE
C         CONFIGURATION.   KEYS(1) BY ITSELF IS ALREADY A
C         TREE OF THE CORRECT FORM SO START BY ADDING
C         KEYS(2)  TO THE TREE
        T END = 1
        DO 100 I = 2,NKEYS
          NEW POS =  KEYS(I)
 100    CALL CREATE (KEYS, NKEYS, T END, NEW POS)
C
COMMENT:  NOW THAT THE TREE HAS BEEN SET UP, PULL THE TOP
C         POSITION OUT, STORE IT IN THE BOTTOM AND FIX UP
C         THE TREE
        T END = N KEYS
 200    BOT POS =  KEYS(T END)
        KEYS (T END) =  KEYS(1)
C       THE TREE IS NOW ONE SPOT SMALLER
        T END = T END  -1
        CALL FIX UP  (KEYS, NKEYS, T END, BOT POS)
        IF ( T END .GE. 2)  GO TO 200
C
COMMENT:  DONE
        RETURN
        END

        SUBROUTINE CREATE  (KEYS, NKEYS, T END, NEW POS)
        INTEGER T END, NKEYS
        REAL KEYS(NKEYS), NEW POS
COMMENT:  THIS SUBROUTINE INSERTS THE KEY "NEW POS"
C         INTO THE PARTIALLY FORMED BINARY TREE STORED IN
C         "KEYS"
        INTEGER I, J, PRED
COMMENT:  STATEMENT FUNCTION FOR PREDECESSOR
        PRED(I) = I/2
C
COMMENT:  THE TREE WILL BE LARGER BY ONE POSITION
        T END = T END + 1
COMMENT:  AT FIRST TRY TO PUT THE NEW KEY ON THE BOTTOM
        I = T END
COMMENT:  HAVE WE LOOKED ALL THE WAY BACK TO THE ROOT?
 100    IF (I .LE. 1)  GO TO 200
COMMENT:  NO, DOES "NEW POS" FIT IN POSITION I
        J = PRED(I)
        IF ( NEW POS .LE. KEYS(J) )  GO TO 200
COMMENT:  NO, 'NEW POS' MUST FIT FURTHER UP THE TREE
        KEYS(I) = KEYS(J)
        I = J
        GO TO 100
COMMENT:  FOUND THE PROPER PLACE FOR "NEW POS".  INSERT IT.
 200    KEYS (I) = NEW POS
        RETURN
        END
```

```
      SUBROUTINE  FIX UP (KEYS, NKEYS, T END, BOT POS)
      INTEGER T END, NKEYS
      REAL KEYS(NKEYS) , BOT POS
COMMENT:   THIS SUBROUTINE ACCEPTS A BINARY TREE WITH A
C          MISSING ROOT AND FIXES IT UP, FINALLY INSERTING
C          "BOT POS" IN THE BLANK SPOT LEFT BY THE FIX UP.
      INTEGER I, J, L SUCC, R SUCC
COMMENT:   STATEMENT FUNCTIONS FOR LEFT SUCCESSOR AND
C          RIGHT SUCCESSOR
      L SUCC(I) = I*2
      R SUCC(I) = I*2 +1
COMMENT:   START AT THE ROOT
      I = 1
COMMENT:   IF I HAS NO SUCCESSORS, WE'RE DONE
  100 IF (L SUCC(I) .GT. T END)  GO TO 300
      J = L SUCC(I)
COMMENT:   IF I HAS JUST ONE SUCCESSOR, GO ON
      IF ( R SUCC(I) .GT. T END )  GO TO 200
COMMENT:   COMPARE VALUES AT THE TWO SUCCESSOR POSITIONS
      IF ( KEYS(J) .LT. KEYS(R SUCC(I)) )  J = R SUCC(I)
COMMENT:   DOES "BOT POS" BELONG HERE?
  200 IF ( KEYS(J) .LE.  BOT POS )  GO TO 300
COMMENT:   SLIDE UP POSITION OF LARGEST SUCCESSOR
      KEYS (I) = KEYS (J)
      I = J
      GO TO 100
COMMENT:   INSERT 'BOT POS'
  300 KEYS (I) = BOT POS
      RETURN
      END
```

This might seem to be a lot of mental effort to produce a sorting algorithm, but in a practical situation it can save an amazing amount of computer time.

To give you a rough idea about how much better this sorting technique is than the one in Section 7 4, let's refresh your memory about the sorting routine there. The way it works is by going through the entire array and finding the largest element. It moves that element to the top and then looks in the rest of the array for the largest remaining element, moves that to the second position and continues. If there are N KEYS values in the array, then we'll make N KEYS searches for the largest element; the first search is through all N KEYS spots in the array, the last is through just one. On the average we look through about N KEYS/2 places. Thus, to sort the array, we go through about N KEYS * (N KEYS/2) steps.

In the sorting scheme we've shown you here, each step we make proceeds not through the entire array but merely along a *path in the binary tree structure*. By looking at some binary trees, you should be able to convince yourself that no path in a binary tree can be longer than $\log_2$ (N KEYS). (An easy way to see this is to observe that the nth horizontal level of a binary tree contains 2^n entries, hence 2^n cannot exceed N KEYS.)

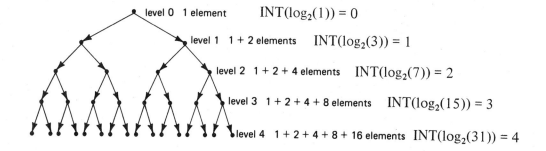

Since we have to search through two paths for each value in the original array (one path to build the tree and another to pull out the largest value and fix up the tree), the total numbers of steps can't be more than

$$2 * N \text{ KEYS} * \log_2(N \text{ KEYS}).$$

Our old scheme takes a number of steps that is proportional to $(N \text{ KEYS})**2$ while our new scheme requires a number of steps that is proportional to N KEYS $* \log_2$ (N KEYS). No matter what the constants of proportionality are, if N KEYS is big enough, our new scheme will take fewer steps than our old scheme. Use the new scheme!

Section 12 4

Program Efficiency

This chapter should have convinced you that some algorithms are faster than others even though they have the same end result. Good programmers who write programs that must deal with large amounts of data or must make large computations *do* concern themselves with developing and using efficient algorithms.

Sometime you will probably run into someone who delights in telling you obscure facts like "Hey, our machine can do a fixed point add in 1.632 microseconds and it takes 10.924 to do a multiply but only .964 to do a shift, so instead of

```
10    ENDPT = 2*NORMAL
```
like you've got, it would be faster to do
```
10    ENDPT = NORMAL + NORMAL
```
and even faster to do
```
10    ENDPT = SHL(NORMAL, 1)
```
and while you're at it, why are you using such long variable names? The scanner has to grind through all those things and, man, that takes time—why not
```
10    E = SHL(N,1)
```
and then you've got all those *comments* in there! Get them out, they just waste time. Listen to me and I'll have you writing *tight code*!"

Let's analyze what you can save by the above suggestions for writing "tight code". If you write the statement using the shift, you'll save ten millionths of a second of computer time every time the statement is executed. At that rate, you would save only one second of computer time even if the statement were executed 100,000 times, an unlikely possibility. Although you might save a fraction of a second of machine time, you would almost certainly *lose* a substantial amount of human time because your program would be harder to understand.

The point we would like to make here is that saving a little time on one statement is rarely worth it. There is a big difference between making your program more efficient by (1) using a good algorithm and by (2) form fitting your program to a specific model of a specific machine. The primary idea behind higher-level languages is that they have a degree of machine independence, that they can be shared by different people using different machines.

PROBLEMS 12

1 Write programs for two or more hash coding storage schemes and compare their behavior. A discussion of such schemes may be found in

> Harold S. Stone, *Introduction to Computer Organization and Data Structure,* McGraw-Hill, 1972, Chapter 11.

Some specific hash coding schemes are in

> J. R. Bell, "The quadratic quotient method: A hash code eliminating secondary clustering," *Comm ACM.* vol. 13, no. 2, 1940, pp. 107–109.
>
> J. R. Bell and C. H. Kaman, "The linear quotient hash code", *Comm ACM,* vol. 13, no. 11, 1970, pp. 675–677.
>
> W. D. Maurer, "An improved hash code for scatter storage", *Comm ACM,* vol. 11, no. 1, 1968, pp. 35–38.
>
> R. Morris, "Scatter storage techniques", *Comm ACM.* vol. 11, no. 1, 1968, pp. 38–44.

2 If you are interested in the searching problem, do some reading on AVL trees. The following articles will give you a start.

> G. M. Adel'son-Velskii and E. M. Landis, "An algorithm for the organization of information", *Dokl. Akad. Nank CCCP, Mathemat.,* vol. 146, no. 2, 1962, pp. 263–266.
>
> Caxton C. Foster, "Information storage and retrieval using AVL trees", *Proc. ACM Nat'l Conf.,* 1965, pp. 192–205.

3 If you are interested in sorting, do some reading on the subject. The following references will give you a start.

> C. A. R. Hoare, "Quicksort", *Comm ACM,* vol. 4, no. 7, 1961, p. 321.
>
> R. W. Floyd, "Tree Sort", *Comm ACM,* vol. 7, no. 12, 1964, p. 701.

D. Knuth, *The Art of Computer Programming,* vol. 3, Addison Wesley, 1973.

J. W. J. Williams "Heapsort", *Comm ACM,* vol. 7, no. 6, 1964, pp. 347–348.

4   Write a program that makes a plot of "number of elements in the array" vs. "average time needed for search" for (a) the sequential search algorithm and (b) the binary search algorithm. Such plots are called *timing diagrams.* Compute the average by timing a separate search for each value in the array and averaging the times.

5   Write a program which makes a timing diagram for (a) the sorting technique of Section 7 4 and (b) the sorting technique of Section 12 3. (To get an average, generate several random-valued arrays.)

6   Find someone who does a lot of sorting and ask what technique he's using. If it's not a tree sort, ask him if he'd be willing to try your tree sort program. Observe the results. (For some very special situations, other sorting techniques may be faster.)

13 SOPHISTICATED USES OF ARRAYS

Section 13 1

Data Structures

Throughout this book we have been emphasizing the idea of breaking down the problem you are trying to program so that it will be easier to understand (more clearly organized), and hence easier to work with. In this chapter we will deal with

> **data structure:** *a group of memory cells organized in some manner.*

an organizational idea which makes programming easier by making the details of your program directly analogous to the details of the problem you want to solve. The idea is to recognize some of the structure (relationships among subparts) of your problem, and after you feel you understand the structure of the problem, to assemble units of information in the computer memory into that structure. We call such assemblages of memory words **data structures**. Every program you have written has used memory cells in some way, so you have been using data structures all along. This is the first time that we will be very conscious of relationships among memory cells, however. Let's look at an example.

Figure 13 1 1(a) contains the same information as Figure 13 1 1(b). Take a look at them. Which one is better? If your problem is "how many mothers are there?" then the organization in Figure 13 1 1(b) is probably best suited. However, if you are faced with the problem of determining more complex family relationships among people, then Figure 13 1 1(a) seems easier to use. Thus, different organizations of the same data may be best suited to different problems.

What is it about Figure 13 1 1(a) that makes it easier to use to answer questions about relationships? One thing is that in the tree (Figure 13 1 1(a)), the closer two names are, the closer is the relationship between them, but there is no way to rearrange the list in Figure 13 1 1(b) so that this is true. In the tree, names along the same vertical line tend to be of the same generation, but this is obviously not true in the list. These and other reasons seem to make it easier to find your way around in the data when it is represented as a tree. More effort has gone into organizing the data in the tree than in the list, but this effort can pay off when the time comes to use the data.

This chapter deals with the organization of data as an important part of programming. Often spending some time and thought organizing your data can result in a program which is not only easier to write and understand but also more efficient.

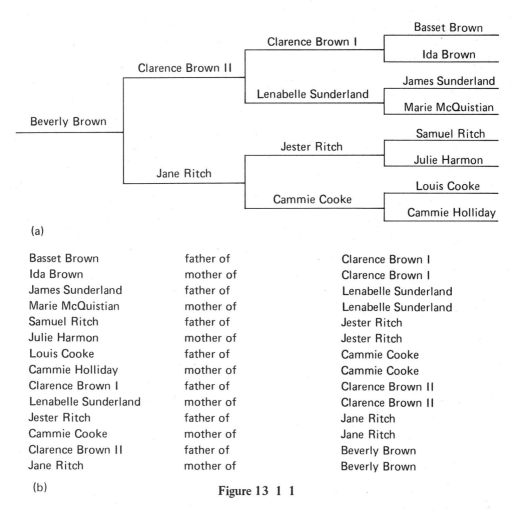

(a)

Basset Brown	father of	Clarence Brown I
Ida Brown	mother of	Clarence Brown I
James Sunderland	father of	Lenabelle Sunderland
Marie McQuistian	mother of	Lenabelle Sunderland
Samuel Ritch	father of	Jester Ritch
Julie Harmon	mother of	Jester Ritch
Louis Cooke	father of	Cammie Cooke
Cammie Holliday	mother of	Cammie Cooke
Clarence Brown I	father of	Clarence Brown II
Lenabelle Sunderland	mother of	Clarence Brown II
Jester Ritch	father of	Jane Ritch
Cammie Cooke	mother of	Jane Ritch
Clarence Brown II	father of	Beverly Brown
Jane Ritch	mother of	Beverly Brown

(b)

Figure 13 1 1

Of course, organizing the data in this way takes some careful thought. We hope that, once you have studied these data structures, you will be able not only to apply them to problems which you encounter, but also to make up new organizations of data suited to whatever problem is at hand.

Section 13 2

Multidimensional Arrays

We have used individual memory cells to store several different kinds of data. As you know, WATFIV automatically maintains an internal organization for each memory cell. This internal organization is different for different types of data. For instance, REAL numbers are stored in a very different way from INTEGERs. Because of this internal organization, each memory cell alone could be considered a data structure, but people usually reserve the term **data structure** for organizations which involve a number of memory cells. We have used such organizations already. When we have had several related items of information, a list of names of members of a club for example, we have stored the items in an array; that is, a data structure consisting of several memory cells grouped together and referred to under the same name. A subscript appended to the name distinguishes one item of the group from another—MEMBER(3) refers to the third memory cell in the array called MEMBER. Because WATFIV includes a special notation for arrays (the subscript notation), they are very easy to use.

There is another data structure for which there is a special notation: the multi-dimensional array. This is a more complicated data structure, but WATFIV alleviates the complication by providing the multiple subscript notation. For example, TABLE(4,7) refers to the memory cell in the fourth row and seventh column of the two-dimensional array TABLE.

Suppose, for a moment, that WATFIV had not provided two-dimensional arrays. How could we organize the data in a one-dimensional array so that we could use it as if it were a two-dimensional array? There are many answers to this question but the one we describe here is the most common. It is important to represent data structures using one-dimensional arrays because in nearly all computers, the one-dimensional array is the only built-in data structure. (A WATFIV compiler organizes two-dimensional arrays using the techniques we will describe.) Perhaps you think it a bit silly to explain, in detail, ways to represent data structures for which WATFIV provides a special notation, but these examples will form an introduction to data structures in terms already familiar to you. Once you understand these, we will go on to describe useful data structures which are not built-in.

If the array is to have M rows and N columns, then it is clear that we need to use M*N memory cells to represent it. Therefore, we declare a one-dimensional array which we call TWODIM in our illustration, with M*N memory cells. We organize this block of cells into N sections, each section having M cells in it. The first section of M cells represents the first column of the two-dimensional array we are creating, the second section represents the second column and so on. (See Figure 13 2 1) Remember, since there are M rows, each column has M elements in it.

If we want to find the place in the array TWODIM which represents the two-dimensional array element in the Ith row and Jth column, we skip down to the Jth section and pick the Ith element in that section. This means that TWODIM(M*(J−1)+I) is the memory cell representing the two-dimensional array element normally designated by the pair of subscripts (I,J). Figure 13 2 1 shows the details for an array with two rows and three columns.

This method of organizing a two-dimensional array is often called the **column major form**; we say that we are storing the array "by columns".

WATFIV stores two-dimensional arrays by columns. It can be helpful to know this when you are using them. For example, suppose you have declared an array REAL A(3,2) in the main program and you CALL a SUBROUTINE with that

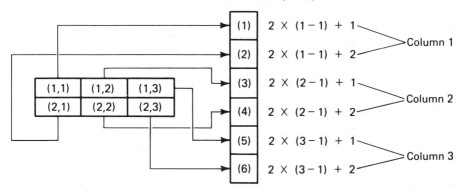

Two-dimensional array using two subscripts

Corresponding position in
one-dimensional array (Column Major Form)
M × (J − 1) + I

(1)	2 × (1 − 1) + 1	Column 1
(2)	2 × (1 − 1) + 2	
(3)	2 × (2 − 1) + 1	Column 2
(4)	2 × (2 − 1) + 2	
(5)	2 × (3 − 1) + 1	Column 3
(6)	2 × (3 − 1) + 2	

| (1,1) | (1,2) | (1,3) |
| (2,1) | (2,2) | (2,3) |

Figure 13 2 1

We can make the array references appear very natural. We simply define an INTEGER *valued function of two arguments (the row and column of the array element to be referenced) which computes the corresponding subscript in the one-dimensional array. For example, if the function is named S and we define it using an arithmetic statement function,*

> •
> •
> •
> ```
> INTEGER S,I,J,M,N
> S(I,J) = M*(J-1) + I
> ```
> •
> •
> •

then TWODIM(S(I,J)) *refers to the (I,J)th element of the M by N array which we are representing.*

array and its dimensions as parameters: CALL SUBR (A,3,2). If the SUB-ROUTINE starts out like this, using N as the *first* length declarator,

```
SUBROUTINE SUBR (B, M,N)
REAL B(N,M)
   •
   •
   •
```

then you would have problems because the SUBROUTINE will place a different organization on the array than does the main program. The diagram below shows the memory cell names as they are in the main program on the left, and their temporary names when the SUBROUTINE is CALLed on the right. You can see that the subscripting is entirely different. This is why it pays to know what you're doing when you use two-dimensional arrays as arguments to subprograms.

```
A(1,1) ┌──────┐ B(1,1)
A(2,1) │      │ B(2,1)
A(3,1) │      │ B(1,2)
A(1,2) │      │ B(2,2)
A(2,2) │      │ B(1,3)
A(3,2) └──────┘ B(2,3)
```

EXERCISES 13 2

1   Draw a figure similar to Figure 13 2 1 showing the representation of a 3 by 4 array.

2   In setting up the column major representation of a two dimensional array with m rows and n columns, what is the role of m? What is the role of n? Why is m more important than n? Could you set up the representation if you knew m precisely, but only knew that n was, say, smaller than 100?

3   There is a similar representation of a two-dimensional array called the **row major form**. In this representation, an array with m rows and n columns is, again, represented by a one-dimensional array with $m \times n$ memory cells. The array is divided into m sections, each section containing n memory cells and representing one row. Work out a formula which, given a subscript pair (I,J) designating the element in the Ith row and Jth column of the matrix, computes the place in the one-dimensional array which corresponds to the (I,J)th element of the matrix. In this row major representation is it more important to know the number of rows or the number of columns?

4   Where do the 1's go?

```
          INTEGER A(4,4)
          CALL ZAPDIA(A,2)
          STOP
          END

          SUBROUTINE ZAPDIA(B,M)
          INTEGER M, B(M,M)
          INTEGER I
   COMMENT:  PUT ONES ON DIAGONAL
          DO 10 I=1,M
    10      B(I,I) = 1
          RETURN
          END
```

314   *WATFIV for Humans*

Section 13 3

Odd-shaped Arrays

It is easy to generalize from the two-dimensional case to see how to represent a three-dimensional array.

Suppose we want to represent an M by N by L three-dimensional array. The first subscript varies between 1 and M, the second between 1 and N, and the third between 1 and L. Therefore, we need M*N*L memory cells to represent the array, and we declare a one-dimensional array THREED with M*N*L memory cells.

> WATFIV *allows arrays of up to 7 dimensions.*

We divide the array into L sections, each section having M*N memory cells. In each of the sections we organize an M by N two-dimensional array in column major form. That is, we divide each of the L sections into N subsections, each subsection having M memory cells. To refer to the (I, J, K)th element of the three-dimensional array we go to the Ith memory cell of the Jth subsection of the Kth section. Then conceptual array element (I, J, K) corresponds to

```
THREED(M*N*(K-1) + N*(J-1) + I)
```

The M*N*(K–1) term moves us to the Kth section of the array, the N*(J–1) term moves us to the Jth subsection of that section, and the I term moves us to the Ith element of that subsection.

Perhaps you can begin to see a general scheme here for representing multi-dimensional arrays. Try to write down the formula for the four-dimensional case, given the range of each subscript.

The two-dimensional array we represented is rectangular in shape. You can easily imagine other shapes for two-dimensional arrays. If you have looked at many road maps, you have no doubt seen a distance chart arranged as a triangular array. This is the data structure we'll discuss now.

Think of the problem faced by a traveling pharmaceuticals salesman in West Texas. His district includes the towns of El Paso, Van Horn, Odessa, Big Spring, Midland, Abilene, Pecos, Lubbock, Amarillo, and Wichita Falls. He lives in Pecos and, since he must travel his route once every month, he wants to plan it carefully so that it will be as economical as possible. In other words, he wants to choose the shortest route, starting and ending in Pecos, which visits all ten of the towns in his district. Fortunately, the corner gas station has a table of intertown distances (Figure 13 3 1).

He wants you to write a program to find the shortest route. The question is, how should you arrange the data from the table in the computer's memory cells? The table looks like a normal two-dimensional array with a missing part. We will call it a **triangular array**. To represent the triangular array, we can use an idea from our representation of rectangular two-dimensional arrays. One method of storing a rectangular two-dimensional array is the row major method (see Exercise 13 2 2); that is, storage "by rows". We divide the array into sections, one section

	Abilene	Amarillo	Big Springs	El Paso	Lubbock	Midland	Odessa	Pecos	Van Horn
Amarillo	285								
Big Springs	110	225							
El Paso	466	581	356						
Lubbock	160	125	100	456					
Midland	150	265	40	316	140				
Odessa	200	315	90	266	190	50			
Pecos	262	377	152	204	252	112	62		
Van Horn	354	469	244	112	344	204	154	92	
Wichita Falls	150	235	260	616	215	355	405	467	559

Figure 13 3 1   Distance Table

for each row. In the rectangular case, each row is the same length so that it is easy to find the beginning of each section in the array. In this new triangular case, each row has a different length, and this complication makes it slightly more difficult to locate the beginning of each section.

Let's look at the details. The first row has one member, the second row has two members, the third, three, and so on up to the ninth row which has nine members. Thus the first section of our one-dimensional array representing this triangular array should have one memory cell, the second section two memory cells, and so on. To find the fourth section, you must skip over the first three. That means skipping over the first row (length one), the second row (length two), and the third row (length three). Altogether you must skip over $1 + 2 + 3$ or 6 memory cells.

In general, to find the beginning of the kth section, you must skip over $1 + 2 + 3 + \ldots + (k - 1) = k*(k-1)/2$ memory cells.

$$
\begin{array}{l}
\left.\begin{array}{lllll}
1 & + \ 2 & + \ 3 & + \ldots + & k \\
+ k & + (k-1) & + (k-2) & + \ldots + & 1
\end{array}\right\} = 2 \times (1 + 2 + 3 + \ldots + k) \\
\hline
\ \ \| \qquad \ \ \| \qquad \ \ \| \qquad\qquad \| \\
(k+1) + (k+1) + (k+1) + \ldots + (k+1) \\
\qquad\qquad = k \times (k+1) \qquad\qquad \dfrac{k(k+1)}{2} = 1 + 2 + \ldots + k
\end{array}
$$

Thus the conceptual triangular array element (I,J) corresponds to

$$TRIANG(I*(I-1)/2 + J)$$

where I, of course, may never be smaller than J. It is interesting that, unlike the case for rectangular arrays, here we don't need to know either the number of columns *or* the number of rows in order to refer to an element in the triangular array. Thus, the triangular array offers a surprising advantage over the rectangular structure.

To set up and use a triangular array, all you need to do is declare an array with as many memory cells as you need, that is, $n(n+1)/2$ memory cells if the array is to have n rows. For our example, since there are ten towns, we need a nine-row triangular array, 45 memory cells in all.

> *Listing all ten towns both vertically and horizontally would result in the chart having ten unnecessary zeros in it.*

The problem we are concerned with is to find the route of shortest length which visits all the towns and which starts and ends in Pecos. We will take a straightforward approach. (This, the **traveling salesman problem,** has been much-studied, and there are more efficient solutions, but we're looking for a simple solution rather than efficiency.) We simply compute the length of every possible route, and choose the shortest one. The difference between routes is the order in which the cities are visited. Therefore, we need a part of our program to step through all the possible orderings of the intermediate cities. This is what we called the "permutation problem" in Section 9 4, and there we wrote a SUBROUTINE which would produce a new ordering of a list each time it was CALLed. We designed the SUBROUTINE so that, if we CALLed it again and again, it would eventually produce all possible orderings of the original list and signal us, through one of its parameters, when it produced the final ordering. That SUBROUTINE can be put to good use here.

Figure 13 3 2 is a flowchart for our program. Try to follow the program using the flowchart as a guide. In the program the towns are referred to by their number in alphabetical order, 1 for Abilene, 2 for Amarillo, . . . , 9 for Van Horn, and 10 for Wichita Falls. We use a FUNCTION to compute the length of a route. The name PERM refers to the SUBROUTINE in Section 9 4.

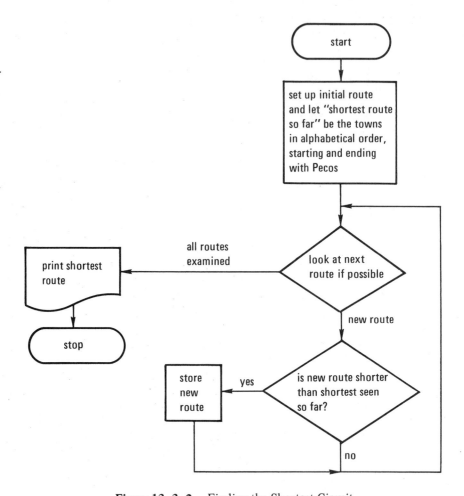

Figure 13 3 2   Finding the Shortest Circuit

You will notice that Pecos (town number 8) is left out of the compile-time initialization of the arrays which store routes the salesman might take. That's because we already know when he'll be in Pecos—he'll leave from there and he'll wind up there.

Our main program uses a FUNCTION LENGTH to discover how many miles it will take to travel a particular route. Since LENGTH must know the distance between towns, it is there that our triangular array appears. The values are entered into the array DIST through compile-time initialization, and the statement function BTWEEN is used to access values to it.

Notice how the compile-time initializations make use of our knowledge about how the arrays are organized, both TOWNS, which is arranged according to WATFIV conventions, and DIST, the triangular one we set up ourselves.

```
COMMENT:  FIND SHORTEST WEST TEXAS ROUTE
        CHARACTER*13 TOWNS(10)/'ABILENE',
      &                         'AMARILLO',
      &                         'BIG SPRING',
      &                         'EL PASO',
      &                         'LUBBOCK',
      &                         'MIDLAND',
      &                         'ODESSA',
      &                         'PECOS',
      &                         'VAN HORN',
      &                         'WICHITA FALLS'/
        INTEGER ROUTE(9) /1,2,3,4,5,6,7,  9,10/
        INTEGER SHORTR(9) /1,2,3,4,5,6,7,  9,10/
        DUMPLIST/STATUS/SHORTR, ROUTE
        INTEGER LENGTH, T
        LOGICAL NEWPRM /.TRUE./
C       GET NEXT ROUTE
  100   CALL PERM(ROUTE,9,NEWPRM)
          IF ( .NOT. NEWPRM )  GO TO 200
C         IF NEW ROUTE IS SHORTER, SAVE IT
          IF ( LENGTH(ROUTE) .LE. LENGTH(SHORTR) )
      &                         CALL STORE(ROUTE, SHORTR, 9)
          GO TO 100
C       TRIED ALL ROUTES--PRINT SHORTEST
  200   PRINT, 'SHORTEST ROUTE (PRINTED BELOW) HAS LENGTH',
      &                    LENGTH(SHORTR)
        PRINT, ' '
        PRINT, 'PECOS'
        DO 300 T=1,9
  300     PRINT, TOWNS(SHORTR(T))
        PRINT, 'PECOS'
        STOP
        END



        INTEGER FUNCTION LENGTH(R)
        INTEGER R(9)
        INTEGER BTWEEN, TOWN1, TOWN2, I, MAXO, MINO
        INTEGER DIST(45)
      &         /285,
      &          110,225,
      &          446,581,356,
      &          160,125,100,456,
      &          150,265, 40,316,140,
      &          200,315, 90,266,190, 50,
      &          262,377,152,204,252,112, 62,
      &          354,469,244,112,344,204,154, 92,
      &          150,235,260,616,215,355,405,467,559/
C    STATEMENT FUNCTION TO COMPUTE SUBSCRIPT FOR TRIANGULAR
C    ARRAY.  THE ROW NUMBER IS ALWAYS 1 SMALLER THAN
C    THE TOWN NUMBER SINCE 'ABILENE' IS NOT ONE OF THE ROWS
        BTWEEN(TOWN1,TOWN2) = (MAXO(TOWN1,TOWN2)-2)*
      &                       (MAXO(TOWN1,TOWN2)-1)/2 +
      &                        MINO(TOWN1,TOWN2)
C    START WITH DISTANCE FROM PECOS (TOWN 8) TO FIRST TOWN
C    IN ROUTE PLUS DISTANCE FROM LAST TOWN TO PECOS
        LENGTH = DIST(BTWEEN(8,R(1)))+DIST(BTWEEN(R(9),8))
C    ADD UP THE REST
        DO 100 I=1,8
  100     LENGTH =LENGTH + DIST(BTWEEN(R(I),R(I+1)))
        RETURN
        END
```

```
      SUBROUTINE STORE(A,B,LEN)
      INTEGER LEN, A(LEN), B(LEN)
      INTEGER I
      DO 100 I=1,LEN
100     B(I) = A(I)
      RETURN
      END
```

output

```
SHORTEST ROUTE (PRINTED BELOW) HAS LENGTH            1482

PECOS
EL PASO
VAN HORN
ODESSA
MIDLAND
LUBBOCK
AMARILLO
WICHITA FALLS
ABILENE
BIG SPRING
PECOS
```

The traveling salesman problem would be a relatively hard one for a beginner to solve, yet the main program above is no harder to follow than the flowchart. Most of the work is done in subprograms, particularly PERM.

EXERCISES 13 3

1 Why not store triangular arrays "by columns"?

2 How would you store an array shaped like this?

```
. . . . .
  . . . .      (upside down
    . . .      triangular array)
      . .
        .
```

3 The traveling salesman program in this section keeps recomputing the length of the shortest route so far. How can this be avoided? Is it worth it?

Section 13 4

Stacks and Queues

To represent a data structure, one must specify interrelationships among its parts. So far, we have specified these interrelationships by altering the method we used to compute subscripts. Thus, the extra information describing the interrelationships has been built into the program. Another alternative is to store information about the data in the memory along with the items of data being stored. We will look at a number of different ways of using memory cells to represent relationships in this chapter. The first is essentially a way of keeping track of a continually changing bunch of things that must be kept in order.

Have you ever had a problem and realized that if only you could solve a sub-problem you could solve the problem and then have begun working on the sub-problem only to realize that if you could solve a sub-problem of the sub-problem, you'd have the answer, etc.? Well, if you have, then you have functioned much as a stack.

Conceptually a **stack** is a storage device which has a top. You may add a new element (piece of data) to the top and you may remove the top element. If you do remove the top element, then the one that was after it in the stack becomes the top. If you keep removing elements until there are no more, the stack is said to be **empty**. We will draw a stack like this

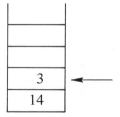

The arrow indicates the top element of the stack. If we remove the top element, the stack would look like this

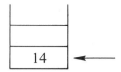

There are broad applications for stacks and they have been given many names: push-down stacks, push-down lists, and LIFO (last–in–first–out) devices.

Just from looking at our drawings of stacks, you may be able to guess how to represent them. We will use a one-dimensional array to provide the storage. We will guess what the maximum number of elements we will ever have to store is and make the array that long.

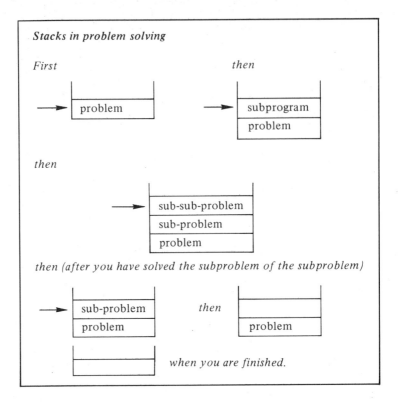

Stacks in problem solving

First

| problem |

then

| subprogram |
| problem |

then

| sub-sub-problem |
| sub-problem |
| problem |

then (after you have solved the subproblem of the subproblem)

| sub-problem |
| problem |

then

| problem |

| | when you are finished.

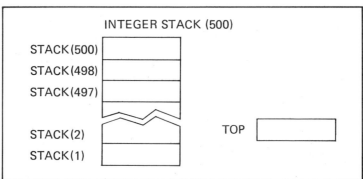

INTEGER STACK (500)

STACK(500)
STACK(498)
STACK(497)

STACK(2)
STACK(1)

TOP

Now all we need is a variable to keep track of the top of the stack. That's easy—we'll just declare an INTEGER variable TOP and let its value be the subscript in the array where the top element is located. Thus TOP represents the arrow in the drawings of stacks. To start off with an empty stack we let TOP be zero. Then we can add a value VAL to the stack with the two statements

```
TOP = TOP +1
STACK(TOP) = VAL
```

and we can remove the top element just as easily.

Our program will be easier to read (and check for errors) if we write subprograms to carry out the processes of ADDing and REMOVing elements from stacks. For example:

```
        SUBROUTINE ADD (STACK, TOP, VALUE)
COMMENT:  ADD THE ELEMENT "VALUE" TO THE "TOP" OF "STACK"
        INTEGER TOP, STACK(500), VALUE
        TOP = TOP +1
COMMENT:  TEST FOR OVERFLOW
        IF ( TOP .LE. 500 )  GO TO 10
        PRINT, 'STACK OVERFLOW WHILE STACKING', VALUE
        STOP
COMMENT:  INSERT THE NEW TOP ELEMENT
  10    STACK(TOP) = VALUE
        RETURN
        END
```

You can write a SUBROUTINE to remove elements in a similar way (see Exercise 13 4 1).

A **queue** is like a line of people politely waiting to buy tickets to see a poetry recital. If you come to the line, you get in the **back**; the man selling tickets deals with the person in **front**. When the person in front has bought tickets, he leaves the line. The most obvious way to represent a queue is a simple extension of the way we handled stacks. We'll just declare an array big enough, and now, instead of having just one variable keeping track of the top, we'll have *two*, one keeping track of the FRONT and one for the BACK.

A Queue

We start FRONT and BACK off with the value zero to represent an empty queue. Now, to add an item VALUE (at the back), we can use the statements

```
BACK = BACK +1
QUEUE(BACK) = VALUE
```

and to remove an item (from the front), we use

```
FRONT = FRONT + 1
VALUE = QUEUE(FRONT)
```

Unfortunately this scheme doesn't work all that well in practice. Suppose we put on one element, then take it off, then put it on, take it off, etc. Even though at any point in time the queue is either empty or else has just one value in it, we will need an infinite number of memory locations. Not very practical.

A cure for this problem is to make the array circular. Study SUBROUTINE QADD to see what we mean. Statement 10 turns the array into a circle by making QUEUE(1) come after QUEUE(500).

```
          SUBROUTINE QADD(QUEUE,FRONT,BACK,VALUE)
          INTEGER QUEUE(500), FRONT, BACK, VALUE
COMMENT:  MOVE BACK
          BACK = BACK +1
COMMENT:  SEE IF WE NEED TO WRAP AROUND
  10      IF ( BACK .GT. 500 )  BACK = 1
COMMENT:  NOW TEST FOR OVERFLOW
          IF ( BACK .NE. FRONT )  GO TO 20
COMMENT:  OVERFLOW...
          PRINT , 'QUEUE OVERFLOW WHEN ADDING', VALUE
          STOP
COMMENT:  ADD IN VALUE
  20      QUEUE(BACK) = VALUE
          RETURN
          END
```

Often you will want to store more than one value in each queue element. For example, if you were writing a simulation of a supermarket and were using queues to represent shoppers waiting at the checkout stands, you might need to store three things for each shopper. Namely, the time the shopper entered the queue (so you can tell how long the shopper had to wait), the number of groceries (so you can tell how long it will take to get checked out), and whether or not the shopper has Tide-XK (so you can tell whether the shopper will be accosted by the people shooting TV commercials in the parking lot).

The solution is very simple—just declare an array for each queue you need and use the same FRONT and BACK values for all of the queues.

```
REAL TIME(500)
INTEGER THINGS(500), FRONT, BACK
LOGICAL TIDE(500)
```

To add in a shopper, just step BACK and insert the appropriate values into TIME(BACK), THINGS(BACK) and TIDE(BACK). The (enlarged) queue would look like this.

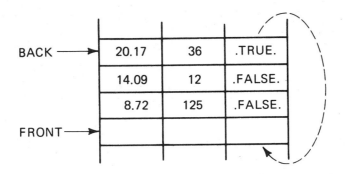

The dotted line is to remind you of our trick for more efficient use of memory space.

EXERCISES 13 4

1. Write a SUBROUTINE called REMOVE which removes the top element from a stack. It will need three arguments, namely the stack, the top, and a variable in which the current stack top element is returned. Make sure your SUBROUTINE won't remove anything from a stack that's already empty; it might implode!

2. If the elements you want to store in the stack are REAL numbers, what would change?

3. Write a SUBROUTINE REMOVE (QUEUE, FRONT, BACK, VALUE) which removes the element at the front of QUEUE, puts its value in VALUE, and incorporates the "wrap-around" usage of the array called QUEUE.

4. Add a test for an empty queue into your SUBROUTINE REMOVE. (If the queue is empty, there's nothing to be removed.)

Section 13 5

Strings

In the last section, we saw data structures which required saving information about how many elements were currently being stored (TOP = the number of elements in a stack, for example). This information was kept separate from the elements being stored. In this section we will see a data structure in which length information is kept right with the elements being stored, and in which other variables will be used to find where subparts of the information are kept.

Imagine that you are responsible for writing a program which processes bills. We'll suppose that, as the bills and checks come in, someone keypunches the amounts on a card and, if the person had a comment (or complaint) written on his bill, that gets punched as well. Your program would update everyone's account on the basis of these cards. If there is a message, then it should be stored along with the person's account, and a list of people who had messages should be printed out so that someone could go over them later.

But now a problem arises—how much space should you leave for messages in the areas where accounts are stored? You know from experience that only a few people will write comments. If you leave the same amount of space for each person's message, then most of the space you set aside will be blank (and wasted). You decide that maybe you could store all the messages in one place and just use one word per account to tell where the message is (if there is one). This way you can set aside a much smaller amount of memory (see Figure 13 5 1).

Everything seems fine now, until it's time to decide how long a space to leave for each message. Some are long like "I wish that next time your man comes he could stay longer because I had such a nice time telling him about my trip uptown and he said he was sorry but he had to rush off and he didn't get to taste my cherry cobbler," and some are short like "@!!?#." The only way to get around leaving a huge space for each message is somehow to store them as variable length chunks. We will call each chunk a *string*.

Strings occur naturally in many nonnumeric computing tasks, linguistic analysis and text editing, for example. String processing is so important that several languages have been developed (notably SNOBOL) especially for dealing with strings. We will describe a way to deal with them in WATFIV.

First estimate the maximum space needed to store all the messages. Then declare an array of that size, *e.g.*,

```
INTEGER STRING(1000)
```

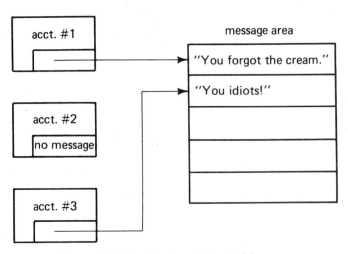

Figure 13 5 1   Storing Strings in Memory

Let's see how to store one message. Suppose it is "Two creams from now on." First, set aside memory cell STRING(1) and then just keep filling letters into successive memory cells in the array until the message is finished. Then put the number of memory cells used by the string into STRING(1).

```
┌──────────────────────────────────────────────────┐
│ Contents of STRING after inserting the message "TWO CREAMS │
│ FROM NOW ON."                                       │
│                                                     │
│         STRING(1)  ┌──────┐                        │
│                    │  24  │                        │
│              (2)   ├──────┤                        │
│                    │  T   │                        │
│              (3)   ├──────┤                        │
│                    │  W   │                        │
│              (4)   ├──────┤                        │
│                    │  O   │                        │
│              (5)   ├──────┤                        │
│                    │  b   │                        │
│              (6)   ├──────┤                        │
│                    │  C   │                        │
│              (7)   ├──────┤                        │
│                    │  R   │                        │
│              (8)   ├──────┤                        │
│                    │  E   │                        │
│                    ├∿∿∿∿∿∿┤                        │
│             (22)   │  O   │                        │
│                    ├──────┤                        │
│             (23)   │  N   │                        │
│                    ├──────┤                        │
│             (24)   │  .   │                        │
│                    └──────┘                        │
│                      ⋮                             │
└──────────────────────────────────────────────────┘
```

┌──┐
│ storing CHARACTERs: CHARACTER information, unlike other │
│ data types, may be stored in memory cells of any type. We are │
│ using this quirk to store two types of information in the array │
│ STRING: (1) the INTEGERs indicating the length of the strings │
│ and (2) the CHARACTERs which make up the messages. │
└──┘

We can reference the string by providing a variable which records where in the array STRING the message starts. The first word of the string tells how long it is, so we know how far to go to find the whole message.

What if we want to add in another message? Well, we soon discover that we had better know where to store the message in the array STRING. We'll create a variable EMPTY that indicates where we can start filling. After the string "Two creams from now on." has been inserted, EMPTY would have the value 25. The following SUBROUTINE is to READ a message from a card, find how long it is (by counting up to the first period), then store the message as a string starting at the position EMPTY in the array STRING, and finally leave the variable NEWSTR with the location at which the new string starts. RDMESS (for ReaD MESSage) could be used each time a message needs to be read. It stores the message in a COMMON area and has one output parameter, the location of the string in the COMMON area.

```
      SUBROUTINE RDMESS (NEWSTR)
      INTEGER NEWSTR
COMMENT:  GET MESSAGE FROM DATA CARD AND STORE AS STRING
      INTEGER LENGTH, S, COLMN, MESS(80), PERIOD/'.   '/
      INTEGER EMPTY, STRING(1000)
      COMMON EMPTY, STRING
COMMENT:  READ IN MESSAGE
      READ 1000, (MESS(COLMN), COLMN = 1,80)
 1000 FORMAT(80A1)
COMMENT:  SEE HOW LONG IT IS
      LENGTH = 1
      DO 200 COLMN = 1,80
        IF ( MESS(COLMN) .EQ. PERIOD )  GO TO 300
  200   CONTINUE
      COLMN = 80
  300 LENGTH = COLMN
COMMENT:  INSERT STRING
      S = EMPTY + 1
C       FILL IN LENGTH--INCLUDE 1 FOR CELL WHICH STORES LENGTH
      STRING(EMPTY) = LENGTH + 1
C       FILL IN CHARACTERS
      DO 400 COLMN = 1,LENGTH
        STRING(S) = MESS(COLMN)
  400   S = S+1
COMMENT:  SET POINTER TO THE STRING
      NEWSTR = EMPTY
COMMENT:  UPDATE "EMPTY" POINTER
      EMPTY = EMPTY + LENGTH + 1
      RETURN
      END
```

Follow through the SUBROUTINE with an example or two.

Sometimes when you go back over something you've written, you want to cut the end of a sentence off because it runs on too long anyway, and sometimes you want to put two sentences together to make a longer message. Let's see how we could do those operations on strings. First, let's take chopping off the end of a string. We'll write a SUBROUTINE CHOP which will chop the last DROPNO characters from the string starting at location SENT in the array STRING.

```
      SUBROUTINE CHOP (SENT, DROPNO)
      INTEGER SENT, DROPNO
      INTEGER LENGTH
      COMMON EMPTY, STRING
      INTEGER EMPTY, STRING(1000)
COMMENT:  FIND HOW LONG STRING IS NOW
      LENGTH = STRING(SENT)
COMMENT:  COMPUTE LENGTH AFTER DROPPING "DROPNO" CHARACTERS
      LENGTH = LENGTH - DROPNO
COMMENT:  STICK IN NEW LENGTH
      STRING(SENT) = LENGTH
      RETURN
      END
```

Next, let's see how we might run two sentences together. Incidentally, this is a widely used string operation called **concatenation**.

We face a problem here. Since we have packed the strings into our array as tightly as possible, we can't just copy the second string into the memory cells immediately following the first string. It usually won't fit without wiping out part of some other string. We'll have to abandon the two original strings and make a copy of the first, then the second, without its length information, then update the new string's length information, and finally, update the variable which pointed to the first string so that now it will point to the beginning of the concatenated result.

```
          SUBROUTINE CONCAT(STR1, STR2)
          INTEGER STR1, STR2
          INTEGER L1, L2, LOWLIM, UPLIM, S, FILL
          COMMON EMPTY, STRING
          INTEGER EMPTY, STRING(1000)
COMMENT:  FIND OUT HOW LONG THE FIRST STRING IS
          L1 = STRING(STR1)
COMMENT:  ALSO THE SECOND STRING
          L2 = STRING(STR2)
COMMENT:  COPY STRING "STR1" TO THE EMPTY REGION
          LOWLIM = EMPTY
          UPLIM = EMPTY + L1 - 1
          S = STR1
          DO 100 FILL = LOWLIM, UPLIM
             STRING(FILL) = STRING(S)
  100     S = S+1
COMMENT:  NOW COPY "STR2" (EXCEPT FOR ITS LENGTH INFO)
          LOWLIM = UPLIM + 1
          UPLIM = LOWLIM + L2 - 2
          S = STR2 + 1
          DO 200 FILL = LOWLIM, UPLIM
             STRING(FILL) = STRING(S)
  200     S = S+1
COMMENT:  SET POINTER TO NEW STRING AND UPDATE LENGTH INFO
          STR1 = EMPTY
          STRING(STR1) = L1 + L2 - 1
COMMENT:  UPDATE "EMPTY" POINTER
          EMPTY = EMPTY + STRING(STR1)
          RETURN
          END
```

You may wonder what happens to all the old strings we abandoned in the CONCAT routine. You might think they're now just wasted space. That's right. A solution to this problem of wasted space is the concept of **garbage collection**. We will not go into this in detail, but the main idea is that if your program tries to create a new string and finds that there's not enough room between EMPTY and the end of the array STRING, it calls a sub-program which rearranges the strings so that all the abandoned ones now become empty space.

You'll get a chance to learn more uses for strings in the problems at the end of the chapter.

EXERCISES 13 5

1 Look at SUBROUTINE RDMESS. Where should a test be placed to prevent trying to store a message which is too long for the available space in memory.

2 If the string starting at S1 looks like:

```
16 C O M E   O N   P E O P L E
```

and S2 looks like:

```
22 S M I L E   O N   Y O U R   B R O T H E R
```

what does the string starting at S1 look like after executing CALL CONCAT(S1,S2)?

3 If the string starting at S1 looks like:

```
60 A S P I R I N   I S   T H E   B E S T   P A I N   R E L I E V E R
   A N D   B A Y E R   I S   1 0 0 %   A S P I R I N
```

and the one starting at S2 looks like:

```
17 T H E   B E S T   A S P I R I N
```

what does the string starting at S1 look like after:

CALL CHOP(S1,48)
CALL CONCAT(S1,S2)?

Section 13 6

Lists

The **linked list** or **plex** data structure is probably useful in more situations than any data structure we've studied so far. Conceptually, a linked list is a number of list elements. Each **list element** has two types of subparts, data and pointers. Data subparts just lie there, waiting to be found, while pointers refer to other list elements. A program can thus follow pointers from one list element to the next, looking patiently for the data it wants.

In our implementation, a list element will consist of a group of memory cells, one cell from each of several arrays. Each cell in a list element will have the same subscript value in its respective array. The array which is used to store pointers must, obviously, be of INTEGER type since it is storing subscript values. Arrays used to store data subparts may be of any appropriate data type.

One common use of lists is in programs simulating real world situations which proceed from "important event" to "important event". For instance, suppose that we wanted to simulate a telephone system in order to estimate the effects of different interconnection schemes. Obviously, fewer circuits are needed between towns than within a given town, but how many should we choose? Too few, and people trying to call from one city to another will get an annoying number of busy-signals. Too many, and we'll waste money on circuits that are unused most of the time.

We won't go into all the details of such a simulation (a really good job of it might require a hundred pages or more); rather we'll concentrate on one small part—a part which demonstrates the use of lists.

Each time a caller from one town gets through to a number in another town, a circuit is tied up. For the purposes of our simulation, we don't care what is said or transmitted over the circuit; all we care about is how long the circuit is in use. Thus, once a circuit is engaged, the next important event is the time it becomes free.

There are also important events associated with calls. Each time a call from town to town is attempted, our program must check to see if a circuit is free. If it is *not*, we record a busy signal and, depending on our model of the callers,

---

Circuit Structure

The chart below shows a possible circuit structure for a cluster of five towns. Each entry indicates the number of circuits from one town to another. Entries on the diagonal show numbers of circuits available for local calls.

	to town 1	2	3	4	5
from town 1	100	30	40	20	40
2	40	120	40	30	40
3	30	30	80	20	30
4	30	30	80	80	30
5	50	50	40	40	100

As you can see, a two-dimensional array would be perfect for storing the number of circuits available. It could be initialized with the total circuit structure. If our simulation attempts a call between towns x and y and box(x,y) is nonzero, indicating a line available, then we decrement box(x,y) to reflect the fact that a line is tied up. If the box is zero, the call can't go through. Similarly, if we encounter the end of a call in our event list, we increment the appropriate circuits-available-box. In this way no box will ever exceed its original value and will always reflect the number of circuits currently available between two points.

---

perhaps enter another upcoming important event corresponding to another attempt at placing the same call. If there is a free circuit, we enter an important event corresponding to the time that circuit will be open again (as noted above).

The program would proceed from important event to important event, keeping a list of upcoming events in temporal order and assembling relevant statistics. By running it with different circuit configurations, we could choose the best combination.

The list of important events could be conceptually organized as shown in Figure 13 6 1.

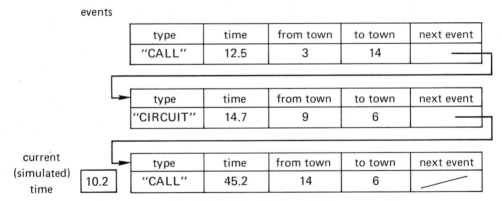

events

	type	time	from town	to town	next event
	"CALL"	12.5	3	14	

	type	time	from town	to town	next event
	"CIRCUIT"	14.7	9	6	

current
(simulated)
time

10.2	type	time	from town	to town	next event
	"CALL"	45.2	14	6	

Figure 13 6 1 An Event List

Each list element has five subparts: four pieces of data and one pointer. To set up such a list we would declare an array for each subpart.

```
CHARACTER*2 TYPE(2000)
REAL TIME(2000)
INTEGER FROM(2000), TO(2000), NEXTEV(2000)
```

In order to create a list element, we simply select a subscript value which has not yet been used (suppose memory cell FREE stores the next such value) and assign data into the arrays. The following assignments create the front two list elements shown in Figure 13 6 1.

```
      TO(FREE) = 6
      FROM(FREE)  = 9
      TIME(FREE) = 14.7
      TYPE(FREE) = 'CR'
C     'CR' = CIRCUIT,  'CL' = CALL
C     GET ANOTHER FREE ELEMENT
      FREE = FREE + 1
C     SET UP POINTER
      NEXTEV(FREE) = FREE - 1
      TO(FREE) = 14
      FROM(FREE) = 3
      TIME(FREE) = 12.5
      TYPE(FREE) = 'CL'
```

Probably you've picked up the main ideas already. Just in case you feel a little shaky about lists, here's a SUBROUTINE ADDEV that will add a new event (a new list element) in the right spot in a list. Figure 13 6 2 shows the effect of using our SUBROUTINE to add a new event which occurs at time 13.0.

```
      CALL ADEV('CL', 13.0, 7, 4, EVENTS)
```

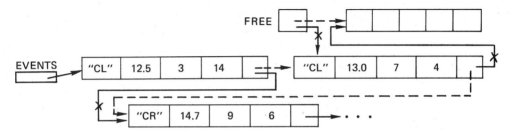

Figure 13 6 2 Inserting an Event Chronologically

```
        SUBROUTINE ADEV (TYP, TIM, F, T, LIST)
        CHARACTER*2 TYP
        REAL TIM
        INTEGER F, T, LIST
COMMENT:  SUBROUTINE TO ADD A NEW ELEMENT INTO "LIST"
C         IN CHRONOLOGICAL ORDER.
C         THE FREE LIST ELEMENTS (ALL LIST ELEMENTS,
C         IN FACT) ARE IN COMMON.
        CHARACTER*2 TYPE(2000)
        REAL TIME(2000)
        INTEGER FROM(2000), TO(2000), NEXTEV(2000), FREE
        COMMON FREE,TIME,FROM,TO,NEXTEV,TYPE
        INTEGER POINTR
C
C       FILL IN DATA PART OF NEW ELEMENT
        TYPE(FREE) = TYP
        TIME(FREE) = TIM
        FROM(FREE) = F
        TO  (FREE) = T
C
C        NOW FIND WHERE TO PUT IT.
C       DOES IT GO AT THE VERY FRONT?
C               NOTE: A POINTER .LE. 0 MEANS END OF LIST
        IF (TIME(FREE).GE.TIME(LIST) .AND. LIST.GT.0) GO TO 10
C       YES...
        NEXTEV(FREE) = LIST
        LIST = FREE
C       DONE... UPDATE FREE AND QUIT
        FREE = FREE + 1
        RETURN
C       DOESN'T GO AT FRONT.  START TRACKING THROUGH THE LIST
   10   POINTR = LIST
C       ARE WE NEAR THE END OF THE LIST?
   20   IF ( NEXTEV(POINTR) .LE. 0 )  GO TO 30
C       DOES IT GO HERE?
        IF ( TIME(FREE).LT.TIME(NEXTEV(POINTR)) )  GO TO 30
C       DIDN'T FIND IT YET--GO ON
        POINTR = NEXTEV(POINTR)
        GO TO 20
C
C       FOUND THE SPOT. INSERT BY MOVING POINTERS
   30   NEXTEV(FREE) = NEXTEV(POINTR)
        NEXTEV(POINTR) = FREE
C       UPDATE FREE
        FREE = FREE +1
        RETURN
        END
```

There are a number of refinements we could add. Probably the most important would be a more sophisticated way of keeping track of free list elements. As it is now, all we can do is throw away list elements that store events which have "occurred". Lists are perfectly suited for recycling, however. If we initially tie all the unused elements together (see Exercise 13 6 1) and remove items from the FREE list by the assignment

$$FREE = NEXTEV(FREE)$$

then we can also insert list elements we are through with back onto the FREE list for reuse. Thus we can simulate an unlimited number of phone calls in our program just as long as the number of events on the event list never exceeds 2000 at any one time.

Another extremely useful property of lists is that they provide you with data structures whose size can be determined by your program according to the needs of the moment. Thus, instead of just maintaining one LIST as in this example, you could maintain several lists, an array of lists perhaps or even a list of lists. Or, if you allow list elements to have two pointers, your lists can have sublists. The programming language LISP is organized around this sort of list structures. If there is a LISP system at your computer center, examine some LISP programs. They will look radically different to you. We promise.

EXERCISES 13 6

1 Write a subprogram which will tie all the list elements in our hypothetical communications system together, leaving a pointer to the front element in memory cell FREE.

2 Write a subprogram which will add the list element pointed to by memory cell DONE to the most accessible (*i.e.*, front) position on the FREE list. (This subprogram can be used for garbage collection.)

3 Say "I love lists." out loud rapidly, five times.

Section 13 7

Free Data Structures

If you've stayed with it this long, you now have the background and understanding needed to devise any sort of data structure you like and write programs that use it. In the hope of giving some encouragement, here's an overview of a strange but powerful data structure that we made up. Just for the occasion.

Instead of having a completely passive data structure, we decided to have data elements act as programs. Then we can write WATFIV statements which not only run those programs but also modify and even write them.

Our basic unit of data will be called a **cluster**, which will have the form of a list and the properties of a program or SUBROUTINE. Each subpart of a cluster (each list element) is called a **sextet** because it has six different pieces of data in it. The first part of a sextet (called ATOMIC) is a LOGICAL value which tells whether the sextet contains a direct command (called an **atomic action**) or a compound command (*i.e.,* a reference to another cluster). If ATOMIC is .TRUE., then the second part of the sextet, the INSTR part, identifies an atomic action; otherwise INSTR points to another cluster. The third part (TEST) designates one of a number of LOGICAL test values to be used in deciding whether to proceed to the LEFT (the sextet pointed to by the fourth part) or to the RIGHT (the sextet pointed to by the fifth part). The sixth part of each sextet (called EOC for End Of Cluster) is a LOGICAL value which comes into play in compound commands.

To illustrate the basic ideas, let's work through the example in Figure 13 7 1. Since ATOMIC in the front sextet is .TRUE., the direct command in INSTR is performed (atomic action 3 in this case). Then, since the value in test cell 2 is .TRUE., we proceed through LEFT to another sextet. There we are told to perform atomic action 1 and use TEST cell 4 to decide whether to proceed LEFT or RIGHT. Since the value in TEST cell 4 is .FALSE., we go on to the sextet named in RIGHT, etc., etc.

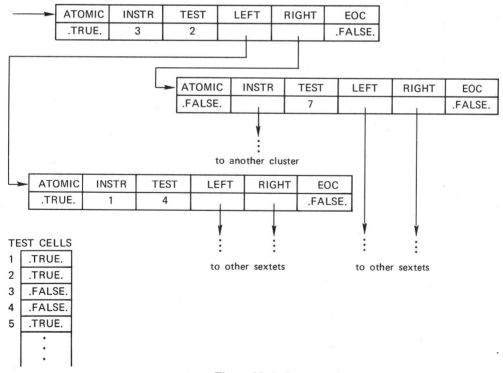

Figure 13 7 1

To create or modify a cluster, we manipulate pointers as in Section 13 6. To be able to carry out the actions described by a cluster, we need a program to interpret clusters and perform atomic actions. The exact nature of these atomic actions depends on the class of problems we wish to solve using clusters.

> *The first six chapters of this book might be thought of as describing the atomic actions of* WATFIV. *When you write A + B, the "+" symbol is a reference to a basic, primitive action.*

To actually *perform* a cluster, our program proceeds to the first sextet. If ATOMIC is .TRUE., then our program must carry out the atomic action named in INSTR, check the value in the cell named in TEST, and proceed to the indicated sextet.

On the other hand, compound commands are more complicated. When one cluster refers to another, the referenced cluster, like a subprogram, must have some way to return to the calling cluster. We will save this return information in the first sextet of the referenced cluster. To avoid losing this information in case a cluster refers to itself, our program will make a complete copy of the cluster before starting to perform its commands. After making the copy and inserting the return information in the first sextet, execution proceeds from the second sextet of the newly copied cluster. Figure 13 7 2 shows a small example showing a reference to a cluster which has just two sextets, its "return" sextet and a sextet invoking atomic action number 3.

An individual sextet, through its LEFT and RIGHT components, may point to any other pair of sextets in a cluster, so that in performing the actions described by a cluster, we can hop all around, going from sextet to sextet. However, in order to simplify the copying process, we require that the memory cells making up all the sextets in a cluster be contiguous. We also require a unique end of cluster mark: the last sextet (the one whose memory cells have the largest array subscript value) must have the value .TRUE. in its EOC component. All other sextets in the cluster should have .FALSE. EOC components. With these conditions, copying a cluster just amounts to copying sextet arrays sequentially up to the one with the .TRUE. EOC component.

The cluster scheme can be applied in many contexts. We've chosen one, a program for making flip-through movies, to illustrate the point. We'll want to print a bunch of "stills", cut them out, stack them, and flip through them to watch our "movie". (Thanks to Sandy Schoichet for this nifty idea.)

All our atomic actions and test cells will be oriented around a 50 by 50 square array which we'll think of as the **scene**. To begin, the scene will have a blank at each spot. Using atomic actions, our cluster will move around the scene placing asterisks and periods in it. One atomic action will print the scene. We will have a

> *There are so many ways to proceed that the choices we've made may seem arbitrary. Feel free to make a version more suited to your desires.*

cursor which gives our current position in the scene as a coordinate pair (u, r) where u stands for "up-down axis" and r for "right-left axis". To move the cursor we will be able to set values for $(\Delta u, \Delta r)$ where Δu is the change in position along u axis and Δr is the change in r.

BEFORE

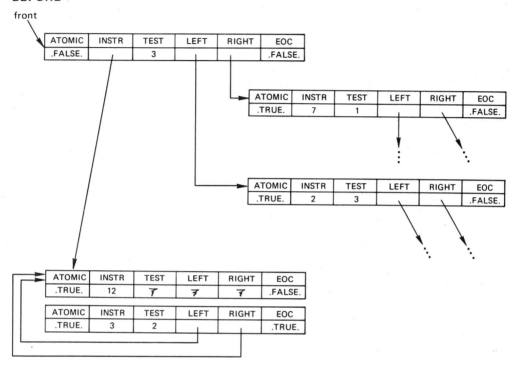

AFTER

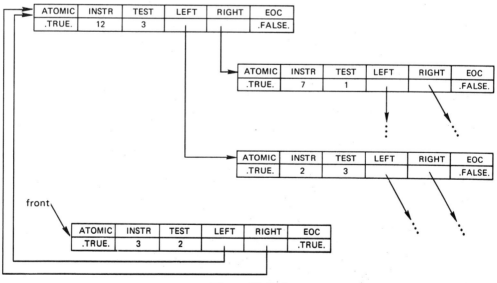

Figure 13 7 2

The atomic actions and test values we decided to use are shown in the boxes.

Atomic Action #	Action
1	move cursor to lower left corner
2	set Δu to 0 and Δr to 0
3	move cursor from (u,r) to $(u+\Delta u, r+\Delta r)$
4	place a character at (u,r)
5	print picture and stop
6	change Δu to $\Delta u+1$
7	change Δu to $\Delta u-1$
8	change Δr to $\Delta r+1$
9	change Δr to $\Delta r-1$
10	don't do anything (useful when an extra test is needed)
11	*if* current character is ".", make it "*" if it's "*", make it "."
12	return from subcluster

Test Cell #	Meaning
1	is this cursor position blank?
2	is the cursor on the top edge?
3	is the cursor on the bottom edge?
4	on left edge?
5	on right edge?
6	on top or bottom edge?
7	on left or right edge?
8	on any edge?
9	when you've gotta go, you've gotta go. (always .TRUE.)
10	is the character "."?

To make sure you see what's going on, verify that the clusters INIT, DIAG, and FILL do what we claim.

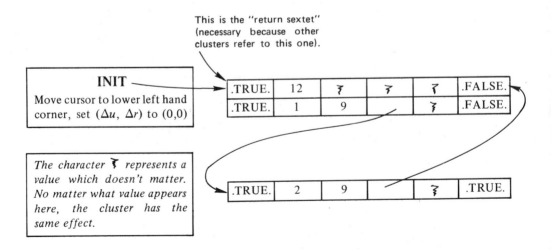

This is the "return sextet" (necessary because other clusters refer to this one).

INIT
Move cursor to lower left hand corner, set $(\Delta u, \Delta r)$ to (0,0)

The character ⸮ represents a value which doesn't matter. No matter what value appears here, the cluster has the same effect.

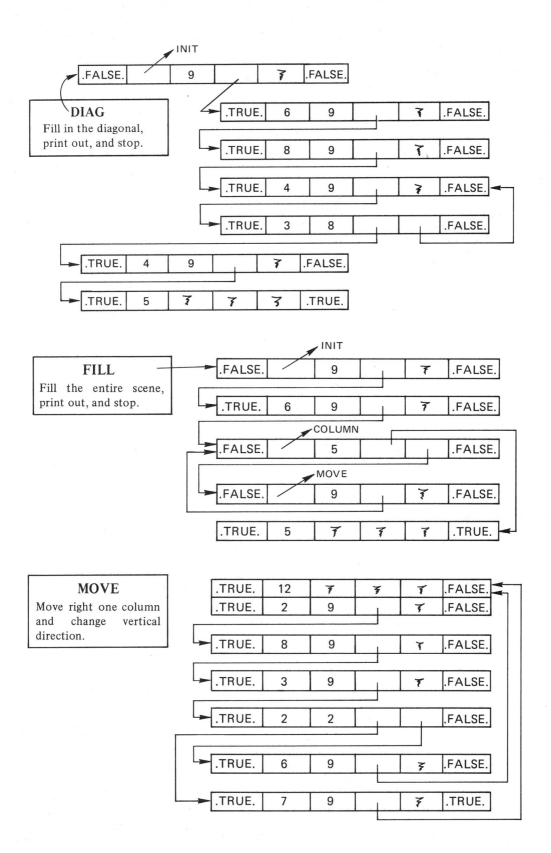

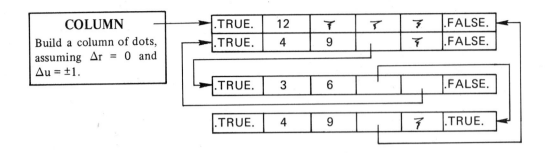

COLUMN Build a column of dots, assuming $\Delta r = 0$ and $\Delta u = \pm 1$.						
.TRUE.	12	⅂	⅂	⅂	.FALSE.	
.TRUE.	4	9		⅂	.FALSE.	
.TRUE.	3	6			.FALSE.	
.TRUE.	4	9		⅂	.TRUE.	

Now let's see how we actually do all these fantasized processes. First, here's SUBROUTINE EXQTE which, given a cluster, carries out the program it represents.

```
        SUBROUTINE EXQTE(CLUSTR)
        INTEGER CLUSTR
COMMENT:THIS SUBROUTINE CARRIES OUT CLUSTERS.
C       IT INCLUDES THE DEFINITIONS OF ALL THE ATOMIC
C       ACTIONS.
C
C       COMMON BLOCK: ARRAYS USED TO MAKE SEXTETS, FREE, ETC.
        LOGICAL ATOMIC(1500),EOC(1500),DEBUG
        INTEGER INSTR(1500),TEST(1500),LEFT(1500),RIGHT(1500),
       +          FREE,UNH
        COMMON ATOMIC,INSTR,TEST,LEFT,RIGHT,EOC,FREE,DEBUG,UNH
        INTEGER ACT,NEWCL,T
        INTEGER U,R,DU,DR
        CHARACTER*1 SCENE(50,50),CHAR
        CHARACTER*1 OLDC
        LOGICAL TESTC(10)
C       INITIALIZE THE SCENE
        DO 10 U=1,50
          DO 10 R=1,50
  10        SCENE(U,R)=' '
        CHAR='.'
C       INITIALIZE THE TEST CELLS.
        DO 11 T=1,10
  11      TESTC(T)=.TRUE.
C
  20    IF (.NOT. DEBUG) GO TO 25
        PRINT,'EXECUTING: ATOMIC,INSTR,ETC.='
        PRINT,ATOMIC(CLUSTR),INSTR(CLUSTR),TEST(CLUSTR)
       +      ,LEFT(CLUSTR),RIGHT(CLUSTR),EOC(CLUSTR)
C       DOES THIS SEXTET REFER TO AN ATOMIC PROGRAM?
  25    IF (ATOMIC(CLUSTR)) GO TO 30
C       REFERENCE TO ANOTHER CLUSTER.  FIRST, DUPLICATE
C       THE NAMED CLUSTER.
          CALL DUPL(INSTR(CLUSTR),NEWCL)
C       NOW COPY INFO INTO FIRST SEXTET OF THE NEW
C       CLUSTER.
        TEST(NEWCL)=TEST(CLUSTR)
        LEFT(NEWCL)=CLUSTR-NEWCL+LEFT(CLUSTR)
        RIGHT(NEWCL)=CLUSTR-NEWCL+RIGHT(CLUSTR)
C
C       CONTINUE FROM THE SECOND SEXTET OF THE NEW CLUSTER.
        CLUSTR=NEWCL+1
        GO TO 20
```

```
C
C       CARRY OUT THE APPROPRIATE ATOMIC ACTION.
  30    ACT=INSTR(CLUSTR)
        IF (DEBUG) PRINT,'CLUSTER#',CLUSTR
        GO TO (100,200,300,400,500,600,700,800,900,1000,
       +       1100,1200),ACT
C
C       ATOMIC ACTION 1:MOVE CURSOR TO LOWER LEFT.
 100    U=1
        R=1
C       NOW ON LEFT AND BOTTOM EDGES
        DO 110 T=1,8
 110       TESTC(T)=.FALSE.
         TESTC(3)=.TRUE.
         TESTC(4)=.TRUE.
         TESTC(6)=.TRUE.
         TESTC(7)=.TRUE.
         TESTC(8)=.TRUE.
         IF (SCENE(U,R) .EQ. ' ') TESTC(1)=.TRUE.
        GO TO 2000
C
C       ATOMIC ACTION 2: SET (DU,DR) TO (0,0)
 200    DU=0
        DR=0
        GO TO 2000
C
C       ATOMIC ACTION 3: MOVE CURSOR
 300    DO 305 T=1,8
 305       TESTC(T)=.FALSE.
        U=U+DU
        IF (U .LT. 50) GO TO 310
          U=50
          TESTC(2)=.TRUE.
          TESTC(6)=.TRUE.
          TESTC(8)=.TRUE.
 310    IF (U .GT. 0) GO TO 320
          U=0
          TESTC(3)=.TRUE.
          TESTC(6)=.TRUE.
          TESTC(8)=.TRUE.
 320    R=R+DR
        IF (R .LT. 50) GO TO 330
          R=50
          TESTC(5)=.TRUE.
          TESTC(7)=.TRUE.
          TESTC(8)=.TRUE.
 330    IF (R .GT. 0) GO TO 340
          R=0
          TESTC(4)=.TRUE.
          TESTC(7)=.TRUE.
          TESTC(8)=.TRUE.
 340    IF (SCENE(U,R) .EQ. ' ') TESTC(1)=.TRUE.
        GO TO 2000
C
C       ATOMIC ACTION 4: PLACE 'CHAR' AT (U,R)
 400    SCENE(U,R)=CHAR
        IF (DEBUG) PRINT,CHAR,'PLACED AT',U,R
        TESTC(1)=.TRUE.
        GO TO 2000
```

```
C
C          ATOMIC ACTION 5: PRINT PICTURE AND STOP
  500      PRINT 510,((SCENE(51-U,R),R=1,50),U=1,50)
  510      FORMAT('1'/(' ',50A1))
           RETURN
C
C          ATOMIC ACTION 6: DU=DU+1
  600      DU=DU+1
           GO TO 2000
C
C          ATOMIC ACTION 7: DECREASE DU BY 1
  700      DU=DU-1
           GO TO 2000
C
C          ATOMIC ACTION 8
  800      DR=DR+1
           GO TO 2000
C
C          ATOMIC ACTION 9
  900      DR=DR-1
           GO TO 2000
C
C          ATOMIC ACTION 10: DO NOTHING WHATSOEVER.
 1000      CONTINUE
           GO TO 2000
C
C          ATOMIC ACTION 11: CHANGE VALUE OF CHAR.
 1100      OLDC=CHAR
           CHAR='.'
           IF (OLDC .EQ. '.') CHAR='*'
           TESTC(10)=.NOT. TESTC(10)
           GO TO 2000
C
C          ATOMIC ACTION 12: SUB CLUSTER RETURN.
C          RECAPTURE SOME FREE SPACE.
 1200      IF (FREE .LT. CLUSTR) PRINT,'RETURN ERROR',FREE
           FREE=CLUSTR
C
C      FINISHED WITH ALL THE ATOMIC ACTIONS--CHECK TEST
C      CELL AND GO ON.
 2000 IF (TESTC(TEST(CLUSTR))) GO TO 2100
C          FALSE, SO TAKE RIGHT SEXTET.
           CLUSTR=CLUSTR+RIGHT(CLUSTR)
           GO TO 20
C
C          TRUE, SO TAKE LEFT SEXTET.
 2100      CLUSTR=CLUSTR+LEFT(CLUSTR)
           GO TO 20
           END
```

SUBROUTINE EXQTE uses another SUBROUTINE called DUPL to make a copy of a cluster referred to by the sextet EXQTE is currently dealing with. Because of our inclusion of EOC in the sextet and our requirement that the sextets in a given cluster occupy consecutive memory cells, writing DUPL is easy. By the way, clusters without this property can be copied, but the copying algorithm is quite complicated.

```
      SUBROUTINE DUPL(CCLUST,COPY)
      INTEGER CCLUST,COPY
C     MAKE A COPY OF A CLUSTER BY CALLING 'SEXTET' UNTIL
C     EOC IS .TRUE.
C     COMMON BLOCK: ARRAYS USED TO MAKE SEXTETS, FREE, ETC.
      LOGICAL ATOMIC(1500),EOC(1500),DEBUG
      INTEGER INSTR(1500),TEST(1500),LEFT(1500),RIGHT(1500),
     +        FREE,UNH
      COMMON ATOMIC,INSTR,TEST,LEFT,RIGHT,EOC,FREE,DEBUG,UNH
      INTEGER CLUST
C     DON'T HURT ARG.
      CLUST=CCLUST
      COPY=FREE
10    CALL SEXTET(ATOMIC(CLUST),INSTR(CLUST),TEST(CLUST),
     +            LEFT(CLUST),RIGHT(CLUST),EOC(CLUST))
      IF (EOC(CLUST)) RETURN
      CLUST=CLUST+1
      GO TO 10
      END
```

Also, we need a SUBROUTINE which lets us define new sextets. This too is very simple, as you see in SUBROUTINE SEXTET.

```
      SUBROUTINE SEXTET(A,I,T,L,R,E)
C     CREATE A NEW SEXTET BY FILLING IN ENTRIES,
C     BUMPING 'FREE'.
      LOGICAL A,E
      INTEGER I,T,L,R
C     COMMON BLOCK: ARRAYS USED TO MAKE SEXTETS, FREE, ETC.
      LOGICAL ATOMIC(1500),EOC(1500),DEBUG
      INTEGER INSTR(1500),TEST(1500),LEFT(1500),RIGHT(1500),
     +        FREE,UNH
      COMMON ATOMIC,INSTR,TEST,LEFT,RIGHT,EOC,FREE,DEBUG,UNH
      IF(DEBUG) PRINT,'NEW SEXTET AT',FREE
      IF (DEBUG) PRINT,A,I,T,L,R,E
      ATOMIC(FREE)=A
      INSTR(FREE)=I
      TEST(FREE)=T
      LEFT(FREE)=L
      RIGHT(FREE)=R
      EOC(FREE)=E
      FREE=FREE+1
      RETURN
      END
```

Now that we can create and perform clusters, let's finish with a big bang by writing a program which makes a movie carrying out the actions in a cluster, modifying the cluster, performing it again, and so on until it has generated 50 scenes. Then, as we said, we'll cut them out and flip through them to watch. The movie will be pretty simple—just three abstract stalks of wheat waving in the abstract, random breeze.

SUBROUTINE INITS creates clusters which draw the basic shape. Notice that we've used loops to generate repeated sequences of sextets.

```
            SUBROUTINE INITS(INIT,WHEAT,SHEAF)
            INTEGER INIT,WHEAT,SHEAF
C           COMMON BLOCK: ARRAYS USED TO MAKE SEXTETS, FREE, ETC.
            LOGICAL ATOMIC(1500),EOC(1500),DEBUG
            INTEGER INSTR(1500),TEST(1500),LEFT(1500),RIGHT(1500),
           +      FREE,UNH
            COMMON ATOMIC,INSTR,TEST,LEFT,RIGHT,EOC,FREE,DEBUG,UNH
            INTEGER MOVER,SEX,TWO
C           DEFINE THE CALLABLE CLUSTER INIT
            INIT=FREE
C           FIRST CREATE THE RETURN SEXTET
            CALL SEXTET(.TRUE.,12,UNH,UNH,UNH,.FALSE.)
C           NOW CREATE A SEXTET TO MOVE CURSOR TO LOWER LEFT.
            CALL SEXTET(.TRUE.,1,9,1,UNH,.FALSE.)
C           FINALLY INSERT COMMAND WHICH ZEROS (DU,DR).
C           SINCE IT FINISHES THE 'INIT' CLUSTER, IT MUST
C           TRANSFER CONTROL BACK TO THE RETURN CELL.
C           ALSO, IT IS THE LAST SEXTET IN 'INIT', SO EOC =.TRUE.
            CALL SEXTET(.TRUE.,2,9,INIT-FREE,UNH,.TRUE.)
C
C           THE BASIC STEP IS TO PLACE A CHARACTER AND MOVE ON.
C           CLUSTER 'TWO' DOES SO TWICE.
            TWO=FREE
            CALL SEXTET(.TRUE.,12,UNH,UNH,UNH,.FALSE.)
            CALL SEXTET(.TRUE.,4,9,1,UNH,.FALSE.)
            CALL SEXTET(.TRUE.,3,9,1,UNH,.FALSE.)
            CALL SEXTET(.TRUE.,4,9,1,UNH,.FALSE.)
            CALL SEXTET(.TRUE.,3,9,TWO-FREE,UNH,.TRUE.)
C           CREATE A CLUSTER TO DRAW A STALK OF WHEAT.
            WHEAT=FREE
            CALL SEXTET(.TRUE.,12,UNH,UNH,UNH,.FALSE.)
            CALL SEXTET(.TRUE.,6,9,1,UNH,.FALSE.)
            CALL SEXTET(.TRUE.,8,10,2,1,.FALSE.)
C           BASE OF STALK IS MADE OF .'S
            CALL SEXTET(.TRUE.,11,9,1,UNH,.FALSE.)
C           NOW CREATE 16 SUCCESSIVE IDENTICAL SEXTETS.
            DO 100 SEX=1,16
              CALL SEXTET(.TRUE.,10,9,1,UNH,.FALSE.)
  100       CALL SEXTET(.FALSE.,TWO,9,1,UNH,.FALSE.)
C           NOW PUT IN THE EAR OF GRAIN.
            CALL SEXTET(.TRUE.,11,9,1,UNH,.FALSE.)
            DO 200 SEX=1,3
  200       CALL SEXTET(.FALSE.,TWO,8,WHEAT-FREE,1,.FALSE.)
            CALL SEXTET(.TRUE.,11,9,WHEAT-FREE,UNH,.TRUE.)
C           'MOVER' IS A CLUSTER WHICH MOVES THE CURSOR FOUR TO
C           THE RIGHT.
            MOVER=FREE
            CALL SEXTET(.TRUE.,12,UNH,UNH,UNH,.FALSE.)
            CALL SEXTET(.TRUE.,8,9,1,UNH,.FALSE.)
            CALL SEXTET(.TRUE.,8,9,1,UNH,.FALSE.)
            CALL SEXTET(.TRUE.,8,9,1,UNH,.FALSE.)
            CALL SEXTET(.TRUE.,8,9,1,UNH,.FALSE.)
            CALL SEXTET(.TRUE.,3,9,1,UNH,.FALSE.)
            CALL SEXTET(.TRUE.,2,9,MOVER-FREE,UNH,.TRUE.)
```

```
C
C      OUR MAIN SCENE IS THREE STALKS OF WHEAT, SO
C      FINALLY WE CREATE A CLUSTER CALLED 'SHEAF'.
       SHEAF=FREE
       CALL SEXTET(.FALSE.,INIT ,9,1,UNH,.FALSE.)
       CALL SEXTET(.FALSE.,WHEAT,9,1,UNH,.FALSE.)
       CALL SEXTET(.FALSE.,INIT ,9,1,UNH,.FALSE.)
       CALL SEXTET(.FALSE.,MOVER,9,1,UNH,.FALSE.)
       CALL SEXTET(.FALSE.,WHEAT,9,1,UNH,.FALSE.)
       CALL SEXTET(.FALSE.,INIT ,9,1,UNH,.FALSE.)
       CALL SEXTET(.FALSE.,MOVER,9,1,UNH,.FALSE.)
       CALL SEXTET(.FALSE.,MOVER,9,1,UNH,.FALSE.)
       CALL SEXTET(.FALSE.,WHEAT,9,1,UNH,.FALSE.)
       CALL SEXTET(.TRUE.,5,UNH,UNH,UNH,.TRUE.)
C      DONE DEFINING CLUSTERS.
       RETURN
       END
```

So far we have a cluster which, when carried out by EXQTE, draws three abstract blades of wheat. Now comes the sneaky part. To make them wave in the abstract breeze, what we'll do is EXQTE the cluster, then have our program make a random change to the cluster WHEAT, and repeat! Hold on to your seat!

```
COMMENT: THIS PROGRAM PRODUCES A MOVIE OF THREE ABSTRACT
C       STALKS OF WHEAT WAVING IN THE ABSTRACT RANDOM BREEZE.
C       IT FIRST USES SUBROUTINE INITS TO CREATE THE INITIAL
C       WHEAT DRAWING CLUSTER, THEN IT ALTERS THAT CLUSTER
C       BY MAKING RANDOM ADDITIONS OF CLUSTER ATOMIC ACTIONS
C       6,7,8, AND 9.
C       COMMON BLOCK: ARRAYS USED TO MAKE SEXTETS, FREE, ETC.
        LOGICAL ATOMIC(1500),EOC(1500),DEBUG
        INTEGER INSTR(1500),TEST(1500),LEFT(1500),RIGHT(1500),
       +        FREE,UNH
        COMMON ATOMIC,INSTR,TEST,LEFT,RIGHT,ECC,FREE,DEBUG,UNH
        INTEGER INIT,INS,HERE,MSEX,PLACE,SAVE,SHEAF,STILL,
       +        WHEAT,SSHEAF
C       'FREE' POINTS TO THE FIRST UNUSED POSITION IN THE
C       ARRAYS USED TO MAKE SEXTETS.
        FREE=1
C       'UNH' IS THE DON'T CARE VALUE.
        UNH=0
C       'DEBUG' CONTROLS A NUMBER OF PRINT STATEMNTS...
        DEBUG=.FALSE.
C       CREATE THE CLUSTERS WHICH MAKE THE BASIC SCENE.
        CALL INITS(INIT,WHEAT,SHEAF)
C       OUR MOVIE CONSISTS OF 50 STILLS.
        DO 1000 STILL=1,50
C       DRAW THE SHEAF
C       'EXQTE' GOBBLES UP ITS ARGUMENT.
        SSHEAF=SHEAF
        CALL EXQTE(SSHEAF)
C       NOW MAKE A CHANGE TO THE CLUSTER 'WHEAT'.
C       'WHEAT' BEGINS AS A CLUSTER OF 41 SEXTETS, 32 OF
C       WHICH MAKE UP THE STALK.  WE WISH TO ALTER ONE OF THE
C       INSTRUCTIONS IN THE STALK TO ACCOUNT FOR BENDING DUE
C       TO THE INTENSE RANDOM BREEZE.
        IF (DEBUG) PRINT,'INIT=',INIT,' WHEAT=',WHEAT
          PLACE=WHEAT+2+INT(RANDOM(X)*5.+12.)*2
          IF (DEBUG) PRINT,'OLD INSTR=',INSTR(PLACE)
          INSTR(PLACE)=RANDOM(X)*5.+6
          IF (DEBUG) PRINT,'NEW INSTR=',INSTR(PLACE),PLACE
   1000 CONTINUE
        STOP
        END
```

The RANDOM number generator we used is just like the one in CHAPTER 7, except that we wrote it as a FUNCTION.

Here are a few stills from our movie.

PROBLEMS 13

1 Verify that WATFIV stores two-dimensional arrays using column major form. Declare a one-dimensional array

INTEGER TEST(16)

in your main program. In each memory cell TEST(*i*), store *i*. Now send TEST as an argument to a SUBROUTINE VERIFY which lists a two-dimensional array

INTEGER A(4, 4)

as a parameter. Within VERIFY, PRINT the values in A, column by column. They should come out 1, 2, 3, 4, 5, 6, 7, . . . , 16.

WATFIV for Humans

2 Redo Problem 1, only this time include a number N as one of SUB-ROUTINE VERIFY's parameters. Use N as a variable dimension, *i.e.,*

INTEGER A(N, N).

Then CALL the SUBROUTINE several times giving N different values. Within VERIFY, PRINT out the values in the array and study how it is arranged in each case.

3 Use our traveling salesman program (Section 13 3 and Section 9 4) on a problem of interest (or practical value) to you. For example, go to a company that makes deliveries of some sort and find out the route their truck takes. Then get a map and find the distances between all stops they must make. See if the route they use really is the shortest. Tell them if it's not.

4 Another odd-shaped array that is sometimes useful is the **polar array**. By computing the subscript properly, a one-dimensional array may be organized into the form shown below.

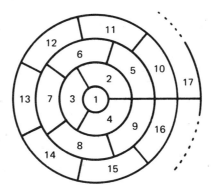

We've chosen this form so that the area that corresponds to each memory cell is about the same. The area of the ring between radius R-1 and radius R is proportional to

$$R^2 - (R-1)^2 = 2R - 1$$

Thus, we've placed 2R−1 locations in each ring of radius R (1 for R = 1, 3 for R = 2, 5 for R = 3, etc.)

We will refer to memory cells in the polar array by giving a value for the radius R, and one for the angle THETA. When THETA is zero, to find our way to the memory cell corresponding to the radius R, we must skip over the first R − 1 rings; thus we must skip over $1 + 3 + 5 + \ldots + (2R - 3)$ locations. The next location will then correspond to the memory cell at radius R and angle 0. Hence, the formula for computing the appropriate array subscript for this cell is

$$(R - 1)^2 + 1$$

Amazing, but true: the sum of the first n odd numbers is n^2

Now all we need is a term to account for non-zero THETAs. Since the ring at radius R has 2R–1 values for the THETA term, the THETA term is

$$((2*R–1) * THETA))/360$$

We have carefully parenthesized the expression so that INTEGER division helps us out.

Thus, given a value R (1 or greater) and a value THETA (0 to 359), we use the memory cell whose subscript is

$$(R – 1)**2 + 1 + ((2*R–1) * THETA)/360$$

Figure out how many memory cells must be in the array when we want to have a polar array whose maximum radius is RMAX. Write a statement function to convert (R, THETA) values into the appropriate array subscripts. Write a program which implements a polar array and test it by first storing values at various (R, THETA) positions and then PRINTing out the array to verify that the values you stored went into the correct positions.

If you feel like it, write a FUNCTION CONVRT that will accept values for THETA in any range and return a value in the proper range (0 to 359). For example,

CONVRT (710) returns 350

and   CONVRT (–90) returns 270

5   Devise a scheme for going from (R, THETA) values to array subscripts which organizes a one-dimensional array into a polar array of the form

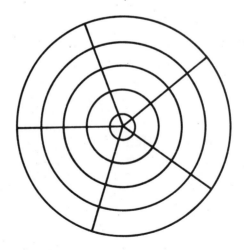

6   Do Problem 8 9 (ringworms) using polar arrays.

7 Queues are often used in situations where a program is receiving much more data than it can cope with at one point in time. A queue can be filled up with data by one subprogram then used in bits and pieces by another subprogram. When the queue is empty, the first subprogram is used to fill it up again, etc.

Of course the situation may be reversed—one subprogram may slowly fill a queue and have another subprogram get rid of the values in it each time the queue becomes full. In cases like this, the queue is often called a *buffer.* Buffers are used by the programs that carry out the I/O statements your program uses.

Redo Problem 10 12 (the one on typesetting ad copy) using a queue to store partially completed lines.

8 Do Problem 10 17 (Morse Code) using queues as buffers.

9 Suppose you are running a supermarket and you have four checkout counters. You would like to run one of them as an "express lane", but you're not sure where to set the limit which determines who may use the express lane. You decide to write a computer simulation and compare the effects of different limits on how quickly 200 shoppers (who buy a random amount of groceries and come to be checked out at random times) get checked out.

Here's the strategy of the program: Let the current time be T. For each shopper, generate two random numbers. The first, T ENTER, gives the time the shopper arrives at the checkout area, and the second, T OUT, gives the length of time it will take for the checker to check the shopper out (once the process starts). For each checkout counter, keep track of the shoppers waiting by using a queue. If there is some shopper already at the head of one of the lines who will be checked out before T NEXT = T + T ENTER, check him out (so that T is now T + T OUT). Keep testing until there are no more to be checked out up to time T NEXT. Then enter the shopper who has arrived (thus making T = T NEXT) using the following strategy:

If the T OUT value associated with this shopper is below the LIMIT, he may enter the express lane if he chooses. Otherwise he should be put in the lane with the fewest people waiting.

Optional: Decide which line the next shopper goes to on a more elaborate basis—perhaps on how many people in a line *and* the T OUT associated with the last person in that line (as if the shopper is also estimating how many groceries the people already in line have).

PRINT the results of your simulation in a form that makes it easy to compare the results. Run the program for several different values of LIMIT.

10 Write a program which creates and maintains a list of people's names and their telephone numbers. Your program should maintain the links in the list so that the names are in alphabetical order. A list element should have the general structure shown below.

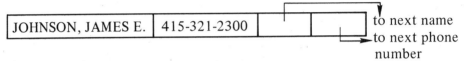

The input for your program should be punched cards in one of two types

    1 new entry card:

      name   phone number

  2 'ALPHABETIC LISTING'

If your program sees a card of type (1) it should add the name and phone number to the list in the appropriate place. If it sees a card of type (2) it should print out all the names and phone numbers in its list in alphabetical order.

Alter your program so that it maintains a doubly linked list. The first link will be unchanged and will order the list according to increasing phone number.

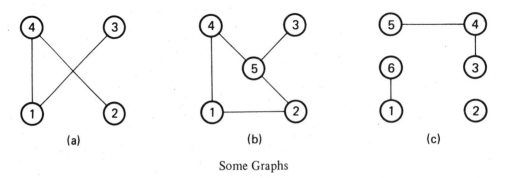

Now your program should accept one more kind of input card:

(3) 'NUMERIC LISTING'

If your program sees a card of type 3 it should PRINT a listing of names and phone numbers in order of increasing phone number.

11 A graph, for the purposes of this problem, is a number of nodes together with a set of line segments connecting some of those nodes.

Some Graphs

A *path* in a graph is a set of its line segments connecting one node to another. A graph is called *connected* if there is a path between each pair of nodes. In the drawing above, (a) and (b) are connected graphs but (c) is not connected. The object of this problem is to write a LOGICAL FUNCTION which decides whether the graph described by its parameters is connected or not.

An easy way to describe a graph is by using a triangular array containing LOGICAL values. The value .TRUE. indicates that a line segment is present between the two nodes determined by the row and column number of that entry in the array; .FALSE. indicates the absence of a connecting segment. Graphs (a), (b), and (c) correspond to triangular arrays (a), (b), and (c). Your LOGICAL FUNCTION should have two parameters: (1) a triangular array describing a graph and (2) an INTEGER indicating the number of nodes of the graph. The FUNCTION should return the value .TRUE. when the graph is connected and .FALSE. otherwise.

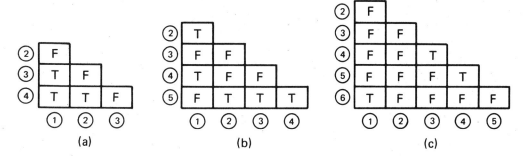

The Same Graphs as Triangular Arrays

Use the following algorithm to determine connectedness.

INITIALIZE: initialize a stack of nodes by placing node 1 on it

HOOK: add to the stack all nodes which are connected to the top element on the stack by a path consisting of a single line segment

DECIDE: (a) if the stack contains all nodes, return the value .TRUE.

(b) if no nodes were added in the HOOK step, return the value .FALSE.

(c) otherwise, repeat from HOOK

12 Devise a data structure with internal links to describe your graphs. Rewrite the algorithm of Problem 11 so that it uses your new data structure rather than the triangular array representation of a graph.

13 Make up a data structure of your own, basing it on some complex real world problem you are interested in. Write down a precise description of how your data structure works. See if you can explain it to someone else in the class. If you can, write the WATFIV statements necessary to implement it. If you can't, your description must not be detailed enough, so try again.

14 Write a program which carries out the logic for the following traffic light system.

The s's in the drawing represent sensors, and the lights should follow the following rules. If no sensors are on, cycle the lights the same as if all sensors were on. If only one sensor is on, let that car go (give him a green light). Traffic on College has priority, so if sensors on College and on Prospect stay on, let more time pass with green for College than green for Prospect. Cars going straight have priority over cars turning.

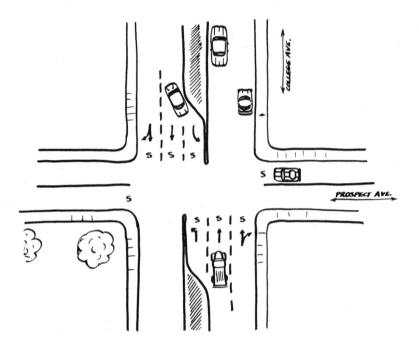

Make up a number of data cards each of which represents a car, and have on the card some representation of which way the car wants to go and what time he arrives at the light. You may ignore yellow lights. Each time the light changes, print out the current situation: *e.g.*, if, at time 10.0, the lights on Prospect are green and there are three cars waiting to proceed North on College and one waiting in the left turn lane to turn west onto Prospect, then print out:

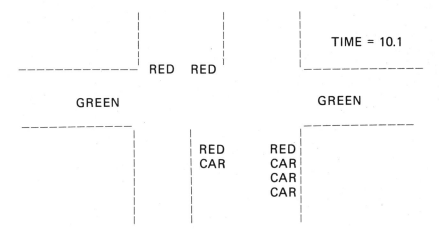

Select some appropriate data structure to store cars that are in the intersection. Queues or lists would do.

15 Write a program to print random sentences. First write a number of rules for generating sentences, using a period at the beginning to distinguish between words that are part of the rules from words which may appear in sentences.

Example

Rule 1	.sentence	=	.nounph	.verb	
Rule 2	.sentence	=	.nounph	.verb	.nounph
Rule 3	.nounph	=	.article	.noun	
Rule 4	.nounph	=	.noun		
Rule 5	.verb	=	BIT		
Rule 6	.verb	=	JUMPED		
Rule 7	.verb	=	SWALLOWED		
Rule 8	.article	=	THE		
Rule 9	.noun	=	HORSE		
Rule 10	.noun	=	COW		
Rule 11	.noun	=	PILL		

Algorithm for forming sentences:

1 Start a stack with .sentence

2 Find the first rule in the stack (*i.e.*, the first word in the list which starts with a period) and replace it by the definition of that rule (*e.g.*, the definition of the rule .article above is THE). If there is more than one definition for the rule, then choose at random *one* of these definitions.

3 If there are no more words in the stack which start with a '.', print out the sentence. Otherwise repeat step 2.

Sophisticated Uses of Arrays

You may want to use two stacks, DONE and WORKIN, to store the partially completed sentences as shown in the example below:

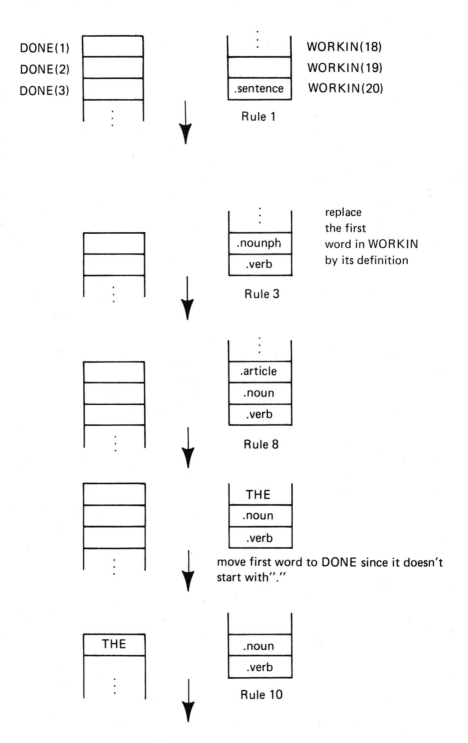

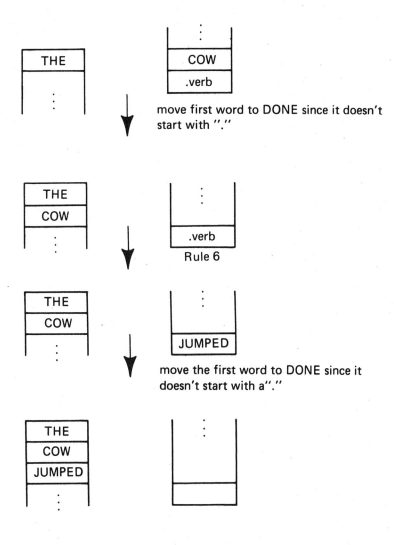

move first word to DONE since it doesn't start with "."

Rule 6

move the first word to DONE since it doesn't start with a"."

*

WATFIV
MiniManual

If you're down in the computer center late at night trying desperately to get a program to run and you can't remember all the options and restrictions associated with DO-loops, look here.

CONTENTS

Definitions

address

a label (symbolic or numeric) identifying a memory cell;

an array **subscript**;

the value of a **pointer**

algorithm

directions for doing something;

more formally: a collection of rules which, when carried out, solve a specified problem in a finite number of steps;

less formally: what all God's chilluns got

alias

alternate name or label;

when a memory cell has several names (through EQUIVALENCE statements) the memory cell is said to have aliases

alphanumeric

alphameric (see **character**)

ANSI Fortran

a computer language defined in standards maintained by the American National Standards Institute, Inc.

array

a collection of memory cells, individual members of which may be referenced by a single identifier followed by a numeric value (the **index** or **subscript**);

the memory cells which comprise a **subscripted variable**

argument

a value which serves as an input to a **subprogram**

assignment compatible

a value is **assignment compatible** with a memory cell name if the value may be legally converted to the type of the memory cell name;

numeric data types are assignment compatible;

CHARACTER*n is assignment compatible with CHARACTER*m

binary I/O

see **unformatted I/O**

bit

a binary digit (0 or 1)

bug

an error;

a statement or pattern of statements which causes an error

byte

a directly addressable eight bit storage element in IBM 360/370 core memory; eight bits of information on an I/O medium or in memory

chad

the material removed to make holes in punched cards or tape

> **warning**: *Use of chad as confetti is* dangerous. *Sharp edges can cause eye injuries. This is* no joke. *Use **chard** instead.*

chard

a vegetable with large leaves and succulent stalks

character

numeric character: a decimal digit, one of

0 1 2 3 4 5 6 7 8 9

alphabetic character: a capitalized letter, one of

A B C D E F G H I J K L M N O P Q R S T U V W X Y Z

alphameric: a numeric or alphabetic character (in some literature, this term is synonymous with "**character**")

special character: one of

. , ' $ + * /) (= b

[where b represents the blank character]

other character: anything not mentioned above that you can find: % ? ! a b c, etc.

compiler

a program which translates WATFIV statements into the lower level language appropriate for your computer

computer

a machine which can perform arithmetic operations, make logical decisions, and perform many other symbol manipulation tasks by automatically following the instructions in a computer program

controller

the part of the conceptual computer which carries out commands;

the part of the conceptual computer other than memory or input/output

debug

to locate and remove **bugs**

default

a value or condition which is assumed unless explicitly overridden

defined

having a value;

having been specified;

for instance, a memory cell's value is **defined** once it has been given a value by an assignment, input statement, or compile-time initialization

disk

a **random access i/o device** containing a stack of spinning magnetic storage plates

double word boundary

a **byte** in IBM 360/370 core memory with an address divisible by eight

documentation

information prepared for humans describing a program or collection of related programs

drum

random access I/O device containing a spinning magnetic recording cylinder

element

one of a collection of things;

an **array element** is a memory cell in an array

executable statement

a statement which is a command to the **controller** rather than an instruction to the **compiler**;

assignment statements of any kind, transfer of control of any kind (including STOP and CONTINUE), input/output of any kind

Fortran

a computer language which either conforms to or closely resembles ANSI Fortran (thus WATFIV may be considered to be Fortran even though it is not strictly compatible with ANSI Fortran)

head

see **read/write head**

identifier

a name (of a simple memory cell, array, subprogram, etc.);

note: some WATFIV error messages use the word **symbol** for **identifier**

I/O device

equipment which reads or writes data on an input or output medium

I/O medium

material used for storing data (*e.g.*, computer paper, 80-column cards, magnetic tape)

index

a label which identifies one of a group of items;

an **array subscript**;

to point out each member of a collection (usually a collection of **array elements**)

initialize

to prepare for a process to begin;

to give starting (initial) values to memory cells

key

in sorting, the values which determine the sorted arrangement are called the **keys**

keyword

a sequence of characters making up a distinguishing part of a WATFIV statement;

for example: STOP
                   DO
                   FORMAT

memory cell

the basic unit of storage in WATFIV;

note: memory cells of differing data types may have different physical sizes in the host machine

mode

type

module

a **program unit** or collection of program units which make a logical subunit of an overall program

multipunch

a pattern of holes created by striking more than one key in the same column of a card;

to create such a pattern by striking several keys while holding down the MLT PCH key

non-executable statement

a statement which is not a command to the **controller**; END, EQUIVALENCE, COMMON, FORMAT, etc.

object

a WATFIV item, element or unit;

i.e., a memory cell, an array, a subprogram, a statement, a constant, etc.

object of a DO-loop

the last statement in the range of a DO statement

operator

+ − * / ** are arithmetic operators;

.NOT. .AND. .OR. are LOGICAL operators

parameter

an **identifier** used to specify the form and type which an **argument** to a **subprogram** will have;

the control variable, initial value, upper bound, or increment of a DO statement

pointer

a memory cell which stores an **address** or **subscript**

precision

the degree to which a value discriminates between measured quantities;

a value correct to two digits is more *precise* than one correct to only one digit since the first discriminates among a hundred possibilities, the second among only ten

program

one or more program units, with or without data, with job control statements;

to write a program

program fragment

part of a program, used to illustrate some particular point

program segment

a program unit

program unit

the main program, a FUNCTION, or a SUBROUTINE;

a sequence of WATFIV statements followed by an END statement;

note: some WATFIV error messages use the equivalent term **program segment**

random access I/O device

an I/O device whose read/write head can move in a nonsequential way, thus making the data retrieval time almost independent of the location of the data on the I/O device (*e.g.,* **disk, drum**)

record

a set of data items treated as a unit; for instance, the sequence of 80 characters on a punched card

recursive

self-referential;

a **recursive** subprogram is one which includes a reference to itself (possibly through some sequence of references to other program units);

using repeated obscenities

simple variable

a memory cell which is not subscripted

specification statement

a non-executable statement;

an instruction to the compiler which provides information about memory cells other than their data type (DATA, EQUIVALENCE, etc.)

statement

a single WATFIV command

structured programming

an approach to programming which leads to understandable, correct computer programs

subprogram

a program unit other than the main program;

a FUNCTION or SUBROUTINE

subscript

a value designating a particular element of an array

subscripted variable

an **array**;

an array **element**

symbol

in WATFIV error messages, same as an **identifier**

temporary

the result of an expression or subexpression which is not assigned directly to a memory cell in the WATFIV program

train

a motive unit, with or without cars, displaying marker lights

type

the interpretation placed on a stored bit pattern, *e.g.,* LOGICAL, INTEGER, REAL, etc.;

mode

typical rule

"This form may be used only if not before the last preceding comma, or in an ASSIGNed GO TO but not before *any* executable statement except STOP or PAUSE when these do not have the optional trailing constant, except that the PAUSE may have an optional trailing unsigned INTEGER constant on odd numbered days."

unformatted I/O

a type of I/O designed for machine-machine communication as opposed to human-machine communication

unsigned INTEGER constant

a nonzero INTEGER constant not preceded by a + or − sign

WATFIV

a computer programming language developed by the Department of Applied Analysis and Computer Science at the University of Waterloo;

WATFIV contains a number of features which are not part of ANSI Fortran; almost all ANSI Fortran programs will run unchanged as WATFIV programs;

WATFIV conforms closely to IBM's Fortran Level G developed for the 360/370 series computers;

WATFIV contains several features, including the CHARACTER*n data type, format-free I/O, and an excellent error message facility, which simplify the process of writing and debugging programs

WATFOR

an earlier version of WATFIV

 "Comma alert";

used to draw attention to obscure places in specific statements where a comma must or may not appear (the triangle points to the place in question)

 forbidden usage;

used to identify illegal, invalid usages

 legitimate usage;

used to identify valid examples

The Price of Freedom from Syntax Errors is Eternal Vigilance

Control Cards

Your computer system has many built-in subsystems. One of those is the WATFIV compiler.

The computer system learns which subsystem you want to use through the job control statements which precede your WATFIV program statements.

It is very likely that the exact procedure for submitting your WATFIV job to the computer system is posted on a bulletin board or taped to the walls somewhere near the keypunches you've used to punch your cards. The deck setup shown in Figure MM 1 will give you some idea what to look for.

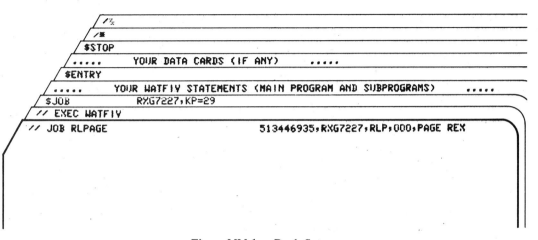

Figure MM 1   Deck Setup

Although some computer centers will ask that you submit WATFIV jobs in a special place and leave off the // JOB and // EXEC WATFIV cards shown in Figure MM 1, most will require those cards (or similar ones) be included in your deck.

The // JOB card gives accounting information to the computer system; the // EXEC WATFIV card tells the computer system that you want to use the WATFIV compiler. At that point, the WATFIV compiler takes over.

The $JOB gives accounting information to the compiler and information about the way you have prepared your program, how long you expect it to run, etc.

The $ENTRY card separates your program from its data cards (if it needs any) and tells the WATFIV compiler to begin execution of your program. $ENTRY is punched in columns one to six; column seven must be blank.

The $STOP card tells the WATFIV compiler that you have no more programs in this deck. It is possible to run several programs in the same // EXEC WATFIV package by repeating the $JOB-statements-$ENTRY-data sequence.

At this point the WATFIV compiler exits from the scene, and the governing computer system takes over. The /* card tells the system that you don't have any more // JOB sequences in this deck.

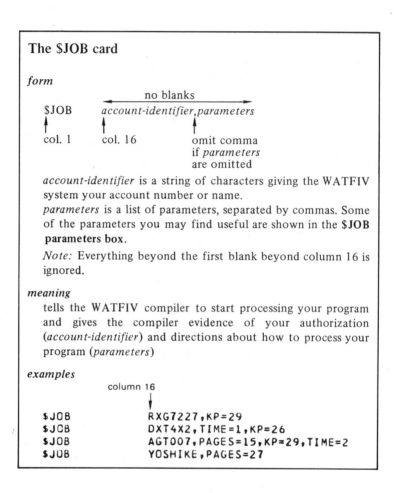

The $JOB card

form

                     no blanks
    $JOB   *account-identifier,parameters*

    col. 1   col. 16   omit comma
                             if *parameters*
                             are omitted

account-identifier is a string of characters giving the WATFIV system your account number or name.

parameters is a list of parameters, separated by commas. Some of the parameters you may find useful are shown in the **$JOB parameters box**.

Note: Everything beyond the first blank beyond column 16 is ignored.

meaning

tells the WATFIV compiler to start processing your program and gives the compiler evidence of your authorization (*account-identifier*) and directions about how to process your program (*parameters*)

examples

              column 16

    $JOB   RXG7227,KP=29
    $JOB   DXT4X2,TIME=1,KP=26
    $JOB   AGT007,PAGES=15,KP=29,TIME=2
    $JOB   YOSHIKE,PAGES=27

$JOB parameters

KP=26   says you have punched your program on a model 026 keypunch (the classic gray metal ones with rounded lines).

KP=29   says you have punched your program on a model 029 keypunch (the modern blue and cream ones with sharp edges). On many systems, KP=29 will be assumed if you omit the KP parameter.

TIME=*minutes*   *minutes,* an unsigned INTEGER constant, is the maximum number of minutes you want your job to run; the compiler will assume some standard time limit if you omit this parameter.

PAGES=*max*   *max,* an unsigned INTEGER constant, is the maximum number of pages you want to allow your program to print; the compiler will assume some standard page limit if you omit this parameter.

There are other parameters, but they are of less interest to the novice.

*

Syntax + Semantics/3

The syntax of a language is its correct grammatical form. Virtually all of the syntax of WATFIV is described herein.

The semantics of a language is the meaning of its grammatical constructs. Some of the semantics of WATFIV is explained herein. The rest is explained in the first thirteen chapters.

Entries have the following general organization.

Major topic category

Specific topic name

   examples of legal usages

   examples of illegal usages, with brief explanations of the error

> precise definition of allowed forms

comments, special things to notice

Material covered by gray shading is either an extension of or in disagreement with standard Fortran as described in ANSI X3.9–1966.

The following IMPLICIT statement indicates the assumptions made about data types in the examples. It is repeated on every pair of facing pages.

```
IMPLICIT CHARACTER*80(A,B), COMPLEX(C),
+        DOUBLE PRECISION(D), INTEGER(I-N),
+        LOGICAL(P,Q), REAL(R-Z)
```

WATFIV Statement Layout

statement field

WATFIV statements may appear anywhere in columns 7 through 72 inclusive. A statement may be continued (in columns 7 through 72 of the next card) by placing any character but zero or blank in column 6 of the next card.

statement label field

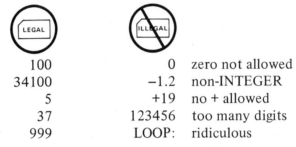

LEGAL	ILLEGAL	
100	0	zero not allowed
34100	−1.2	non-INTEGER
5	+19	no + allowed
37	123456	too many digits
999	LOOP:	ridiculous

An unsigned, non-zero INTEGER with up to 5 digits placed anywhere in columns 1 to 5

comments

A 'C' in column 1 identifies that entire card as a comment. The contents will be included in the program listing but are otherwise ignored.

A multiple card comment must have a 'C' in column 1 of each card.

A "zigamorph" character (multipunch 12-11-0-7-8-9) on a card causes the remainder of that card to be treated as a comment.

blanks

```
REAL WAR PER          REAL WARPER           REAL WAR,PER
DO 1 K=1,12    is      DO1K=1,2     but not   DO 1 K =1-12
'HI THERE'   equivalent 8HHI THERE  equivalent 'HITHERE'
5HBLECH        to      'BLECH'         to     6H BLECH
```

Blank characters are ignored in the statement field and label field except with CHARACTER*n constants.

multiple statements

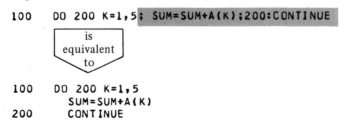

```
100    DO 200 K=1,5; SUM=SUM+A(K);200:CONTINUE
```

is equivalent to

```
100    DO 200 K=1,5
       SUM=SUM+A(K)
200    CONTINUE
```

More than one statement may be crammed onto one card. A semicolon (;) terminates a statement. If a statement label appears in columns 7–72, it must be followed by a colon (:). Continuations work as usual. (The label field on a continuation card must be blank.)

data

To avoid confusion with WATFIV control cards like $JOB or $STOP, data cards must not have a $ sign in column 1.

Data cards may use all 80 columns at the programmer's pleasure depending only on the FORMAT describing the data card layout.

Constants

A constant is a fixed value involving no computation.

INTEGER constant

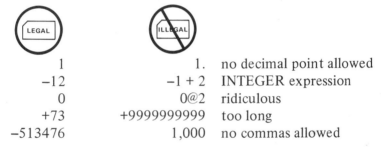

LEGAL	ILLEGAL	
1	1.	no decimal point allowed
−12	−1 + 2	INTEGER expression
0	0@2	ridiculous
+73	+9999999999	too long
−513476	1,000	no commas allowed

May include a leading + or −, otherwise all numeric characters.

INTEGER constants must be in the range −2147483648 to 2147483647.

REAL constant

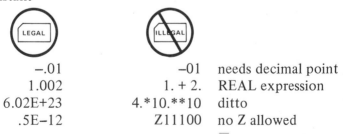

LEGAL	ILLEGAL	
−.01	−01	needs decimal point
1.002	1. + 2.	REAL expression
6.02E+23	4.*10.**10	ditto
.5E−12	Z11100	no Z allowed

May include a leading + or − ; contains up to 7 digits, excluding optional decimal point shift factor; must have a decimal point. A decimal point shift factor is an E followed by an INTEGER constant in the range −78 to 75.

COMPLEX constant

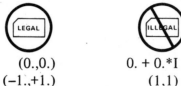

(0.,0.)	0. + 0.*I	REAL expression
(−1.,+1.)	(1,1)	components must be REALs
(24.0E+1, 9.)		

Two REAL constants, enclosed by parentheses, separated by a comma. First REAL is the real part, second REAL the imaginary part.

DOUBLE PRECISION constants

3.1415926	4	INTEGER
+1.0D0	1,000.0	no commas allowed
−7.7777D−20	3.2E19	REAL

Like a REAL constant except may have up to 16 numeric digits before the optional shift factor. Shift factor is written with a D instead of E and must be in the range −78 to 75.

LOGICAL constant

| .TRUE. | TRUE | needs periods |
| .FALSE. | NO | not even close |

Corresponds to two valued logic. The periods at each end distinguish LOGICAL constants from identifiers.

CHARACTER constant

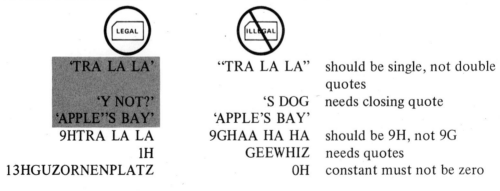

'TRA LA LA'	"TRA LA LA"	should be single, not double quotes
'Y NOT?'	'S DOG	needs closing quote
'APPLE''S BAY'	'APPLE'S BAY'	
9HTRA LA LA	9GHAA HA HA	should be 9H, not 9G
1H	GEEWHIZ	needs quotes
13HGUZORNENPLATZ	0H	constant must not be zero

A string (sequence) of any sort of characters. There are two forms—the newer form simply encloses the string in single quotes (apostrophes). The older form (often called a **Hollerith constant**) requires that you count the characters in the constant and write that number, followed by an H, before the string.

Hollerith notation

form
    $nHc_1c_2 \ldots c_n$
    n is an unsigned INTEGER constant
    c_i is a character

meaning
    provides an alternative notation to the CHARACTER constant
    '$c_1c_2 \ldots c_n$';
    included in WATFIV for historical reasons

examples

```
A1=4HBONG
A2='BONG'
B1=4HATOM
B2='ATOM'
```

Note: After the computer performs these four assignments, A1 and A2 contain the same values, B1 and B2 also contain identical values

four equivalent FORMATs:

```
1000    FORMAT('1','CHECKING ACCOUNT SUMMARY')
2000    FORMAT(1H1,24HCHECKING ACCOUNT SUMMARY)
3000    FORMAT('1CHECKING ACCOUNT SUMMARY')
4000    FORMAT(25H1CHECKING ACCOUNT SUMMARY)
```

The analysis of the 1880 U.S. Census was not completed by 1890. The 1890 census was finished before 1900, thanks in large part to equipment invented by Herman Hollerith.

```
IMPLICIT CHARACTER*80(A,B), COMPLEX(C),
+       DOUBLE PRECISION(D), INTEGER(I-N),
+       LOGICAL(P,Q), REAL(R-Z)
```

375

Hexadecimal constant

LEGAL	ILLEGAL	
Z0	Z-1	no sign allowed
ZABCF	–ZABCF	no sign allowed
Z0001FF	Z0001FH	H is not a hexadecimal digit
Z34790E		

The character Z followed by at least one hexadecimal digit (*i.e.*, a numeric character or one of A B C D E F) forms a hexadecimal constant.

Normally used as a convenient way to initialize memory cells to specific bit patterns in compile-time initialization statements.

Not a WATFIV data type.

May not be used where it could be confused with *identifier*.

statement label constant

See Subprograms

Memory Allocation

Memory can be allocated in single chunks (unsubscripted memory cells) or larger blocks (arrays). The compiler needs to know the data type of the values to be stored in the memory cells at the time of allocation because different types need memory cells of different lengths. The type can be declared explicity in a declaration statement or assumed according to the implicit typing rules.

Declaration of array parameters in subprograms doesn't involve memory allocation but takes the same form as memory allocating declarations.

Identifiers

LEGAL	ILLEGAL	
A1	1A	starts with number
BAT MAN	BRUCE WAYNE	too long
HNGRY	%GREED	illegal character
RST	R, S-T	illegal characters
X12345	X1234567	too long
SLOPE		

Up to 6 characters long, consisting of alphanumeric characters. Must begin with an alphabetic character. Used for memory cell names, subprogram names, etc. If the KP=29 option is in effect, the character $ may be used anywhere in an identifier, as if it were another alphabetic character.

Simple variable name

An identifier; an unsubscripted memory cell name

subscripted variable

A(1,2,3)	A<1,2,3>	angle brackets not allowed
COST(M,N+2)	COSTLINESS(M,N)	name too long
TYPE(23)	(23)TYPE	name must go first

An identifier followed by from one to seven subscripts, separated by commas, enclosed in parentheses. Don't use the identifier FORMAT to name an array.

Explicit type declarations

```
INTEGER M,N,LOT(25)
REAL XYLO
LOGICAL PLATO(2,4,8)
COMPLEX C1,C2
DOUBLE PRECISION DRIFT(14),D12,DWARF2
CHARACTER ATLAS,BAR(132,2)
```

```
INTERGER M,N,LOT(25)      misspelling
REAL 3.14159              must be an identifier, not a constant
LOGICAL(2,4,8)PLATO       array length info comes after identifier
DEVIOUS C1,C2             not a type
REAL YNOT(0)              array length may not be zero
INTEGER K(+2)             array length must be unsigned
```

In subprograms, variables may be used as length declarators for array parameters. The variable length declarators must either be parameters themselves or members of COMMON regions available to the subprogram

Explicit type declarations—Optional lengths

```
INTEGER*2 M,N,LOT(25)
REAL*8 X,Y*4,YAZ
LOGICAL*1 PLATO(2,4,8)
CHARACTER*132 A,B
COMPLEX CAT*16(20)
```

```
IMPLICIT CHARACTER*80(A,B), COMPLEX(C),
+        DOUBLE PRECISION(D), INTEGER(I-N),
+        LOGICAL(P,Q), REAL(R-Z)
```

```
INTEGER*8 M,N,LOT(25)          illegal length option
REAL*8 X,Y*47,YAZ              ditto
LOGICAL*3 PLATO(2,4,8)         ditto
CHARACTER*512 A,B              ditto
COMPLEX CAT(20)*16             length option goes before array info
DOUBLE PRECISION*16 DWARF2     no length option allowed
```

Memory cells may be of several different lengths. Useful for saving memory, increasing accuracy, or different length CHARACTER values. An asterisk (*) followed by an unsigned INTEGER constant, known as a **type length modifier**, may follow a type (INTEGER, REAL, etc.), or an identifier, or both. Optional length after an identifier over-rides optional length after *type*.

WATFIV Data Types

type	type length modifiers	remarks
INTEGER	*2 *4	$-32768 \leq$ INTEGER*2 ≤ 32767 *4 is default
REAL	*4 *8	*4 is default *8 same as DOUBLE PRECISION
COMPLEX	*8 *16	*8 is default *16 is double precision COMPLEX
DOUBLE PRECISION	no options	same as REAL*8
LOGICAL	*1 *4	*4 is default
CHARACTER	*n where $1 \leq n \leq 255$	*1 is default

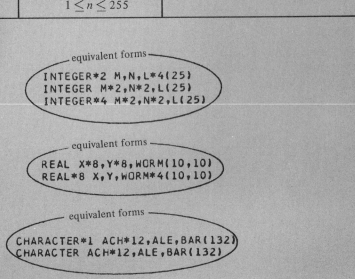

equivalent forms
```
INTEGER*2 M,N,L*4(25)
INTEGER M*2,N*2,L(25)
INTEGER*4 M*2,N*2,L(25)
```

equivalent forms
```
REAL X*8,Y*8,WORM(10,10)
REAL*8 X,Y,WORM*4(10,10)
```

equivalent forms
```
CHARACTER*1 ACH*12,ALE,BAR(132)
CHARACTER ACH*12,ALE,BAR(132)
```

Explicit Type Declarations—Initialization

```
INTEGER M/0/,N/-1/,LCT(25)
REAL*8 XENO(3)/0.0,2*1.0/
COMPLEX COMMIE/(0.0,0.0)/
LOGICAL P*1(20)/20*.FALSE./
CHARACTER BUMP*1(3)/'0','1','2'/
```

```
INTEGER M/3.0/,N/2*1/,LOT(25)      too many constants for N
REAL*8 XENO/0.0,2*1.0/(3)          constants must follow array info
COMPLEX COMMIE//
LOGICAL P(20)/20*.FALSE./*1        misplaced length option
```

An element in the list following *type* which does not correspond to a sub-program parameter may be given an initial value by following it with a list of one or more constants enclosed by slashes (/). The constants must agree in *type* with the memory cells they will initialize. An unsigned INTEGER constant followed by an asterisk (*) is a **replication factor**.

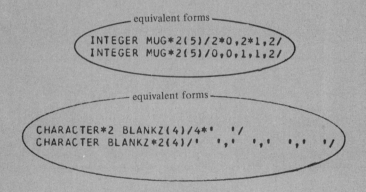

```
─── equivalent forms ───
INTEGER MUG*2(5)/2*0,2*1,2/
INTEGER MUG*2(5)/0,0,1,1,2/

─── equivalent forms ───
CHARACTER*2 BLANKZ(4)/4*'  '/
CHARACTER BLANKZ*2(4)/'  ','  ','  ','  '/
```

> *There are at least 240 different styles of* WATFIV *explicit type declarations, ranging from*
>
> INTEGER ICH
>
> *to*
>
> REAL*8 X*4,Y(20),Z*4(2)/1.0,1,0/

If you are reading this because you got error message
>   DA-0, DA-1, or DA-5,
vent your rage by hitting here hard.

IMPLICIT CHARACTER*80(A,B), COMPLEX(C),
+   DOUBLE PRECISION(D), INTEGER(I-N),
+   LOGICAL(P,Q), REAL(R-Z)

Type Statement (declaration)

$type\ a_1{}^*t_1(s_1)/d_1/,a_2{}^*t_2(s_2)/d_2/,\ldots a_n{}^*t_n(s_n)/d_n/$

type is a WATFIV data type (see chart, WATFIV data types, preceding)

a_i is an identifier

t_i is a data type length modifier consistent with *type*

s_i is a list of up to seven length declarators for the array a_i (must be unsigned INTEGER constants unless a_i is a parameter name in the current subprogram)

d_i is a list of s_i constants of a data type consistent with the type of a_i. $/d_i/$ must be omitted if a_i is a parameter name in the current subprogram

note: $^*t_i$, (s_i), and-or $/d_i/$ may be omitted

Implicit Type Declarations

If an identifier does not appear in a type statement of any kind, then

| if it begins with A through H, O through Z, or $ } | it is assumed to be REAL*4 |

| if it begins with I through N } | it is assumed to be INTEGER*4 |

Explicitly Implicit Type Declarations—the IMPLICIT statement

```
IMPLICIT COMPLEX*16(A,X-Z)
IMPLICIT REAL($),INTEGER(A-M,Z)
IMPLICIT LOGICAL*1(T-W),REAL(X,Y,Z)
IMPLICIT CHARACTER*10(A,F-K)
```

```
EXPLICIT LOGICAL(A-Z)
IMPLICIT REAL(Z-A)
ILLICIT CHARACTER(1-2)
```

IMPLICIT statement

IMPLICIT $t_1(r_1), t_2(r_2), \ldots, t_n(r_n)$

t_i is a WATFIV data type

r_i is a letter A, B, C, $\ldots$, Z or $ or a letter range x-y where x is a letter alphabetically preceding y

At most one IMPLICIT statement may appear per program unit. In the main program it must be the first statement; in subprograms it must be the second statement (*i.e.*, the first statement after the SUBROUTINE or FUNCTION statement).

Any explicit type declaration over-rides implicit typing assumptions.

Warning: An IMPLICIT statement will alter the type of built-in FUNCTIONs, causing undesirable effects unless countered by explicit typing.

The $ sign follows Z in alphabetic ordering.

Don't use the $ sign if the KP=26 $JOB card option is in effect.

A good, safe idea: Explicitly type the names of all the FUNC-TIONs you use, including built-in ones.

example
```
INTEGER IABS
REAL SQRT
COMPLEX CMPLX,CABS
```

Specification Statements

A **type statement** declares the data type associated with a list of memory cells. **Specification statements** give additional information about memory cells. For this reason, specification statements should follow declarations of the memory cells involved. Otherwise implicit typing is used temporarily and problems often ensue because different types of memory cells have different lengths.

> *If you're lucky, you can sometimes get away with specifications preceding declarations. For example, if X and Y are EQUIVA-LENCEd before they are declared to be of type INTEGER*4, there will be no problem because INTEGER*4 and REAL*4 memory cells are the same size (four bytes) and REAL*4 would be the implicit type assumed at EQUIVALENCE statement.*

COMMON Statement

LEGAL — sequence of COMMON statements

```
COMMON A(3),M,X,R(10)
COMMON /BLK1/Y,B//T(100)
```

ILLEGAL — sequence

```
COMMON A,M,X
COMMON /BLK/X,Y
```
a variable may appear in only *one* COMMON block

> ### COMMON Statement
>
> COMMON/a_1/$list_1$/a_2/$list_2$/ . . . /a_n/$list_n$
>
> a_k is an identifier or blank.
> $list_k$ is a list of unsubscripted memory cell names or array names separated by commas.
> If a_1 is a blank, the first two slashes may be omitted. An array name in $list_k$ may be followed by a length declarator if its length is not declared elsewhere.

COMMON statements establish regions of memory which are **global** in the sense that they are accessible to any program unit. Each of these regions has a name. One legal name is the blank name; this region is known as the **blank common** region. Regions with nonblank names are known as **labelled COMMON** regions. A program unit gains access to a COMMON region via a COMMON statement naming that region and the memory cells therein.

> **COMMON** *Names: Each subprogram (or main program) which uses a* COMMON *region must declare the region with a* COMMON *statement. A* COMMON *region is a collection of contiguous storage units. The names referring to these storage units may differ in different subprograms. It is the* order *of the memory cell and array names in the* COMMON *statement which determines which names will be associated with which storage units.*

382

> COMMON *Safety: To be safe, for each* COMMON *region, punch a "COMMON deck" of memory cell and array declarations and a single* COMMON *statement. Duplicate the deck for each program unit that uses the* COMMON *region.*

If a program unit contains COMMON statements referring to the same COMMON region more than once, the memory cells involved are sequentially included in the region in the order in which they occur in the COMMON statements.

Compile-time initialization of memory cells in COMMON regions should be done with DATA statements following the COMMON statement. Initializations prior to the COMMON statement are errors.

Simple INTEGER memory cells in COMMON regions may be used as length declarators in subprogram array parameters.

EQUIVALENCE statements may extend COMMON regions by adding more memory cells to the end of the regions. EQUIVALENCE statements implying new starting points for COMMON regions are in error.

COMMON regions are always started on double word boundaries. Thus, alignment problems for double word memory cells, DOUBLE PRECISION (REAL*8), COMPLEX, and COMPLEX*16 (double double-word), can be avoided by placing these cells at the beginning of the region, then single word cells, REAL*4, INTEGER*4, LOGICAL*4, then half word cells, INTEGER*2, and finally CHARACTER*n and LOGICAL*1 cells. Contents of double word and single word cells which are not aligned on proper word boundaries will have to be aligned before arithmetic can be performed; this increases the time needed to run your program.

Different COMMON regions may not overlap in the computer memory. Therefore, two different COMMON regions may not both contain the same memory cell.

Array sizes may be declared in COMMON statements, but array size information may only be given *once* in a program unit.

EQUIVALENCE statement

```
EQUIVALENCE (A,B)
EQUIVALENCE (X,Y,R),(D(10),C(387,2))
```

```
EQUIVALENCE (X)
EQUIVALENCE (A,B)(T,Z)
```

EQUIVALENCE statement

*EQUI*VALENCE *(list$_1$), (list$_2$), . . . , (list$_n$)*

list$_k$ is a list of memory cell names (possibly subscripted with a constant subscript) or array names. Not more than one of the elements in *list$_k$* can be in a COMMON statement.

```
IMPLICIT CHARACTER*80(A,B), COMPLEX(C),
+       DOUBLE PRECISION(D), INTEGER(I-N),
+       LOGICAL(P,Q), REAL(R-Z)
```

An EQUIVALENCE statement may imply an extension on the end of a COMMON region but may not imply any other rearrangement in a COMMON region.

> *If it is 3 A.M. and you're still here because you used an* EQUIVALENCE *statement, it serves you right.*

EQUIVALENCE statements may cause alignment problems with double word and single word cells.

Compile-time initialization should take place after all aliases for the memory cell in question have been established.

DIMENSION Statement

Array sizes may be specified in a DIMENSION statement. The data types of the arrays concerned should be previously established, unless implicit types are being used.

```
DIMENSION A(10)
DIMENSION X(10,15),Y(103)
```

```
DIMENSION X          lacks array length info
DIM Y(10)            no abbreviations allowed
DIMENSION A,B(10,12)
```

> **DIMENSION Statement**
>
> DIMENSION *list*
>
> *list* is a list of array declarators like those which may be used in type statements.

Array length information may only be given once in a program unit.

DATA Statement

```
DATA X/1.72/,Y/3.17/
DATA A,P/'?',.TRUE./,C/(0.0,1.0)/
INTEGER MT(10)
DATA MT(3),MT(1),MT(10)/1,0,0/
DATA MT/0,1,1,0,2,5*0/
DATA (MT(I),I=1,4)/0,1,1,0/
DATA N/4/,(MT(I),I=1,N)/0,1,1,0/
```

```
DATA X/Y/          no variables allowed in constant list
DATA X/1.2,3.7/    more constants than memory cells
DATA X,Y/1.0/      more memory cells than constants
DATA X/1/          data types don't match
```

Compile-time initializations should be described with DATA statements when the memory cells involved appear in (prior) COMMON or EQUIVALENCE statements.

DATA statements should follow declarations of the initialized memory cells.

DATA statements should follow COMMON and EQUIVALENCE information on the initialized memory cells.

Implied do list parameters (lower bound, upper bound, increment) are usually constants, but they may be simple INTEGER memory cells provided these cells have had previous compile-time initializations.

BLOCK DATA Subprogram

```
BLOCK DATA
REAL YES
LOGICAL PRAPS
COMMON /SETUP/ YES, PRAPS
DATA PRAPS/.TRUE./
END
```

```
BLOCK DATA
REAL YES
LOGICAL PRAPS
COMMON /SETUP/ YES, PRAPS
PRAPS=.TRUE.                 no executable
END                         statements
                            allowed
```

In a program which uses COMMON regions in memory, it is sometimes convenient to summarize all compile-time initializations of cells in COMMON regions in one section of the program. A BLOCK DATA subprogram may be used for this purpose.

A BLOCK DATA subprogram begins with the statement BLOCK DATA. It has no other name associated with it.

The body of a BLOCK DATA subprogram may contain *only* comments, type statements (declarations), COMMON, DATA, EQUIVALENCE, and DIMENSION statements. In addition the first statement after BLOCK DATA may be an IMPLICIT statement.

Expressions

Arithmetic Expressions

```
20.
3*INT(SQRT(X+Y))+1
ZN(14)+Z1(I*J,3)/X
-(X**Y)*(3.14/(Y+X))
+RATS
```

```
M*-4              adjacent operators not allowed
X+'4'             CHARACTER value cannot be added
X*(Y/(1.4/T)      parentheses not balanced
```

The number and data type of arguments in a FUNCTION reference must correspond to the function definition.

The number of and values of subscripts in an array reference must correspond to the array length declarators.

> Subscripts may have non-INTEGER data types. Numeric subscripts are converted to INTEGER subscripts by the usual conversion rules (see Conversion Chart, on page 390). The first byte of LOGICAL and CHARACTER*n type subscripts is converted, as an unsigned binary number, to an INTEGER subscript.

precedence

An arithmetic expression is evaluated in the following order:

1. evaluate expressions in parentheses
2. ** exponentiations
3. * / multiplication or division
4. + – addition or subtraction (both binary and unary)
5. When faced with two operators at the same level, if they are exponentiations, proceed right to left, otherwise proceed left to right

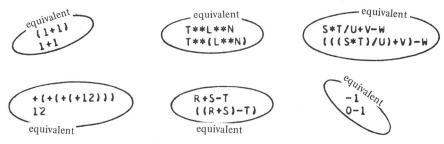

A unary + or – is equivalent to a binary + or – with 0 as the first operand.

```
IMPLICIT CHARACTER*80(A,B), COMPLEX(C),
+       DOUBLE PRECISION(D), INTEGER(I-N),
+       LOGICAL(P,Q), REAL(R-Z)
```
387

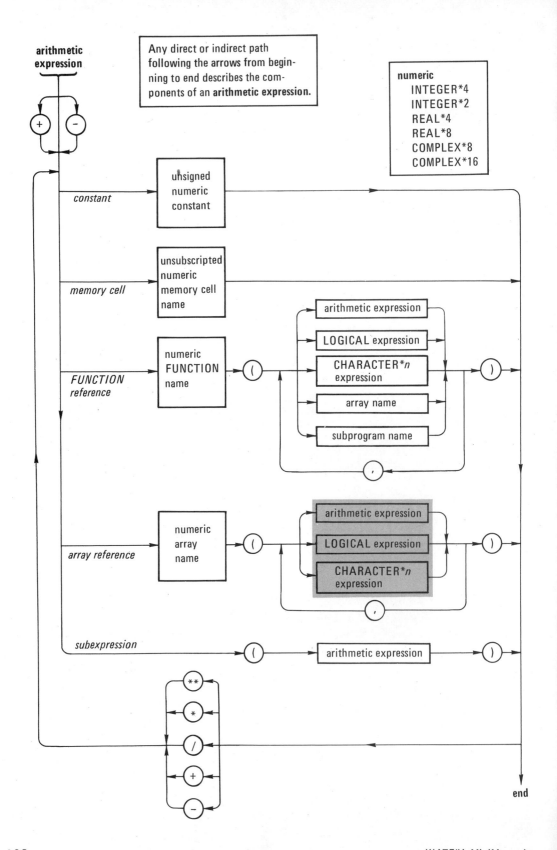

arithmetic expression

Any direct or indirect path following the arrows from beginning to end describes the components of an **arithmetic expression**.

numeric
- INTEGER*4
- INTEGER*2
- REAL*4
- REAL*8
- COMPLEX*8
- COMPLEX*16

constant — unsigned numeric constant

memory cell — unsubscripted numeric memory cell name

FUNCTION reference — numeric FUNCTION name (arithmetic expression / LOGICAL expression / CHARACTER*n expression / array name / subprogram name ,)

array reference — numeric array name (arithmetic expression / LOGICAL expression / CHARACTER*n expression ,)

subexpression — (arithmetic expression)

** * / + −

end

Types of Arithmetic Expressions

If an arithmetic expression contains constants, memory cell names, array names, and function references all of the same type *t*, the expression is of type *t*.

If the above case does *not* hold, the expression is of mixed mode (or mixed type). The type of the expression then is the type of the longest, most complicated operand.

It is illegal to attempt to raise a negative value to a REAL or DOUBLE PRECISION power.

exponentiation A**B				
type of A \ type of B	INTEGER	REAL	DOUBLE PRECISION	type of result COMPLEX
INTEGER	INTEGER	REAL	DOUBLE	⊘
REAL	REAL	REAL	DOUBLE	⊘
DOUBLE PRECISION	DOUBLE	DOUBLE	DOUBLE	⊘
COMPLEX	COMPLEX	⊘	⊘	⊘

All other mixed mode operations (+, −, *, /) are legal and produce a result according to the following principles:

1 Conversions are made locally, that is, the two numbers involved in the operation being performed determine the type of the result.

2 Conversion is made in the direction of the longest, most intricate type.

types involved	result	example
INT *op* REAL	REAL	2*3.14159
INT *op* COMPLEX	COMPLEX	(1.0,1.0)/2
REAL*4 *op* REAL*8	REAL*8	1.*3.0D2
COMPLEX*8 *op* REAL*8	COMPLEX	(1.0,1.0)*3.1416D+1

troublesome cases

2/3*1.0	evaluates to 0.0	left to right; 2/3 is zero
−1**N	evaluates to −1	exponentiation first
1./3.+0.D0	≠ 1.D0/3.	due to conversion rules
3000*3000*3000*1.0	≠ 1.0*3000*3000*3000	INTEGER overflows are ignored for some reason

I = 1.234E+50 results in an incorrect value being placed in I (the correct value won't fit). Tough luck.

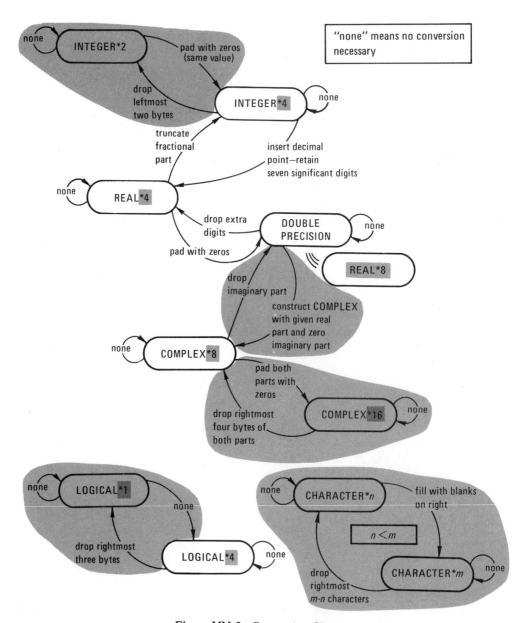

To deduce the result of a conversion from type *a* to type *b*, start from the type *a* oval and follow the arrows along the most direct route to the type *b* oval, noting conversions as you go.

If you can't get to *b* from *a*, the conversion is not allowed.

"none" means no conversion necessary

Figure MM 2 Conversion Chart

LOGICAL Expressions

```
.TRUE.
PLATO(2*3)
QUIZIT .OR. X .LT. 10.7
POOBEE .AND. .NOT. POOBEE
X*Y .GT. 3.1  .AND.  I .NE. O
A .EQ. 'JOHNSON'
A .GT. 'SMITH'
```

```
X .AND. Y .LT. 3.14      X isn't of type LOGICAL
QUIZIT .EQ. .TRUE.       QUIZIT AND .TRUE. are neither
                         numeric nor CHARACTER*n
```

See comments about array and FUNCTION references in **Arithmetic Expressions** above.

Relational operators (.EQ., .NE., LT., etc.) cannot have COMPLEX or LOGICAL operands.

LOGICAL operators (.NOT., .AND., and .OR.) can have LOGICAL operands *only*.

Comparisons between CHARACTER*n values are made character by character from the left until a difference in the strings is found. (Trailing *blanks* in the longer string are ignored.) Ordering on individual characters corresponds to the unsigned binary integer representations of the characters. This implies alphabetical ordering of letters with blank being smaller than any letter.

LOGICAL*1 and LOGICAL*4 values may be freely mixed.

precedence

A LOGICAL expression is evaluated in the following order:

1 evaluate terms in parentheses
2 evaluate relational expressions
3 .NOT.
4 .AND.
5 .OR.

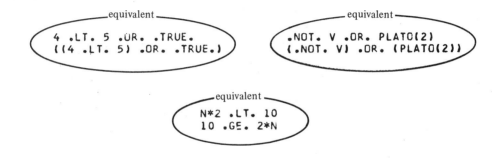

```
IMPLICIT CHARACTER*80(A,B), COMPLEX(C),
+       DOUBLE PRECISION(D), INTEGER(I-N),
+       LOGICAL(P,Q), REAL(R-Z)
```

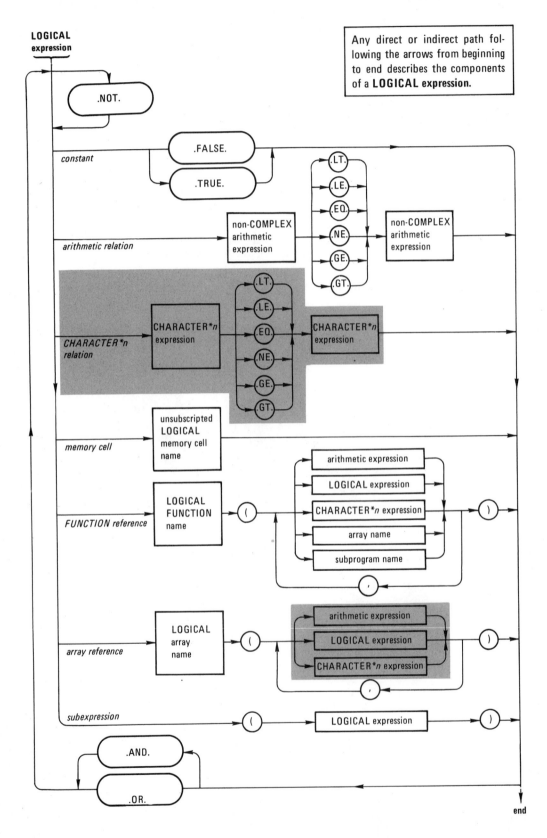

LOGICAL expression

Any direct or indirect path following the arrows from beginning to end describes the components of a **LOGICAL expression**.

.NOT.

constant
- .FALSE.
- .TRUE.

arithmetic relation
- non-COMPLEX arithmetic expression
- .LT. .LE. .EQ. .NE. .GE. .GT.
- non-COMPLEX arithmetic expression

CHARACTER*n relation
- CHARACTER*n expression
- .LT. .LE. .EQ. .NE. .GE. .GT.
- CHARACTER*n expression

memory cell
- unsubscripted LOGICAL memory cell name

FUNCTION reference
- LOGICAL FUNCTION name
- (arithmetic expression / LOGICAL expression / CHARACTER*n expression / array name / subprogram name)

array reference
- LOGICAL array name
- (arithmetic expression / LOGICAL expression / CHARACTER*n expression)

subexpression
- (LOGICAL expression)

.AND.
.OR.

end

CHARACTER*n Expressions

```
'23 PEAS PER KNIFE'
14HLOVIN SPOONFUL
A(14)
B
```

```
'BEA'+'TLES'       you can't add strings
```

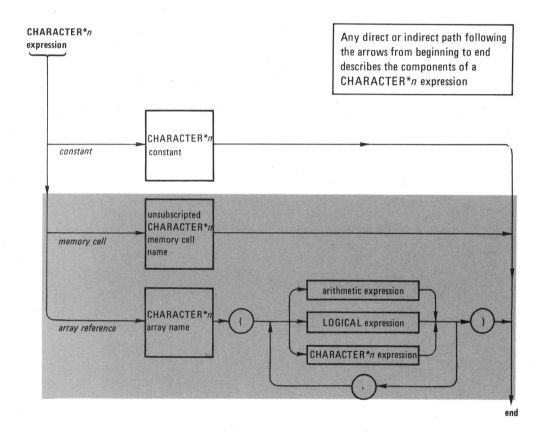

Any direct or indirect path following the arrows from beginning to end describes the components of a CHARACTER*n expression

See remarks on array references under **Arithmetic Expressions** above.

CHARACTER*n Operators

There are no CHARACTER*n operators. If you think you are using one, you're in trouble.

There aren't any CHARACTER*n valued FUNCTIONs either.

```
IMPLICIT CHARACTER*80(A,B), COMPLEX(C),
+       DOUBLE PRECISION(D), INTEGER(I-N),
+       LOGICAL(P,Q), REAL(R-Z)
```

Assignment

Assignment Statement

```
SIMPLE=1.7*2+IABS(-2)
ROOST(SIMPLE)=0.
CAZZIE=(1.0,1.0)*2.
A='%'
QUES=N .LE. 10
```

```
SIMPLE=.TRUE.      illegal conversion—SIMPLE is REAL
ROOST(2)='TWO'     illegal conversion—ROOST is REAL
A=2*3              illegal conversion—A is CHARACTER*n
```

Assignment statement

$v = expr$

v is a memory cell name, possibly subscripted, and *expr* is an expression whose data type is assignment compatible with v.

If v and *expr* are not of the same data type but are assignment compatible, then *expr* is evaluated and the result is converted to the type of v. See the Conversion Chart, Figure MM 2, under Arithmetic Expressions.

Assignment of LOGICAL values involves moving only one byte of information, even if the variable involved is LOGICAL*4. Thus P=Q changes only the first byte of the LOGICAL*4 memory cell P whether Q is of type LOGICAL*4 or LOGICAL*1.

Multiple Assignment

```
M=N=J=124*(N+1)
A=B='BOUFFARD'
```

```
M=N=124*(N+1)=J
```
expression must be on the right

Multiple Assignment

$$v_1 = v_2 = v_n = expr$$

v_i is a memory cell name, possibly subscripted
expr is an expression whose data type is assignment
compatible with each v_i

$$v_1 = v_2 = \cdots v_n = expr$$

is equivalent to

$$v_n = expr$$
$$v_{n-1} = v_n$$
.
.
.
$$v_1 = v_2$$

```
S=F=G=2*3.14
```
is equivalent to
```
G=2*3.14
F=G
S=F
```

Because of data type conversions, the order of the assignments, $v_2, \ldots, v_n$ may affect the value assigned to v_i.

```
N=M=F=4.7
```

N	4
M	4
F	4.7

is not equivalent to

```
N=F=M=4.7
```

N	4
M	4
F	4.0

```
IMPLICIT CHARACTER*80(A,B), COMPLEX(C),
+       DOUBLE PRECISION(D), INTEGER(I-N),
+       LOGICAL(P,Q), REAL(R-Z)
```

Transfer of Control

The default flow of control is sequential, from statement to statement. This flow may be altered by control statements.

GO TO

```
GO TO 1000
GO TO 7543
```

```
GO TO *-1
GO TO F007      not legal statement labels
GO TO N
```

> ### GO TO s
>
> s is the statement label of an executable statement within the same program unit.

Computed GO TO

```
GO TO (10,20,20),JAX
GO TO (10,10,20,47,92,10),LOIN
```

```
GO TO (10,10,20,47,92,10),2*LOIN      2*LOIN isn't a simple memory cell name
GO TO (10,20,20) JAX                  needs a comma
```

> ### Computed GO TO Statement
>
> GO TO $(s_1, s_2, \ldots, s_n), v$
>
> s_i is a statement label
> v is an unsubscripted INTEGER memory cell name

Control is transferred to the vth statement label in the list.

If the value of v is not in the range 1 to n, then no transfer of control is performed (*i.e.*, the statement is ignored, and the usual sequential control resumes).

Each s_i must be the label of an executable statement in the current program unit.

ASSIGNed GO TO

```
ASSIGN 20 TO IBIS
ASSIGN 40 TO JAX
GO TO JAX,(10,40,92)
GO TO IBIS,(20,40)
```

```
ASSIGN IBIS=20
ASSIGN 42*3 TO JAX     42*3 isn't a statement label
GO TO JAX(10,40,92)    needs a comma
GO TO IBO(2),(10,10,30) control variable may not be subscripted
```

ASSIGN Statement

ASSIGN *s* TO *v*

s is a statement label
v is an unsubscripted INTEGER*4 memory cell name

The label *s* must be the label of an executable statement in the current program unit.

The memory cell *v* must also be used in an ASSIGNed GO TO statement.

ASSIGNed GO TO Statement

GO TO *v*, $(s_1, s_2, \ldots, s_n)$

v is an unsubscripted INTEGER*4 memory cell name
s_i is a statement label

Each s_i must be the label of an executable statement in the current program unit.

The memory cell *v* must have been given one of the values s_i by an ASSIGN statement.

```
IMPLICIT CHARACTER*80(A,B), COMPLEX(C),
+       DOUBLE PRECISION(D), INTEGER(I-N),
+       LOGICAL(P,Q), REAL(R-Z)
```
397

Logical IF

```
IF (P) STOP
IF (NUML .EQ. 10) PRINT, LINE
IF (3.14159 .GE. X) GO TO 10
IF (XRAY .LT. 0.0) XRAY=-XRAY
```

```
IF P STOP                              needs parentheses
IF (P) IF (3 .EQ. 4) GO TO 10          IF may not have another as right part
IF (JJ .LT. 3 .OR. .GT. 1) X=2.        not a legitimate logical expression
IF (P),STOP                            unwanted comma
```

Logical IF Statement

If (*logexpr*) *stmt*

logexpr is any LOGICAL valued expression
stmt is any executable statement except a DO or Logical IF

The statement *stmt* is performed only when *logexpr* is .TRUE..

Unless *stmt* is performed and alters the flow of control, the next statement performed is the one following the logical IF.

The following construction serves no purpose which couldn't be served by omitting the IF statement.

```
       IF (N .EQ. 10) GO TO 100
100    X=EXP(Y)
```

If you have used such a construction, (*i.e.*, a conditional transfer to the next statement in sequence), change your program to say what you meant.

Arithmetic IF

```
IF (IBIS-10) 10,10,20
IF (X*100.-25.*Y) 9,10,11
IF (2.+XRAY) 1,20,20
```

```
IF (IBIS .GT. 10) 10,10,20      cross between LOGICAL and arith. IF
IF X*100.-25.*Y 9,10,11         needs parentheses
IF (2.+XRAY),1,20,20            extra comma
```

Control is transferred to one of the statement labels: s_{neg} if *arithexpr* has a negative value, s_{zero} if *arithexpr* has a zero value, and s_{pos} if *arithexpr* has a positive value.

Each of the statement labels must designate an executable statement in the current program unit.

The value of *arithexpr* cannot be COMPLEX.

DO Statement

```
DO 10 KAZ=ICE9,MONOID,3
DO 2700 IK=52,97
DO 999 LAMB=1,100,1
```

```
DO 10 X=ICE9,MONAD(2),3      bound may not be subscripted
DO 2700 I7=52,95+2           95+2 not legal
DO 999 LAMB=100,1,-1         increment may not be negative (or zero)
DO 999,LAMB=1,100,1
```

The **range** of a DO-loop is the statements after the DO statement up to and including statement *s*, the **object** of the DO-loop.

The statements in the range are repeated once for each value of the index *v* in sequence beginning at *v* = *start* and increasing in steps of *increment* as long as *v* doesn't exceed *bound*. Thus the DO statement

```
DO 100 I=3,9,4
```

would cause the statements in its range to be performed twice, first for I = 3, then for I = 7.

```
IMPLICIT CHARACTER*80(A,B), COMPLEX(C),
+        DOUBLE PRECISION(D), INTEGER(I-N),
+        LOGICAL(P,Q), REAL(R-Z)
```
399

> If *bound* is smaller than *start,* the statements in the range will be performed once with $v = start$. (This degenerate case is only semilegal.)

It is illegal to transfer from outside the range of a DO-loop to arrive inside the range without passing through the DO statement itself, thus setting the index to the value *start.* This implies that no GO TO or arithmetic IF outside the range of a particular DO-loop may list a destination inside the range. (The one exception to this rule, the extended range construction, is so awkward that we'll not discuss it.) It also implies that DO-loops cannot be partially overlapped as shown below.

```
        DO 100 I=1,10
        DO 200 J=1,10
100         CONTINUE
200         CONTINUE
```

DO-loops may be nested to a depth of 255.

If a DO-loop terminates normally (*i.e.,* by performing the object statement with v equal to the last value indicated by the DO parameters), then the index v no longer has a value.

On the other hand, if a DO-loop terminates by exiting via a GO TO or arithmetic IF before normal termination, then the index v still has the last value it took while the DO-loop was being performed.

All of the DO parameters, *start, bound, increment,* must be strictly positive.

Any attempt in the range of a DO-loop to change the value of the v, *start, bound,* or *increment* is an error.

If nested DO-loops have the same object statement, any transfer to the object statement is considered to refer to the end of the *innermost* loop, thus such transfers from anywhere except within the range of the innermost loop are illegal.

CONTINUE

```
        CONTINUE
100     CONTINUE
```

```
        PROCEED
        CONTINUE 100
```

A CONTINUE statement instructs the controller to proceed in the usual control sequence. It is in the class of executable statements.

> CONTINUE is the purest statement.

CONTINUE statements are often used as objects of DO-loops.

STOP and PAUSE

```
STOP
STOP 10
PAUSE
PAUSE 20
PAUSE 'THAT REFRESHES'
```

```
STOP AT ONCE
STOP 'HAVE A BEER'
STOP 10*2
REFRESH
```

STOP and PAUSE Statements

STOP
STOP *n*
PAUSE
PAUSE *n*
PAUSE *message*

n is an unsigned INTEGER constant up to five digits long
message is a CHARACTER*n* constant

STOP terminates execution of your program.

> STOP is the most powerful statement

STOP *n*, on most systems, is equivalent to STOP. On some systems, it causes the indicated value to appear on the operator's console or the printed output.

PAUSE, on most systems, is equivalent to CONTINUE. On some systems, it causes temporary termination of your program, sends the constant (if given) to the operator's console, and resumes execution at the statement after the PAUSE on a signal from the operator.

Subprogram Control Statements

CALL and RETURN are covered under the heading **Subprograms**.

END

```
END
```

```
100  END          no label allowed
     ENDS HERE
```

The END statement is not executable.

END instructs the compiler to stop compiling the current program unit and prepare to compile another program unit.

```
IMPLICIT CHARACTER*80(A,B), COMPLEX(C),
+        DOUBLE PRECISION(D), INTEGER(I-N),
+        LOGICAL(P,Q), REAL(R-Z)
```

FORMATs

A FORMAT describes an I/O record.

FORMAT Statement

```
10    FORMAT(' 1 ')
1505 FORMAT(I3,A5,2G11.2/A10)
2307 FORMAT(' ',2('NO.',I3,' IS NOT',L2/))
```

```
      FORMAT('1')                   needs statement label
1505 FORMAT(3*I2)                   *not legal
2307 FORMAT(' ',2(2I123PF7.0))      ambiguous, needs comma
```

> ### FORMAT Statement
>
> FORMAT (*spec*)
>
> *spec* is a list of FORMAT descriptors (*i.e.,* data descriptors literal descriptors, spacing descriptors, slashes, or groups of these) separated by commas. Slashes serve as delimiters, so commas should be omitted around slashes. Commas may also be omitted if it doesn't cause ambiguity. Every FORMAT must have a statement label.

A FORMAT statement must always be labeled.

The (*spec*) part of a FORMAT may be stored in an array as a series of Hollerith (CHARACTER*n) values. This array may then be used as a **variable FORMAT** in an I/O statement.

Data Descriptors

> See Chapter 10 for further details.

G11.4   G3.7   *d* must be smaller than *w*
G20.7   GW.D   *w* and *d* can't be variables
G28.16
G10

> **G*w***   INTEGER, REAL, DOUBLE PRECISION, or LOGICAL field
> **G*w.d*** of width *w;* *d* significant digits for REAL output

I10	IK	w must be a constant
I3	I+2	no sign allowed
I22	I3.2	no decimal point allowed

> **Iw** INTEGER field of width w

F10.0	F3.7	d must be smaller than w
F8.1	FN.K	w and d must be constants
F30.16		

> **F$w.d$** REAL or DOUBLE PRECISION field of width w; d decimal places on output

E15.7	E10.7	$w-d$ must be at least 7
E12.3		

> **E$w.d$** REAL field of width w; scientific notation with d significant digits on output

D15.7	D20.16	$w-d$ must be at least 7
D23.16		

> **D$w.d$** DOUBLE PRECISION field of width w; scientific notation with d significant digits on output

> *For* COMPLEX *or* COMPLEX*16 *values, use two* REAL *or* DOUBLE PRECISION *data descriptors.*

```
IMPLICIT CHARACTER*80(A,B), COMPLEX(C),
+       DOUBLE PRECISION(D), INTEGER(I-N),
+       LOGICAL(P,Q), REAL(R-Z)
```
403

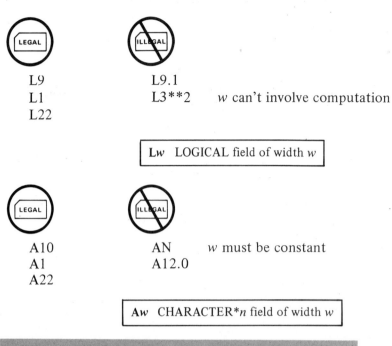

L9
L1
L22

L9.1
L3**2   *w* can't involve computation

| **L***w*   LOGICAL field of width *w* |

A10
A1
A22

AN   *w* must be constant
A12.0

| **A***w*   CHARACTER**n field of width *w* |

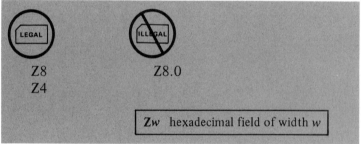

Z8
Z4

Z8.0

| **Z***w*   hexadecimal field of width *w* |

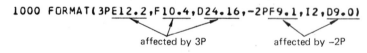

1000 FORMAT(3PE12.2,F10.4,D24.16,−2PF9.1,I2,D9.0)

affected by 3P   affected by −2P

| ***s*P**   scale factor; shifts decimal point in subsequent REAL or DOUBLE PRECISION fields; *s* may be negative |

Literal Descriptors

Literal descriptors are simply CHARACTER**n constants used in FORMATs. (See MiniManual **Constants** section.)

On output, the *n* characters in the literal descriptor are transmitted directly to the output record. On input, the *n* characters in the corresponding field in the input record replace the characters in the literal descriptor.

> *What!?!*
> *Yes! The* FORMAT *itself is altered when the* READ *transmits characters to the literal descriptor.*

Spacing Descriptors

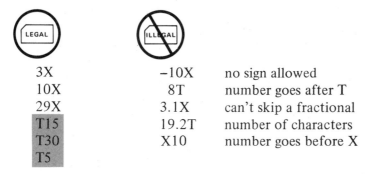

LEGAL	ILLEGAL	
3X	−10X	no sign allowed
10X	8T	number goes after T
29X	3.1X	can't skip a fractional
T15	19.2T	number of characters
T30	X10	number goes before X
T5		

> *n*X skip the next *n* characters in the I/O record
> T*n* move to *n*th character in the I/O record

Repeat Specifications, Groups, and Record Separators

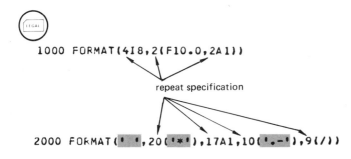

```
1000 FORMAT(4I8,2(F10.0,2A1))
```
repeat specification

```
2000 FORMAT(' ',20('*'),17A1,10('.-'),9(/))
```

zero not allowed
```
9999 FORMAT(+4I8,0G10.2)
```
no sign allowed

A **repeat specification** is an unsigned INTEGER constant *n* (not exceeding 255) which is placed immediately to the left of a data descriptor or a group of FORMAT descriptors. Its effect is the same as that of writing the data descriptor or group *n* times (separated by commas, of course).

subgroup
```
1000 FORMAT(3(I2,A4), 2(3I1,4(A2,A3)) )
```
group   group

```
2000 FORMAT(3(I2,A4,2(A1,I3,2(I1,A1))))
```
nested too deeply

```
      IMPLICIT CHARACTER*80(A,B), COMPLEX(C),
     +         DOUBLE PRECISION(D), INTEGER(I-N),
     +         LOGICAL(P,Q), REAL(R-Z)
```

A format descriptor **group** is a parenthesized list of FORMAT descriptors. Groups may be nested to a depth of two in the *spec* list in a FORMAT statement.

When there are more I/O list elements than data descriptors in the FORMAT, the FORMAT scan is repeated, starting from its **rightmost group**, including the group's repeat specification if it has one. In other words, the repeat scan starts at

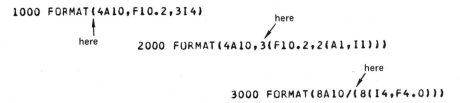

```
1000 FORMAT(4A10,F10.2,3I4)
```
here

```
2000 FORMAT(4A10,3(F10.2,2(A1,I1)))
```
here

```
3000 FORMAT(8A10/(8(I4,F4.0)))
```
here

the repeat specification preceding the left parenthesis which matches the next to last right parenthesis in the FORMAT. If there are no groups in the FORMAT, the repeat scan starts at the beginning of the FORMAT.

```
1000 FORMAT(8A10/3I4)
```
This FORMAT describes two data cards

```
2000 FORMAT('1',A50/'0',10G11.4/)
```
This FORMAT describes three output lines. Each one contains a carriage control character. The last line is totally blank.

A **slash** (/) is used in a FORMAT to separate one record description from another. It must be used whenever a FORMAT describes more than one I/O record (*e.g.*, more than one output line or more than one data card).

I/O Statements

I/O statements are used to bring values into the computer memory (input) or to transmit values from the computer memory. The values brought into the memory by input statements are often read from punched cards, but may be read from other storage devices. Similarly, values transmitted from memory are often written on paper, but may be written on other storage media.

Input list

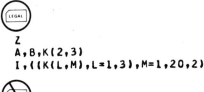

```
Z
A,B,K(2,3)
I,((K(L,M),L=1,3),M=1,20,2)
```

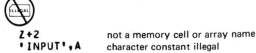

```
Z+2            not a memory cell or array name
'INPUT',A      character constant illegal
```

Input statements use input lists to designate the memory cells in which to store the values obtained from the input device.

Memory cells in an input list are given values in the order in which they occur in the list.

An input list may contain *memory cell names* (possibly subscripted), *array names* (implying all the elements in the array are elements in list, ordered from the lowest subscript to the highest), or implied DO lists.

Output list

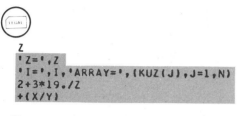

```
Z
'Z=',Z
'I=',I,'ARRAY=',(KUZ(J),J=1,N)
2+3*19./Z
+(X/Y)
```

```
(SQRT(2.)+1.)/R     may not begin with parenthesis
A;B;C               semicolon illegal
```

An output list has the same form as an input list except that its elements may be computed values (*i.e.,* arithmetic or logical expressions) or constants as well as memory cells. One exception: expressions must not begin with a parenthesis.

Implied DO list

```
(K(J),J=1,3)
(A,2,ICE9=1,13,4)
(A,ICE9,RAMP(ICE9),ICE9=32,N,M)
((LAMBDA(I,J),I=1,10),J=10,100,10)
```

```
((LAMB(ICH),ICH,ICH=1,10),(SHEEP(ICK),ICK,ICK=1,10),L=1,2)
```

```
(K(X),X=1,20)                       X is not an INTEGER
(A,2,ICE9=1,10+N,4)                 10+N illegal
((LAMBDA(I,J),I=1,10)J=10,100,10)   needs a comma
```

```
IMPLICIT CHARACTER*80(A,B), COMPLEX(C),
+       DOUBLE PRECISION(D), INTEGER(I-N),
+       LOGICAL(P,Q), REAL(R-Z)
```

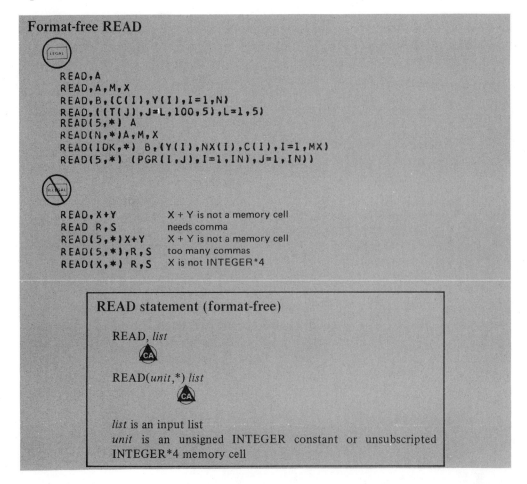

Implied DO list

$$(list,\ i = k_1,\ k_2)$$
$$(list,\ i = k_1,\ k_2,\ k_3)$$

list is an input list if the implied DO list is part of an input statement and an output list if it's part of an output statement.

i is an unsubscripted INTEGER memory cell name

k_1, k_2, and k_3 are nonzero unsigned INTEGER constants or unsubscripted INTEGER memory cell names

Implied DO lists may be nested.

The INTEGER memory cell i is called the **index** or **control** variable. It takes the **initial value** k_1, then increases to the **upper bound** k_2 by **increments** of k_3 or by increments of one if k_3 is omitted. Thus the implied DO list has the effect of repeating its *list* part several times ($1 + (k_2 - k_1)/k_3$ times, to be exact) with all occurrences of the control variable i replaced by the appropriate value in each repetition of the *list*.

Format-free READ

```
READ,A
READ,A,M,X
READ,B,(C(I),Y(I),I=1,N)
READ,((T(J),J=L,100,5),L=1,5)
READ(5,*) A
READ(N,*)A,M,X
READ(IDK,*) B,(Y(I),NX(I),C(I),I=1,MX)
READ(5,*) (PGR(I,J),I=1,IN),J=1,IN))
```

```
READ,X+Y          X + Y is not a memory cell
READ R,S          needs comma
READ(5,*)X+Y      X + Y is not a memory cell
READ(5,*),R,S     too many commas
READ(X,*) R,S     X is not INTEGER*4
```

READ statement (format-free)

READ, *list*

READ(*unit*,*) *list*

list is an input list
unit is an unsigned INTEGER constant or unsubscripted INTEGER*4 memory cell

Transfers values from data cards or other input device (*unit*) into memory cells

unit = 5 is normally the card reader (check with local experts)

Values on data cards must be separated by blanks or commas.

CHARACTER*n values on data cards must be surrounded by quote marks (*e.g.*, 'CHARACTER*23 DATA VALUE')

Values on data cards (records on the input *unit*) must match with the data type of corresponding memory cells in *list*.

Data values for the memory cells in *list* may be on one or several data cards.

READ will continue until values have been found on data cards for each memory cell in *list*. An error message will be issued if the data cards (records) are exhausted before enough data values are found.

Format-free PRINT/WRITE

```
PRINT,A
PRINT,4,X**2,T(3),+(X+1)**2
PRINT,SQRT(X),(Y(I),EXP(Y(I)),I=1,N)
PRINT,'TABLE OF TEMPERATURES'
PRINT,' '
PRINT,((T(J),J=L,100,5),L=1,5)

WRITE(6,*)A
WRITE(N,*) 4,X**2,T(3),+(X+1)**2
WRITE(6,*)'EXPONENTIALS ',(Y(I),EXP(Y(I)),I=1,N)
WRITE(ITP,*) ((T(J),J=L,N,ISTP),L=1,ISTP)
```

```
PRINT                  needs output list
PRINT 'PIZZA',SIZE     needs comma
PRINT,(X-Y)**2         expression may not start with parenthesis

WRITE(6,*)             needs output list
WRITE(*,6) A           * misplaced
WRITE(6,*),X,Y         extra comma
WRITE(N,*)(X-Y)**L     expression may not start with parenthesis
```

PRINT/WRITE statements (format-free)

PRINT, *list*

WRITE(*unit*,*) *list*

list is an output list
unit is an unsigned INTEGER constant or unsubscripted INTEGER*4 memory cell

---

Transmits values to paper output or other output medium (designated by *unit*) such as punch cards, magnetic tape, etc.

list cannot be omitted.
PRINT transmits values to the line printer.

unit = 6 normally designates the line printer (check with local experts)
unit = 7 normally designates the card punch (check with local experts)

Expressions in *list* must not begin with parentheses.

Values are written on one line (record), if possible.
Multiple lines (records) are used when necessary.

Output FORMATs associated with data types in format-free PRINT/WRITE

INTEGER	I12, 1X
REAL	E16.7, 1X
DOUBLE PRECISION	D38.16, 1X
COMPLEX	'(' E16.7 ',' E16.7 ')' 1X
COMPLEX*16	'(' D28.16 ',' D28.16 ')' 1X
LOGICAL	L8, 1X
CHARACTER*n	An, 1X

Format-free PUNCH

```
PUNCH,A
PUNCH,4,X**2,T(3),+(X+1)**2
PUNCH,'EXPONENTIALS ',(Y(I),EXP(Y(I)),I=1,N)
PUNCH,'TABLE OF TEMPERATURES'
PUNCH,' '
PUNCH,((T(J),J=L,100,5),L=1,5)
```

```
PUNCH                    needs output list
PUNCH 'PIZZA',SIZE       needs comma
PUNCH,(X-Y)**2           expression may not begin with parenthesis
```

PUNCH Statement (format-free)

PUNCH, *list*

list is an output list

Transmits values to punched card output

list cannot be omitted

Expressions in a *list* must not begin with parentheses

Values are punched on one card if possible. Multiple cards are used as necessary. The first column of the punched card is skipped.

Values are punched under control of data descriptors as shown under format-free PRINT/WRITE above.

Formatted READ

```
READ 1000,A
READ 2000,(Y(K),K=1,N)
READ AFMT,A,M,X
READ(5,1000) A
READ(5,AFMT)A,M,X
READ(NT,2010)B,(Y(K),K=L,LU,3)
READ(NT,1000,ERR=999)X
READ(5,2000,END=457)(Y(K),K=1,6)
READ(5,3000,END=943,ERR=857)X,A
```

```
READ(5,9999)X+Y        X + Y is not a memory cell
READ(5,9898),A,B,C     extra comma
READ(X,1000)A,B,C      X is not an INTEGER*4
READ,1000,A            too many commas
READ 1000 A            not enough commas
READ(5,9987,END=N) X   N is not a legal statement label
```

READ Statement (formatted)

READ *f, list*

READ *f*

READ (*unit, f*) *list*

READ(*unit, f,* END = *s*) *list*
READ(*unit, f,* ERR = *t*) *list*
READ(*unit, f,* ERR = *t*) *list*
READ(*unit, f,* ERR = *t,* END = *s*) *list*

list is an input list (may be omitted in forms containing *unit*)
f is a FORMAT statement number or an array containing the (*spec*) part of a FORMAT statement represented by CHARACTER*n values.
unit is an unsigned INTEGER constant or unsubscripted INTEGER*4 memory cell
s and *t* are statement labels

Transfers values from data cards or other input medium (*unit*) to memory

```
IMPLICIT CHARACTER*80(A,B), COMPLEX(C),
+        DOUBLE PRECISION(D), INTEGER(I-N),
+        LOGICAL(P,Q), REAL(R-Z)
```

The card reader is the implied input device for the READ *f, list* and READ *f* forms.

unit = 5 is normally the card reader (check with local experts)

The FORMAT *f* describes the layout of the input records.

If *list* is omitted, one data card (record) is skipped (on the input *unit*)

All characters in a CHARACTER*n* field (A data descriptor) are part of the resulting value. In other words, an A field is delimited by field boundaries, not by quote marks.

CHARACTER*n* values may be stored in a memory cell of any data type. In all other cases, the data type of the value on the input medium must match the data type of the corresponding memory cell in the *list*.

The *list* is the driving force; all memory cells in *list* will be given values. The system issues an error message if the input *unit* runs out of records before the *list* is completed.

END = *s* causes a transfer to statement *s* if the READ encounters an end of file.

ERR = *t* causes a transfer to statement *t* in case of certain kinds of transmission errors or bad data (parity errors).

Formatted PRINT/WRITE

```
PRINT 1000
PRINT 2000,4,X**2,EXP(1.0)
PRINT 3000,(Y(I),(Z(I,J),J=1,N),I=1,M)
PRINT AFMT,B,Z(4,3)

WRITE(6,1000) A
WRITE(NT,2000) 'PI=',ATAN(1.0)*4.0
WRITE(7,ASKFMT) (M(I),I=1,N)
WRITE(6,4621)
WRITE(A,2032) X
```

```
PRINT,1000,A          extra comma
PRINT 1000 'SAUSE'    needs another comma
WRITE(6,2000) (3-X)*2 expression may not start with parenthesis
WRITE(X,1000) Y(3)    X must be INTEGER*4 or CHARACTER*n
```

Transmits values to paper output or other output medium (designated by *unit*) such as punched cards, magnetic tape, etc.

PRINT transmits values to the line printer.

unit = 6 normally designates the line printer

unit = 7 normally designates the card punch (check with local experts)

Expressions in *list* must not begin with parentheses.

The line printer always uses the first transmitted character on a line as the carriage control. The carriage control character is not printed.

carriage controls

blank	single space
0 (zero)	double space
–	triple space
1	eject (print at top of next page)
+	overprint previous line

The *list* is the driving force. All values in *list* are sent to the output device.

If *list* is omitted, the characters sent to the output device are the literal descriptors and spacing descriptors in f which precede the first data descriptor in f.

Data types of values in *list* must match corresponding data descriptors in f.

Core-to-core READ

```
READ(A,1000)N,Z,(Y(I),I=1,N)
READ(B(3),2000) M
READ(B(M),AFMT) X,Y(3),Z
```

```
READ(X,1000) N,Z        X isn't of CHARACTER*n type
READ(A,1000,ERR=457)X   ERR and END conditions can't be used
```

Core-to-core READ

READ(*c, f*) *list*

c is a CHARACTER*n memory cell or array
f is a FORMAT statement label or an array containing a variable
FORMAT
list is an input list

Transfers information from one area of memory, CHARACTER*n memory cell(s), to another area, the input *list*. During transfer, the information is converted from records of *n* CHARACTERs to other data types according to the FORMAT *f*.

If *c* is an unsubscripted memory cell, there is one record available. If *c* is an array or array element, then the number of records available is the number of memory cells in the array or the number of memory cells in the array from the array element designated to the end of the array.

If *list* specifies more records than are available in *c*, you get error UN-E. Check *c* and *list*.

The core-to-core READ is useful for converting data of type CHARACTER*n to other data types.

Core-to-core WRITE

```
WRITE(A,1000)X,Y(3),Z
WRITE(B(3*I),2000),X,SQRT(X)
WRITE(B(1),LFT),(Y(I),I=1,N)
```

```
WRITE(X,1000) Y(2)   X isn't of CHARACTER type
```

Core-to-core WRITE

> WRITE(*c, f*) *list*
>
>
>
> *c* is a CHARACTER*n memory cell (possibly subscripted) or array
> *f* is a FORMAT statement label or an array containing a variable FORMAT

Transfers information from one area of memory, the output *list,* to another area, CHARACTER*n memory cell(s). During transfer, the information is converted to records of *n* CHARACTERs according to the FORMAT *f*.

If *c* is an unsubscripted memory cell, there is one record available. If *c* is an array or array element, then the number of records available is the number of memory cells in the array or the number of memory cells in the array from the designated array element to the end.

The core-to-core WRITE is useful for converting computed values to the CHARACTER*n data type.

NAMELIST statement

```
NAMELIST /GRP/A,M,Y /PARAM/Z,Y,T,P
NAMELIST /RATES/ RM,RT
```

```
NAMELIST /NGD/AX,T,/GRP/Y      extra comma
NAMELIST /RST/P,QT /PST/R,M/   trailing slash illegal
NAMELIST /SBS/A,Y(3),Q        subscript illegal (entire array must be included)
NAMELIST /GRP/A,GRP,X         GRP used in two different meanings
```

> ### NAMELIST statement
>
> NAMELIST /*name₁*/*list₁*/*name₂*/*list₂*/ . . . /*name_n*/*list_n*
>
>
>
> *name_i* is an identifier
> *list_i* is a list of unsubscripted memory cell names or array names separated by commas (these are the members of the NAMELIST *name_i*)

Sets up groups of memory cells to be used for I/O purposes

One memory cell or array may be in several NAMELISTs.

Subprogram formal parameter names may not be members of NAMELISTs.

```
IMPLICIT CHARACTER*80(A,B), COMPLEX(C),
+       DOUBLE PRECISION(D), INTEGER(I-N),
+       LOGICAL(P,Q), REAL(R-Z)
```
415

Declarations and specifications involving memory cells in any *list$_i$* must precede the NAMELIST statement.

NAMELIST READ

```
READ (5,GRP)
READ(NT,PARAM)
READ(5,GRP,END=987)
READ(NT,GRP,ERR=503,END=600)
```

> GRP *and* PARAM *are* NAMELISTs *in these examples.*

```
READ(5,GRP)A,X,M    no input list allowed
READ GRP            parentheses and unit needed
```

NAMELIST READ statement

READ(*unit, name*)
READ(*unit, name,* END = *s*)
READ(*unit, name,* ERR = *t*)
READ(*unit, name,* END = *s*, ERR = *t*)
READ(*unit, name,* ERR = *t*, END = *s*)

unit is an unsigned INTEGER constant or unsubscripted INTEGER*4 memory cell
name is an identifier which has been declared as the name of a NAMELIST
s and *t* are statement labels

Transmits values from NAMELIST data cards (records) to memory cells in a NAMELIST

NAMELIST data

 column 2
↓

```
&GRP A='BLT', &END
```

```
&RATES RM=104,108,203,207,209,
       RT=11,15,12,22,37,
&END
&PARAM   Z=1.94E16,Y=16*0.0,
         P=.TRUE.,,T(3)=4.7, &END
```

 column 2
↓

```
&GRP A='BLT' &END          comma required after each data specification
```

```
&RATES RM=104,108,203,207,209
RT=11,15,12,22,37,                      column one of each card must be blank
&END

&PARAM   Z=1.914E16 ,&END   trailing blank makes constant too large (1.914E160)
```

NAMELIST data

&*name* b $c_1 = v_1, c_2 = v_2, \ldots, c_n = v_n$, &END

name is the name of a NAMELIST
b is at least one blank
c_i is a memory cell (a subscript must be a constant) or array
v_i is a constant or list of constants whose type(s) is consistent with c_i. Constants must be separated by commas and may be repeated by a repeat factor (an unsigned INTEGER constant followed by an asterisk). The number of constants in v_i cannot exceed the number of memory cells in c_i.

NAMELIST data may be continued over several cards (records).

Each NAMELIST data card (record) must have a blank in the first column.

No imbedded blanks are allowed in constants or names.

Names may not be split over card boundaries.

Trailing blanks (before the comma) in numeric v_i's are treated as zeros.

Memory cells in the NAMELIST which are not mentioned on the NAMELIST data cards remain unchanged by the NAMELIST READ, thus providing a convenient way to initialize memory cells which usually take some default value placed in the memory cell by compile-time initialization or via an assignment statement prior to the NAMELIST READ.

NAMELIST WRITE

```
WRITE(6,GRP)
WRITE(LTP,PARAM)
```

GRP *and* PARAM *have been declared to be* NAMELISTs.

```
WRITE(6,GRP)X,Y,Z      no output list allowed
WRITE GRP              needs parentheses and unit
```

NAMELIST WRITE statement

WRITE(*unit, name*)

unit and *name* are as in the NAMELIST READ

NAMELIST WRITEs provide a convenient way to dump groups of memory cell values for debugging purposes.

```
IMPLICIT CHARACTER*80(A,B), COMPLEX(C),
+        DOUBLE PRECISION(D), INTEGER(I-N),
+        LOGICAL(P,Q), REAL(R-Z)
```
417

NAMELIST output looks pretty much like NAMELIST data except the &END always appears on a separate card.

If NAMELIST output is punched on cards or written on some other medium which can be used as input, its form is suitable for NAMELIST READ statement processing.

DUMPLIST statement

```
DUMPLIST /GRP/A,M,Y /PARAM/Z,Y,TP
DUMPLIST /FINSTA/ XCOORDS,YCOORDS,TIME
```

```
DUMPLIST /NGD/A,X,T,/GDP/Y      extra comma
DUMPLIST/SBS/X,Y(3),Q           no subscript allowed (whole array
                                must be included)
```

DUMPLIST statement

DUMPLIST $/name_1/list_1/name_2/list_2/\ldots/name_n/list_n$

$name_i$ is an identifier
$list_i$ is a list of unsubscripted memory cell or array names separated by commas (these are the members of the DUMPLIST $name_i$)

Prints values of memory cells in DUMPLIST groups in case of error termination of program.

DUMPLISTs are printed in the same form as NAMELIST output.

Some error terminations (*e.g.*, a time limit under some circumstances) may fail to invoke the DUMPLISTs.

Declarations and specifications involving memory cells in any $list_i$ must precede the DUMPLIST statement.

Unformatted READ

```
READ(9) N,(A(I),I=1,N)
READ (ILP)BIGARA
READ(17)
```

```
READ(4*I)A       unit can't be an expression
READ (X) A       unit must be of type INTEGER*4
```

Unformatted READ statement

READ(*u*) *list*
READ(*u*, END = *s*) *list*
READ(*u*, END = *s*, ERR = *t*) *list*
READ(*u*, ERR = *t*) *list*
READ(*u*, ERR = *t*, END = *s*) *list*

u, the unit number, is an INTEGER constant or unsigned INTEGER*4 memory cell name
list is an input list which may be omitted
s and *t* are statement labels

If *list* is omitted, one record is skipped.

If *list* doesn't exhaust a full record, the rest of the record is skipped.

Unformatted WRITE

```
WRITE(11) N,(P(I),I=1,N)
WRITE(ILP) X,GIGARA
```

```
WRITE(6) N,(A(I),I=1,N)
```
the line printer can deal with CHARACTER output only

Unformatted WRITE

WRITE(*u*)*list*

u and *list* are as in the unformatted READ

An **unformatted record** is what is written by a single unformatted WRITE statement.

I/O Device Positioning

```
REWIND 9
REWIND NT
BACKSPACE JP
ENDFILE 17
```

```
REWIND(9)
BACKSPACE,3
```
no parentheses allowed
no comma allowed

```
IMPLICIT CHARACTER*80(A,B), COMPLEX(C),
+       DOUBLE PRECISION(D), INTEGER(I-N),
+       LOGICAL(P,Q), REAL(R-Z)
```

> REWIND *unit*
> BACKSPACE *unit*
> ENDFILE *unit*
>
> *unit* is an unsigned INTEGER constant or unsubscripted INTEGER*4 memory cell

REWIND positions the I/O head of *unit* at the point where data begins or may begin.

BACKSPACE positions the I/O head at the beginning of the record immediately preceding the present record, or at the beginning of the data if the current record is the first record.

ENDFILE places an end-of-file mark on *unit* at the current position of the I/O head.

DEFINE FILE Statement

```
DEFINE FILE 16(512,10,L,KURSE)
DEFINE FILE 10(2000,5,E,LUMP)
```

```
DEFINE FILE 16(512,N,L,KURSE)      Size must be a constant
CREATE FILE 10(2000,5,F,LUMP)      F is not a legal mode, CREATE is illegal
```

> ### DEFINE FILE Statement
>
> DEFINE FILE *list*
>
> *list* is a list of structured array declarators separated by commas

> ### Structured Array Declarator
>
> *a (len, size, mode, cursor)*
>
> *a,* the structured array name, is an unsigned INTEGER constant corresponding to the unit number (data set reference number) established for the structured array
> *len,* the array length, is an unsigned INTEGER constant specifying the number of elements in the structured array
> *mode* is E, U, or L depending on whether the array elements are to be stored in a formatted form, unformatted form, or a mixture of the two, respectively (yes, E, U, or L. Really.)
> *size* is an unsigned INTEGER constant specifying the size of a structured array element—size is specified in characters (bytes) in modes E and L and in words (four-character storage units) if the mode is U
> *cursor* is a subscripted INTEGER memory cell name which will be used to store the current position of the read/write head

DEFINE FILE statement declares name and layout of structured array (*i.e.*, direct access file)

Information structured according to a user-provided FORMAT may be stored on and retrieved from a random access I/O device. Records in a **direct access file** are referenced with an index similar to an array subscript. For this reason we refer to a direct access file as a **structured array**.

Declarations and specifications involving memory cells in any file defined must precede the DEFINE FILE statement.

Direct Access WRITE

```
WRITE(16'ICE+2,105) (KAZ(J),J=1,10)
WRITE(10'KOUNT,AFMT) A,B
```

```
WRITE(16'ICE+2,105) (KURSE,KAZ(J),J=1,10)
```
KURSE, the *cursor* for structured array 16, may not appear in the output *list* (see DEFINE FILE)

Direct Access WRITE Statement

WRITE(*a's, f*) *list*
WRITE(*a's, f*)
WRITE(*a's*) *list*

a, the structured array name, is an unsigned INTEGER constant or unsubscripted INTEGER*4 memory cell name
s, the subscript, is a positive INTEGER valued expression
f, the FORMAT, is a FORMAT statement label or the name of an array containing a variable FORMAT
list is an output list

Stores a structured array element on a direct access I/O device

Values from the *list* are stored in the *s*th element of the structured array *a* (according to FORMAT *f* if *a* is a FORMATted direct access file).

The *cursor* memory cell for the structured array *a* should not appear in *list*.

Direct Access READ

```
READ(16'ICE,305) KAZ
READ(10'KOUNT/2,AFMT) A,B
```

```
READ(10'KOUNT/2,AFMT,ERR=N) A,B
```
N is not a statement label

```
IMPLICIT CHARACTER*80(A,B), COMPLEX(C),
+        DOUBLE PRECISION(D), INTEGER(I-N),
+        LOGICAL(P,Q), REAL(R-Z)
```
421

Subprograms

SUBROUTINEs

```
SUBROUTINE DIV(I,J)
SUBROUTINE PRN
SUBROUTINE MULRET(X,*,A,C,*)
SUBROUTINE BYLOC(/A/)
```

```
SUBROUTINE S(A(3))      illegal parameter
SUBROUTINE RT(X(K))     illegal parameter
SUBROUTINE (X,Y,Z)      no name
SUBROUTINE X(1.3,T)     illegal parameter
```

┌───┐
│ **SUBROUTINE Statement**   │
│   │
│ SUBROUTINE *name* ($p_1, p_2, \ldots, p_n$)   │
│ SUBROUTINE *name*   │
│   │
│ *name,* the name of the SUBROUTINE, is an identifier │
│ p_k, a parameter, is an identifier, or an identifier enclosed in a │
│ pair of slashes indicating a call-by-location parameter, or an │
│ asterisk (*) indicating a multiple-return parameter │
└───┘

The body of a SUBROUTINE, that is, the statements between the SUBROUTINE statement and the END statement, must contain at least one RETURN.

A SUBROUTINE, unlike a FUNCTION, has no *type.*

CALL Statement

```
    CALL DIV(3,N)
    CALL PRN
    CALL ST(Y**2,&379,ABS(X))
    CALL SRT(A,N)
```

```
    CALL DIV(3 N)      needs comma to separate arguments
    CALL PRN(   )      if PRN takes no arguments, leave off parentheses
    CULL SRT(A;N)      misspelling
```

CALL Statement

CALL *name* $(a_1, a_2, \ldots, a_n)$
CALL *name*

name is the identifier for the SUBROUTINE being invoked
a_k, an argument, is a constant, expression, a memory cell name,
an array name, the name of an EXTERNAL subprogram, or a
statement number constant. Its type must agree with that of the
corresponding parameter in the SUBROUTINE statement

EXTERNAL Statement

```
    EXTERNAL SIN,COS,USERFN
    EXTERNAL ALOG
```

```
    REAL X(10)
    EXTERNAL X      only subprograms can be external
```

EXTERNAL Statement

EXTERNAL *list*

list is a list of FUNCTION and/or SUBROUTINE names separated by commas

---

Whenever a subprogram name (*i.e.,* FUNCTION or SUBROUTINE name) is used
as an argument in a CALL statement or FUNCTION reference, that subprogram
name must be declared to be EXTERNAL. Otherwise it may be interpreted as a
local memory cell under the implicit typing rules.

```
IMPLICIT CHARACTER*80(A,B), COMPLEX(C),
+         DOUBLE PRECISION(D), INTEGER(I-N),
+         LOGICAL(P,Q), REAL(R-Z)
```

Statement Number Constants

```
CALL S(&379,&942)
CALL RT(X,&100,T)
```

```
K=&379              {statement number constants
Y=FN(X,&100)        {may be used only in CALL statements
```

Statement Number Constant

&*s*

s is a statement label in the current program unit

Statement number constants may be used *only* in CALL statements to indicate alternate return points.

The ampersand (&) must be replaced by the $ sign when the KP=26 $JOB card option is in effect.

FUNCTION Statement

```
INTEGER FUNCTION NXT(X,Y)
LOGICAL FUNCTION PER(AS,BE,CEE)
REAL FUNCTION XTM(Z,I)
COMPLEX FUNCTION CDV(C1,C2)
REAL FUNCTION DT*8(X)
FUNCTION D(X,Y,Z)
```

```
REAL FUNCTION RND           a FUNCTION must have at least one parameter
REAL FUNCTION RND()         a FUNCTION must have at least one parameter
FUNCTION Z(3)               illegal parameter
REAL*8 FUNCTION DT(X)       misplaced length modifier
REAL FUNCTION DT*27(X)      illegal length modifier
```

FUNCTION Statement

type FUNCTION *name*($p_1, p_2, \ldots, p_n$)
type FUNCTION *name**t($p_1, p_2, \ldots, p_n$)
FUNCTION *name*($p_1, p_2, \ldots, p_n$)

type is any data type except CHARACTER (no length modifier is allowed, however)
name, the FUNCTION name, is an identifier
t, an unsigned INTEGER constant, is a data type length modifier consistent with *type*
p_k, a parameter, is an identifier or an identifier enclosed in a pair of slashes indicating a call-by-location parameter

Throughout the computation described in the body of the FUNCTION, the *name* of the FUNCTION is used like a memory cell name, the value of the FUNCTION is the value of its *name* when a RETURN statement in the body of the FUNCTION is performed. There must be at least one RETURN in a FUNCTION.

> If you place a length modified data type before the word FUNCTION, as in
>
> ```
> REAL*8 FUNCTION DT(X)
> ```
>
> the compiler will mistake the FUNCTION statement for a declaration statement, treat your FUNCTION definition as a main program, issue error message VA-0 telling you that variable name FUNCTI has been truncated to six characters, and error message SV-4 telling you that the length declarators for array FUNCTI cannot be variables. So don't try it.

FUNCTION Reference

```
X=SIN(Y**2+1.3)
M=3**MIN0(MAX0(I,2*K),-10)
PRINT,CMPLX(4.1*X,Y)
IF (COS(X) .LT. 0.0) GO TO 100
```

```
SIN(0.0)=0.0      sin(0.0) is not a memory cell, it's a value
READ,ALOG(1.7)    ALOG(1.7) is not a memory cell, it's a value
```

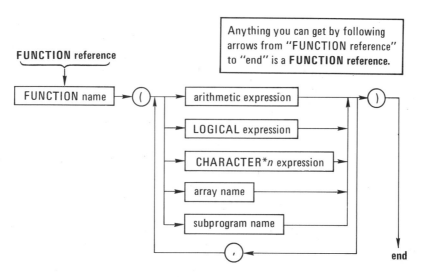

Anything you can get by following arrows from "FUNCTION reference" to "end" is a **FUNCTION reference**.

The number of arguments in a FUNCTION reference must be consistent with the FUNCTION definition.

The data type of the arguments in a FUNCTION reference must be the same as the data types of the corresponding parameters in the FUNCTION definition.

When you forget to declare an array, the compiler often mistakes references to the array for FUNCTION references (errors FN-2, SR-0, SF-1, SF-2, SF-3, SF-4, SF-5).

```
IMPLICIT CHARACTER*80(A,B), COMPLEX(C),
+        DOUBLE PRECISION(D), INTEGER(I-N),
+        LOGICAL(P,Q), REAL(R-Z)
```

RETURN Statement

```
RETURN
RETURN 2
```

```
RETURN 2*N    2*N is not an unsigned INTEGER constant
```

RETURN Statement

RETURN
RETURN *n*

n is an unsigned INTEGER constant indicating a RETURN to the statement number constant in the CALL statement corresponding to the *n*th asterisk in the SUBROUTINE statement

restriction
The multiple-return form, RETURN *n*, is valid only in SUBROUTINEs, not FUNCTIONs.

A RETURN statement returns control to the place where the subprogram was called.

A subprogram may have several RETURN statements.

Multiple ENTRY Points

```
ENTRY DPT(X)
ENTRY RX(Y)
ENTRY JTQ
ENTRY F(X,/A/,N)
ENTRY S(/X/,K,*)
```

```
ENTRIES A,B        ech!
ENTRY,RX(Y)        comma error
ENTRY S(3.14,X)    constant illegal
```

ENTRY Statement

ENTRY *name*($p_1, p_2, \ldots, p_n$)
ENTRY *name*

name is an identifier
p_k, a parameter, is an identifier, an identifier enclosed in slashes indicating a call-by-location parameter, or an asterisk (*) indicating a multiple-return parameter.

An ENTRY statement sets up an alternate point of entry in a SUBROUTINE or FUNCTION. References to the ENTRY *name* (CALLs or FUNCTION references) begin execution at the statement following the ENTRY.

Arguments in a reference to an ENTRY *name* must match in number and type with the parameters in the ENTRY statement.

The parameters in an ENTRY statement need not be the same as those at other points in the same SUBROUTINE or FUNCTION, but if some of the same parameters appear at two entry points, both references should be of the same kind (call-by-value or call-by-location).

> *If it's 2 A.M. and your program bombed because you used the* ENTRY *statement, let it be a lesson to you.*

Explicit typing won't work for parameters in ENTRY statements unless you place the type statements immediately after the ENTRY (a WARNING will be issued, but it'll work).

ENTRY *names* in FUNCTIONS are treated like variables EQUIVALENCEd to the FUNCTION *name*, and may be used to give the FUNCTION its value. They need not all be of the same data type, but if they aren't you're asking for trouble.

If ENTRY *name* has been invoked by a CALL statement, then a RETURN *n* statement refers to the *n*th multiple-return parameter in the parameter list of ENTRY *name*.

Statement Functions

```
POS(X)=X .GT. 0.0
P(Q1,Q2)=(Q1 .AND. Q2) .OR. .NOT. PI
TRUNC(X)=FLOAT(INT(X))
IN(X,Y,Z)=AMAX1(X,Y,-Z,U,1.0)
HI(ISCUS)=2**ISCUS
CROTAT(C)=C*(0.0,1.0)
```

```
P(4.7)=.TRUE.     illegal parameter
P(Q1,Q2)=3.9      illegal type conversion
B(ARCH)='B'       CHARACTER valued functions aren't allowed
```

> ### Statement Function Definition
>
> $f(p_1, p_2, \ldots, p_n) = expr$
>
> f, the function name, is an identifier
> p_i, a parameter name, is an identifier
> *expr*, the function's value, is an expression whose data type may be converted to the type of the identifier f

```
IMPLICIT CHARACTER*80(A,B), COMPLEX(C),
+        DOUBLE PRECISION(D), INTEGER(I-N),
+        LOGICAL(P,Q), REAL(R-Z)
```
427

The type of _f_ must be established prior to the statement function definition. All statement function definitions must appear before any executable statement in the program unit.

Statement functions are local to the program unit where they are defined, hence they cannot be referenced in other program units and cannot be listed in EXTERNAL Statements.

When you forget to declare an array, the compiler often mistakes references to the array for statement function definitions since they are formally the same. (Errors FN-2, SR-0, SF-1, SF-2, SF-3, SF-4, SF-5).

The _expr_ part of a statement function definition may refer to _previously defined_ statement functions only.

References to statement functions are made in the same way as references to external FUNCTIONs.

Parameters in statement functions may not be placeholders for subprograms or array names. Thus, F(X,G)=G(X) is not a legal statement function definition.

Built-in FUNCTIONs plus
Other Helpful FUNCTIONs

Built-in FUNCTIONs are ones provided along with the WATFIV compiler. To use them in your program you need merely use a type declaration to specify their type of result (see last column of the table) and then write their name followed by appropriate arguments. For example, to take the logarithm of 3.141592653589793:

```
REAL*8 DLOG
PRINT ,'LOG OF PI=',DLOG(3.141592653589793)
STOP
END
```

In the table, the first column shows the form of a reference to the FUNCTION, the second column describes the computation the FUNCTION performs, and the third column indicates the type of the result. The type and number of arguments each FUNCTION expects are indicated by these letters:

$a*4$	any type of length 4 bytes
$i*2$	INTEGER*2
$i*4$	INTEGER
$r*4$	REAL
$r*8$	REAL*8 or DOUBLE PRECISION
$c*8$	COMPLEX
$c*16$	COMPLEX*16

In some cases description needs to differentiate between specific arguments. In such cases a subscript is used as in CMPLX (r_1*4, r_2*4).

A few of the built-in FUNCTIONs allow two or more arguments, and the number of arguments may vary from one FUNCTION reference to the next. In those cases we write the formal FUNCTION reference with dots in the argument list, *e.g.*, MAX0 $(i_1*4, i_2*4, \ldots, i_n*4)$, to indicate that a variable number of arguments are allowed.

FUNCTION reference	value computed	type of value
absolute value		
IABS ($i*4$)	absolute value of $i*4$, $\lvert i*4 \rvert$	INTEGER
ABS ($r*4$)	absolute value of $r*4$, $\lvert r*4 \rvert$	REAL
DABS ($r*8$)	absolute value of $r*8$, $\lvert r*8 \rvert$	REAL*8
CABS ($c*8$)	modulus of $c*8$ SQRT (REAL ($c*8$)**2 +AIMAG ($c*8$)**2)	REAL
CDABS ($c*16$)	modulus of $c*16$	REAL*8
COMPLEX operations		
CMPLX (r_1*4, r_2*4)	convert to COMPLEX, $r_1*4+r_2*4\sqrt{-1}$	COMPLEX
DCMPLX (r_1*8, r_2*8)	convert to COMPLEX	COMPLEX*16
REAL ($c*8$)	real part of $c*8$	REAL
AIMAG ($c*8$)	imaginary part of $c*8$	REAL
CONJG ($c*8$)	complex conjugate of $c*8$, CMPLX (REAL($c*8$), –AIMAG ($c*8$))	COMPLEX
DCONJG ($c*16$)	complex conjugate of $c*16$	COMPLEX*16
type conversion		
DBLE ($r*4$)	DOUBLE PRECISION version of $r*4$	REAL*8
SNGL ($r*8$)	REAL*4 version of $r*8$	REAL
FLOAT ($i*4$)	REAL version of $i*4$	REAL
DFLOAT ($i*4$)	REAL*8 version of $i*4$	REAL*8
IFIX ($r*4$)	Convert argument to an INTEGER,	INTEGER
HFIX ($r*4$)	dropping any fractional part, convert	INTEGER*2
INT ($r*4$)	result to proper type.	INTEGER
AINT ($r*4$)		REAL
IDINT ($r*8$)		INTEGER
remainder		
IDIM (i_1*4, i_2*4)	i_1*4 – MIN0 (i_1*4, i_2*4)	INTEGER
DIM (r_1*4, r_2*4)	r_1*4 – AMIN1 (r_1*4, r_2*4)	REAL
MOD (i_1*4, i_2*4)	remainder in division $i_1*4 - (i_1*4/i_2*4)*i_2*4$	INTEGER
AMOD (r_1*4, r_2*4)	r_1*4 – AINT (r_1*4/r_2*4)*r_2*4	REAL
DMOD (r_1*8, r_2*8)	REAL*8 version of AMOD	REAL*8
sign		
ISIGN (i_1*4, i_2*4)	sign of i_2*4 times IABS (i_1*4)	INTEGER
SIGN (r_1*4, r_2*4)	sign of r_2*4 times ABS (r_1*4)	REAL
DSIGN (r_1*8, r_2*8)	sign of r_2*8 times DABS (r_1*8) **NOTE**: in WATFIV, the sign of zero is taken to be +.	REAL*8

FUNCTION reference	value computed	type of value
MAX0 $(i_1*4, i_2*4, \ldots, i_n*4)$	largest of $i_1*4, \ldots, i_n*4$ $n \geqslant 2$	INTEGER
AMAX1 $(r_1*4, \ldots, r_n*4)$	largest of $r_1*4, \ldots, r_n*4$ $n \geqslant 2$	REAL
DMAX1 $(r_1*8, \ldots, r_n*8)$	largest of $r_1*8, \ldots, r_n*8$ $n \geqslant 2$	REAL*8
MAX1 $(r_1*4, \ldots, i_n*4)$	INT (AMAX1 $(r_1*4, \ldots, r_n*4)$) $n \geqslant 2$	INTEGER
AMAX0 $(i_1*4, \ldots, i_n*4)$	FLOAT (MAX0 $(i_1*4, \ldots, i_n*4)$) $n \geqslant 2$	REAL
MIN0 $(i_1*4, \ldots, i_n*4)$	smallest of $i_1*4, \ldots, i_n*4$ $n \geqslant 2$	INTEGER
AMIN1 $(r_1*4, \ldots, r_n*4)$	smallest of $r_1*4, \ldots, r_n*4$ $n \geqslant 2$	REAL
DMIN1 $(r_1*8, \ldots, r_n*8)$	smallest of $r_1*8, \ldots, r_n*8$ $n \geqslant 2$	REAL*8
MIN1 $(r_1*4, \ldots, r_n*4)$	INT (AMIN1 $(r_1*4, \ldots, r_n*4)$) $n \geqslant 2$	INTEGER
AMIN0 $(i_1*4, \ldots, i_n*4)$	FLOAT (MIN0 $(i_1*4, \ldots, i_n*4)$) $n \geqslant 2$	REAL
AND $(a_1*4, \ldots, a_n*4)$	bit-by-bit logical "and" of $a_1*4, \ldots, a_n*4$ $n \geqslant 2$	REAL
OR $(a_1*4, \ldots, a_n*4)$	bit-by-bit logical "or" $n \geqslant 2$	REAL
EOR $(a_1*4, \ldots a_n*4)$	bit-by-bit "exclusive or" $n \geqslant 2$	REAL
COMPL $(a*4)$	1's complement of $a*4$	REAL
EXP $(r*4)$	e^{r*4}	REAL
DEXP $(r*8)$	e^{r*8}	REAL*8
CEXP $(c*8)$	e^{c*8}	COMPLEX
CDEXP $(c*16)$	e^{c*16}	COMPLEX*16
ALOG $(r*4)$	natural logarithm of $r*4$	REAL
DLOG $(r*8)$	natural logarithm of $r*8$	REAL*8
CLOG $(c*8)$	principle value of $\log_e (c*8)$	COMPLEX
CDLOG $(c*16)$	principle value of $\log_e (c*16)$	COMPLEX*16
ALOG10 $(r*4)$	base 10 logarithm of $r*4$	REAL
DLOG10 $(r*8)$	base 10 logarithm of $r*8$	REAL*8

maximum, minimum

bit operations

exponential

logarithm

e is the base of natural logarithms

FUNCTION reference	value computed	type of value
ERF ($r*4$)	error function $$\frac{2}{\sqrt{\pi}} \int_{o}^{r*4} e - s^2 \, ds$$	REAL
DERF ($r*8$)	DOUBLE PRECISION error function	REAL*8
ERFC ($r*4$)	1.0 – ERF ($r*4$)	REAL
DERFC ($r*8$)	1.0D0 – DERF ($r*8$) **NOTE**: ERF (x) is twice the integral from 0 to $\sqrt{2x}$ of the Normal (standard Gaussian) curve.	REAL*8
GAMMA ($r*4$)	$\int_{0}^{\infty} e - s \, s^{-1 + r*4} ds$; $\Gamma (n + 1) = n\Gamma(n)$	REAL
DGAMMA ($r*8$)	$\Gamma(r*8)$	REAL*8
ALGAMA ($r*4$)	ALOG (GAMMA ($r*4$))	REAL
DLGAMA ($r*8$)	DLOG (DGAMMA ($r*8$))	REAL*8
SQRT ($r*4$)	square root of $r*4$	REAL
DSQRT ($r*8$)	square root of $r*8$	REAL*8
CSQRT ($c*8$)	principle value of $\sqrt{c*8}$ (positive real part)	COMPLEX
CDSQRT ($c*16$)	principle value of $\sqrt{c*16}$ (positive real part)	COMPLEX*16

statistical functions — ERF through DLGAMA
square root — SQRT through CDSQRT

FUNCTION reference	value computed	type of value
SIN ($r*4$)	sine of $r*4$ radians	REAL
DSIN ($r*8$)	sine of $r*8$ radians	REAL*8
CSIN ($c*8$)	sine of $c*8$ radians	COMPLEX
CDSIN ($c*16$)	sine of $c*16$ radians	COMPLEX*16
COS ($r*4$)	cosine of $r*4$ radians	REAL
DCOS ($r*8$)	cosine of $r*8$ radians	REAL*8
CCOS ($c*8$)	cosine of $c*8$ radians	COMPLEX
CDCOS ($c*16$)	cosine of $c*16$ radians	COMPLEX*16
TAN ($r*4$)	tangent of $r*4$ radians	REAL
DTAN ($r*8$)	tangent of $r*8$ radians	REAL*8
COTAN ($r*4$)	cotangent of $r*4$ radians	REAL
DCOTAN ($r*8$)	cotangent of $r*8$ radians	REAL*8
ARSIN ($r*4$)	angle ($-\frac{\pi}{2}$ to $\frac{\pi}{2}$) whose sine is $r*4$	REAL
DARSIN ($r*8$)	angle ($-\frac{\pi}{2}$ to $\frac{\pi}{2}$) whose sine is $r*4$	REAL*8
ARCOS ($r*4$)	angle (0 to π) whose cosine is $r*4$	REAL
DARCOS ($r*8$)	angle (0 to π) whose cosine is $r*8$	REAL*8
ATAN ($r*4$)	angle ($-\frac{\pi}{2}$ to $\frac{\pi}{2}$) whose tangent is $r*4$	REAL
DATAN ($r*8$)	angle ($-\frac{\pi}{2}$ to $\frac{\pi}{2}$) whose tangent is $r*8$	REAL*8
ATAN2 (r_1*4, r_2*4)	arctan (r_1*4/r_2*4) in the quadrant of the vector (r_1*4, r_2*4)	REAL
DATAN2 (r_1*8, r_2*8)	arctan (r_1*8/r_2*8) in the quadrant of the vector (r_1*8, r_2*8) **NOTE:** you'll save trouble if you use ATAN2 and DATAN2 instead of ATAN and DATAN whenever possible.	REAL*8
SINH ($r*4$)	hyperbolic sine of $r*4$	REAL
DSINH ($r*8$)	hyperbolic sine of $r*8$	REAL*8
COSH ($r*4$)	hyperbolic cosine of $r*4$	REAL
DCOSH ($r*8$)	hyperbolic cosine of $r*8$	REAL*8
TANH ($r*4$)	hyperbolic tangent of $r*4$	REAL
DTANH ($r*8$)	hyperbolic tangent of $r*8$	REAL*8

trigonometric functions (bracket spanning SIN through DATAN2)

hyperbolic functions (bracket spanning SINH through DTANH)

Some Other Helpful FUNCTIONs

If you see one you need, copy it whole since these are *not* part of the WATFIV Library.

```
      INTEGER FUNCTICN ROOF(ARG)
      REAL ARG
COMMENT: 'ROOF' RETURNS THE SMALLEST INTEGER WHICH IS NOT
C     LESS THAN ARG (ROUND UP).
      ROOF=INT(ARG)
      IF (ARG .LE. 0.0) RETURN
      IF (ARG .EQ. FLOAT(INT(ARG))) RETURN
      ROOF=ROOF+1
      RETURN
      END

      INTEGER FUNCTION FLOOR(ARG)
      REAL ARG
COMMENT: 'FLOOR' RETURNS THE LARGEST INTEGER WHICH IS NOT
C     GREATER THAN ARG (ROUND DOWN).
      FLOOR=INT(ARG)
      IF (ARG .GE. 0.0) RETURN
      IF (ARG .EQ. FLOAT(INT(ARG))) RETURN
      FLOOR=FLOOR-1
      RETURN
      END

      INTEGER FUNCTION ROUND(ARG)
      REAL ARG
      REAL SIGN
COMMENT: CLASSICAL ROUNDING
      ROUND=INT(ARG+SIGN(.5,ARG))
      RETURN
      END

      REAL FUNCTION DREAL*8(C)
      COMPLEX*16 C
COMMENT: RETURN THE REAL PART OF C WHERE C IS
C     DOUBLE PRECISICN COMPLEX BY FORCING A TYPE
C     CONVERSION.
      DREAL=C
      RETURN
      END

      REAL FUNCTION DIMAG*8(C)
      COMPLEX*16 C
COMMENT: SNEAK IMAG PART INTO REAL PART AND FORCE TYPE
C     CONVERSION TO RETURN IMAGINARY PART OF THE DOUBLE
C     PRECISION COMPLEX VALUE C.
      DIMAG=(0.0,-1.0)*C
      RETURN
      END

      REAL FUNCTION POS(ARG)
      REAL ARG
COMMENT: IF ARG .GE. 0 THEN ARG, ELSE 0.
      POS=ARG
      IF (ARG .LT. 0.) POS=0.
      RETURN
      END
```

```
      REAL FUNCTION SGN(ARG)
      REAL ARG
COMMENT: +1,0, OR -1 ACCORDING TO WHETHER 'ARG' IS
C        .GT., .EQ., OR .LT. ZERO.
      SGN=+1.
      IF (ARG .GT. 0.) RETURN
      SGN=-1.
      IF (ARG .LT. 0.) RETURN
      SGN=0.
      RETURN
      END
```

*

Error Messages

ASSEMBLER LANGUAGE SUBPROGRAMS

AL-0   MISSING END CARD ON ASSEMBLY LANGUAGE OBJECT DECK

AL-1   ENTRY-POINT OR CSECT NAME IN AN OBJECT DECK WAS PREVIOUSLY DEFINED. FIRST DEFINITION USED

BLOCK DATA STATEMENTS

BD-0   EXECUTABLE STATEMENTS ARE ILLEGAL IN BLOCK DATA SUBPROGRAMS

BD-1   IMPROPER BLOCK DATA STATEMENT

CARD FORMAT AND CONTENTS

CC-0   COLUMNS 1-5 OF CONTINUATION CARD ARE NOT BLANK.
PROBABLE CAUSE: STATEMENT PUNCHED TO LEFT OF COLUMN 7

CC-1   LIMIT OF 5 CONTINUATION CARDS EXCEEDED

CC-2   INVALID CHARACTER IN FORTRAN STATEMENT.
A '$' WAS INSERTED IN THE SOURCE LISTING

CC-3   FIRST CARD OF A PROGRAM IS A CONTINUATION CARD.
PROBABLE CAUSE: STATEMENT PUNCHED TO LEFT OF COLUMN 7

CC-4   STATEMENT TOO LONG TO COMPILE (SCAN-STACK OVERFLOW)

CC-5   A BLANK CARD WAS ENCOUNTERED

CC-6   KEYPUNCH USED DIFFERS FROM KEYPUNCH SPECIFIED ON JOB CARD

CC-7   THE FIRST CHARACTER OF THE STATEMENT WAS NOT ALPHABETIC

CC-8   INVALID CHARACTER(S) ARE CONCATENATED WITH THE FORTRAN KEYWORD

CC-9   INVALID CHARACTERS IN COLUMNS 1-5. STATEMENT NUMBER IGNORED.
PROBABLE CAUSE: STATEMENT PUNCHED TO LEFT OF COLUMN 7

CC-A   CONTROL CARDS MAY NOT BE CONTINUED

COMMON

CM-0   THE VARIABLE IS ALREADY IN COMMON

CM-1   OTHER COMPILERS MAY NOT ALLOW COMMONED VARIABLES TO BE INITIALIZED IN OTHER THAN A BLOCK DATA SUBPROGRAM

CM-2   ILLEGAL USE OF A COMMON BLOCK OR NAMELIST NAME

FORTRAN TYPE CONSTANTS

CN-0   MIXED REAL*4, REAL*8 IN COMPLEX CONSTANT; REAL*8 ASSUMED FOR BOTH

CN-1   AN INTEGER CONSTANT MAY NOT BE GREATER THAN 2,147,483,647 (2**31-1)

CN-2   EXPONENT ON A REAL CONSTANT IS GREATER THAN 2 DIGITS

CN-3   A REAL CONSTANT HAS MORE THAN 16 DIGITS. IT WAS TRUNCATED TO 16

CN-4   INVALID HEXADECIMAL CONSTANT

CN-5   ILLEGAL USE OF A DECIMAL POINT

CN-6   CONSTANT WITH MORE THAN 7 DIGITS BUT E-TYPE EXPONENT, ASSUMED TO BE REAL*4

CN-7   CONSTANT OR STATEMENT NUMBER GREATER THAN 99999

CN-8   AN EXPONENT OVERFLOW OR UNDERFLOW OCCURRED WHILE CONVERTING A CONSTANT IN A SOURCE STATEMENT

COMPILER ERRORS

CP-0   COMPILER ERROR — LANDR/ARITH
CP-1   COMPILER ERROR. LIKELY CAUSE: MORE THAN 255 DO STATEMENTS
CP-4   COMPILER ERROR — INTERRUPT AT COMPILE TIME, RETURN TO SYSTEM

CHARACTER VARIABLE

CV-0   A CHARACTER VARIABLE IS USED WITH A RELATIONAL OPERATOR
CV-1   LENGTH OF A CHARACTER VALUE ON RIGHT OF EQUAL SIGN EXCEEDS THAT ON LEFT. TRUNCATION WILL OCCUR
CV-2   UNFORMATTED CORE-TO-CORE I/O NOT IMPLEMENTED

DATA STATEMENT

DA-0   REPLICATION FACTOR IS ZERO OR GREATER THAN 32767. IT IS ASSUMED TO BE 32767
DA-1   MORE VARIABLES THAN CONSTANTS
DA-2   ATTEMPT TO INITIALIZE A SUBPROGRAM PARAMETER IN A DATA STATEMENT
DA-3   OTHER COMPILERS MAY NOT ALLOW NON-CONSTANT SUBSCRIPTS IN DATA STATEMENTS
DA-4   TYPE OF VARIABLE AND CONSTANT DO NOT AGREE. (MESSAGE ISSUED ONCE FOR AN ARRAY)
DA-5   MORE CONSTANTS THAN VARIABLES
DA-6   A VARIABLE WAS PREVIOUSLY INITIALIZED. THE LATEST VALUE IS USED. CHECK COMMONED AND EQUIVALENCED VARIABLES
DA-7   OTHER COMPILERS MAY NOT ALLOW INITIALIZATION OF BLANK COMMON
DA-8   A LITERAL CONSTANT HAS BEEN TRUNCATED
DA-9   OTHER COMPILERS MAY NOT ALLOW IMPLIED DO-LOOPS IN DATA STATEMENTS

DEFINE FILE STATEMENTS

DF-0   THE UNIT NUMBER IS MISSING
DF-1   INVALID FORMAT TYPE
DF-2   THE ASSOCIATED VARIABLE IS NOT A SIMPLE INTEGER VARIABLE
DF-3   NUMBER OF RECORDS OR RECORD SIZE IS ZERO OR GREATER THAN 32767

DIMENSION STATEMENTS

DM-0   NO DIMENSIONS ARE SPECIFIED FOR A VARIABLE IN A DIMENSION STATEMENT
DM-1   THE VARIABLE HAS ALREADY BEEN DIMENSIONED
DM-2   CALL-BY-LOCATION PARAMETERS MAY NOT BE DIMENSIONED
DM-3   THE DECLARED SIZE OF ARRAY EXCEEDS SPACE PROVIDED BY CALLING ARGUMENT

DO LOOPS

DO-0   THIS STATEMENT CANNOT BE THE OBJECT OF A DO-LOOP
DO-1   ILLEGAL TRANSFER INTO THE RANGE OF A DO-LOOP
DO-2   THE OBJECT OF THIS DO-LOOP HAS ALREADY APPEARED
DO-3   IMPROPERLY NESTED DO-LOOPS
DO-4   ATTEMPT TO REDEFINE A DO-LOOP PARAMETER WITHIN THE RANGE OF THE LOOP
DO-5   INVALID DO-LOOP PARAMETER
DO-6   ILLEGAL TRANSFER TO A STATEMENT WHICH IS INSIDE THE RANGE OF A DO-LOOP
DO-7   A DO-LOOP PARAMETER IS UNDEFINED OR OUT OF RANGE

DO-8	BECAUSE OF ONE OF THE PARAMETERS, THIS DO-LOOP WILL TERMINATE AFTER THE FIRST TIME THROUGH
DO-9	A DO-LOOP PARAMETER MAY NOT BE REDEFINED IN AN INPUT LIST
DO-A	OTHER COMPILERS MAY NOT ALLOW THIS STATEMENT TO END A DO-LOOP

EQUIVALENCE AND/OR COMMON

EC-0	EQUIVALENCED VARIABLE APPEARS IN A COMMON STATEMENT
EC-1	A COMMON BLOCK HAS A DIFFERENT LENGTH THAN IN A PREVIOUS SUBPROGRAM: GREATER LENGTH USED
EC-2	COMMON AND/OR EQUIVALENCE CAUSES INVALID ALIGNMENT. EXECUTION SLOWED. REMEDY: ORDER VARIABLES BY DECREASING LENGTH
EC-3	EQUIVALENCE EXTENDS COMMON DOWNWARDS
EC-4	A SUBPROGRAM PARAMETER APPEARS IN A COMMON OR EQUIVALENCE STATEMENT
EC-5	A VARIABLE WAS USED WITH SUBSCRIPTS IN AN EQUIVALENCE STATEMENT BUT HAS NOT BEEN PROPERLY DIMENSIONED

END STATEMENTS

EN-0	MISSING END STATEMENT: END STATEMENT GENERATED
EN-1	AN END STATEMENT WAS USED TO TERMINATE EXECUTION
EN-2	AN END STATEMENT CANNOT HAVE A STATEMENT NUMBER. STATEMENT NUMBER IGNORED
EN-3	END STATEMENT NOT PRECEDED BY A TRANSFER

EQUAL SIGNS

EQ-0	ILLEGAL QUANTITY ON LEFT OF EQUALS SIGN
EQ-1	ILLEGAL USE OF EQUAL SIGN
EQ-2	OTHER COMPILERS MAY NOT ALLOW MULTIPLE ASSIGNMENT STATEMENTS
EQ-3	MULTIPLE ASSIGNMENT IS NOT IMPLEMENTED FOR CHARACTER VARIABLES

EQUIVALENCE STATEMENTS

EV-0	ATTEMPT TO EQUIVALENCE A VARIABLE TO ITSELF
EV-2	MULTI-SUBSCRIPTED EQUIVALENCED VARIABLE HAS BEEN INCORRECTLY RE-EQUIVALENCED. REMEDY: DIMENSION THE VARIABLE FIRST

POWERS AND EXPONENTIATION

EX-0	ILLEGAL COMPLEX EXPONENTIATION
EX-1	I**J WHERE I = J = 0
EX-2	I**J WHERE I = 0, J .LT. 0
EX-3	0.0**Y WHERE Y .LE. 0.0
EX-4	0.0**J WHERE J = 0
EX-5	0.0**J WHERE J .LT. 0
EX-6	X**Y WHERE X .LT. 0.0, Y .NE. 0.0

ENTRY STATEMENT

EY-0	ENTRY-POINT NAME WAS PREVIOUSLY DEFINED
EY-1	PREVIOUS DEFINITION OF FUNCTION NAME IN AN ENTRY IS INCORRECT
EY-2	THE USAGE OF A SUBPROGRAM PARAMETER IS INCONSISTENT WITH A PREVIOUS ENTRY-POINT
EY-3	A PARAMETER HAS APPEARED IN AN EXECUTABLE STATEMENT BUT IS NOT A SUBPROGRAM PARAMETER

| EY-4 | ENTRY STATEMENTS ARE INVALID IN THE MAIN PROGRAM |
| EY-5 | ENTRY STATEMENT INVALID INSIDE A DO-LOOP |

FORMAT
SOME FORMAT ERROR MESSAGES GIVE CHARACTERS IN WHICH ERROR WAS DETECTED

FM-0	IMPROPER CHARACTER SEQUENCE OR INVALID CHARACTER IN INPUT DATA
FM-1	NO STATEMENT NUMBER ON A FORMAT STATEMENT
FM-2	FORMAT CODE AND DATA TYPE DO NOT MATCH
FM-4	FORMAT PROVIDES NO CONVERSION SPECIFICATION FOR A VALUE IN I/O LIST
FM-5	AN INTEGER IN THE INPUT DATA IS TOO LARGE
	(MAXIMUM = 2,147,483,647 = $2**31-1$).
FM-6	A REAL NUMBER IN THE INPUT DATA IS OUT OF MACHINE RANGE (1.E–78, 1.E+75)
FM-7	UNREFERENCED FORMAT STATEMENT
FT-0	FIRST CHARACTER FOR VARIABLE FORMAT IS NOT A LEFT PARENTHESIS
FT-1	INVALID CHARACTER ENCOUNTERED IN FORMAT
FT-2	INVALID FORM FOLLOWING A FORMAT CODE
FT-3	INVALID FIELD OR GROUP COUNT
FT-4	A FIELD OR GROUP COUNT GREATER THAN 255
FT-5	NO CLOSING PARENTHESIS ON VARIABLE FORMAT
FT-6	NO CLOSING QUOTE IN A HOLLERITH FIELD
FT-7	INVALID USE OF COMMA
FT-8	FORMAT STATEMENT TOO LONG TO COMPILE (SCAN-STACK OVERFLOW)
FT-9	INVALID USE OF P FORMAT CODE
FT-A	INVALID USE OF PERIOD (.)
FT-B	MORE THAN THREE LEVELS OF PARENTHESES
FT-C	INVALID CHARACTER BEFORE A RIGHT PARENTHESIS
FT-D	MISSING OR ZERO LENGTH HOLLERITH ENCOUNTERED
FT-E	NO CLOSING RIGHT PARENTHESIS
FT-F	CHARACTERS FOLLOW CLOSING RIGHT PARENTHESIS
FT-G	WRONG QUOTE USED FOR KEY-PUNCH SPECIFIED
FT-H	LENGTH OF HOLLERITH EXCEEDS 255
FT-I	EXPECTING COMMA BETWEEN FORMAT ITEMS

FUNCTIONS AND SUBROUTINES

FN-1	A PARAMETER APPEARS MORE THAN ONCE IN A SUBPROGRAM OR STATEMENT FUNCTION DEFINITION
FN-2	SUBSCRIPTS ON RIGHT-HAND SIDE OF STATEMENT FUNCTION. PROBABLE CAUSE: VARIABLE TO LEFT OF EQUAL SIGN NOT DIMENSIONED
FN-3	MULTIPLE RETURNS ARE INVALID IN FUNCTION SUBPROGRAMS
FN-4	ILLEGAL LENGTH MODIFIER
FN-5	INVALID PARAMETER
FN-6	A PARAMETER HAS THE SAME NAME AS THE SUBPROGRAM

GO TO STATEMENTS

GO-0	THIS STATEMENT COULD TRANSFER TO ITSELF
GO-1	THIS STATEMENT TRANSFERS TO A NON-EXECUTABLE STATEMENT
GO-2	ATTEMPT TO DEFINE ASSIGNED GOTO INDEX IN AN ARITHMETIC STATEMENT
GO-3	ASSIGNED GO TO INDEX MAY BE USED ONLY IN ASSIGNED GO TO AND ASSIGN STATEMENTS

GO-4   THE INDEX OF AN ASSIGNED GO TO IS UNDEFINED OR OUT OF RANGE, OR INDEX OF COMPUTED GO TO IS UNDEFINED

GO-5   ASSIGNED GO TO INDEX MAY NOT BE AN INTEGER*2 VARIABLE

HOLLERITH CONSTANTS

HO-0   ZERO LENGTH SPECIFIED FOR H-TYPE HOLLERITH

HO-1   ZERO LENGTH QUOTE-TYPE HOLLERITH

HO-2   NO CLOSING QUOTE OR NEXT CARD NOT A CONTINUATION CARD

HO-3   UNEXPECTED HOLLERITH OR STATEMENT NUMBER CONSTANT

IF STATEMENTS (ARITHMETIC AND LOGICAL)

IF-0   AN INVALID STATEMENT FOLLOWS THE LOGICAL IF

IF-1   ARITHMETIC OR INVALID EXPRESSION IN LOGICAL IF

IF-2   LOGICAL, COMPLEX OR INVALID EXPRESSION IN ARITHMETIC IF

IMPLICIT STATEMENT

IM-0   INVALID DATA TYPE

IM-1   INVALID OPTIONAL LENGTH

IM-3   IMPROPER ALPHABETIC SEQUENCE IN CHARACTER RANGE

IM-4   A SPECIFICATION IS NOT A SINGLE CHARACTER. THE FIRST CHARACTER IS USED

IM-5   IMPLICIT STATEMENT DOES NOT PRECEDE OTHER SPECIFICATION STATEMENTS

IM-6   ATTEMPT TO DECLARE THE TYPE OF A CHARACTER MORE THAN ONCE

IM-7   ONLY ONE IMPLICIT STATEMENT PER PROGRAM SEGMENT ALLOWED. THIS ONE IGNORED

INPUT/OUTPUT

IO-0   I/O STATEMENT REFERENCES A STATEMENT WHICH IS NOT A FORMAT STATEMENT

IO-1   A VARIABLE FORMAT MUST BE AN ARRAY NAME

IO-2   INVALID ELEMENT IN INPUT LIST OR DATA LIST

IO-3   OTHER COMPILERS MAY NOT ALLOW EXPRESSIONS IN OUTPUT LISTS

IO-4   ILLEGAL USE OF END= OR ERR= PARAMETERS

IO-5   INVALID UNIT NUMBER

IO-6   INVALID FORMAT

IO-7   ONLY CONSTANTS, SIMPLE INTEGER*4 VARIABLES, AND CHARACTER VARIABLES ARE ALLOWED AS UNIT

IO-8   ATTEMPT TO PERFORM I/O IN A FUNCTION WHICH IS CALLED IN AN OUTPUT STATEMENT

IO-9   UNFORMATTED WRITE STATEMENT MUST HAVE A LIST

JOB-CONTROL CARDS

JB-0   CONTROL CARD ENCOUNTERED DURING COMPILATION; PROBABLE CAUSE: MISSING $ENTRY CARD

JB-1   MIS-PUNCHED JOB OPTION

JOB TERMINATION

KO-0   SOURCE ERROR ENCOUNTERED WHILE EXECUTING WITH RUN = FREE

KO-1   LIMIT EXCEEDED FOR FIXED-POINT DIVISION BY ZERO

KO-2   LIMIT EXCEEDED FOR FLOATING-POINT DIVISION BY ZERO

KO-3   EXPONENT OVERFLOW LIMIT EXCEEDED

KO-4	EXPONENT UNDERFLOW LIMIT EXCEEDED
KO-5	FIXED-POINT OVERFLOW LIMIT EXCEEDED
KO-6	JOB-TIME EXCEEDED
KO-7	COMPILER ERROR—EXECUTION TIME: RETURN TO SYSTEM
KO-8	TRACEBACK ERROR. TRACEBACK TERMINATED
KO-9	CANNOT OPEN WATFIV .ERRTEXTS. RUN TERMINATED
KO-A	I/O ERROR ON ERROR TEXT FILE

LOGICAL OPERATIONS

| LG-0 | .NOT. WAS USED AS A BINARY OPERATOR |

LIBRARY ROUTINES

LI-0	ARGUMENT OUT OF RANGE DGAMMA OR GAMMA. (1.382E−76 .LT. X .LT. 57.57)
LI-1	ABS(X) .GE. 175.366 FOR SINH, COSH, DSINH OR DCOSH OF X
LI-2	SENSE LIGHT OTHER THAN 0, 1, 2, 3, 4 FOR SLITE OR 1, 2, 3, 4 FOR SLITET
LI-3	REAL PORTION OF ARGUMENT .GT. 174.673, CEXP OR CDEXP
LI-4	ABS(AIMAG(Z)) .GT. 174.673 FOR CSIN, CCOS, CDSIN OR CDCOS OF Z
LI-5	ABS(REAL(Z)) .GE. 3.537E15 FOR CSIN, CCOS, CDSIN OR CDCOS OF Z
LI-6	ABS(AIMAG(Z)) .GE. 3.537E15 FOR CEXP OR CDEXP OF Z
LI-7	ARGUMENT .GT. 174.673, EXP OR DEXP
LI-8	ARGUMENT OF CLOG OR CDLOG IS ZERO
LI-9	ARGUMENT IS NEGATIVE OR ZERO, ALOG, ALOG10, DLOG OR DLOG 0
LI-A	ABS(X) .GE. 3.537E15 FOR SIN, COS, DSIN OR DCOS OF X
LI-B	ABSOLUTE VALUE OF ARGUMENT .GT. 1, FOR ARSIN, ARCOS, DARSIN OR DARCOS
LI-C	ARGUMENT IS NEGATIVE, SQRT OR DSQRT
LI-D	BOTH ARGUMENTS OF DATAN2 OR ATAN2 ARE ZERO
LI-E	ARGUMENT TOO CLOSE TO A SINGULARITY, TAN, COTAN, DTAN OR DCOTAN
LI-F	ARGUMENT OUT OF RANGE DLGAMA OR ALGAMA. (0.0 .LT. X .LT. 4.29E73)
LI-G	ABSOLUTE VALUE OF ARGUMENT .GE. 3.537E15, TAN, COTAN, DTAN, DCOTAN

MIXED MODE

MD-0	RELATIONAL OPERATOR HAS LOGICAL OPERAND
MD-1	RELATIONAL OPERATOR HAS COMPLEX OPERAND
MD-2	MIXED MODE — LOGICAL OR CHARACTER WITH ARITHMETIC
MD-3	OTHER COMPILERS MAY NOT ALLOW SUBSCRIPTS OF TYPE COMPLEX, LOGICAL OR CHARACTER

MEMORY OVERFLOW

MO-0	INSUFFICIENT MEMORY TO COMPILE THIS PROGRAM. REMAINDER WILL BE ERROR CHECKED ONLY
MO-1	INSUFFICIENT MEMORY TO ASSIGN ARRAY STORAGE. JOB ABANDONED
MO-2	SYMBOL TABLE EXCEEDS AVAILABLE SPACE. JOB ABANDONED
MO-3	DATA AREA OF SUBPROGRAM EXCEEDS 24K — SEGMENT SUBPROGRAM
MO-4	INSUFFICIENT MEMORY TO ALLOCATE COMPILER WORK AREA OR WATLIB BUFFER

NAMELIST STATEMENTS

NL-0	NAMELIST ENTRY MUST BE A VARIABLE, NOT A SUBPROGRAM PARAMETER
NL-1	NAMELIST NAME PREVIOUSLY DEFINED
NL-2	VARIABLE NAME TOO LONG
NL-3	VARIABLE NAME NOT FOUND IN NAMELIST

NL-4   INVALID SYNTAX IN NAMELIST INPUT
NL-6   VARIABLE INCORRECTLY SUBSCRIPTED
NL-7   SUBSCRIPT OUT OF RANGE

PARENTHESES

PC-0   UNMATCHED PARENTHESIS
PC-1   INVALID PARENTHESIS NESTING IN I/O LIST

PAUSE, STOP STATEMENTS

PS-0   OPERATOR MESSAGES NOT ALLOWED: SIMPLE STOP ASSUMED FOR STOP, CONTINUE ASSUMED FOR PAUSE

RETURN STATEMENT

RE-1   RETURN I, WHERE I IS OUT OF RANGE OR UNDEFINED
RE-2   MULTIPLE RETURN NOT VALID IN FUNCTION SUBPROGRAM
RE-3   VARIABLE IS NOT A SIMPLE INTEGER
RE-4   A MULTIPLE RETURN IS NOT VALID IN THE MAIN PROGRAM

ARITHMETIC AND LOGICAL STATEMENT FUNCTIONS

PROBABLE CAUSE OF SF ERRORS – VARIABLE ON LEFT OF = WAS NOT DIMENSIONED

SF-1   A PREVIOUSLY REFERENCED STATEMENT NUMBER APPEARS ON A STATEMENT FUNCTION DEFINITION
SF-2   STATEMENT FUNCTION IS THE OBJECT OF A LOGICAL IF STATEMENT
SF-3   RECURSIVE STATEMENT FUNCTION DEFINITION: NAME APPEARS ON BOTH SIDES OF EQUAL SIGN. LIKELY CAUSE: VARIABLE NOT DIMENSIONED
SF-4   A STATEMENT FUNCTION DEFINITION APPEARS AFTER THE FIRST EXECUTABLE STATEMENT
SF-5   ILLEGAL USE OF A STATEMENT FUNCTION NAME

SUBPROGRAMS

SR-0   MISSING SUBPROGRAM
SR-1   SUBPROGRAM REDEFINES A CONSTANT, EXPRESSION, DO-PARAMETER OR ASSIGNED GO TO INDEX
SR-2   THE SUBPROGRAM WAS ASSIGNED DIFFERENT TYPES IN DIFFERENT PROGRAM SEGMENTS
SR-3   ATTEMPT TO USE A SUBPROGRAM RECURSIVELY
SR-4   INVALID TYPE OF ARGUMENT IN REFERENCE TO A SUBPROGRAM
SR-5   WRONG NUMBER OF ARGUMENTS IN A REFERENCE TO A SUBPROGRAM
SR-6   A SUBPROGRAM WAS PREVIOUSLY DEFINED. THE FIRST DEFINITION IS USED
SR-7   NO MAIN PROGRAM
SR-8   ILLEGAL OR MISSING SUBPROGRAM NAME
SR-9   LIBRARY PROGRAM WAS NOT ASSIGNED THE CORRECT TYPE
SR-A   METHOD FOR ENTERING SUBPROGRAM PRODUCES UNDEFINED VALUE FOR CALL-BY-LOCATION PARAMETER

SUBSCRIPTS

SS-0   ZERO SUBSCRIPT OR DIMENSION NOT ALLOWED
SS-1   ARRAY SUBSCRIPT EXCEEDS DIMENSION
SS-2   INVALID SUBSCRIPT FORM
SS-3   SUBSCRIPT IS OUT OF RANGE

STATEMENTS AND STATEMENT NUMBERS

ST-0	MISSING STATEMENT NUMBER
ST-1	STATEMENT NUMBER GREATER THAN 99999
ST-2	STATEMENT NUMBER HAS ALREADY BEEN DEFINED
ST-3	UNDECODABLE STATEMENT
ST-4	UNNUMBERED EXECUTABLE STATEMENT FOLLOWS A TRANSFER
ST-5	STATEMENT NUMBER IN A TRANSFER IS A NON-EXECUTABLE STATEMENT
ST-6	ONLY CALL STATEMENTS MAY CONTAIN STATEMENT NUMBER ARGUMENTS
ST-7	STATEMENT SPECIFIED IN A TRANSFER STATEMENT IS A FORMAT STATEMENT
ST-8	MISSING FORMAT STATEMENT
ST-9	SPECIFICATION STATEMENT DOES NOT PRECEDE STATEMENT FUNCTION DEFINITIONS OR EXECUTABLE STATEMENTS
ST-A	UNREFERENCED STATEMENT FOLLOWS A TRANSFER
ST-B	STATEMENT NUMBER MUST END WITH COLON. STATEMENT NUMBER WAS IGNORED

SUBSCRIPTED VARIABLES

SV-0	THE WRONG NUMBER OF SUBSCRIPTS WERE SPECIFIED FOR A VARIABLE
SV-1	AN ARRAY OR SUBPROGRAM NAME IS USED INCORRECTLY WITHOUT A LIST
SV-2	MORE THAN 7 DIMENSIONS ARE NOT ALLOWED
SV-3	DIMENSION OR SUBSCRIPT TOO LARGE (MAXIMUM $10**8-1$)
SV-4	A VARIABLE USED WITH VARIABLE DIMENSIONS IS NOT A SUBPROGRAM PARAMETER
SV-5	A VARIABLE DIMENSION IS NOT ONE OF SIMPLE INTEGER VARIABLE, SUBPROGRAM PARAMETER, IN COMMON

SYNTAX ERRORS

SX-0	MISSING OPERATOR
SX-1	EXPECTING OPERATOR
SX-2	EXPECTING SYMBOL
SX-3	EXPECTING SYMBOL OR OPERATOR
SX-4	EXPECTING CONSTANT
SX-5	EXPECTING SYMBOL OR CONSTANT
SX-6	EXPECTING STATEMENT NUMBER
SX-7	EXPECTING SIMPLE INTEGER VARIABLE
SX-8	EXPECTING SIMPLE INTEGER VARIABLE OR CONSTANT
SX-9	ILLEGAL SEQUENCE OF OPERATORS IN EXPRESSION
SX-A	EXPECTING END-OF-STATEMENT

TYPE STATEMENTS

TY-0	THE VARIABLE HAS ALREADY BEEN EXPLICITLY TYPED
TY-1	THE LENGTH OF THE EQUIVALENCED VARIABLE MAY NOT BE CHANGED REMEDY: INTERCHANGE TYPE AND EQUIVALENCE STATEMENTS

I/O OPERATIONS

UN-0	CONTROL CARD ENCOUNTERED ON UNIT 5 AT EXECUTION. PROBABLE CAUSE: MISSING DATA OR INCORRECT FORMAT
UN-1	END OF FILE ENCOUNTERED (IBM CODE IHC217)
UN-2	I/O ERROR (IBM CODE IHC218)
UN-3	NO DD STATEMENT WAS SUPPLIED (IBM CODE IHC219)

UN-4	REWIND, ENDFILE, BACKSPACE REFERENCES UNIT 5, 6 OR 7
UN-5	ATTEMPT TO READ ON UNIT 5 AFTER IT HAS HAD END-OF-FILE
UN-6	AN INVALID VARIABLE UNIT NUMBER WAS DETECTED (IBM CODE IHC220)
UN-7	PAGE-LIMIT EXCEEDED
UN-8	ATTEMPT TO DO DIRECT ACCESS I/O ON A SEQUENTIAL FILE OR VICE VERSA. POSSIBLE MISSING DEFINE FILE STATEMENT (IBM CODE IHC231)
UN-9	WRITE REFERENCES 5 OR READ REFERENCES 6 OR 7
UN-A	DEFINE FILE REFERENCES A UNIT PREVIOUSLY USED FOR SEQUENTIAL I/O (IBM CODE IHC235)
UN-B	RECORD SIZE FOR UNIT EXCEEDS 32767, OR DIFFERS FROM DD STATEMENT SPECIFICATION (IBM CODE IHC233, IHC237)
UN-C	FOR DIRECT ACCESS I/O THE RELATIVE RECORD POSITION IS NEGATIVE, ZERO, OR TOO LARGE (IBM CODE IHC232)
UN-D	AN ATTEMPT WAS MADE TO READ MORE INFORMATION THAN LOGICAL RECORD CONTAINS (IBM CODE IHC236)
UN-E	FORMATTED LINE EXCEEDS BUFFER LENGTH (IBM CODE IHC212)
UN-F	I/O ERROR – SEARCHING LIBRARY DIRECTORY
UN-G	I/O ERROR – READING LIBRARY
UN-H	ATTEMPT TO DEFINE THE OBJECT ERROR FILE AS A DIRECT ACCESS FILE (IBM CODE IHC234)
UN-I	RECFM IS NOT V(B)S FOR I/O WITHOUT FORMAT CONTROL (IBM CODE IHC214)
UN-J	MISSING DD CARD FOR WATLIB. NO LIBRARY ASSUMED
UN-K	ATTEMPT TO READ OR WRITE PAST THE END OF CHARACTER VARIABLE BUFFER
UN-L	ATTEMPT TO READ ON AN UNCREATED DIRECT ACCESS FILE (IHC236)

UNDEFINED VARIABLES

UV-0	VARIABLE IS UNDEFINED
UV-3	SUBSCRIPT IS UNDEFINED
UV-4	SUBPROGRAM IS UNDEFINED
UV-5	ARGUMENT IS UNDEFINED
UV-6	UNDECODABLE CHARACTERS IN VARIABLE FORMAT

VARIABLE NAMES

VA-0	A NAME IS TOO LONG. IT HAS BEEN TRUNCATED TO SIX CHARACTERS
VA-1	ATTEMPT TO USE AN ASSIGNED OR INITIALIZED VARIABLE OR DO-PARAMETER IN A SPECIFICATION STATEMENT
VA-2	ILLEGAL USE OF A SUBROUTINE NAME
VA-3	ILLEGAL USE OF A VARIABLE NAME
VA-4	ATTEMPT TO USE THE PREVIOUSLY DEFINED NAME AS A FUNCTION OR AN ARRAY
VA-5	ATTEMPT TO USE A PREVIOUSLY DEFINED NAME AS A SUBROUTINE
VA-6	ATTEMPT TO USE A PREVIOUSLY DEFINED NAME AS A SUBPROGRAM
VA-7	ATTEMPT TO USE A PREVIOUSLY DEFINED NAME AS A COMMON BLOCK
VA-8	ATTEMPT TO USE A FUNCTION NAME AS A VARIABLE
VA-9	ATTEMPT TO USE A PREVIOUSLY DEFINED NAME AS A VARIABLE
VA-A	ILLEGAL USE OF A PREVIOUSLY DEFINED NAME

EXTERNAL STATEMENT

XT-0	A VARIABLE HAS ALREADY APPEARED IN AN EXTERNAL STATEMENT

*

Answers to Exercises

ANSWERS TO EXERCISES 1 3

1 Making "Pineapple Sliders"—Verbal Description

Sift together

    1 cup all purpose flour

    1 tsp. baking powder

    1/4 tsp. salt

In a separate bowl mix together (with wire whip)

    2 eggs

    1/2 cup granulated sugar

    1/2 cup brown sugar

Add

    1 tsp. vanilla

    1/2 cup chopped walnuts

    1 8 oz. can, crushed, unsweetened pineapple (drained)

Slowly add the flour mixture and blend thoroughly.

Bake in a slightly greased 8" square aluminum pan for 30 minutes at 350°.

Cool on rack for 5 minutes and cut into bars.

Roll in confectioner's sugar while warm.

"Pineapple Sliders" courtesy of C.M. Drotos.

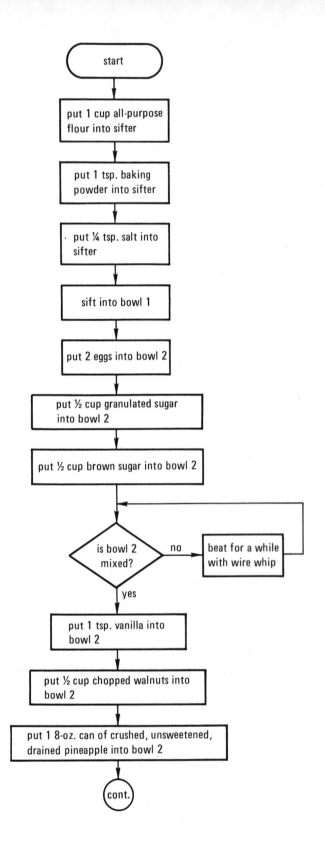

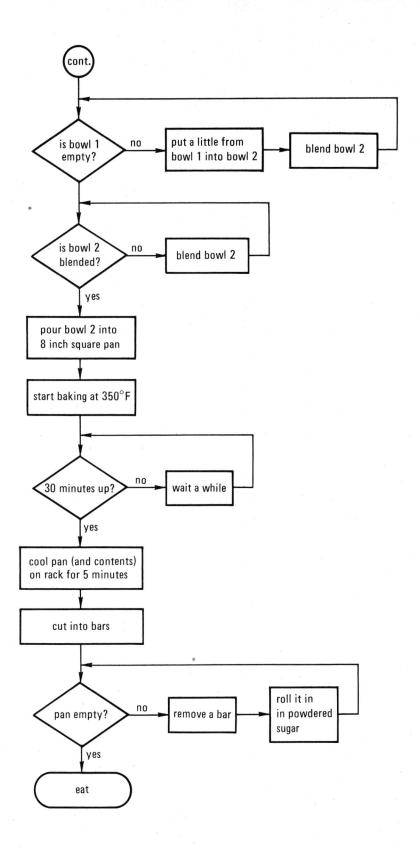

ANSWERS TO EXERCISES 1 4

3 controller: executes statements of program

memory: cells in which instructions and data are stored

I/O: provides for communication between human and computer

4 The memory cell is a device which stores information; its name allows us to locate it for purposes of examining or changing its contents; its value is what's in it at a point in time.

ANSWERS TO EXERCISES 1 5

1 Add the following statement between STATEMENT 1 and STATEMENT 2

STATEMENT 1.5 Look at the value in memory cell B. If it is less than zero, stop.

2 We will need several memory cells: SUM to store the running total of the numbers, N to keep track of the number of numbers, NUM to store the numbers, one at a time, and ST1, ST2, . . . , ST9 in which to store the statements.

card number	memory cell which stores this statement	statement
1	ST1	Store 0 in SUM
2	ST2	Store 0 in N
3	ST3	Remove top card from the card reader stack; copy the number on it into NUM. Discard the card. (If there were no cards, get next instruction from ST7.)
4	ST4	Look at the values in NUM and SUM, add them together, and store the result in SUM.
5	ST5	Look at the value in N, add 1 and store the result in N.
6	ST6	Get your next instruction from ST3.
7	ST7	Look at the values in SUM and N, divide the former by the latter, and store the result in SUM.
8	ST8	Send the string "AVERAGE IS", followed by the number in SUM to the printer.
9	ST9	Stop.
10	none	Comment: End of program. Now comes the data.
11	none	14
12	none	17
13	none	3
14	none	-4
15	none	8

3 We will need several memory cells: LONGEST to store the longest name seen, NAME to store the names on the cards, one at a time, and ST1, ST2, . . . , ST6 to store the statements of the program.

card number	memory cell which stores the statement	statement
1	ST1	Remove the top card from the card reader stack and copy the character string on it into LONGEST. Discard the card.
2	ST2	Remove the top card from the card reader stack and copy the value on it into NAME. Discard the card. (If there were no cards on the card reader stack, get your next instruction from ST5.
3	ST3	Look at the strings in LONGEST and NAME and copy the longer one into LONGEST.
4	ST4	Get your next instruction from ST2.
5	ST5	Send the string "THE LONGEST NAME IS", followed by the value of LONGEST, to the printer.
6	ST6	Stop
7	none	Comment: End of program. Now comes the data.
8	none	J E Birk
9	none	D E Farmer
10	none	P Das
11	none	P G McCrea
12	none	C C Cheung
13	none	D L Milgram

ANSWERS TO EXERCISES 2 1

1 23SKIDOO is illegal because it starts with a digit.

SKIDOO23, BATMAN13, TONY THE TIGER and FORTRAN are illegal because they have more than six characters.

TORQUE and JUICE are legal memory cell names.

2 INTEGER VERYLONG is illegal because the memory cell name is too long.

INTERGER Q is illegal because INTEGER is misspelled.

3 `INTEGER AJAX, FOAM`

4 41.7, 31.8, −493.1 are not INTEGERs.

5 `CHARACTER*47 A, B, C`

6 They are all legitimate and have lengths 14, 1, 5, 7, 11, and 16, respectively.

ANSWERS TO EXERCISES 2 2

1   A and B are 10 and 2, respectively.

2   Memory cell B takes on the values 24, 3, and −38 at successive points in time (B contains only one of the values at a time, of course).

3   −AT = 2 and CAT + DOG = FIGHT are illegal because their left hand sides are expressions rather than memory cell names. CAT + DOG − 3, of course, is hopelessly illegal since it doesn't even have an assignment operator.

4   SOUP contains, at successive points in time, the values 15, 61, 1, 2, and 0.

5
```
INTEGER FIRST
FIRST = 2
FIRST = FIRST*4
FIRST = FIRST + 1
```

6   A │ WAIT │   B │ WALK │   P │ , │

7   B is assigned a value containing 15 characters, but only 6 will fit. The first six characters, "RUMPLE", are put in B and a warning message is issued.

8   A, B, C, and D are TO*b*OWE, TOO*b*WE, *b*BATS*b*, and BATS*bb*. respectively (*b* stands for blank). Note that no two of the values are the same. Blank characters are significant parts of CHARACTER*n* values.

ANSWERS TO EXERCISES 2 3

1   The second is illegal because the expression (X + Y)*2 starts with a parenthesis. The others are OK.

2
```
      PRINT, 'BASE PRICE    $', 4127
      PRINT, '     RADIO    $', 232
      PRINT, '   SPOILER    $', 248
      PRINT, ' '
      PRINT, 'TOTAL PRICE   $', 4127 + 232 + 248
      PRINT, '         TAX  $', +(4127 + 232 + 248)/50
      PRINT, ' '
      PRINT, 'PLEASE PAY CASHIER    $', 4127+232+248+
     +                                 (4127+232+248)/50
      STOP
      END
```

```
output

BASE PRICE    $          4127
     RADIO    $           232
   SPOILER    $           248

TOTAL PRICE   $          4607
       TAX    $            92

PLEASE PAY CASHIER    $        4699
```

ANSWERS TO EXERCISES 2 4

1 data for bank balance program

   data

```
             125
             427
            2792
           13200
             942
          -23726
               0
```

   output

```
    NEW BALANCE IS          6490 CENTS
```

2 READ, A, A + B, 2 is illegal; A + B and 2 are values, not memory cell names.

   PRINT A, B is illegal; it needs a comma after PRINT.

   PRINT, (A + B) is illegal, (A + B) starts with a parenthesis. The others are OK.

3
```
    INTEGER A, B, C, D
    READ, A, B, C, D
    PRINT, A+B+C+D
    STOP
    END
```

   data
```
10 15  7 13
```

   output
```
       45
```

ANSWERS TO EXERCISES 3 2

1 The first two statements are OK.

   The third statement contains the illegal relation .EG.

   The fourth statement contains the illegal relation .SGT.

   The last statement lacks parentheses and has an illegal comma. It should look like this

```
IF ( Y .EQ. 0)  GO TO 20
```

2
```
    INTEGER BALNCE, TRANS
    READ, BALNCE
20  READ, TRANS
    IF ( TRANS .EQ. 0 )  GO TO 30
    BALNCE = BALNCE - TRANS
    GO TO 20
30  PRINT, BALNCE
    STOP
    END
```

```
        data
         45603
         7836
        -2539
         4525
          4522
        -7542
               0


        output
                38801
```

ANSWERS TO EXERCISES 3 3

1 `IF ( PRICE .GT. 99999.0 )  GO TO 20`

   Note: It is not wise to test for exact equality of REALs because they are represented to limited precision.

2
```
        INTEGER FIVES
        FIVES = 0
10      FIVES = FIVES + 5
          PRINT, FIVES
          IF ( FIVES .LT. 100 )  GO TO 10
        STOP
        END
```

   output
```
                 5
                10
                15
                20
                25
                30
                35
                40
                45
                50
                55
                60
                65
                70
                75
                80
                85
                90
                95
               100
```

3 Change the loop as shown below. (*Note:* we don't recommend this in practice. It is not straightforward and involves extra calculation which could affect accuracy.)

```
          .
          .
          .
10     READ, PRICE, WGT
          SUM = SUM + PRICE/WGT
          N = N + 1
          IF ( PRICE .GT. 0.00 )  GO TO 10
C      FIX SUM AND N TO GET RID OF PHONEY VALUE
          SUM = SUM - PRICE/WGT
          N = N - 1
          .
          .
          .
```

4 The loop in the bank balance program of Section 3 2 and the one of the Exercise 3 have the same post-test form, following our loop writing suggestions. However, they both unfortunately add phoney values into the sums they are computing. In the bank balance program the phoney value didn't affect the sum, which was lucky. In the detergent program, the SUM and N were both affected by the extra iteration and had to be corrected after exit from the loop. Besides taking time and making the program obscure, the extra computation could cause inaccuracies. For these reasons, the loop which avoids adding the phoney values seems better, even though it doesn't quite follow the loop writing suggestions. *Note:* it's not too far off base to think of the IF statement testing for termination values right after the READ as a part of the READing process, a "conditional READ" in a sense. In this sense, the loop which avoids extra iteration is a pre-test loop.

ANSWERS TO EXERCISES 3 4

1 With length 78, whatever string the user punches on the card (80 columns, with 2 columns taken up by quote marks) will fit into the memory cell.

```
2      CHARACTER*78 NAME
          INTEGER BALNCE, TRANS
100    READ, NAME
          IF ( NAME .EQ. 'END OF DATA' )  STOP
          PRINT, ' '
          PRINT, NAME
          READ, BALNCE
          PRINT, BALNCE, 'PREVIOUS BALANCE'
          PRINT, 'TRANSACTIONS'
150    READ, TRANS
          IF ( TRANS .EQ. 0 )  GO TO 160
          IF ( TRANS .GT. 0 )  PRINT, TRANS
          IF ( TRANS .LT. 0 )  PRINT, -TRANS,'DEPOSIT'
          BALNCE = BALNCE - TRANS
          GO TO 150
160    PRINT,        BALNCE , 'FINAL BALANCE'
          GO TO 100
          END
```

```
data
'F. DAVID LESLEY'
 45632
  2298
  3354
-29155
  5439
  0000
'VERNOR VINGE'
 33252
  2203
-32941
  2211
  0000
'END OF DATA'

output
F. DAVID LESLEY
        45632 PREVIOUS BALANCE
TRANSACTIONS
         2298
         3354
        29155 DEPOSIT
         5439
        63696 FINAL BALANCE

VERNOR VINGE
        33252 PREVIOUS BALANCE
TRANSACTIONS
         2203
        32941 DEPOSIT
         2211
        61779 FINAL BALANCE
```

ANSWERS TO EXERCISES 4 2

1 12 + 2 and 4 * 2 are INTEGER expressions; the term constant is restricted to values involving no computations and no memory cells.

12.75, 1.0, −127.5, are REAL constants. The others are INTEGER constants.

2 2 and +2 are INTEGER constants

−2.01E3.2 and 300E30. contain illegal decimal point shift factors

−22E+30 will be accepted as a REAL constant even though it doesn't have a decimal point.

3 REALs in WATFIV are of a fixed, finite precision; hence, they are actually a restricted form of rational numbers.

ANSWERS TO EXERCISES 4 3

1 The expression is evaluated like 0 −1**4. Exponentiations are performed before subtractions; hence, the result is −1.

2 MOUSE + (CAT*(DOG**2))
   ((SEX+DRUGS)−(SKIN*FLICK))+(BUSTER**(BROWN**SHOES))
   (ROCK/ER)/FELLOW

3 Negative values can't be raised to REAL powers

4 2.0, 2.0, 0.0, 4.0, 4.0

5 AB is a single identifier in WATFIV.

ANSWERS TO EXERCISES 4 4

1 `IABS(MINO(-2, -3, 149*79675/1888))`

```
IABS(              -3                )
```

3

2 Replace the 4 statements between the comments by the statement

```
PRINT, 'LARGEST IS',
+         AMAX1(ALOG(1.E+2),SQRT(144.),SIN(3.14159))
```

ANSWERS TO EXERCISES 4 6

1 a (2.8, −7.4)

b (−1.0, 0.0)

c the COMPLEX number whose real part is the value contained in A and whose imaginary part is the value of B

d the complex conjugate of ZETA

2 No

ANSWERS TO EXERCISES 4 7

1 All of them

2 *'bbbbbbbb'* (8 blanks)
'147*SQRT' (and a warning)
'WENDOVER' (and a warning)
'NORTHERN' (and a warning)

3 CENTURION

ANSWERS TO EXERCISES 4 8

1 .TRUE.
.TRUE.
.FALSE.
.TRUE.
.FALSE.
.TRUE.

2 `IF ( X .GT. 0 .AND. X .LT. 10 ) STOP`

3 `IF ( X .GT. 10 .OR. X .LT. 0 ) STOP`

4 `(A .AND. .NOT. B) .OR. (B .AND. .NOT. A)`

5 You would need to change the declaration

```
INTEGER A, B, C
```

to

```
REAL A, B, C
```

so the program would make A, B, and C be REAL memory cells. Also, statement 200 should be changed. Because of the loss of accuracy caused by finite memory cell length, REALs should not be compared for strict equality. Better and safer would be

```
200  PYTHAG = ABS( (A**2+B**2-C**2)/C**2 ) .LE. 1.E-6
```

which gives PYTHAG the value .TRUE. if A**2 + B**2 equals C**2 to within the accuracy of REAL numbers—a little more than six decimal places.

ANSWERS TO EXERCISES 6 1

1 If the values in memory cells I and J are the same and that value is a legal subscript for B, then B(I) and B(J) denote the same cell.

2

0	1	1	2	3
5	8	13	21	34

3

B(3) = B(I)	legal; but since I has the value 3, nothing is changed
B(I) = B(I-1)	legal; changes value of B(3) to value contained in B(2)
B(J) = B(2*I)	legal; changes value of B(7) to value contained in B(6)
B(2*I) = B(J+4)	illegal; B(J + 4) refers to B(11), which doesn't exist
B(4) = B(J-1) + B(I*J-21)	illegal; B(I*J−21) refers to B(0), which doesn't exist
B(1.7) = 0	legal; fractional part of REAL subscript is ignored, hence the value of B(1) becomes zero

4 No arrays would be needed, as shown in the program below.

```
COMMENT--PROGRAM TO LIST THE WESTERN STATES, THEIR
C        SALES TAX RATES, AND THE AVERAGE RATE OVER THE
C        WESTERN STATES
         CHARACTER*10 S
         REAL T, SUM, AVE
         INTEGER N
C
         SUM = 0.0
         N = 0
  100 READ, S, T
         PRINT, S, T
         SUM = SUM + T
         N = N+1
         IF ( N .LT. 11 ) GO TO 100
```

```
C
      AVE = SUM/11.0
C
      PRINT, ' '
      PRINT, 'AVERAGE WESTERN STATES SALES TAX IS', AVE
      STOP
      END
```

data

'WASHINGTON'	0.045
'IDAHO '	0.03
'MONTANA '	0.00
'OREGON '	0.04
'WYOMING '	0.03
'CALIFORNIA'	0.06
'NEVADA '	0.03
'UTAH '	0.04
'COLORADO '	0.03
'ARIZONA '	0.04
'NEW MEXICO'	0.04

output

WASHINGTON	0.4500000E-01
IDAHO	0.3000000E-01
MONTANA	0.0000000E 00
OREGON	0.4000000E-01
WYOMING	0.3000000E-01
CALIFORNIA	0.6000000E-01
NEVADA	0.3000000E-01
UTAH	0.4000000E-01
COLORADO	0.3000000E-01
ARIZONA	0.4000000E-01
NEW MEXICO	0.4000000E-01

AVERAGE WESTERN STATES SALES TAX IS   0.3499997E-01

5 REAL A(10)	legal
INTEGER A(13-2)	illegal; no computation allowed in length declarator
INTEGER A(I)	illegal; no variable allowed in length declarator
REAL A(150), BOK(3472)	legal
REAL X(15.0)	illegal; length declarator must be INTEGER
LOGICAL QS(23), PS(47)	legal

ANSWERS TO EXERCISES 6 2

1 We need 12 cells in the arrays because the information on the 'END DATA' card will have to be stored somewhere. Since there will be up to 11 response cards, we need 12 cells to include the information from the 'END DATA' card.

2 The READ list includes an element of the array T; therefore, the card must contain a value to put into that memory cell.

3 Change the STORE DATA and COMPUTE AVERAGE sections of the program as shown below.

```
C          STORE DATA
        SUM = 0.0
        N = 0
 100    READ, S(N+1), T(N+1)
        IF ( S(N+1) .EQ. 'END DATA' )  GO TO 200
        SUM = SUM + S(N+1)
        N = N+1
        GO TO 100
 200    AVE = SUM/N
```

4 Since N will be zero when the computer reaches the COMPUTE AVER-AGE section of the program the computer will attempt to divide by zero, resulting in an error. To avoid this, change the statements between statements 200 and 210 in the program to the ones below.

```
 200    IF ( N .NE. 0)  GO TO 205
        PRINT, 'NO DATA FOR TAX PROGRAM'
        STOP
 205    SUM = 0.0
        K = 1
```

5 Change the statement GO TO 100 in the STORE DATA section of the program to the following sequence of statements.

```
IF ( N .LE. 11 )  GO TO 100
  PRINT, 'ONLY', N-1, 'RESPONSE CARDS ALLOWED'
  PRINT, 'YOU HAVE INCLUDED TOO MANY'
  STOP
```

6 Increase the length of the arrays S and T to 51.

7
```
COMMENT--PROGRAM TO LIST THE WESTERN STATES WITH
C          BELOW AVERAGE SALES TAX RATES
        CHARACTER*10 S1,S2,S3,S4,S5,S6,S7,S8,S9,S10,S11
        REAL T1,T2,T3,T4,T5,T6,T7,T8,T9,T10,T11, SUM, AVE
C
C       SET ALL TAX RATES TO ZERO SO THAT UNUSED CELLS
C       WILL NOT CONTRIBUTE TO SUM IN STATEMENT 200
        T1 = T2 = T3 = T4 = T5 =    0.0
        T6 = T7 = T8 = T9 = T10=T11=0.0
```

```
C
C       STORE DATA AND ACCUMULATE SUM
        SUM = 0.0
        N = 0
        READ, S1 , T1
        IF ( S1  .EQ. 'END DATA' )  GO TO 200
        N = N+1
        READ, S2 , T2
        IF ( S2  .EQ. 'END DATA' )  GO TO 200
        N = N+1
        READ, S3 , T3
        IF ( S3  .EQ. 'END DATA' )  GO TO 200
        N = N+1
        READ, S4 , T4
        IF ( S4  .EQ. 'END DATA' )  GO TO 200
        N = N+1
        READ, S5 , T5
        IF ( S5  .EQ. 'END DATA' )  GO TO 200
        N = N+1
        READ, S6 , T6
        IF ( S6  .EQ. 'END DATA' )  GO TO 200
        N = N+1
        READ, S7 , T7
        IF ( S7  .EQ. 'END DATA' )  GO TO 200
        N = N+1
        READ, S8 , T8
        IF ( S8  .EQ. 'END DATA' )  GO TO 200
        N = N+1
        READ, S9 , T9
        IF ( S9  .EQ. 'END DATA' )  GO TO 200
        N = N+1
        READ, S10, T10
        IF ( S10 .EQ. 'END DATA' )  GO TO 200
        N = N+1
        READ, S11, T11
        IF ( S11 .EQ. 'END DATA' )  GO TO 200
        N = N+1
C
200     AVE = (T1+T2+T3+T4+T5+T6+T7+T8+T9+T10+T11)/N
C
        PRINT, 'STATES WITH BELOW AVERAGE SALES TAX'
        PRINT, ' '
        IF ( T1  .LE. AVE .AND. N .GE. 1  ) PRINT, S1
        IF ( T2  .LE. AVE .AND. N .GE. 2  ) PRINT, S2
        IF ( T3  .LE. AVE .AND. N .GE. 3  ) PRINT, S3
        IF ( T4  .LE. AVE .AND. N .GE. 4  ) PRINT, S4
        IF ( T5  .LE. AVE .AND. N .GE. 5  ) PRINT, S5
        IF ( T6  .LE. AVE .AND. N .GE. 6  ) PRINT, S6
        IF ( T7  .LE. AVE .AND. N .GE. 7  ) PRINT, S7
        IF ( T8  .LE. AVE .AND. N .GE. 8' ) PRINT, S8
        IF ( T9  .LE. AVE .AND. N .GE. 9  ) PRINT, S9
        IF ( T10 .LE. AVE .AND. N .GE. 10 ) PRINT, S10
        IF ( T11 .LE. AVE .AND. N .GE. 11 ) PRINT, S11
        STOP
        END
```

```
data
'WASHINGTON'     0.045
'IDAHO      '    0.03
'MONTANA    '    0.00
'OREGON     '    0.04
'WYOMING    '    0.03
'CALIFORNIA'     0.06
'NEVADA     '    0.03
'UTAH       '    0.04
'COLORADO   '    0.03
'ARIZONA    '    0.04
'NEW MEXICO'.    0.04
'END DATA   '    0.00
```

output
```
STATES WITH BELOW AVERAGE SALES TAX

IDAHO
MONTANA
WYOMING
NEVADA
COLORADO
```

Imagine changing this program to handle all fifty states!

```
8  COMMENT--MAKE A BAR GRAPH FROM DISTANCE DATA.
        INTEGER BAR(6), NUMB
        REAL DIST
   COMMENT--INITIALIZE BAR HEIGHTS
        BAR(1) = BAR(2) = BAR(3) = 0
        BAR(4) = BAR(5) = BAR(6) = 0
   COMMENT--READ IN A DISTANCE.  IF IT'S NEGATIVE, THEN
   C         THERE ARE NO MORE DISTANCES IN THE DATA.
    10    READ, DIST
            IF ( DIST .LT. 0.0 )  GO TO 200
   C         CONVERT THE DISTANCE INTO AN INTEGER. DROP FRACTION.
            NUMB = DIST
   C         INCREMENT APPROPRIATE BAR COUNTER
            IF ( NUMB .LE. 5 )  GO TO 20
              PRINT, 'DISTANCE', DIST, 'IS OUT OF RANGE.'
              GO TO 10
    20        BAR(NUMB+1) = BAR(NUMB+1) + 1
              GO TO 10
   COMMENT--STOP READING CARDS.  WE'RE READY TO PRINT.
    200  PRINT, ' '
         PRINT, 'BAR          HEIGHT'
         PRINT, ' 0', BAR(1)
         PRINT, ' 1', BAR(2)
         PRINT, ' 2', BAR(3)
         PRINT, ' 3', BAR(4)
         PRINT, ' 4', BAR(5)
         PRINT, ' 5', BAR(6)
         STOP
         END
```

```
        data
        1.9
        0.4
        0.9
        3.9
       17.5
        2.8
        4.5
        4.1
        3.2
        5.8
        6.9
        4.5
        3.7
        2.9
        5.2
       -1.0


        output
        DISTANCE     0.1750000E 02 IS OUT OF RANGE.
        DISTANCE     0.6900000E 01 IS OUT OF RANGE.

        BAR          HEIGHT
         0              2
         1              1
         2              2
         3              3
         4              3
         5              2
```

ANSWERS TO EXERCISES 6 4

```
  1  COMMENT--PROGRAM TO PRINT POLITICAL POLL SUMMARIES
            REAL POLL(7,5), AVERGE, SUM
            INTEGER COLUMN, ROW, I
      C     STORE DATA
            I = 1
     100    READ, ROW, COLUMN, POLL(ROW,COLUMN)
            I = I+1
            IF ( I .LE. 35 )  GO TO 100

      C
      C     COMPUTE AVERAGE SUPPORT IN EAST-WEST SLICES OF AREA
      C
      C     START WITH ROW 1 AND AVERAGE ONE ROW AT A TIME
            ROW = 1
     200    SUM = 0.0
            COLUMN = 1
     250    SUM = SUM + POLL(ROW,COLUMN)
            COLUMN = COLUMN + 1
            IF ( COLUMN .LE. 5 )  GO TO 250
      C     FINISHED SUMMING ROW--COMPUTE AVERAGE
            AVERGE = SUM/5.0
            PRINT, 'THE AVERAGE SUPPORT IN SLICE', ROW
            PRINT, 'FROM THE NORTH IS', AVERGE, 'PER CENT'
            PRINT, ' '
            ROW = ROW + 1
            IF ( ROW .LE. 7 )  GO TO 200

      C
      C
            PRINT, ' '
      C
      C
```

2 C   COMPUTE AVERAGE SUPPORT IN SOUTHEAST QUARTER
  C   START WITH ROW 4 AND AVERAGE ONE HALF ROW AT A TIME
        ROW = 4
300   SUM = 0.0
          COLUMN = 1
350   SUM = SUM + POLL(ROW,COLUMN)
            COLUMN = COLUMN + 1
            IF (COLUMN .LE. 3) GO TO 350
          ROW = ROW + 1
          IF (ROW .LE. 7) GO TO 300
        PRINT, 'AVERAGE SUPPORT IN SOUTHEAST QUARTER IS',
       +   SUM/(4.0*3.0)
        STOP
        END

data
    1   1   21.0
    1   2   35.3
    1   3   27.4
    1   4   47.8
    1   5   35.2
    2   1   28.7
    2   2   34.5
    2   3   45.7
    2   4   45.3
    2   5   51.4
    3   1   38.7
    3   2   45.2
    3   3   48.7
    3   4   68.7
    3   5   57.5
    4   1   22.1
    4   2   35.8
    4   3   25.8
    4   4   22.1
    4   5   12.8
    5   1   18.9
    5   2   46.2
    5   3   14.3
    5   4   10.5
    5   5   08.3
    6   1   12.4
    6   2   14.8
    6   3   22.3
    6   4   34.1
    6   5   28.4
    7   1   16.8
    7   2   24.7
    7   3   27.5
    7   4   29.2
    7   5   19.7

output

```
THE AVERAGE SUPPORT IN SLICE            1
FROM THE NORTH IS    0.3334000E 02 PER CENT

THE AVERAGE SUPPORT IN SLICE            2
FROM THE NORTH IS    0.4112000E 02 PER CENT

THE AVERAGE SUPPORT IN SLICE            3
FROM THE NORTH IS    0.5175995E 02 PER CENT

THE AVERAGE SUPPORT IN SLICE            4
FROM THE NORTH IS    0.2372000E 02 PER CENT

THE AVERAGE SUPPORT IN SLICE            5
FROM THE NORTH IS    0.1963998E 02 PER CENT

THE AVERAGE SUPPORT IN SLICE            6
FROM THE NORTH IS    0.2239999E 02 PER CENT

THE AVERAGE SUPPORT IN SLICE            7
FROM THE NORTH IS    0.2357999E 02 PER CENT


AVERAGE SUPPORT IN SOUTHEAST QUARTER IS    0.5750000E 01
```

3 Add the declarations

```
INTEGER FOR, AGIN, SBLOCK, EBLOCK
REAL RFOR, RAGIN
```

and change statement 100 to the following sequence of statements

```
100  READ, SBLOCK, EBLOCK, FOR, AGIN
C        COMPUTE SUBSCRIPTS CORRESPONDING TO BLOCK NUMBERS
         ROW = SBLOCK/100 - 20
         COLUMN = EBLOCK/100 - 47
C        CONVERT VOTES FOR AND AGAINST TO REALS FOR DIVISION
         RFOR = FLOAT(FOR)
         RAGIN = FLOAT(AGIN)
         POLL(ROW,COLUMN) = 100.0*RFOR/(RFOR+RAGIN)
```

4 `INTEGER A(100,3), B(3,100),I`   legal; declares two INTEGER arrays A and B

`REAL QRT(3,49)`   legal; declares a REAL array QRT

`LOGICAL P(10), Q(4,2)`   legal; declares two LOGICAL arrays P and Q

`REAL X(N,100)`   illegal; length declarators must be constants

5 `A(4,2) = 0`   legal

`B(4,2) = 1`   illegal; 4 is too large

`A(3,50) = 0`   illegal; 50 is too large

`I = 10`

`Q(I/3,I-8) = .TRUE.`   legal

`P(8) = Q(3,2)`   legal

ANSWERS TO EXERCISES 6 5

1 There are many ways this can be done. One is to replace the statement
AGECD = AGE – 17 in the input section by the following series of statements.

```
          INTEGER C(12,3,2)
          INTEGER AGE
          CHARACTER*10 AFIL
          CHARACTER*5  HAIR
          INTEGER AGECD, AFILCD, HAIRCD, S
C
C         INITIALIZE COUNTERS
          AGECD = 0
  100     AGECD = AGECD + 1
             C(AGECD,1,1) = 0
             C(AGECD,2,1) = 0
             C(AGECD,3,1) = 0
             C(AGECD,1,2) = 0
             C(AGECD,2,2) = 0
             C(AGECD,3,2) = 0
             IF ( AGECD .LT. 12 )  GO TO 100
C
C         GET DATA AND COMPUTE CLASS COUNTS
  200     READ, AGE, AFIL, HAIR
             IF ( AGE .EQ. 0 )  GO TO 300
             IF ( (AGE .GE. 18 .AND. AGE .LE. 29)
        +    .AND. (AFIL .EQ. 'REPUBLICAN'
        +             .OR. AFIL .EQ. 'DEMOCRAT'
        +                .OR. AFIL .EQ. 'OTHER')
        +    .AND. (HAIR .EQ. 'LONG'
        +             .OR. HAIR .EQ. 'SHORT') )  GO TO 210
               PRINT, 'INVALID DATA', AGE, AFIL, HAIR
               GO TO 200
  210        AGECD = AGE - 17
             AFILCD = 3
             IF ( AFIL .EQ. 'REPUBLICAN' )  AFILCD = 1
             IF ( AFIL .EQ. 'DEMOCRAT ' )  AFILCD = 2
             HAIRCD = 1
             IF ( HAIR .EQ. 'LONG ' ) HAIRCD = 2
             C(AGECD,AFILCD,HAIRCD) = C(AGECD,AFILCD,HAIRCD) + 1
             GO TO 200
```

2
```
  300     PRINT, 'THERE ARE',
        +        C(29-17,1,2)+C(29-17,2,2)+C(29-17,3,2),
        +        '29-YEAR-OLD LONG HAIRED MEMBERS'
C
C
          PRINT, ' '
```

3
```
          S = C(21-17,1,1)+C(21-17,1,2)+
        +     C(21-17,2,1)+C(21-17,2,2)+
        +     C(21-17,3,1)+C(21-17,3,2)
          PRINT, 'THERE ARE', S, '21-YEAR-OLD MEMBERS'
C
          STOP
          END
```

data

18	'DEMOCRAT '	'LONG '
20	'OTHER '	'LONG '
26	'DEMOCRAT '	'LONG '
24	'DEMOCRAT '	'LONG '
21	'OTHER '	'SHORT'
21	'REPUBLICAN'	'LONG '
27	'REPUBLICAN'	'SHORT'
27	'DEMOCRAT '	'SHORT'
20	'OTHER '	'LONG '
23	'DEMOCRAT '	'LONG '
22	'OTHER '	'LONG '
28	'DEMOCRAT '	'LONG '
22	'DEMOCRAT '	'SHORT'
27	'REPUBLICAN'	'SHORT'
18	'DEMOCRAT '	'SHORT'
22	'DEMOCRAT '	'SHORT'
29	'DEMOCRAT '	'LONG '
25	'REPUBLICAN'	'LONG '
26	'OTHER '	'SHORT'
24	'DEMOCRAT '	'LONG '
21	'OTHER '	'SHORT'
18	'OTHER '	'LONG '
29	'DEMOCRAT '	'SHORT'
18	'DEMOCRAT '	'SHORT'
29	'REPUBLICAN'	'LONG '
24	'DEMOCRAT '	'LONG '
0	' '	' '

output

```
THERE ARE          2 29-YEAR-OLD LONG HAIRED MEMBERS

THERE ARE          3 21-YEAR-OLD MEMBERS
```

ANSWERS TO EXERCISES 6 6

1
```
   READ, A(1), A(2), A(3), A(4)
   PRINT, A(4), A(6), A(8), A(10), A(12)
   PRINT, A(2), A(6), A(10)
   READ, B(1,1), B(2,1), B(3,1), B(4,1),
  +      B(1,2), B(2,2), B(3,2), B(4,2)
   PRINT, Q, R, S, B(3,1), A(1), S, B(3,2), A(2), BC,
  +       A(1), A(2), A(3), A(4)
```

2
```
   PRINT, (A(I), I=1,5)
   PRINT, (A(I), I=2,10,2)
   PRINT, (I,A(I), I=1,4)

   READ, ( (B(I,J),I=2,3), J=1,3)
```
                        or
```
   READ, (B(2,J), B(3,J), J=1,3)
```

3   `PRINT, (A(J), J=1,N-1)`   N−1 is illegal; expressions not allowed as implied do list parameters

    `READ, (J, A(J), J=1,N)`   implied do list parameters may not be changed while the list is being used, This READ would change J by giving it a value from a data card.

    `PRINT, (A(J), J=1,C(N))`   C(N) is illegal; only constants and *simple* INTEGER variables may be parameters in implied do lists

4 The index K in the implied do list starts at a positive value (the value of ROW) gets incremented by SIZE for each repetition. Therefore, by the time K has been incremented SIZE times, it will exceed N because ROW + SIZE*SIZE is greater than N

5 Declare an INTEGER memory cell SPACE and assign it the value (12 − SIZE)/2 after SIZE has been computed. Change the PRINT statement to

```
PRINT, ('    ',K=1,SPACE), (STR(K),K=ROW,N,SIZE)
```

6 Declare an INTEGER memory cell called STARS and change the lines after statement 300 to those shown below.

```
      STARS = (5*SIZE+3)/2
C     PRINT ASTERISKS FOR TOP ROW--DIVIDE BY 2 BECAUSE
C     '*' PRINTS AS '* '
      PRINT, ('*', K=1,STARS)
C     PRINT ROWS--BEGIN AND END WITH ASTERISKS
  310 PRINT, '*', (STR(K), K=ROW,N,SIZE), '*'
      ROW = ROW + 1
      IF ( ROW .LE. SIZE ) GO TO 310
C     PRINT ASTERISKS ON BOTTOM LINE
      PRINT ('*', K=1,STARS)
      STOP
      END
```

ANSWERS TO EXERCISES 7 2

1 The first two are legal.

The third is illegal. The name POMEGRANATE is too long.

The fourth is illegal. A parameter must be listed by name only. If it is an array, the parameter declarations will say so. If it is only a memory cell, it doesn't need a subscript.

2 They are all legal.

3 It would PRINT the line

    9   16   25

4 It would PRINT

    `A= DOG NONE BAT`

5 It would PRINT

```
SIZES:
        TINY        0.7500000E 01
        BIG         0.1200000E 02
        HUGE        0.1800000E 02
```

6 All you need to do is add this statement at the beginning

```
SUBROUTINE ROMAN (ARABIC, ROMNUM, NUMSYM)
```

and delete the READ statement and the last PRINT statement. Then replace both of the GO TO 100 statements by RETURN statements.

7 Change the statement assigning REM a value to

```
REM = MOD(DIVDND,DIVSOR)
```

ANSWERS TO EXERCISES 7 3

1 Testing for equality of REALs is a risky practice because REAL numbers are the results of physical measurements and physical measurements are never exact. In addition, the computer uses approximations to the REAL numbers you write, some of which can't be represented exactly in the notation the computer uses. Therefore, it makes sense to test for equality of REALs only up to a given precision related to the precision in our measurements. Our FUNCTION EQUAL tests for equality to three decimal places. Changing the number 0.5E–3 to 0.5E–2 reduces the precision of the test to two decimal places.

Usually, physical measurements are accurate not to a given number of decimal places, but instead to some number of significant digits. Therefore a test for equality to a percentage of the size of the numbers being compared would make more sense. The function EQUAL below tests for equality to one part in a hundred.

```
        LOGICAL EQUAL (X,Y)
        REAL SIZE
COMMENT:  COMPUTE RANGE OF NUMBERS TO BE COMPARED
        SIZE = AMAX1(ABS(X),ABS(Y))
COMMENT:  IF BOTH ARE EXACTLY 0.0, THEY'RE EQUAL
        EQUAL = .TRUE.
        IF ( SIZE .EQ. 0.0 ) RETURN
COMMENT:  TEST FOR EQUALITY TO ONE PART IN A HUNDRED
        EQUAL = ABS(X-Y)/SIZE .LT. 0.01
        RETURN
        END
```

2 The cell A will take the values 1.0, 4.0, and then 1.0 again.

3 A FUNCTION must have *at least one parameter*.

4 On zero or negative arguments, FACT returns the value 1.

5
```
REAL FUNCTION OURABS(A)
REAL A
OURABS = A
IF ( OURABS .LT. 0.0 ) OURABS = -OURABS
RETURN
END
```

```
6   INTEGER FUNCTION C(Q,R)
    INTEGER Q, R
    INTEGER FACT
    C = FACT(Q)/(FACT(R)*FACT(Q-R))
    RETURN
    END
```

ANSWERS TO EXERCISES 7 4

1 ONE: legal
   TWO: legal
   THREE: illegal—LENGTH isn't in the parameter list of SUBROUTINE
   THREE, so it can't be used as an array size declarator in THREE's para-
   meter declarations.

2 It is illegal to change the value of an array size declarator. Thus, the
   statement N = N + 1 is illegal.

3 Change the FUNCTION LOCBIG so that the second IF statement
   becomes

```
   IF ( A(I) .LT. A(LOCBIG) )  LOCBIG = I
```

   Note: it would also be nice, although not strictly necessary, to change the
   name of the FUNCTION (and all references to it) to LOCSM since it now
   LOCates the SMallest element in the array.

4 After execution of the CALL statement, the cells ONE and TWO would
   both have whatever value TWO had before execution of the CALL statement.

5 The statement CALL BADSWT (1, 2) lists two constant *values* as arguments, yet the SUBROUTINE BADSWT *changes* the values of the arguments given to it. It is illegal to change the value of a constant.

ANSWERS TO EXERCISES 8 1

1 NUMBER   SQUARED   CUBED
      1   1   1
   will be PRINTed, since the test to see if the index has executed the upper
   bound is placed *after* the statements in the range (post-test).

2 In no way

3 As near as we can tell, eight.   LINE
                                       LINE
                                       LINE
                                       LINE
                                       LINE
                                       LINE
                                       LINE
                                       LINE

ANSWERS TO EXERCISES 8 2

1 Chapter 3:
      None of the loops were counting loops, so DO-loops wouldn't be
      appropriate.

470   *Answers to Exercises*

Section 6 1:

Both the READ loop and the PRINT loop in the last program are counting loops and could profitably be written as DO-loops.

Section 6 2:

The loop which computes the average and the PRINT loop are counting loops and would make good DO-loops. The READ loop, on the other hand, is not a counting loop. It's termination condition does not test the loop index, N, against a predetermined count.

Section 6 4:

All the loops in the political poll program are counting loops and are, therefore, good candidates for DO-loops.

Section 6 5:

The loops of statements 100 and 310 should be written as DO loops, but not the READ loop of statement 200.

Section 6 6:

The READ loop in the poet's program is not a counting loop because its termination condition does not depend on N reaching a predetermined count. Similarly the loop computing SIZE isn't a counting loop. The PRINT loop, however, is a counting loop and would make a good DO-loop.

2 Change all references to memory cell MINIM to MAX, change the COMMENTs appropriately, and most important, change the IF statement in the range of the DO-loop to

```
IF ( ROSE(HERE) .LE. MAX )   GO TO 300
```

3 Add an INTEGER memory cell NUMB, then use these statements (or equivalent)

```
COMMENT:   THERE'S ONLY BEEN ONE ELEMENT SC FAR, SO THE FIRST
C          ELEMENT IS THE SMALLEST, AND THE CURRENT MINIMUM
C          HAS BEEN ENCOUNTERED ONLY ONCE.
           MINIM = ROSE(1)
           NUMB = 1
C
C          LOOK AT ALL THE OTHER ELEMENTS IN "ROSE" LOOKING FOR
C          SMALLER VALUES.  KEEP TRACK OF THE NUMBER OF TIMES THE
C          CURRENT MINIMUM HAS BEEN ENCOUNTERED.
           DO 300 HERE = 2,N
             IF ( ROSE(HERE) .GT. MINIM )   GO TO 300
             IF ( ROSE(HERE) .LT. MINIM )   GO TO 200
C            CURRENT MINIMUM ENCOUNTERED ANOTHER TIME
             NUMB = NUMB + 1
             GO TO 300
C            FOUND A NEW SMALLEST VALUE--UPDATE.
  200        MINIM = ROSE(HERE)
             NUMB = 1
  300      CONTINUE
C     DONE
           PRINT, NUMB, 'ROSES HAVE', MINIM, 'PETALS.'
           PRINT, 'NONE HAVE FEWER.'
           STOP
           END
```

ANSWERS TO EXERCISES 9 1

```
1 a   GO TO (10, 20, 30), K
  b   GO TO (200,200,100,100,200), I
```

2 Change
```
    IF ( DICE .EQ. 7 )  GO TO 20
```
to
```
    IF ( DICE .EQ. 7 .OR. DICE .EQ. 11)  GO TO 20
```

ANSWERS TO EXERCISES 9 2

```
1 COMMENT:  NOW SORT ON HEIGHTS.
            CALL INDSRT(HGT,X,N)
            PRINT, 'CHILDREN BY INCREASING HEIGHT'
            PRINT, 'NAME            AGE        WEIGHT        HEIGHT'
            I = 1
      410   PRINT, NAME(X(I)), AGE(X(I)), WGT(X(I)), HGT(X(I))
            I = I+1
            IF ( I .LE. N )  GO TO 410
```

2 Put a test to assure that N never gets larger than 100 (the length of our arrays) in the loop that READs in the data.

3 No, it won't cause an error. As long as N does not exceed the actual declared length of the array (100 here), the SUBROUTINE can just use the lower parts of the array (up to position N) with no problem. However, this can cause unexpected problems when the array is multidimensional. That's covered in Chapter 13.

ANSWERS TO EXERCISES 9 3

1 Replace statement 500 and following by the statements below

```
COMMENT:  PRINT WINNER OR WINNERS
  500   NWNNRS = 1
  510   IF ( TIME(NWNNRS) .NE. TIME(NWNNRS+1) )  GO TO 550
        NWNNRS = NWNNRS +1
        GO TO 510
  550   PRINT, 'WINNING ELAPSED TIME:', TIME(1)
        IF ( NWNNRS .NE. 1 )  GO TO 560
        PRINT, 'WINNING CAR:'
        GO TO 570
  560   PRINT, 'WINNING CARS:'
  570 C = 1
  575 PRINT, CAR(C)
        C = C + 1
        IF ( C .LE. NWNNRS )  GO TO 575
     STOP
     END
```

2 Probably the most reasonable thing to do is every time a card with a 0.0 time on it comes in, to change it to 100.0 before storing it in the array

```
IF ( T .LE. 0.0 )  T = 100.0
```

Otherwise when the SORT routine is called, all the disqualified cars would be at the top of the standings.

3 The odd thing about

$$\text{IF (TIME(C) .LE. 99.)} s_1$$
$$\text{IF (TIME(C) .GT. 99.)} s_2$$

is that if the first test has a .TRUE. result, then we don't even need to carry out the second test, it *must* be .FALSE.. Similarly, if at some point in time the first test is .FALSE., that automatically means the second will be .TRUE.. Therefore, there's no need to ever make the second test. We could just as well have

$$\text{IF (TIME(C) .LE. 99.) GO TO 5000}$$

$$s_2$$
$$\text{GO TO 6000}$$
$$5000 \quad s_1$$
$$6000 \quad \ldots$$

Somehow, though, the first way we wrote it, with two IF statements, seems much easier to read.

4 An appropriate subprogram would be

```
        SUBROUTINE OUTPUT (CAR, TIME, HOWMNY)
        INTEGER CAR(HOWMNY), HOWMNY
        REAL TIME(HOWMNY)
COMMENT:  THIS SUBPROGRAM PUTS OUT THE CURRENT STANDINGS.
        INTEGER C
          PRINT, ' '
          PRINT, '          STANDING          CAR          TIME'
          C = 1
  400     IF ( TIME(C) .LE. 99.0 )  PRINT, C,CAR(C),TIME(C)
  410     IF ( TIME(C) .GT. 99.0 )  PRINT, C, CAR(C), 'DISQ.'
          C = C+1
          IF ( C .LE. HOWMNY )  GO TO 400
        RETURN
        END
```

5 The parameter declarations should be changed to reflect the fact that 'KEYS' will now contain REAL numbers. Instead of

$$\text{INTEGER N, KEYS(N), OTHER(N)}$$

we'd have

$$\text{INTEGER N, OTHER(N)}$$
$$\text{REAL KEYS(N)}$$

In addition, write another SUBROUTINE which interchanges the values in two REAL cells and CALL it in place of SWITCH (see next page).

```
      SUBROUTINE SORT (KEYS, OTHER, N)
      INTEGER N,            OTHER(N)
      REAL  KEYS(N)
COMMENT:   ARRANGE THE VALUES IN 'KEYS' AND 'OTHER' INTO
C              INCREASING ORDER ACCORDING TO 'KEYS'
      INTEGER TOP, SMLEST
      INTEGER LOCSML
      TOP = 1
C     FIND SMALLEST NUMBER IN 'KEYS' BETWEEN 'TOP' AND 'N'.
 100  SMLEST = LOCSML(KEYS, TOP, N)
C         INTERCHANGE KEYS(TOP) WITH KEYS(SMLEST)
          CALL RSWICH (KEYS(TOP), KEYS(SMLEST))
C         TO AVOID MESSING UP THE CORRESPONDENCE BETWEEN
C         VALUES IN 'KEYS' AND VALUES IN 'OTHER', MAKE AN
C         IDENTICAL INTERCHANGE IN 'OTHER'.
          CALL ISWICH (OTHER(TOP), OTHER(SMLEST))
C         INCREMENT 'TOP' TO REFLECT NEW TOP OF UNSORTED
C         PORTION OF ARRAYS.
          TOP = TOP + 1
          IF ( TOP .LT. N )  GO TO 100
      RETURN
      END

      INTEGER FUNCTION LOCSML (A, FROM, TO)
      INTEGER FROM, TO, A(TO)
COMMENT:  LOCATE THE SMALLEST VALUE IN 'A' BETWEEN A(FROM)
C            AND THE END OF THE ARRAY.
      INTEGER I
      LOCSML = FROM
      I = FROM + 1
 100  IF ( I .GT. TO )  RETURN
          IF ( A(I) .LT. A(LOCSML) )  LOCSML = I
          I = I + 1
          GO TO 100
      END

      SUBROUTINE RSWICH (A,B)
      REAL A, B
      REAL COPYA
      COPYA = A
      A = B
      B = COPYA
      RETURN
      END

      SUBROUTINE ISWICH (A,B)
      INTEGER A, B
      INTEGER COPYA
      COPYA = A
      A = B
      B = COPYA
      RETURN
      END
```

ANSWERS TO EXERCISES 9 4

```
1  1 2 3 4 5
   2 3 5 4 1
   3 2 5 4 1
   5 4 2 3 1
   5 4 3 1 2
```

2	1	2	3	TRANFORMWATE
	1	3	2	TRANWATEFORM
	2	1	3	FORMTRANWATE
	2	3	1	FORMWATETRAN
	3	1	2	WATETRANFORM
	3	2	1	WATEFORMTRAN

ANSWERS TO EXERCISES 10 1

1 single spaced from previous line:

$$bbb14b74bbbbbb{-}6$$

2 single spaced from previous line:

$$b100b900bbbb9bb0$$

blank line

$$bbbbbbbb10$$

3 There are many possibilities; two of them are below.

```
      PRINT 1000, 47, 102
 1000 FORMAT('1', G6.0, G8.0)
```

and

```
      PRINT 1000, 4,7, 1,0,2
 1000 FORMAT('1', G5.0,G1.0, G6.0,G1.0,G1.0)
```

4 As you can see, the data descriptor G6.0, which corresponds to PRINT list element 10009428, doesn't leave enough room to print out the value. This is an error condition, and the field specified by the erroneous data descriptor is filled with asterisks to warn us of the error. Thus we get the following line:

$$bb4037{*}{*}{*}{*}{*}{*}bbbb98$$

5 single spaced from previous line:

$$bbb500.bbbbb51bb7.932E{-}07$$

ANSWERS TO EXERCISES 10 2

1 `1000 FORMAT(G10.0,G15.0,G5.0)`

2 $b14137b4963b{-}192$

3 A [1]   B [34]   C [927.1]

4 A [103]   B [4092]   C [7.1]

5 D [349.7]   E [.047]   F [9.3E+40]

All blanks in numeric input fields are interpreted as zeros. The last blank in the third field makes the decimal point shift factor 40 instead of 4.

ANSWERS TO EXERCISES 10 4

1 starting at the top of a page

```
SOME COMPUTATIONS

THE PRODUCT OF 493 AND 846 IS   417078
THE PRODUCT OF 493 AND 846 IS   493*846

THE SUM 4392+6947=11339
```

2
```
      PRINT 1000, A, B, A+B
1000 FORMAT('0',G11.4,'+',G11.4,'=',G11.4)
```

ANSWERS TO EXERCISES 10 5

1 single spaced from previous line

bbbbbb3bbb30
bbbbbbb3bbb20

2 DOLARS 49 CENTS 7

3 DOLARS 7 CENTS 49

ANSWERS TO EXERCISES 10 6

1 1000 – 1001 aren't equivalent.

1001 is equivalent to:

```
1001 FORMAT(' ', I3, G12.2, I3, G12.2, I3, G12.2)
```

Each of the other pairs is equivalent.

ANSWERS TO EXERCISES 10 7

1 The FORMAT describes a record of 90 characters for the card reader, but cards are records of only 80 characters.

2 The value for A should be punched in the columns 1 to 10 of the first card and the value for B in columns 11 to 20 of that card. The values for C and D and for E and F should be punched in the same way on cards 2 and 3, respectively.

3 Recall that the repeat starts from the repetition factor 2. Starting at the top of a page:

```
NAME        CODE

FRED****    OF****
JUNE****    AL****
JANE****    TA****
TED ****    SB****
```

4   There are many possibilities. Two of them are shown below.

```
1000 FORMAT(A10, 10X, G10.0, 10X, G10.0, 10X, G10.0/ 4G5.0)
2000 FORMAT(A10, 3(10X,G10.0)/ 4G5.0)
```

A possible disadvantage with the FORMAT 2000 is that if you want to read several pairs of cards with the same layout in one READ statement, the READ statement repeats from the group 3(10X, G10.0). Thus, the cards after the first pair would be read improperly.

5
```
      PRINT 5000
5000 FORMAT('1', 100(/' ','FORMAT IS A TRICKY LANGUAGE'))
```

Note: this actually starts on the *second* line of a new page.

6   Double space, then

```
IN FIRST PLACE WAS BARBER
THERE WERE 2 TIED FOR IT

IN FIRST PLACE WAS MOODY
THERE WERE
```

Not a particularly well done FORMAT.

ANSWERS TO EXERCISES 11 2

1
```
LOGICAL EXOR, ONE, TWO
EXOR(ONE, TWO) = (ONE .AND. .NOT. TWO) .OR.
+                    (TWO .AND. .NOT. ONE)
```

2
```
REAL SDIST, X1,Y1, X2,Y2
SDIST(X1,Y1, X2,Y2) = SQRT( (X1-X2)**2 + (Y1-Y2)**2 )
```

3
```
REAL ADIST, X1,X2, Y1,Y2
ADIST(X1,Y1, X2,Y2) = ABS(X1-X2) + ABS(Y1-Y2)
```

4
```
REAL TRNCD, R1,R2
TRNCD(R1,R2) = AINT(R1/R2)
```

5
```
RNDDIV(I,J) = ISIGN(1,I)*ISIGN(1,J)*
&                INT(ABS(FLOAT(I)/FLOAT(J))+0.5)
```

ANSWERS TO EXERCISES 11 3

1   None of the answers is correct. The EXTERNAL statement appears in the program unit which has a subprogram reference in which an argument is the name of another subprogram.

ANSWERS TO EXERCISES 11 4

```
1   INTEGER A1/10/, R1
    INTEGER A2/10/, R2
    CALL DV1 (A1,A1,R1)
    CALL DV2 (A2,A2,R2)
    PRINT, R1, 'DOESN''T EQUAL', R2
    STOP
    END

    SUBROUTINE DV1( DVN , QUO , REM)
    INTEGER DVN, QUO, REM
    QUO = DVN/3
    REM = DVN - 3*QUO
    RETURN
    END

    SUBROUTINE DV2(/DVN/,/QUO/, REM)
    INTEGER DVN, QUO, REM
    QUO = DVN/3
    REM = DVN - 3*QUO
    RETURN
    END
```

```
output
        1 DOESN'T EQUAL            -6
```

ANSWERS TO EXERCISES 11 6

1   Change the two assignment statements putting values into SKIP(2) and SKIP(5) to the following core-to-core WRITEs.

```
       WRITE (SKIP(2),1000) 11-N
       WRITE (SKIP(5),1000) N
  1000 FORMAT(I4)
```

The array DIGIT is no longer needed.

ANSWERS TO EXERCISES 11 9

1   A:18, B:1
    A:1, C(1):7, C(2):7, C(3):7, D:4.0
    A:3, E:5.0, F(1):5.0, F(2):5.0, F(3):5.0, F(4):5.0
    illegal: E is REAL and can't have the value 2, an INTEGER.
    C(2):2—no other cells initialized
    A:2, C(2):3—legal because A is initialized first.

ANSWERS TO EXERCISES 11 10

1

	ONE	TWO	THREE

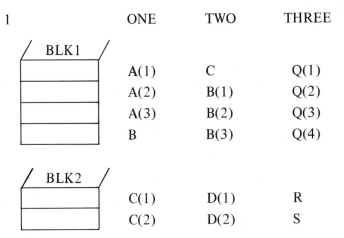

	ONE	TWO	THREE
BLK1	A(1)	C	Q(1)
	A(2)	B(1)	Q(2)
	A(3)	B(2)	Q(3)
	B	B(3)	Q(4)
BLK2	C(1)	D(1)	R
	C(2)	D(2)	S

2 It will print the values of A, B, C, D, E, and F, which will be 2.0, 1.0, 2.0, 3.0, 1.0, and 3.0, respectively.

ANSWERS TO EXERCISES 11 11

1 A, X, Y(1)
   B, Y(2)
   C(1), Y(3)
   C(2), Y(4)

ANSWERS TO EXERCISES 13 2

1

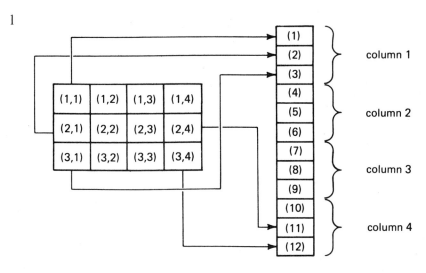

2 In order to reference elements (in a two-dimensional array) "by columns," you must know *how long* the columns are. (It doesn't matter how long the rows are.) An *m* by *n* two-dimensional array has columns of length *m*. Therefore, you could set up the array as long as you knew *m* and an upper bound on the total amount of room you'd need for the array. Thus, knowing *m* exactly and that $n \leqslant 100$ is enough.

3 (I, J) corresponds to element N*(I−1)+J
Note that N is the value you need to know precisely.

4

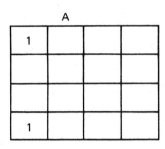

i.e. in A(1,1) and A(4,1)

ANSWERS TO EXERCISES 13 3

1 You would not want to store a triangular array by columns because then you would need to know how long the first column is in order to skip around it to reference the other columns.

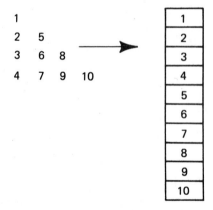

If the first column has four elements, then

$$(row, col) \longrightarrow \frac{4*(4+1)}{2} - \frac{(5-col)*(6-col)}{2} + row - col + 1$$

2 Store it by columns. Then

$$(row, col) \longrightarrow \frac{col*(col-1)}{2} + row$$

3 It's probably not worth it. Even if the shortest route were recomputed the maximum number of times, it would add less than 25% to the running time since less than that proportion of each loop iteration is spent in recomputing the shortest route length. Your time would be far better spent in fixing up the permutation generator, since it is fairly slow, or better yet in reducing (by more careful analysis) the number of routes you need to look at.

ANSWERS TO EXERCISES 13 4

1
```
        SUBROUTINE REMOVE (STACK, TOP, VALUE)
        INTEGER TOP, STACK(500), VALUE
COMMENT:  ROUTINE TO REMOVE TOP ELEMENT OF A PUSH DOWN STACK
C       FIRST MAKE SURE THERE'S SOMETHING TO REMOVE
        IF ( TOP .GT. 0 )  GO TO 10
C         STACK ALREADY EMPTY
          PRINT, 'TRIED TO REMOVE A VALUE FROM AN EMPTY STACK'
          STOP
C         GET THE VALUE--MOVE TOP DOWN ONE
   10     VALUE = STACK(TOP)
          TOP = TOP - 1
          RETURN
        END
```

2 The declaration of the array STACK would have to be changed to REAL. Also the parameter VALUE in SUBROUTINEs ADD and REMOVE must be a REAL.

3
```
        SUBROUTINE REMOVE (QUEUE, FRONT, BACK, VALUE)
        INTEGER QUEUE(500), FRONT, BACK, VALUE
COMMENT:  "FRONT" MOVES ONE PLACE
        FRONT = FRONT + 1
COMMENT:  WRAP AROUND IF NECESSARY
        IF ( FRONT .GT. 500 )  FRONT = 1
COMMENT:  GET "VALUE"
        VALUE = QUEUE(FRONT)
        RETURN
        END
```

4 Add a test to see if FRONT equals BACK right after the wrap around statement.

ANSWERS TO EXERCISES 13 5

1 Near the bottom just before the statement

```
EMPTY = EMPTY + LENGTH + 1
```

2

| 37 | C | O | M | E | | O | N | | P | E | O | P | L | E | | S | M | I | L | E | | O | N | | Y | O | U | R | | B | R | O | T | H | E | R |

3

| 28 | A | S | P | I | R | I | N | | I | S | | T | H | E | | B | E | S | T | | A | S | P | I | R | I | N |

ANSWERS TO EXERCISES 13·6

1
```
        SUBROUTINE BEGIN
        CHARACTER*2 TYPE(2000)
        REAL TIME(2000)
        INTEGER FROM(2000), TO(2000), NEXTEV(2000)
        COMMON TIME,FROM,TO,NEXTEV,TYPE
        INTEGER PT
COMMENT:  PUT AN  END OF LIST SYMBOL IN THE LAST ELEMENT
        NEXTEV(2000) = 0
C       FILL IN THE REST
        DO 10 PT = 1,1999
   10      NEXTEV(PT) = PT + 1
C       MAKE "FREE" POINT TO THE FIRST ELEMENT
        FREE = 1
        RETURN
```

2
```
        SUBROUTINE CLENZ(DONE)
        INTEGER DONE
        CHARACTER*2 TYPE(2000)
        REAL TIME(2000)
        INTEGER FROM(2000), TO(2000), NEXTEV(2000)
        COMMON TIME,FROM,TO,NEXTEV,TYPE
C       TIE IN
        NEXTEV(DONE) = FREE
C       RE-POINT FREE
        FREE = DONE
        RETURN
        END
```

3   "I luv lisds, Ilse of Lidzt, eye love-uls, #*@!!"

INDEX

```
C        QUICK REFERENCE INDEX
C
C        TYPICAL STATEMENT          PAGE NO.
C
C  DECLARATION STATEMENTS
         INTEGER A, BASS, C12            23, 53
         REAL RATE, SPEED               55
         CHARACTER*5 TITLE, SPACE       23, 72
         LOGICAL PLATO, KANT            77
         REAL X/0.0/,Y/1.234/           83
         INTEGER COUNT (100)            98
         REAL POLL (10, 20)             105
C        THIS IS A COMMENT              32
         END                            32
         SUBROUTINE CLEAR (TXT, A, B)   135
         REAL FUNCTION FIRST (LIST, S, F) 145
         DIST (RATE, TIME) = RATE*TIME  244
C
C  ASSIGNMENT AND I/O STATEMENTS
         A=1                            25
         QWKREF=THANKS**DDM             59
         BASS=R/T*2+C(4)**C12           57
         TITLE='QWIK'                   71
         P=.FALSE.                      77
         P=A .LT. 0 .OR. B .GT. 1.0     77
         READ, A, B, C                  35
         PRINT, A, B, C*2               31
         READ, (COUNT(H), H=1, 20)      115
         PRINT, (H, COUNT(H), H=1, 10)  115
C
C  CONTROL STATEMENTS
         STOP                           32
         GO TO 100                      40
         IF (A .LT. 10) GO TO 200       41
         IF ('DOG' .EQ. C) GO TO 300    49
         IF (A .LT. 0 .OR. B .GT. 1.0)
     +      PRINT, 'HELP'               77
         GO TO (10, 20, 30, 10, 20), JTH 182
         CALL SUBR (R*B, 'FINIS')       132
         RETURN                         135
         DO 500 I=1, 10                 164
         J=J+1
500      CONTINUE                       168
         DO 600 J=1, N, 2               167
         Z(J) = COS (ATAN(FLOAT(J)*PI/4.0)) 63
600      Z(J+1)=SIN(PI*Z(J))            63
```

†

Notes

Notes

Notes

Notes

Notes

Notes

Notes

Notes

Notes

Notes